When Elvis Died

by
Neal and Janice Gregory

James Prendergast Library Association
509 Cherry Street
Jamestown, New York 14701

Communications Press, Inc.
Washington, D.C.

Grateful acknowledgment is made to the following newspapers for permission to reprint their editorials: *The Asheville Citizen*, Asheville, North Carolina; *The Atlanta Constitution*, Atlanta, Georgia; *The Atlanta Journal*, Atlanta, Georgia; *The Record* (Bergen County), Hackensack, New Jersey; *The Daily Herald*, Biloxi-Gulfport, Mississippi; *The Birmingham News*, Birmingham, Alabama; *The Idaho Statesman*, Boise, Idaho; *The Boston Globe*, Boston, Massachusetts; *Buffalo Evening News*, Buffalo, New York; *The Charleston Gazette*, Charleston, West Virginia; *The Charlotte Observer*, Charlotte, North Carolina; *The Chattanooga Times*, Chattanooga, Tennessee; *Chicago Daily News*, Chicago, Illinois; *Chicago Sun-Times*, Chicago, Illinois; *Chicago Tribune*, Chicago, Illinois; *The Cleveland Press*, Cleveland, Ohio; *The Plain Dealer*, Cleveland, Ohio; *The State*, Columbia, South Carolina; *The Dallas Morning News*, Dallas, Texas; *Dayton Daily News*, Dayton, Ohio; *The Denver Post*, Denver, Colorado; *The Des Moines Register*, Des Moines, Iowa; *Detroit Free Press*, Detroit, Michigan; *Fort Worth Star-Telegram*, Fort Worth, Texas; *Greensboro Daily News*, Greensboro, North Carolina; *The Greenville News*, Greenville, South Carolina; *The Hartford Courant*, Hartford, Connecticut; *The Honolulu Advertiser*, Honolulu, Hawaii; *The Honolulu Star-Bulletin*, Honolulu, Hawaii; *The Indianapolis Star*, Indianapolis, Indiana; *The Knoxville Journal*, Knoxville, Tennessee; *Lexington Herald*, Lexington, Kentucky; *Arkansas Democrat*, Little Rock, Arkansas; *The Courier-Journal*, Louisville, Kentucky; *The Commercial Appeal*, Memphis, Tennessee; *Memphis Press-Scimitar*, Memphis, Tennessee; *The Meridian Star*, Meridian, Mississippi; *Miami Herald*, Miami, Florida; *The Milwaukee Journal*, Milwaukee, Wisconsin; *Milwaukee Sentinel*, Milwaukee, Wisconsin; *The Montgomery Advertiser*, Montgomery, Alabama; *Nashville Banner*, Nashville, Tennessee; *The Tennessean*, Nashville, Tennessee; *The Virginian-Pilot*, Norfolk, Virginia; *Sentinel-Star*, Orlando, Florida; *Pensacola Journal*, Pensacola, Florida; *The Philadelphia Inquirer*, Philadelphia, Pennsylvania; *Arizona Republic*, Phoenix, Arizona; *The Pittsburgh Press*, Pittsburgh, Pennsylvania; *Press Herald*, Portland, Maine; *The Oregonian*, Portland Oregon; *Nevada State Journal*, Reno, Nevada; *Richmond Times-Dispatch*, Richmond, Virginia; *The Morning Star*, Rockford, Illinois; *St. Louis Post-Dispatch*,, St. Louis, Missouri; *Deseret News*, Salt Lake City, Utah; *The Salt Lake Tribune*, Salt Lake City, Utah; *The San Diego Union*, San Diego, California; *San Francisco Examiner*, San Francisco, California; *The Times*, Shreveport, Louisiana; *The Spokesman-Review*, Spokane, Washington; *The News Tribune*, Tacoma, Washington; *The Tampa Tribune*, Tampa, Florida; *The Arizona Daily Star*, Tucson, Arizona; *Daily Journal*, Tupelo, Mississippi; *The Washington Star*, Washington, D.C.; *Wilmington Morning Star*, Wilmington, North Carolina; *The Intelligencer*, Wheeling, West Virginia; and to *The Commercial Appeal* also for permission to reprint the cartoon by William Garner.

To Jenny, Kate, and Chuck,
who cooperated in this venture
with patience and enthusiasm

Authors' Note

When Elvis died, people around the world beseiged the news media for information. Some journalists and broadcasters, those who viewed Presley as a simple entertainer from a bygone era, were caught short by the public reaction. Others knew the death would provoke an intense response, but even these did not expect such a profound outpouring from so many segments of society.

While the event did not carry with it the trauma of an assassination or the stately pomp accompanying the death of a government leader, Elvis's passing clearly struck deep chords, especially among working people and among those of the Presley generation, whatever their station in life. Three years after his death, countless individuals still remember where they were and how they felt when they heard the news that Elvis had died.

Many critics and many who view themselves as protectors of culture were reluctant to view Elvis as a quality entertainer or as a person of any importance. The widespread public reaction to his death made such views superfluous and unleashed a full scale effort by many—including academics and the elite of the media—to chronicle and explain Elvis Presley's impact on an entire generation. Washington, D.C. is a city where the media are studied as assiduously as news events themselves. From this setting, we recognized the coverage of Elvis's death as a major event in media history and a reflection of a significant milestone in twentieth century popular culture.

Combing through the extensive files of the Library of Congress confirmed the breadth of the Presley phenomenon. Through interviews and travels, we began to get an understanding of his deep and pervasive impact. Our research took us back to the Southern towns that were his roots and his musical foundation. Opinion varies on whether his impact came in spite of—because of—or in addition to—his slicked hair and sideburns and his hip-swiveling, hard-driving rock style. But it is clear that Presley's music drew heavily from the strong heritage of two potent minorities, the poor whites and poor blacks of the American South. An understanding of that heritage helps to explain his durability in a field where so many others soared and fell, usually quickly.

No one can yet give a full accounting of the Presley phenomenon. But through an analysis of the reaction to his death, we can begin. Many have projected an image of Elvis fans as a separate group—fanatical, garish, and usually screaming hysterically. But his death also brought forth the ordinary fan— the established citizen, the symphony player, the high government official, the casual observer—persons who simply enjoyed the music and acknowledged the Presley preeminence in popular culture. As David Brinkley remarked. "It didn't even matter a great deal whether you liked Elvis or not. He was a part of our lives...Elvis Presley *changed* things."

For assistance in writing this book, we would like to express our appreciation to many people. First, we thank the many reporters and broadcasters who responded enthusiastically to our inquiries and took the time to relate their personal experiences and to give us their insights into the Presley phenomenon. Our gratitude also goes to the patient personnel of the Library of Congress, especially to those who staff the reading rooms of the Music Division and Newspapers and Current Periodicals; to Richard Bancroft and others of the British Library and the BBC Library; and to Nancy Patty and her associates at the Memphis Public Library. For sharing their personal reflections of Elvis, Janelle McComb, Todd Slaughter, Eddie Fadal, and Wanda Davis Lewis have our special thanks. We acknowledge the assistance of Kathryn Ebert, Lyte Fozard, Gerd Ritchie, and Steve Ruud in translating many articles from the European press. There were gracious hosts in Memphis—Sarah and Charles Burns, Jane and Sidney Genette, Ann and George Grider, who gave us an insight into the attitudes of the city—and in Heanor, where Kate and Ray Fletcher provided us with a unique European view of the cultural impact of Elvis. For advice on sources and for reading the manuscript and making suggestions we thank Jim Brown, Ralph Hutto, Don McLeod, Griffin Smith, Red Swift, and Charles Thompson. And to those whose continuing efforts brought this book to reality—Mary Louise Hollowell, Chuck Culhane, Edmond Smith, Dominick and Janet Anfuso, and Bill Brown—many, many thanks.

—Neal and Janice Gregory
Washington, D.C., July 12, 1980

Contents

Midafternoon at a morning newspaper is an easygoing time of day, particularly at a paper like *The Commercial Appeal*, the venerable journal that since 1840 has chronicled the life and times of Memphis, Tennessee, and the small towns and rural areas of the surrounding Midsouth. Reporters are telephoning in from their beats, giving their editors verbal reports that may become tomorrow's news. There is no sense of crisis; deadline for the first edition is still three or four hours away.

The afternoon of Tuesday, August 16, 1977, was such a time until shortly after three o'clock. Les Seago, who heads the Memphis bureau of the Associated Press, wandered into *The Commercial Appeal* newsroom from his office at the rear of the building. He was trying to confirm a rumor.

He heard that an ambulance driver had dropped off a patient at Baptist Memorial Hosptial. The driver saw Elvis Presley, apparently dead, being carried into the emergency room. He called a friend on the *Jonesboro Sun* with the news, but the small afternoon paper in northeastern Arkansas had just gone to press. So the friend had passed the tip on to the state AP bureau in Little Rock, which, in turn, telephoned the information to Seago.

Metro Editor Angus McEachran and his colleagues around the city desk shook their heads: No, they hadn't heard anything. It sounded like just another Elvis story.

Seago returned to the AP office, and McEachran began scanning the home edition of the *Memphis Press-Scimitar*, the afternoon competition that had just arrived from the pressroom next door. Seago's message did not interrupt his routine; he had heard it before. Since he first joined the newspaper as a copyboy some sixteen years earlier, McEachran had heard almost everything about the entertainer: Elvis had been killed in a car wreck ... his plane had crashed ... he'd been shot by a jealous boyfriend ... he'd been thrown off his motorcycle ... or his horse ... Elvis had drowned in a submarine.

Elvis was a home-town boy. He was good to his mamma. He gave away millions. He was a Memphis institution. Since his first record in 1954, since that spectacular television appearance, since his first movie, since he was drafted, since he got out of the Army, since his marriage, since his divorce—Elvis was there, always the subject of gossip and rumor, always news.

From across the desk, however, Shirley Downing, the assistant city editor, said maybe they should check this one out. A reporter had just called her from the police station saying he had heard that Presley was in the emergency room at Baptist.

McEachran reluctantly agreed. He called a friend at the hospital, someone who could quickly and quietly give the newspaper accurate information. Apologizing for the interruption, he asked if a check could be made at the emergency room. Within minutes, the source called back:

"Elvis isn't in the emergency room. He's in the morgue."

Knocking over a mug of coffee as he wheeled around in his chair, McEachran shouted across to the managing editor, James McDaniel, "By God, Elvis is really dead."

Throughout the cavernous city room—at the copy desk, in the sports department, in the women's section, on the business desk—heads looked up. And the room got quiet.

No one recalls exactly how long the eerie silence lasted, but Shirley Downing broke the spell when she ripped the now-useless daily assignment sheet from her clipboard and used it to mop up the puddle of coffee from the city desk.

It did not get quiet again for a long time.

When Elvis Died

1

Emergency at Graceland

That Tuesday afternoon seemed typical for Memphis in August. A sticky, smothering blanket of Southern summer heat lay over the city, while occasional clouds seemed to promise residents the relief of an afternoon shower. The night before, a spectacular gas explosion in a hardwood drying kiln and the resulting three-alarm fire had wiped out a lumber yard at the north end of downtown. Political factions continued old squabbles at City Hall, and the city's teachers were locked in a tough negotiating session with the school board. But the only really unusual occurrence in Memphis was the gathering of sixteen thousand Shriners for their annual convention.

Fezzes, mock-Arabian baggy pants, and shirts with puffed sleeves dotted the emptiness of the Mid-America Mall, the new pedestrian walkway that used to be Main Street. Some of the visitors rode motorcycles, exploded firecrackers, and engaged in hi-jinks that always enliven meetings of the fraternal order. But most of the middle-aged men and their ladies sought relief from the oppressive heat in the swimming pools or the air-conditioned bars and lobbies of the city's hotels and motels, where every room was sold out.

The usual throng of tourists had driven out Elvis Presley Boulevard (Highway 51 South) towards the Mississippi state line to see Graceland, the home of Elvis Presley. As a local tourist attraction, the entertainer's

13.7-acre estate was second only to the Mississippi River, whose broad sweep seen from Riverside Drive is a spectacular sight. Surrounded by a five-foot wall of natural stone, the centerpiece of the estate is a white-columned mansion sitting on a grassy rise one hundred yards away from the busy highway. Shrubbery and trees conceal a swimming pool, gardens, and the complex of offices, garages, and stables that stand behind the house. Unlike the region's other famous homes—the antebellum mansions of Natchez, Andrew Jackson's Hermitage in Nashville, or William Faulkner's Rowan Oak in nearby Oxford, Mississippi—Graceland was not open to the public.

But the fans came anyway, to peer through the famous wrought-iron gate with notes of music cast in metal adorning the filigree, to gaze past the curving driveway towards the house where their idol lived. The owner of a real estate office in the shopping center across the street said that since Elvis bought the house in 1959, a crowd of people was around the estate, day and night. During most of the daylight hours, a Presley was at the gatehouse—Elvis's Uncle Vester, brother to his father Vernon. For most of two decades, Vester Presley was the security guard who identified with the fans. He would pose for pictures, chat with them about the Presley family, sometimes pack them into his jeep and drive them up closer to the house so they could snap photographs. Through the years, the more daring visitors would snatch a handful of grass or a twig from a tree—any memento to prove their pilgrimage to Memphis. They usually hoped that Elvis himself would come out of the house, sign autographs or wave from his horse, although this had not happened often in recent years. Nevertheless, cameras were always ready; Elvis fans were a special breed whose faith never wavered.

Vester estimated he already had escorted about fifteen hundred persons to the house for photo sessions that day when, about 2:30 p.m., he got a call from "one of the boys" who constantly surrounded Elvis. The caller told Vester not to leave the gate because there was an emergency at the house and an ambulance was coming.

"Well as soon as I heard the siren," Vester recalled, "I opened the gate so they wouldn't have to stop. They didn't even slow down. I don't know how long they were up there. Of course, I was nervous. I knew somebody was real sick up there, but I had no idea who it was. I had the gate open when the ambulance started back out going to the hospital."

At first he feared for his mother, Minnie Mae Presley, Elvis's eighty-three-year-old grandmother, or his sister, Delta Mae Biggs, both of whom lived in the big house; or for his brother, Vernon, Elvis's father, who had been in poor health lately but came over to Graceland each day to direct the administrative details of his son's multimillion-dollar entertainment empire. As the Memphis Fire Department ambulance roared north away from the gate toward the city, Vester went into the gatehouse and called his daughter Patsy to find out what was happening.

"Daddy, don't ask me right now," she said. "Elvis is in bad shape. He may be dead."

No one will ever know precisely what happened to Elvis during the morning hours of August 16. But shock and grief sometimes kindle a desire to ferret out every fact and detail possible, as though these tidbits of knowledge might fill up the emptiness and relieve the sense of loss. The death of Elvis set off just such a reaction.

"There are so many unanswered questions about Elvis' death for which I must find answers," Vernon Presley said later in an article in *Good Housekeeping* magazine. "How long had he been lying on the floor before his body was discovered? Why hadn't somebody at Graceland wondered where he was and if he was all right? These are two of the questions I want answered. I know he hadn't been able to sleep the night before he died and had played racquet ball at about four or five in the morning. Then what happened? I want to know?"

So did the legions of fans—whose insatiable appetite for all the minute details of their hero's death was fed by all elements of the media, which published and transmitted every iota of information available— facts and hearsay—about the entertainer's last hours and the protracted international emotional binge that followed the news.

Conflicting stories were common. The county medical examiner, Dr. Jerry T. Francisco, a forensic pathologist, said the death was caused by "coronary arrythmia," an erratic heartbeat. In the confusing days that followed, gossip and innuendo, fueled by publicity surrounding a newly-published book by three former Presley bodyguards, provoked rumors that Elvis died of drug abuse.

Both Memphis newspapers, other local media, and the wire services initially reported that the body had been discovered in the mansion by Joe Esposito, Presley's Brooklyn-born road manager and his only close associate not from Memphis. Two days later, Ginger Alden, the beautiful dark-haired woman who said she was to be the next Mrs. Presley, told *The Commercial Appeal* in a copyrighted story that she, not Esposito, had found the body in the posh bathroom on the second floor.

"I said, 'Elvis,' and he didn't answer, so I opened his bathroom door and that's when I saw him in there," she told a reporter a few hours after the funeral. "I slapped him a few times and it was like he breathed once when I turned his head. I raised one of his eyes and it was just blood-red but I couldn't move him."

Alden supplied more graphic details a few weeks later in a story she sold to the *National Enquirer*: "His eyes were closed but his face was a purplish color and swollen-looking. His tongue was sticking out of his mouth and he'd bitten down on it. I raised one eyelid and the eye ball was blood red—no white at all—and just staring vacantly. I searched for signs of breathing but there weren't any. I leaned back for a few moments in shock."

She said she then called bodyguard Al Strada, who was on duty at the time. He surveyed the situation and immediately telephoned Esposito, who was in the office behind the house. At 2:33 p.m., the dispatcher for the Memphis Fire Department put out an alert: "Unit Six, respond to 3764 Elvis Presley Boulevard. Party having difficulty breathing. Go to the front gate and go to the front of the mansion."

Dr. George Nichopoulos, a close friend who had treated Elvis for eleven years, said he was at Doctors Hospital, some five minutes away, when he was summoned to the mansion. He, too, supplied details in a copyrighted interview published in *The Commercial Appeal*:

"I called out there and talked to Joe, I guess. He answered the phone and said the Fire Department ambulance was there and Elvis was still breathing he thought, but they were going to take him to the hospital. I got there [when] they had just put him in the ambulance, and I got in the ambulance and they were bag breathing him."

Charlie Crosby, driver of the ambulance, had told the *Memphis Press-Scimitar* that Nichopoulos was in the bathroom giving cardiopulmonary resuscitation (CPR) when he and his partner arrived at the mansion. He said it took five people to lift Elvis onto a stretcher.

The atmosphere of urgency at Graceland makes discrepancies in reports of the traumatic event understandable. Most of those on hand that day had special relationships extending far beyond the normal ties of blood or employment. As the ambulance arrived, word of the tragedy had spread through the house, and as many as twenty people had gathered on the southwest corner of the second floor in the singer's suite—the massive bedroom and the adjoining plush-carpeted bathroom that served also as a lounge, equipped with a reclining chair with sunlamp and reading light. Relatives, secretaries, members of the household staff, and the "Memphis mafia," that group of hangers-on and good old boys that Elvis kept around him to serve as bodyguards, valets, and reminders of his youth, clustered around. All felt grief, helplessness, and a sense of panic as they realized that the man who had been the focal point of their lives was not responding to the ministrations of the emergency medical team.

By 2:56 p.m., the ambulance crew had delivered its passenger to the emergency room at Baptist Hospital, only twenty-three minutes after the driver received the call. A skilled team of professionals, who knew only that a *"white male, approximately forty, under CPR, no response"* had arrived at the hospital, took over from the paramedics.

Doctor Nichopoulos, during the seven-minute, high-speed ambulance ride, pleaded, "Come on, Presley, breathe. Breathe for me." Finally he gave up and halted the frantic efforts of the emergency room team. At 3:30 p.m., he officially declared his patient dead. The hospital made the public announcement at four o'clock. Elvis Presley, the "king of rock and roll," was dead at the age of 42.

Public reaction already had started.

2

The Word Goes Out

Since he had come to Memphis two years earlier, Les Seago had averaged at least one call a week from Associated Press clients, saying variously that they had it on good authority that Elvis was either dead, dying of some obscure disease, married, or about to be married. Would Memphis please check it out?

Here we go again, thought Seago, as he sat alone in the one-room office of the wire service down the hall from *The Commerical Appeal's* sports department, pondering the roundabout rumor he had received from Little Rock. He had just completed a radio split, a series of brief items of information that broadcasters use in reporting their hourly news breaks. Because nothing dramatic was happening, preparing the usually routine radio copy had turned into a real chore. Now, here was a call saying Elvis was dead. Briefly he debated setting the news tip aside while he caught up with some of the bureau's administrative details, but his reporter's instinct told him to check it out.

His source of information on matters involving Elvis's health was Maurice Elliott, vice-president for public affairs at Baptist Memorial Hospital, the largest facility in the city's huge medical complex. Elvis's hospital stays had become more frequent in recent years—an eye infection, fatigue, problems of the digestive system, nothing that appeared to be serious. But Elliott could be counted on to confirm or deny that Elvis indeed was a patient. The ideal hospital spokesman, he had an easygoing camaraderie with members of the Memphis news media. He was someone who could help a reporter untangle a complicated medical story, and he would suffer any reporter's question, no matter how preposterous, particularly when it involved the city's most famous resident.

"Hey, Maurice," Seago began, "I've got another one of those calls about Presley."

Immediately the reporter sensed he was onto something out of the ordinary. The touch of humor was missing from Elliott's response. Instead of calling him "Elvis," as he always had in the past, he said: "I can confirm that Mr. Presley is in our emergency department and that he is being treated for respiratory distress." Then he added: "Beyond that, I can't tell you anything more."

Seago called the general desk of the Associated Press in New York and said he was onto a big story. He dictated a short bulletin saying Elvis was in the hospital suffering from respiratory problems. Then he started calling other sources—the police station, the fire department, an unlisted number at Graceland, Baptist Hospital again. No one knew anything concrete. He checked *The Commercial Appeal*'s city room to find out if the reporters there knew anything; then he went back to his telephone.

Dan Sears of radio station WMPS called, saying, "You can take it from me. It's true." With most stories, this would have been enough. Seago regarded Sears as one of the city's best newsmen. But not on this one. The source had to be official. A dozen years earlier, a predecessor at the Memphis AP bureau had moved a story saying civil rights activist James Meredith had been "shot dead" on a march through Mississippi. While Meredith had indeed been shot by a sniper, his wounds were superficial, and the timing of the bulletin meant that each of network television's evening news programs relayed the error simultaneously to millions of viewers, precipitating scattered violence and demonstrations.

As he cradled the phone on his shoulder seeking some official confirmation of the news he felt in his gut was true, Seago composed a death bulletin on the video-screen terminal that transmits his stories to the AP network. New York called two or three times, asking if he had made any progress, finally igniting the short fuse to his temper: "I'm here by myself; I can't make any progress with you people calling me!"

The most promising source seemed to be a lieutenant in the police department's homicide bureau. Seago had talked with him twice and he had seemed willing to share any information he could obtain. But on the next call Seago was told the officer had left the building.

"Is there anyone else who can talk with me?" Seago's voice had a touch of panic. "I'm trying to find out about Elvis Presley."

The secretary replied: "Well, I have a statement that I can give you."

And that was it. The elusive official confirmation had just been pulled from her typewriter. As she finished reading the statement, Seago thanked her and pushed the "send" button on his terminal. The bulletin was on its way. He then dialed the desk in New York and repeated the news. He told them more copy was coming as soon as possible.

A backgrounder on the entertainer which his colleague Marian Fox had prepared six months earlier was stored in the computer. Seago called it up on the screen, supplied a hasty rewrite and update, and in minutes had a full obituary moving on the wire. In retrospect, his solitary ordeal had seemed to him like hours, but only twenty minutes had elapsed since the call from Little Rock.

Upstairs, on the fifth floor of the squat, red-brick building that looked more like a warehouse than the home of the two Memphis newspapers, Seago's competition would experience a similar, difficult struggle to obtain details on the year's biggest story.

Through the sixties and seventies, Memphis had been in the forefront of major news developments—civil rights confrontations, medical research, municipal labor strife, politics, the assassination of Martin Luther King, Jr., and now the death of Elvis Presley. Yet the city was far removed from the main line of the nation's news circuits. To the Associated Press and United Press International, Memphis was a poor relation compared with their bureaus in Nashville or Atlanta.

Each wire service had assigned three persons to its Memphis operations. Providing service seven days a week on an eight-to-midnight basis, the reporters' schedules sometimes overlapped, but they usually had to staff the offices alone, filing a lot of routine copy such as cotton market quotations, weather information, and radio briefs. In general, they rarely got a chance to leave the building to cover a story but had to rely on interviewing their sources by telephone or rewriting copy provided by the two daily newspapers. Just as the AP's office was housed near the editorial offices of *The Commercial Appeal*, the United Press International bureau was two floors above, adjoining the city room of the *Memphis Press-Scimitar*.

Nanci Albritten arrived at the UPI bureau shortly before 3:00 p.m., quickly wrote the afternoon Tennessee radio summary, and began to take stock of the day's activities. Susan White, the bureau chief, was vacationing in Nashville; Craig Schwed, the other UPI employee assigned to Memphis, had just gone off duty. Fresh out of college and a brief stint with a Gainesville, Florida, radio station, Schwed had been on the job for just over a week. It looks as if he is going to work out just fine, Albritten thought, as she reviewed the copy he had filed that morning. Then the telephone rang.

Albritten doesn't remember exactly who it was, but the caller—probably a newsman from one of the twenty-six Memphis radio stations served by the wire service—told her that Elvis Presley had been taken to Baptist Hospital. Her first reaction was: Here's the Baptist Hospital syndrome again. Call Maurice Elliott, get confirmation, file the story, answer queries from papers all over the world, keep checking on his condition. If Elvis is there for a while, write a feature story on the flowers, the teddy bears, and the other gifts that the fans will send by the hundreds. Elvis always provided good copy; she'd been through this routine before.

But the caller startled her with the comment that this was not just another trip to the hospital. He said it looked bad. "There was some urgency in his voice," Albritten recalled. "I don't believe he knew anything more than that, but it frightened me a little bit."

Albritten immediately confirmed that Baptist Hospital indeed had admitted the singer. She filed an "Urgent" report to that effect, with no explanation of the cause of his illness. Recalling a story she had filed two months earlier when Presley was hospitalized, she threw in a couple of background paragraphs about his previous health problems. She then called the emergency room, where the nurse on duty declined to give a report on the patient's condition, suggesting she call Maurice Elliott's office. This struck her as highly unusual; someone would always give you a brief condition report—good, stable, serious, critical, something.

What if Elvis died? Albritten knew she was in a unique position, the only UPI reporter in the Memphis bureau. But she knew if she filed the story, if she—to use newspaper parlance—were the reporter to kill Elvis on a national wire, she had better be sure of her facts. If she were wrong, she could just hang up her career.

She called Elliott's office and was put on "hold" indefinitely. She reviewed her files and found an unlisted number for Graceland. It was still good. A man answered; his voice was strange. Later, Albritten thought he probably was in a state of shock, but she identified herself and asked a series of questions: Can you confirm that Elvis is ill? What is the medical problem this time? What is his condition?

"Ma'am, I can't tell you anything," he replied. "You'll have to talk to Mr. Vernon."

Could she speak with Vernon Presley, the singer's father? Was he there?

"I can't tell you anything," he said and hung up the phone.

Now convinced that Elvis was either dead or dying, Albritten called the Nashville bureau, alerting her colleagues there to the developing story. She told them she strongly suspected that Elvis was going to die and they should make detailed plans for reporting the event while they still had time. While she tracked down some reliable source, would they please call up the previously written obituary from the computer system and update it for possible use? No, she was not totally alone; a technician had just arrived to repair an old Model 40 printer, the "click-clack" teletype the bureau kept for back-up use. He was working noisily on the other side of the small room, frequently dropping tools, stumbling over boxes, and generally adding to the confusion. She assured the Nashville bureau she would report back as soon as possible.

Meanwhile, she was getting a flurry of phone calls. Several broadcasters told her the singer's condition was worsening quickly. One said he heard that Elvis had died. Could UPI confirm?

Frustrated by her inability to get details from the hospital or Graceland, Albritten suddenly thought of the police. She went right to the top and called Police Director Winslow "Buddy" Chapman. When she reached him, he confirmed it immediately: Elvis had died at Baptist Hospital, apparently from a heart attack.

"I got the bulletin on the screen," Albritten recalled. "And for God only knows, the thing would not move off the screen. It seemed like it was about ten minutes of insanity, just absolute electronic insanity. They poll when the computer is absorbing what you've printed—what you've typed out. And I could not get a poll."

The fault lay not with UPI but with overloaded telephone circuits. Already the communications problems in Memphis were beginning as friends throughout the city called each other repeating the bulletins that were flashing on local television screens and interrupting radio broadcasts.

Albritten finally moved her bulletin out, attributing the news to Police Director Chapman. At the same time, she relayed her story by telephone to Nashville, only to learn that the four- thousand-word, prewritten Presley obituary UPI had been holding in storage in its regional computer facility in Atlanta had been "un-held," accidentally erased last February. No one had rewritten it, and the Nashville bureau had nothing to follow the bulletin.

Would she please go through the Presley file and provide anything she could? Jack Warner of the Atlanta bureau would write the story. Albritten felt panic. She was answering the phone calls from clients, stringers, and the public. They added little information; most of them wanted confirmation of the tragic news or more details.

"I started typing from scratch, just sheer scratch," she recalled. "As fast as I could, anything I could get my hands on about the man and his career and his life, which is staggering, to say the least. It just blew my mind, that's for sure. The idiocy of it all."

There were some bright moments. She considered Jack Warner the best writer in the company, and she knew that he could take the worst situation in the world and at least write a passable report. She reached Craig Schwed who had gone home instead of stopping off for a beer as originally planned. She told him to get over to Baptist Hospital and start phoning in anything he could. But the phone system was becoming impossible to manage.

At the request of South Central Bell, Albritten moved a story asking everybody in Memphis to limit calls to emergencies. The heavy traffic on the lines was blocking telephone equipment. She felt that most of the calls were being directed to her office. The rotary system was backing up with calls, so that as each line was freed, another call came in. Desperate, she ran next door to the *Press-Scimitar*'s morgue and hired the librarian to manage the phones.

Schwed soon checked in from Baptist Hospital and she told him to file his reports directly to Atlanta. The Nashville bureau located Susan White and already she was flying back to Memphis. Someone was answering the phones. Help was on the way. To Albritten, it looked as if everything was under control.

Even the bumbling repairman was almost finished with his work on the old printer. Then, as she resumed her frantic writing, the glass plate he was fitting over the teletype keys crashed to the floor. Her loud scream vented the frustration of the afternoon.

At the time, no one could be concerned with anything other than getting the story. The inevitable question of who broke the story first would come later. The question is a matter of some dispute. The honor probably goes to Dan Sears of WMPS, although he is not particularly proud of his scoop.

It was about two minutes before 3:00 p.m., when Sears finished up the "five-before-the-hour" newscast. As he waited for a recorded commercial to end so that he could tack on the latest stock quotations and the weather forecast, a staff assistant handed him a note saying Elvis had died at Baptist Hospital.

"Ah, another rumor," he said to his messenger, a new employee at the station. "Where'd you get this?"

"From the hospital," she replied.

"You mean they made an announcement?"

"Yes, they called—"

The commercial ended. Sears swiveled back to his microphone and introduced his bulletin: "This has just been handed to me."

He signed off the news segment, then, as the music came up, he walked over to the news tickers. He got an uneasy feeling; no Presley stories were moving on the wire.

"You know," he recalled later, "if you're handed a note from the newsroom, you assume it is coming across the wire. But we had a new girl working in the newsroom, and all she had was a tip over the phone from a nurse at Baptist Hopsital. It hadn't been checked at all. We had never heard of—this lady did not leave her name—we had never heard of her before. And you know how critical it was. We had no idea we were right. We were just lucky."

Even luckier were the news staff at WHBQ-TV, Channel 13, the city's ABC affiliate. "We were the first in the world with the news," said Gordon Wilson, the station's executive news producer. "I remember it well, because my heart was in my throat, hoping we were right."

The station's first tip came early. The source was the police dispatcher, calling a friend with the news that something unusual was happening at Graceland. Someone had called for an ambulance, and a police car was heading toward the singer's estate. No one was really certain whether Elvis was in town, but any unusual activity at the Presley mansion was news. Kathy Wolfe, news assignments editor for the television station, sent a photographer to Baptist Hospital, the hospital the Presley family favored. During the three years she had covered the police beat before her current assignment, Wolfe had developed some good contacts. Now she started calling them to find out what was happening.

Meanwhile, a secretary in the program director's office was talking with a close friend, the wife of a high-ranking police official, when the officer got word on his police radio that an ambulance was on the way to Graceland. Suddenly the officer's wife said, "Oh God, I've got to get off the phone. They think Elvis may be dead."

Wolfe called the police director's office and was told that an officer at the hospital had confirmed that Presley was definitely dead. It was 3:00 p.m., just minutes after the ambulance had arrived at the hospital.

"I simply asked the direct question, 'Is he dead?'" Wolfe recalled. "We knew it had to be Elvis, although I had no reason to suppose that he was dead. But they were being so secretive. I thought he must have had a massive coronary or something, but when I said, 'Is he dead?' they thought I knew. Rather than lie and be accused later of lying, they simply admitted it, and I had my story."

But because of the gravity of the news, Wolfe had to get a solid, second confirmation. By 3:15 p.m. she had got another police source to talk with her. But he also asked not to be quoted; the official announcement had to come from higher up or from the hospital.

She was ready to go on the air, but it took another fifteen minutes to get the announcement to the public. News Director Don Stevens was on vacation, which meant that there was no one in the news department authorized to make the decision to interrupt programming. Wolfe and Gordon Wilson finally got the go-ahead from the program director. They first planned to present a crawl, the projection of a moving sentence across the bottom of the video screen. But one of the reporters, Jack Chestnut, came into the booth and asked if they wanted him to go on live.

With no script, he stepped in front of the camera and repeated the words Kathy Wolfe had given him: "Ladies and gentlemen, Eyewitness News interrupts regular programming. We have just learned through reliable sources that Elvis Presley has been pronounced dead at Baptist Hospital."

The time was 3:32 p.m.

Wolfe said she was glad they had waited the extra two minutes when they later learned that Nichopoulos had officially pronounced Presley dead at half past three.

A moment of anxiety came about fifteen minutes later when WMC-TV, Channel 5, the region's oldest station and the outlet with the largest news staff, interrupted its programming to announce that Elvis was in critical condition at Baptist Hospital. But the momentary uncertainty ended as the wire services finally moved the definitive stories. The stations began developing their evening news broadcasts.

Anyone familiar with journalism in Memphis knew the death of Elvis was a major story, but the veteran newsmen were completely unprepared to cope with those first few hours. Their only frame of reference for a local story with such national importance was the assassination of Martin Luther King, Jr., nine years earlier. But that was more like a disaster, a major police story. It was not unlike the night Russwood Park burned down: The home of the Memphis Chickasaws' baseball team was located in the middle of the Medical Center, and the flames that suddenly erupted and engulfed the old stadium threatened nearby hospitals and their patients. The editors knew how to handle this kind of news story—pull out all the stops and deploy the competent staff to cover all the angles. With Presley's death, however, the police could not serve as the ready source of complete information. Nor was there anyone else to fill this role.

Many editors and reporters who had been in Memphis for some time at first thought the story would be handled like the death on October 16, 1954, of Edward Hull Crump—"Boss" Crump, who had ruled Memphis through his fabled political machine for more than a half century. But that story was planned for weeks: Boss Crump was eighty-years-old and in failing health. Both newspapers had set up a death watch in front of his midtown home on Peabody Avenue, resorting to such tactics as bribing a medical attendant to lower a bedroom shade when the benevolent dictator had breathed his last breath. A watching reporter was thus alerted to call his paper with the news.

The two newspapers divided the hours of the printing plant they shared; if Crump died before six o'clock in the evening, the story belonged to the *Press-Scimitar*; if after six, *The Commercial Appeal.* When the news of his death flashed at 4:53 p.m., the afternoon paper quickly reached the streets with an "extra," the regular final edition with a new front-page wrapper around it and the banner headline announcing Crump's death. The obituary already was set in type; editors only needed to fill in the information fixing the time and place.

But the times were different in 1977. Not only had Elvis changed the music and mores of his generation; technology and economics had changed the newspaper business. Even though the *Press-Scimitar* again had "rights" to the pressroom and the plant's delivery mechanisms, no one even considered publishing an extra with its sure-fire street sales. Newspapers were not sold that way in Memphis anymore, and the economics of the Cincinnati-based Scripps-Howard newspaper chain—owners of the two papers—provided no chance to attempt one. Radio and television had become the media with the instant message, and there was nothing in type anyway.

Only the *Press-Scimitar*, with a full night still ahead, had the luxury of time. Its final edition already was on the streets, and Clark Porteous, the afternoon paper's veteran mainstay, was in the Federal Building pressroom when he got a call to come in and write the obituary for the next day's paper. Porteous, whose gray mustache and everpresent pipe give him a slightly Faulknerian look, knew the city and its times better than any other active Memphis journalist. For thirty years he had covered the city and the region, exploring the political and social scene. He was a utility man for the *Press-Scimitar*, filling in when the city hall reporter was on vacation, covering political campaigns, announcing a new industrial development project, reporting on a murder trial. Through the years he had declined editing posts, preferring the notebook and typewriter. Porteous had the added skill of being the paper's best rewrite man, taking the notes that other reporters dictated over the phone and quickly translating them into succinct, understandable prose for the late-breaking stories that appeared in the afternoon paper.

But for this story, he had time to ponder the wealth of material. Porteous later said he felt like he was beginning research for *Gone With the Wind* when he sat down with the Presley file from the newspaper's morgue. The file was enormous—twenty years of clippings, press releases, photographs, and notes. Included was the first interview Elvis ever gave: "The Front Row" column by movie critic Edwin Howard on August 30, 1956, when "That's All Right (Mama)" was released locally by Sun Records. There were dozens of articles by Bill E. Burk and photographs by William Leaptrot, who had attended Humes High School with Elvis and maintained an entree to Graceland through the years, and hundreds of "This Evening" columns by the late Robert Johnson, onetime movie critic and longtime political reporter who had boosted Elvis's career from the beginning. There were the hard news stories—Elvis being drafted, the death of his mother, his contributions to charity, his selection by the Junior Chamber of Commerce as one of the nation's ten outstanding young men of the year. And there were record and movie reviews and stories about the fans who had flocked to the city every day.

Porteous took the file and began to write. After the first couple of paragraphs giving the known details ("Elvis Presley was found dead yesterday . . . of an apparent heart attack"), he began to weave his story, producing more than eight full columns of copy that began on page one the next day under the headline: "A Lonely Life Ends/On Elvis Presley Boulevard." *Press-Scimitar* Editor Milton Britten said it was probably the best thing anyone wrote about the singer's death during the entire hectic week.

While Porteous wrote, others around him swirled in a sea of frantic activity. Communications problems mounted at the Memphis Publishing Company building. The big switchboard, located in a screened area at the rear of *The Commercial Appeal's* city room, was swamped with incoming calls. The two operators who route calls to the two newspapers and to the advertising and circulation departments had all lights blinking and no outgoing dial tones. When a caller did get through, it was usually a voice asking: "Is it true?" And there were the overseas calls—from Europe, Japan, South Africa, New Zealand, the Philippines. These proved more time-consuming, with language or idiomatic barriers and the intricacies of foreign operators linking their callers into the American telephone network.

At *The Commercial Appeal*, Metro Editor Angus McEachran began to mobilize his reporters, plugging each person's normal assignment into the Elvis story—the police reporters, the medical writer, feature writers, the TV critic, the entertainment editor, an editorial writer, the cartoonist. "We were just snowed under," he recalled. "We put almost everybody we had on it." Reporters and photographers were dispatched to the hospital, to Graceland, and, later, to Memphis Funeral Home. Personnel in the newspaper morgue began to organize the file of material, particularly the incredible number of photographs the paper had taken of the entertainer through the years. Editors pressed into service the direct-dial, straight-line telephones that were not connected to the switchboard, along with the radio telephones linked to the automobiles of the paper's photographers. A little less than three hours remained un-til deadline for the first edition of the next day's paper.

Radio and television stations faced even more pressing deadlines.

3

Airwaves of Grief

Wire service bulletins interrupted radio programming throughout the country. In the eastern time zone the news came during the afternoon rush hour as commuters were heading home. These are the hours when radio stations have the most listeners and seek the highest ratings so that they can charge more for commercial advertising minutes. Tragic news always travels quickly, but the timing of the initial announcements meant that most people heard of Elvis's death before sitting down to dinner or watching the evening news on television.

After the initial bulletins, the stations had to fill the demand for more news—details of the death, recapitulations of his career, local angles, reminiscences, interviews, and commentaries. Since most radio programming is recorded music, the vast Elvis catalogue provided most stations with a natural response to the news. But the few stations that have an all-news format had a special problem. Even though there were reams of wire copy to read, the story needed music. At one such station, WCBS-AM in New York, the staff borrowed records from the FM affiliate and produced a five-minute tribute which was repeated several times over the next few days. WIP in Philadelphia played "Love Me Tender" as background for its newscasts.

Those stations which use a talk format, with provocative questions drawing responses from listeners through telephone conversations, had no trouble filling the air time. Fans expressing shock and sorrow jammed phone lines as they remembered their youth. Callers told of seeing Elvis live in concert, watching his movies, buying his records, and collecting the memorabilia that were part of growing up in the fifties. Many of the callers were crying, creating special problems for the personalities who were on the receiving end of the mass outpouring of grief. Almost every person who called Chicago's WJJD wanted to deliver a short tribute to Elvis. Suburban Philadelphia's WBUX in Doylestown tried to run its regular sports phone-in program, but the callers wanted to talk about Elvis.

"Dialogue Line," the talk-show on Baltimore's WCBM, normally gets twenty-five to thirty-five respondents to its questions. But Tuesday night's "What effect did Elvis have on your life?" brought 470 callers, all favorable. One woman said that she had given birth three and a half hours earlier and had named the baby Elvis; another said she was defying her husband and going to Memphis for the funeral under threat of divorce. The station provided a full night of Elvis music starting at seven o'clock and lasting until Thursday morning.

Elaine Camphonse, a fan in Virginia, wrote the Presley fan club in England that she was unable to sleep and kept twirling the radio dial. "EVERY station had Elvis," she said. "I got stations in St. Louis, Salt Lake City, New York, Pittsburgh, Philly, Chicago, North Carolina, and you name it. The sounds kept fading in and out—some of the shows were all music and some were talk shows, and some a combination. People kept calling the DJs. They said there had never been anything like that in their lives. This was repeated Wednesday night and, to a lesser extent, Thursday night. The whole country was in shock. Even non-Elvis fans felt bad and as if something important had gone out of their lives."

Whatever their programming format, numerous radio stations shuffled schedules and revamped programming to make some sort of immediate response to the news. In Buffalo, talk personality Shane made live telephone calls to persons who had known Elvis. WPGC, the top-rated rock station in Washington, D.C., went on the air with a half-hour special, then played an Elvis record each hour for the rest of the day. On the West Coast at KJR in Seattle, the receptionist reported the switchboard lit up continuously starting at 3:00 p.m., local time. "There's a rumor going around here at Plant No. 2 at Boeing that he's dead," said one caller. "Is it true?" *Billboard* reported the news had thrown the big Los Angeles market into a "frenzy." Radio stations, competing for the listeners on the freeways, at the beaches, and around swimming pools, responded with detailed reporting of the event and many of the singer's recordings. KMET in Los Angeles broke the news and immediately began a one-hour tribute. KIOI ran a three-hour tribute later syndicated by Drake-Chennault Enterprises. KHJ, billing itself as the "Top 40 Giant," played at least one Presley record an hour.

In New York City, the three powerful stations owned and operated by each of the major networks focused on the Elvis story. WNBC produced a one-hour special. WABC, which broadcasts throughout the East with 50,000 watts of power, played Elvis records all night. The Reverend Peter Madori, who conducts a special program involving rock and religion on Sunday mornings, broadcast a special program. And at WCBS-FM, a station oriented toward nostalgia music, Dick Heatherton began playing Presley records and continued for six hours with no commercials.

Because of the importance of disc jockeys and their promotion of records as part of the Elvis story, CBS Television sent a camera crew to WHN, New York's big country-music station, to film disc jockey Bobby Wayne at work. The news electrified the staff at WHN, where listener surveys consistently named Elvis the favorite male artist. Program Director Ed Salamon had taken the afternoon off, but the station tracked him down at a movie theater near Fort Lee, New Jersey, where he was watching *Star Wars* with his ten-year-old son. He stopped by his home and pulled out all the Elvis recordings from his extensive collection, then headed back to the city against the rush-hour traffic. WHN's news department began interviewing people who had known Elvis or worked with him during the past two decades. Singer T. G. Sheppard told how Presley had given him his first touring bus, and members of the Jordanaires reminisced about singing back-up on the legendary concert tours. "Every production studio, every tape recorder, every telephone that we had in the studio was devoted to Elvis," Salamon recalled. "The switchboard was jammed with people wanting to know more, wanting to hear more, wanting to be a part, wanting to share this experience. And it was just a huge collective experience for all of them."

Other stations that use country music as their principal staple found equally heavy demand for Elvis's music. WDKA in Nashville announced the singer's death at 4:20 p.m., local time, and began playing his records continuously for the rest of the day. Switchboards of other stations in the city that is the world capital of country music were jammed with incoming calls. "It was as if the music had died," said David Tower, news director at Nashville's WLAC. "Callers would not let us stop playing his records."

Chicago's big country music station, the NBC-owned-and-operated WMAQ, began a live tribute at 5:00 p.m. that continued for two hours. WYNA in Raleigh, North Carolina, made every third record an Elvis song.

WPEN in Philadelphia played an hour of Elvis music, then asked fans to comment. From the first announcement at 5:35 p.m., the station's four Pennsylvania lines and two New Jersey lines were ringing steadily. Brandon Brooks, the station's only newsman on the evening shift, said: "We had a lot calling and saying, 'I'm 35 years old,' and we had a lot saying, 'I'm only 16, but I loved him.' "

Jim LaBarbara, who works under the name, "The Music Professor," at WLW in Cincinnati, had just gone off the air when a newsman showed him the wire copy. LaBarbara, who had recently completed a twenty-four-hour taped history of rock and roll, went back on the air in an effort to give historical perspective to Elvis's life.

"I've never seen any performer's death affect so many people," said Steve King of WLS, Chicago's top-rated rock-and-roll station. "Callers ranged in age from 9 to the 60s: all felt as if they had lost a member of the family."

The news affected Steve Goddard, a twenty-five-year-old disc jockey for San Diego's KCBQ, in a deeply personal way. He had been an Elvis fan since he was nine-years-old, and he owned a personal collection of some four hundred Elvis records. "I was on the air when I heard the news bulletin," he recalled. "It was as if someone had hit me over the head with a sledge-hammer. It was a hard day."

Twelve staffers at WAYS, the station in Charlotte, North Carolina, with the strongest rock and roll tradition, got together a six-hour special, borrowing records to add to the station's holdings and calling around the country for interviews. The special went on the air at 6:00 p.m. All commercials were eliminated, costing the station $2,600 in revenues. Stan Kaplan, president of the station, said Presley was to radio what Arnold Palmer was to golf. Charlotte's 50,000-watt station, WBT-AM, presented a four-hour special at eight o'clock Tuesday night, with Bob Lacey, the station's top morning disc jockey, anchoring the program. A Greensboro radio station received 2,400 names in a fifteen-hour period when it asked listeners if they wanted their names added to a mailgram the station was sending to the Presley family. It took a secretary five hours to type the thirty-five-foot long mailgram.

Peggy Kendricks, who claimed she was South Florida's number one fan, had seen Elvis's last Miami concert in a body cast. She was one of those taping comments for a two-hour tribute on WAXY, a golden-oldie station. At WTAL in Tallahassee, every other record from the time Elvis died until midnight Wednesday was a Presley record. Tom Allen, program director of WVOJ in Jacksonville, had to use records from his own private collection to keep up with listener demands. Jacksonville's gospel music station—WBIX—secured an interview with Mae Boren Axton, composer of "Heartbreak Hotel."

Boston's WROR-FM, which features golden-oldies, presented a three-hour salute to Elvis. "We felt like we had to do something," said Al Feinberg, music and program director. "This is his station in town. He's like a part of the family. Elvis has been an integral part of our format. We've been flooded with phone calls from fans who were dazed and upset."

Station WDEE in Detroit began playing Elvis music nonstop, interspersed with bulletins from Memphis and comments from listeners. Program Director Tom Collins marveled at the sincerity of the callers: "It's like they lost a mother or a father. They hardly talk without sobbing."

Sales secretary Danielle Strubhar also reported a lot of tears at KSON in San Diego where she was drafted to help answer the deluge of phone calls. "A lot of women were crying about it," she said, "and I was one of them. My own reaction was 'It just can't be true.'" Her station broadcast a twelve-hour documentary "The Elvis Presley Story" from 6:00 p.m. to midnight on Tuesday and Wednesday. The program had first been aired on the station in 1971.

"Many people called just to talk about it," said Jim Ashbury of WFLA in St. Petersburg. "They only wanted to tell someone how much they liked him."

That same sentiment prevailed in Honolulu where K108 began a twenty-four-hour show dedicated to Elvis. "The phone never stopped ringing," said disc jockey Andy Riley. "We got hundreds of calls for requests and from people who just wanted to talk about him and remember."

And in Chapel Hill, North Carolina, Jay Orr, a young Mississippian, was thrown into absolute panic as he read the news ticker at the University of North Carolina's WUNC. The student announcer was preparing for a career as a musicologist, and he knew this was the biggest story of the year for the world of music; yet the station's library had no Elvis records. He frantically called fellow students, only to hear them say that Elvis was before their time; they did not own any of his records.

While most people heard of Elvis's death from radio or from conversations with friends, they turned to television for confirmation of the news.

Data from Arbitron, which samples the number of television viewers every quarter-hour and assigns ratings to the competing programs, show a huge jump in the number of homes with television sets turned to the evening news shows during the dinner hour on the night of August 16, 1977. In New York, where the three networks broadcast their news shows in direct competition from seven until seven-thirty in the evening, the HUT-ratings (homes using television) hit forty-six and forty-nine percent for the two quarter-hour segments, compared with thirty-four and thirty-two percent on the previous Tuesday night. In Los Angeles, where the network news shows are staggered and do not have head-to-head competition, HUT ratings showed an even more dramatic jump. In the evening's six to seven-thirty time slot, the numbers started at fifty-two and rose to fifty-eight. A week earlier the figures were thirty-six to forty-four.

By network standards, Elvis's death was a late-breaking story, the news coming just over an hour before the feed to local stations around the country began. Reporters and film crews had been dispatched to Memphis, but there was no time for them to file reports for a 6:30 p.m. transmission from New York. News executives had to make decisions — where to place the story in relation to the other news of the day and what sort of film, tape, or other visuals to use.

The reporting of Elvis's death reveals the impact such decisions can have on the success or failure of a network news team. It is more than just a popularity contest. A continued drop in ratings can mean the loss of millions of dollars of advertising revenue. This loss of revenue means less money to cover stories, hire top talent, and produce succeeding programs. High ratings, conversely, add to the network's prestige and to the

morale of its employees, and they mean increased advertising revenue
for each advertising minute.

Viewers preferences for evening news shows influence their choices
for other special events programming, and the news shows represent a
strong lead-in to the prime time programming that is the dominant force
in the advertising marketplace.

For more than a decade the *CBS Evening News with Walter Cronkite*
led the ratings, and most people turned their dials to the local CBS channel on August 16. But the opening CBS headlines did not mention the
story from Memphis. Millions of viewers, not finding the information
they sought, immediately tuned out the video eye and switched to one of
the other networks.

At Rockefeller Center there was no question of the day's top story.
Not only did NBC news executives rewrite the lineup in order to lead the
Nightly News with the Presley death, they also immediately put in mo-
tion plans for a late-night news special on Elvis which would delay the
Tonight show for a half hour.

David Brinkley was in charge at NBC, as he had been been for most
of the years since 1956 when he and Chet Huntley were teamed to
anchor the Democratic and Republican presidential nominating conventions. Until CBS assumed the dominant role in the mid-sixties, the
Huntley-Brinkley Report had been the most-watched network news program on television. Here was a story to which Brinkley could relate. The
veteran broadcaster's style, slightly irreverent with the unique cadence
and the accents of his Carolina youth, was particularly well-suited to
reporting the death of the prime popular culture phenomenon of the century.

Brinkley narrated the lead item, tracing Elvis's career and devoting
almost three minutes to the piece. The report featured a film clip of the
1973 special Elvis had done for NBC. Also included were films of his
wedding and of a young Presley singing "Hound Dog." Brinkley closed
the opening segment with the announcement that NBC News would present a special that evening.

News executives at ABC had also picked the Presley death as the
day's number one news story, but they were caught short by Brinkley's
announcement of a late-night special. During the half-hour broadcast,
hurried telephone calls were made and efforts to obtain materials got
underway. Just before sign off, Harry Reasoner was able to announce

that ABC would also feature a half-hour news special on the late singer following the late-evening local news.

ABC devoted two minutes to its lead story on the *Evening News*, with Reasoner announcing the news from Memphis and reporter James Walker providing a recap of Presley's career. ABC also used a film clip of Elvis singing "Hound Dog," this one taken from an early TV appearance.

Arbitron's sampling of viewers in New York and Los Angeles revealed that the CBS decision not to lead with the story on Elvis gave the Cronkite show its lowest ratings in years. Two yardsticks dominate the television surveys—the "rating" or percentage of the total potential television market watching the program, and the "share," that portion of those actually watching TV who are tuned to a specific program.

In New York that night, the *CBS Evening News* garnered only a rating of five and an eleven share. ABC and NBC each scored ratings of eight with a seventeen share. Prospects for the usually top-rated CBS were no better across the country. KNXT,which broadcasts CBS news in Los Angeles at six o'clock local time, had a rating of eight with a fifteen share. Its competitors, showing local news at that hour and leading with stories of Elvis and Hollywood reaction to the news, were registering an eleven with a twenty-one (KNBC) and a fourteen with a twenty-seven share (KABC). An hour later, KNXT was showing a movie to a seven rating and a thirteen share, while the network news shows on KNBC were registering a nine rating and a sixteen share and on KABC, an eleven with a twenty share.

Why the decision at CBS not to lead with the Elvis story?

Over two years and several hundred news programs later, the principals of that evening's broadcast remembered the event well, although they differed in interpretations of how the decision was made.

Roger Mudd, who was filling in for the vacationing Walter Cronkite, opened the broadcast with the news that former President Ford had endorsed the Panama Canal treaties and urged ratification of them by the Senate. Six and a half minutes into the program, after a commercial break, CBS allotted one minute and ten seconds to the Elvis story, using still photos from the singer's career and a voice-over of Elvis singing "Hound Dog."

"It was a very hard call that night," said Burton Benjamin Jr., the program's executive producer. "We had a distinct scarcity of materials and we thought the other story was terribly important, the Panama Canal. If I had it all to do over again—it's like the Satchel Paige rule:

Who knows what you would have done. It's hindsight. I got a lot of praise for it in some quarters, and some of our competitors thought it was a bad decision. So I apparently was fairly close to being right."

At CBS, as well as at the other networks, there is a certain collegiality about the selection of news. About 2:30 each afternoon, reports have been received from correspondents around the world about what tape or film is available, and the wire services have been scanned for late-breaking stories. A half-dozen people—the anchor, the executive producer, the news editor, and others—sit down and sketch out an early lineup of the stories that will fill that evening's twenty-six-minute time slot.

"We go through all of the available stories and we argue back and forth about what should be the lead and what shouldn't be the lead," Mudd explained, "and if you led with this, what should you do next, because you have those unavoidable commercials that stop you in midflight. So when we go into one of those meetings, everybody says their piece and we try to leave the room so that everybody feels that we have got the best combination, that no one has any strong feelings or objections."

News Editor Lee Townsend, who tracked stories from day to day and made sure that no story was overlooked and that the broadcast had some coherence, saw the Presley story move on the wire. Feeling that this was an added starter among the previously agreed-on stories, he showed it to Mudd and the two of them took the copy into the fishbowl, the glass office that looks out onto the newsroom, to Ron Bond, producer in charge of the broadcast that night.

This was the best story of the day, they told Bond, suggesting that he tear up the lineup and open the show with Presley. The producer's reaction set them back on their heels. With a great deal of feeling Bond let them know that there was no way he would lead with the story.

Surprised at the emotional response, Mudd and Townsend beat a hasty retreat. But as the wire services continued to churn out Presley copy, the potential public interest reinforced their initial instincts. Mudd recalled:

"Lee and I went back a second time to Ron and said, 'We really think we ought to do this,' and again we got this very strenuous opposition. And when you get that sort of intransigence or resistance to doing something, you don't like to force your way through somebody. And, as a substitute myself, I didn't want to call in a preemtive strike and make it difficult for the rest of the summer. So, I think now, despite our better judgement, we yielded to Bond."

Burton Benjamin, meanwhile, was scrambling around trying to get material for the segment on Presley, wherever it was slotted. Ironically, CBS had film from Elvis's last concert tour, set for a two-hour special program in the fall. But Colonel Tom Parker, Presley's manager, could not be located.

"It was right in the house, right back in our tape room," Benjamin observed. "And, of course, we would have had the best material, but there was no way we could spring it. And the lawyers said it had to have Parker's permission, and we couldn't find Parker. So there it sat. And the temptation always is, 'Oh hell, let's use it and worry about the lawsuits later,' but that's not always very prudent. So we did not use it."

Benjamin acknowledged that the decision on a lead may have been different if CBS had been able to use the concert footage or to find materials other than stills and record album covers to illustrate the story. And he also admitted his surprise at the attention the media focused on Presley after his death: "I've been astonished at how this legend continues, and I can't describe it. I don't know whether it is because he was such a luminous star or there's some necrophilia involved. I had no idea that he had that much popularity. Let me give you an example: Maybe six months later, Bing Crosby died and there was nothing like that. This was indeed a phenomenon as far as I'm concerned."

Ron Bond, while insisting that "my own feeling was that it wasn't the lead that night," did not remember anyone else having made a strong argument to the contrary, especially since no decent material had been available.

"People have asked me this before, 'Why did we play it like that?' " Bond added. "I think it got hyped. And, you know, we didn't hype. And that's not a bad thing to say. But—I don't know. It was a judgement call. It may well have been a wrong one. I may have been out of tune with the national consciousness. On the other hand, my suspicion has always been that I was right."

Benjamin also said he got many questions from industry associates about his news judgment in the days following Presley's death, but he shrugs it off:

"If on my epitaph it reads: 'This is the man who did not lead with Elvis Presley,' I can live with that."

4

Elvis: Front Page

There was a tornado alert and a driving rainstorm underway as Susan White ran into the Nashville airport, getting the last seat aboard a flight to Memphis. Arriving at the UPI Bureau in Memphis just before 7:00 p.m., she passed Nanci Albritten in the doorway. Her colleague was heading for Baptist Hospital and a press conference where the results of a preliminary autopsy were to be announced.

"We all knew that the death of Elvis was a front page story," said White. "But what we didn't anticipate was that editors wanted four, five, six, seven sidebars to go along with it."

The sidebar, the accompanying story with a slightly different slant on the same general subject, is a staple of print journalism. It became more important as newspapers shifted to shorter, snappier formats. Instead of a single lengthy piece providing all the details, reporters broke up the major story and rounded it out with various sidebars.

Editors in New York and Atlanta were asking Memphis for separate stories on Elvis's health, his finances, his family, and his girlfriends. A researcher in New York was compiling a list of all Elvis's number one records. Someone in Los Angeles was listing his films. The many stories, illustrated with a myriad of file photos, would fill many columns in the nation's newspapers over the next few days.

White looked at the request list and sat down in the middle of the bureau floor with the huge Elvis file in her lap. She started dealing the clippings and notes out like cards, putting them in piles for potential sidebars. Then she picked up a stack and started writing.

Meanwhile, for three hours, the crowd had been growing at the emergency entrance of Baptist Memorial Hospital, spilling along the sidewalks and into the parking lot. The local media were there with cameras and microphones. People with strained looks on their faces stared at the glass doors. The stunned atmosphere pervaded the hospital, engulfing visitors as well as the regular employees. Knots of nurses, technicians, and orderlies formed at hallway intersections, at elevator entrances, and at nurses' stations on each floor and engaged in whispered conversations. A single subject was on their minds.

Craig Schwed had dictated his description of the scene to UPI in Atlanta and was prepared to move on to Graceland where crowds were gathering as well. In the best newspaper tradition, he had lifted a white hospital coat from a passing cart, and he presented it to Albritten when she arrived to relieve him. Slipping it on, she headed toward the pathology department. With an uncanny stroke of luck she walked into the lab where the Presley autopsy had just ended. The body was in an adjoining room, and as she realized that she had hit the mark, she tried to maintain her composure and blend in with the assorted medical personnel who were milling about. Men in green coats, the words "refrigeration technician" embroidered on their breast pockets, and several white-coated personnel were occupied with charts and conversation. Albritten's subterfuge was short-lived; the reporter's notebook she was clutching gave her away. Someone came up and politely escorted her back out into the hall.

With time to kill—she had almost a half hour before the press conference was scheduled to begin—Albritten found a telephone and checked in with Jack Warner, the deskman in Atlanta. He told her to keep a line open so that she could relay the hospital statements as soon as possible. If necessary, he said, pay somebody big money to stand there with the telephone and just hold it. To Albritten, the importance of the story took a quantum leap: In her years with frugal UPI this was the most extravagant thing she had ever heard. She located a bank of telephones in a waiting room just down the corridor from the conference room. She paid an incredulous grandmother and a small boy ten dollars to hold one of the phones until she returned from the press conference.

About a dozen reporters and an equal number of hospital personnel crowded into the small conference room where Dr. Jerry Francisco, the county medical examiner, and Dr. George Nichopolous described the day's events. There were assorted questions about the time the body was found and the resuscitation efforts. But most of the comments focused on the cause of death.

It was here that Francisco announced his initial findings and his conclusion that death was caused by "cardiac arrhythmia." He explained the term as "severely irregular heartbeat" and, responding to questions, he said it was "just another name for a form of heart attack." He said there was "no indication of any drug abuse of any kind," no needle tracks on the arms or damage to the nose from cocaine use. "There was severe cardiovascular disease present," Francisco added. "He had a history of mild hypertension and some coronary artery disease. These two diseases may be responsible for cardiac arrhythmia, but the precise cause was not determined. Basically it was a natural death. The precise cause of death may never be discovered."

Most of the afternoon papers in the country had closed down for the day when the news flashed from Memphis. Final editions are printed earlier nowadays, in part because extra time is needed to transport papers to growing suburban residential areas, far removed from center-city printing plants. Only a few West Coast papers were able to print the news that Elvis had died *today*. The *Seattle Times* ran the AP story in a single column ("Elvis/Presley/Dies/At 42") in the lower right corner of page one. The *Anchorage Times* led with the story of a meeting by labor leaders on the Alaska pipeline, but the editors placed a one-column photo of Elvis and the accompanying story at the top left of the page.

The *Los Angeles Herald-Examiner*, in its many editions during the day, ran headlines about the violent windstorms and flooding that were ravaging Southern California. The news from Memphis made the Sunset edition, the last run of the day. "Elvis Presley Dies" was the full banner headline above the Associated Press story.

It was the *San Francisco Examiner* that set a benchmark for other papers to emulate, however. The editors scrapped the existing front page and began pulling together material on Presley.

Reporter Art Harris recalled standing by the wire service machines in the *Examiner* newsroom when the bulletin moved:

"I realized that everyday people whose lives are built around the stuff of movie magazines and so-called frivolous events would be hit hard. Elvis represented the one ray of hope for millions of Americans. I just knew this news had to be the critical event of the week, if not the — whatever news cycle you consider, not just the day. And, apparently the editor agreed with me."

The editor, Reg Murphy, was, like Harris, a native of Georgia. Though he had been in San Francisco only two years, he was acutely aware of the thousands of transplanted Southerners and Midwesterners who lived throughout the Bay Area. They clung to the red-clay memories of their home states, and Murphy knew Elvis's death would strike responsive chords within them. They were the plain working people of the region and an integral part of the newspaper's circulation, even if the promoters of conventions and tourism who touted the cosmopolitan image the city projects to the world often ignored them.

Across the top of the *Examiner*'s front page the headline blazed: "Elvis Presley Dies." Above was a smaller headline: "Heart attack, doctor says." A photo of a performing Presley was included and a story combining the early AP and UPI stories read out from a subhead: "Unconscious/at his mansion/in Memphis." A paragraph in boldface type headed "The Presley legend in photos: Page 6" called attention to a page of photographs and a hastily written story recalling the entertainer's last Bay Area concert, an appearance in April 1976 at the Cow Palace.

Several thousand extra copies of the final edition were run off, and all were snapped up by workers heading home by bus, automobile, rapid-rail, and cablecar.

The *Examiner* provided fuller coverage in all its editions the next day. Art Harris wrote a rich reminiscence from his experience in 1975, covering a four-day convention of Elvis fans that coincided with Presley's appearance at the Omni in Atlanta. He had chronicled the efforts of Lulubelle and Roxanne, prototypes of Everywoman, and their struggles to see their idol, to touch him, to tell him of their love—only to be defeated by the security forces that ringed his hotel and the concert arena. Reporter Larry Kramer found the "ultimate fan," Naomi Frisby, a thirty-nine-year-old housewife and country band bass player who lived in Milpitas. "I've been crazy about Elvis for twenty-one years," she said, showing off her fifteen scrapbooks of memorabilia. Mrs. Frisby is president of the Elvis Now Society, a fan club of thirty-five members (the maximum number her living room will hold) with another one hundred on its mailing list.

Editors around the country began planning for the next day's paper, facing choices of what stories to give what play. While practically all agreed that Elvis's death was a major story, just how did it stack up with the rest of the day's news? Several cities had important local stories, but the international scene was rather quiet. There were only two major new developments out of Washington that day—the Panama Canal treaty fight and reports that Federal District Court Judge Frank Johnson of Alabama was President Carter's choice to become director of the Federal Bureau of Investigation. Former President Gerald Ford had endorsed the ratification of the treaties. But the Senate, along with most of the rest of official Washington, was taking a holiday from the August heat, and aside from predictable reactions from the conservative foes of ratification, there was no one around to assess the Ford action.

News judgment is a subtle thing, influenced by the editor's instinct that one story is more important than another. Even those editors who lacked any enthusiasm for Presley or his music knew this was not a routine obituary. For one thing, the wire services were focusing a lot of attention on the story. For another, local interest was strong. Telephones in the newsroom were ringing constantly with calls from hysterical fans and ordinary citizens. Almost every major city had some local involvement with Elvis. Even if he had not appeared there in person—and for twenty years he had given numerous public appearances in arenas throughout the country—his performance in some not-too-distant city had made news. Every performance was an event, always sold out, always evoking reactions. Now Elvis was dead, and once again he was news.

Never before had so many newspapers led their front pages with a report that someone other than a head of state had died.

In New York, the *Daily News* had no hesitation about how to handle the late-breaking news. A flattering photo from the Associated Press and the headline "Elvis Presley/Dies at 42" dominated the front page. The caption under the photo read "Elvis Presley, one of the pioneers of rock and roll, dies in Memphis. Stories on page 2; other pictures in the centerfold." The tabloid, with more than two million readers, is the nation's largest daily newspaper, and the Elvis story supplanted the "Son of Sam" murder stories that had boosted circulation in recent weeks.

"Elvis: Idol of Millions," a three-part series by reporter Alton Slagle, gave a detailed account of the entertainer's life. The series found its way into many other newspapers through syndication by the newspaper's news service.

At *The New York Times*, some mild panic occurred when editors discovered no one had prepared an advance obituary. The assignment for writing one went to Molly Ivins, a Texan who had joined *The Times* a year earlier after editing the *Texas Observer*, a weekly political journal.

"I've never written harder or faster in my life," Ivins recalled, acknowledging major assistance from the newspaper's research department. "It was one of those real, right-down-to-the-deadline, crash-bang things where they were ripping the copy out of the typewriter take by take. *The Times* normally has obits in the can of anyone that's important; but, of course, no one had expected Elvis to die that young."

For Ivins, the hardest task was adhering to the newspaper's style and writing "Mr. Presley" for each reference to the singer. She related the known facts about his death and provided a retrospective of his career, from the days "Mr. Presley toured in rural areas under the sobriquet, 'The Hillbilly Cat.'" She also gave due credit to Colonel Tom Parker, "a character of P. T. Barnum proportions," as the guiding force behind the Presley career, recalling his credo: "Don't explain it, just sell it." Ivins's distinctive article was moved by The New York Times News Service, and it was the comprehensive piece that led the front pages of dozens of the nation's major newspapers the next day.

The Times bracketed the obituary by Ivins with a lengthy analysis by rock critic John Rockwell ("Presley Gave/Rock Its Style"), and the two articles and a two-column photo of Elvis, from his 1973 NBC Television special, were played at the top left of page one. While not the newspaper's lead story, the positioning of the photo and articles by the nation's most prestigious newspaper was considered astounding in media circles, and *The Times*'s action influenced magazine editors, broadcasters, and other journalists in their perception of the importance of Presley's death.

The Los Angeles Times ran three photos of Elvis at the top of its front page. Underneath was the obituary by Ted Thackrey, Jr.: "Elvis Presley Dies at 42/Legend of Rock 'n' Roll Era." Also on page one was an analysis by Robert Hilburn, the newspaper's pop music critic. *The Washington Post* led with the news that an Alabama judge was expected to head the FBI and gave second play to a story out of Yugoslavia,

"Brezhnev Hints at 'Positive Turn' In U.S. Relations." But a three-column box in the center of the front page contained a photo of Elvis from 1974 and the beginning of the obituary which jumped to a full page inside. The front of the paper's "Style" or feature section was given over to a huge face shot of Presley and two features—"In the End, He Was Wholesome Enough for Memphis" by Henry Mitchell and "All Shook Up on the Day the '50s Died" by Marian Clark.

Newspapers all across the country used banner headlines, often accompanied by subheadings, multicolumn pictures, or boxed stories—or all of these eye-catching journalistic techniques—on their front pages. The layouts fairly shouted the news and reflected the common themes of Presley's impact, of the outpouring of grief, and of questions about the cause of Presley's death. This included *The Boston Globe* with its story "Elvis is dead at 42" and *The Boston Herald-American* with a similar head boxed in green; *The Indianapolis Star* banner head "Elvis Dead at 42; Started Rock Music Era" and subhead "From Truck Driver to Millionaire"; the *Milwaukee Sentinel* "Rock King Elvis Presley Dies"; *The Milwaukee Journal* Elvis Fans Mourn Idol's Death at 42"; and in Madison the *Wisconsin State Journal* three-column color photo captioned "The late, great Elvis Presley."

The Philadelphia Inquirer headlined "Elvis Presley 'The King' Dies at 42" across its front page, and a note called attention to stories inside. *The Evening Bulletin* ran a color photograph and a boxed story and pictures across the top of page one under the headlines: "Elvis dies/Rock Legend Had Humble Start" and "His Fans/Mourn/'The King.'" Across the river in South Jersey, *The Courier Post*, published in Cherry Hill, New Jersey, ran a banner headline, "Doctors deny drugs killed Presley," along with a four-column color studio photo of Elvis.

Aside from one column detailing a local murder, *The Plain Dealer* in Cleveland gave over the entire top half of its front page to " 'King of Rock'/Presley, 42, dies." At the other end of the state *The Cincinnati Enquirer* ran an index and news summary down column one; the rest of the front page was bordered in black. A photo, taken at a recent local concert, was captioned: "... mature, heavier Elvis still thrilled audience." The headline read: "Drug Use Discounted/'King' Presley, 42,/Dies of Heart Attack." A boxed index referred to a full page of stories and pictures inside, and at the fold was a banner headline: "Fans Shocked, Numbed By Elvis' Sudden Death."

In every part of the country—at *The Des Moines Register,* the (Portland) *Oregon Journal,* the *Chicago Tribune, The San Diego Union,* the *Jackson Daily News, The Morning News* of Paterson, New Jersey, and the *Honolulu Advertiser*—full banner headlines were used. *The San Antonio Light* used red type and an exclamation point in its headline above the masthead: " 'The King' Is Dead!"

Probably the nation's most interesting front page was the *Nashville Banner.* The entire upper right quarter of the page was yellow sheet music with green notes and the words to "Blue Suede Shoes." The title of the song was "Elvis 1935-1977." Superimposed over this was a cut-out color photo taken at the singer's only Nashville concert (July 1, 1973). Down the left side of the page were four parallel headlines: "Elvis," "Lisa," " 'Twas True," and "Grief," all locally written stories that were syndicated through the Gannett newspapers, the nation's largest chain. Gannett's flagship paper, the *Democrat and Chronicle* in Rochester, New York, ran a photograph of Elvis from his last performance in that city— at the War Memorial on May 25—and an index to the additional stories inside. The lead headline took up five of the six columns across the top of page one.

A photo of the singer's last local appearance also highlighted the *Chicago Tribune's* front page. Elvis was shown acknowledging cheers from a capacity crowd at the Chicago Stadium on October 14, 1976. Page one also included an analysis by rock music critic Lynn van Matre and a boxed index to the Presley items inside: an assessment of Elvis's movies by critic Gene Siskel, the reaction of show business personalities by columnist Aaron Gold, and a full page of Elvis pictures. Above the paper's masthead, however, a headline cited a story on the inside pages that was to play a counterpoint to much of the media's coverage for the next few days: "Reveal Elvis' Drug Use and Violence/Associates Tell All in New Book."

The *Tribune's* reference was to a review of *Elvis: What Happened?,* a 332-page paperback which Ballantine Books had published with little fanfare on August 1. The initial press run had been four hundred thousand, but within six hours of Elvis's death, the publisher had gone back to press for another two hundred fifty thousand copies. By week's end, K-Mart, the big discount department store chain, had placed an order for two million copies, the largest single book order in history. The book was the product of reporter Steve Dunleavy, who said he culled the material from three hundred hours of taped interviews with three bodyguards that Presley had fired—Red West, Sonny West, and Dave Hebler. Advertised as "the dark other side of the brightest star in the world," the book was a series of bizarre tales alleging that Elvis had a pathological obsession with guns and that he believed he had extraordinary psychic and religious powers. But the most sensational aspect of the narrative was an allegation of widespread use of drugs by the entertainer. "He takes pills to go to sleep," Red West says in the book. "He takes pills to get up. He takes pills to go to the john, and he takes pills to stop him from going to the john. ... He is a walking pharmaceutical shop."

When Dunleavy began interviewing the bodyguards, he was a reporter for the *National Star,* the sensational weekly tabloid owned by Rupert Murdoch, the Australian press magnate. He persuaded Murdoch to scrap a planned series of articles so that he could expand the interviews into a book. Now Dunleavy was a reporter for the *New York Post,* also owned by Murdoch, and from that position he appeared on NBC's late-night nationwide television special on Elvis and on *Good Morning America* on ABC television, where Geraldo Rivera took him to task for smearing Elvis's reputation.

A serialization of the book began Wednesday afternoon in the *Post,* under the headline, "Millions/Mourn/Presley," with a photo captioned: "The decline is apparent in an older, heavier Elvis Presley as he appeared in a recent concert appearance." Across the bottom of the New York tabloid's front page was a boxed "Exclusive: New book tells of his decline in a drug nightmare. 'Elvis: What Happened?' 4-page pullout begins on P. 33."

The three bodyguards called a Los Angeles press conference to deny they were trying to capitalize on Presley's death and to point out that the book had been written long before his death. Dave Hebler told reporters Elvis was "a tormented man, a victim of himself, the image and the legend." While several papers retrieved the review copies of the book they had discarded and ran stories about its publication, the most extensive publicity surrounding *Elvis: What Happened?* came from *Chicago Sun-Times* columnist Bob Greene. The talented young writer, whose column is syndicated in dozens of major papers, had interviewed Sonny West only hours before Presley's death in what he called "the first newspaper interview on the subject ever given by a member of Presley's entourage."

Greene first heard of the book on Monday of that week and called Ballantine's public relations office, not just to do a story on the book but to interview one of the bodyguards. He was given Sonny West's telephone number, and the next day he called, asked a series of questions, and wrote a story based on the interview. He then called RCA Records, seeking some Presley spokesman to rebut the accusations that had been made, but to no avail. Ralph Otwell, the *Sun-Times* editor, said the piece should go on the front page the next day, and he had it cleared by the company's lawyers. Greene then took the copy upstairs to the Field Newspaper Syndicate where it was scheduled to be sent out over the wire that night under the headline, "Elvis: He's in Danger of Losing His Life." When he returned to his desk, Greene was approached by Otwell who said, "I suppose you've heard . . . Elvis just died." The reporter recalled later that he began to tremble as he looked at the column he held in his hand. Phrases were inserted to give the reader a hint of what had happened, and all references to Elvis were changed to the past tense. But the original plans to run the column on page one the next day stood. Greene and his editors insist the decision was strictly a news judgment.

The tabloid-size *Sun-Times* devoted most of its front page to a large photo of Presley, the headline "Elvis is dead," and a quote: " 'Come on, Presley, breathe. Breathe for me . . .'—Desperate doctor on way to hospital. Full coverage inside." The start of Bob Greene's column spread across the bottom of the page. Pages three, four, and five were given over to the Presley story, with wire coverage, features reprinted from *The Washington Post*, and local reaction. But the Greene column produced the loudest indignation—angry telephone calls and letters from fans who shared the feelings of ancient Greeks who wanted to kill the messenger who brought bad news. Ironically, Greene was an intense Presley fan. "Outside of my own family," he said, "Elvis was the greatest single influence of my life."

The Associated Press moved a story quoting from Greene's interview with Sonny West, and his column was given prominent play in other newspapers, most notably *The Washington Star*, which led its early editions with it. The headline over the column ran the width of the paper: "Elvis Presley—a Life Plagued by Drugs, Fear and Loneliness," and it provoked a storm of protest, including a full page of letters to the editor criticizing the paper's lack of taste and sensitivity. The *San Francisco*

Chronicle also played the story on page one and reported more than five hundred complaining telephone callers that morning.

Most of the reporters assigned to the Presley story became aware of the book, and Les Seago at the Memphis AP recalls the scramble to try to read it in the hours after Elvis died. "I think I read it in snatches," he said, "while I was going to the bathroom, things like that, so I would know what the talk was all about." Questions of drug usage came into play at the Tuesday night press conference by the medical examiner, and the book and its allegations were the subject of conversation by many of the fans who were gathering in Memphis.

Although *The Commercial Appeal* usually carried Bob Greene's column, the editors elected not to run his interview with Sonny West. The Memphis newspaper did note in its lead story on Wednesday morning that there were initial reports that homicide officers had investigated reports of a death due to drug overdose. Reporter Lawrence Buser also quoted the emphatic denial from the county medical examiner that there was "no indication of any drug abuse of any kind." During the next few months, the paper published a story on laboratory test results from the autopsy which strongly suggested that drugs had played a part in the death. There were interviews with Dr. Francisco and Dr. Nichopoulos, and stories in *The Commercial Appeal* which raised the drug questions again, were duly reported by the two wire services. But, as UPI's Albritten noted, "They were played once and then put aside, like a stone sinking into the water." In August 1978, the *National Enquirer* ran a story charging that drug abuse and not a heart attack was the cause of Elvis's death; Representative Robert Dornan of California placed the article in the *Congressional Record*, but there was little notice. It was almost two years after Elvis's death before the drug issue received national media attention through an investigative report by producer Charles Thompson and reporter Geraldo Rivera on ABC Television's *20/20*. In the hours following the first news from Memphis, however, drugs were only a minor sidelight in the developing story.

"Death Captures Crown of Rock and Roll" was the headline on the front page of *The Commercial Appeal*, and the paper became a collector's item. The first rule of journalism is that all news is local, and this was clearly the biggest local story that ever hit the city. "We were afloat on a sea of hysteria," said James McDaniel, the managing editor. "We figured we had the greatest story in the world. There were calls from

London and Paris—people wanting our story before it was even written." He and Editor Michael Grehl increased the number of pages that had been planned. As the night wore on and the original stories were updated and new ones were added, they began to speculate on how many extra papers should be printed. An increase of twenty thousand was authorized, then thirty thousand. Finally, an extra sixty thousand were printed.

When McDaniel finally left the office around midnight, he saw no cars stopped in front of the Memphis Publishing Company building, and he had a sinking feeling that they might be stuck with the extra newspapers. On almost any evening, there would be cars pulling over to the curb, their drivers buying early editions of the morning paper. But he had passed by during a unique lull in the Union Avenue traffic; by seven o'clock the next morning, every paper had been sold. There were reports of news racks being looted and of people following carrier boys along their routes, taking the papers from front porches before residents could retrieve them. Copies of the historic newspaper were being sold for five and ten dollars to out-of-town fans who had just arrived at Graceland. Copies sold for more than fifty dollars in Dallas and New York, and the *Wall Street Journal* reported that a copy later sold in London for three hundred dollars.

The editors had rejected the use of color on the front page, electing instead to feature a 1974 photograph by David Darnell of a smiling Elvis, sunglasses pushed up on his forehead, signing autographs. Below the fold were an AP story on the selection of Judge Johnson to head the FBI, the regular front page humor column by Lydel Sims, an index, and the weather report. Everything else was about Elvis—the lead story announcing the news and the city's reaction; a biographical sketch ("Elvis Went/From Rags/To Riches"); and a commentary on his music and his career by critic Walter Dawson, who noted that Elvis began as "an artist who couldn't be pigeonholed" and ended as "one who was unclassifiable." There was also a photo of the hearse taking the body from the hospital and the accompanying story, "Are You Sure There's No Mistake?/—The Desired Answer Never Came."

The newspaper maxim about local news was not confined to Memphis. Editors throughout the country began seeking out local reaction and local angles to the staggering news from Memphis that was dominating the wires. The subject of the most frequently appearing local sidebar was record sales. In city after city, record stores were selling out of Elvis records—singles, tapes, albums, anything with the Presley voice.

Newsday reported signs posted in the giant New York area Sam Goody record store chain: "Due to circumstances beyond our control, we are currently out of all Elvis Presley records." Rain checks were offered, but many distraught customers were convinced that since Elvis was gone, there would be no more records. On the West Coast, a clerk at the Licorice Music Store told *The San Diego Union* that an old gray-haired couple had bought the last copy of "Moody Blue." Denise Wolfe said the store sold out of Elvis's new album within an hour after his death was reported. *The Atlanta Constitution* said the Record Bar reported several customers buying nine or ten copies of "Moody Blue," which had been recorded on blue vinyl and was thought to be a particularly significant collector's item.

Former radio personality Tommy Edwards, who had been master of ceremonies the first time Elvis appeared in Cleveland (in a show headlined by Roy Acuff), told *The Plain Dealer* it was the biggest day in the seventeen years he had operated the Record Haven shop. He said he had fifty-six different titles in stock, the largest in the area, a total of three hundred albums. By the end of the day, only two Christmas albums remained in stock.

"Elvis Fans clean out area stores" was a headline on the business page of *The Dallas Morning News*. The story surveyed area stores and reported that the Dallas RCA office had ordered $250,000 in Presley albums after writing orders all night. *The Des Moines Register* interviewed John Swenson, sales manager of the RCA regional office in Minneapolis, who said one wholesaler had ordered 42,000 copies of "Moody Blue." "I was with Capitol when the Beatles hit," said Swenson, "and this is very similar to that. Of course, with the Beatles, we had only one piece of product, and here we've got 21 years worth." Stan Lewis, a veteran record distributor and owner of six local retail stores in Shreveport, Louisiana, told *Billboard* his entire stock of 25,000 albums was sold in a day. It took him four hours to get through to the RCA sales office to order 150,000 more.

Papers in the cities where Elvis had been scheduled to appear in concert during the next few days interviewed managers of the sold-out arenas and fans holding the now-useless tickets. The first stop was to have been Portland, Maine, and the *Press-Herald* gave the story full play, interviewing the fan who was first in line to buy tickets, a clerk in a record store who sold eight records in the first ten minutes after the news, and the manager of a theater that had lined up a Presley film festival to be held in conjunction with the concerts in the Cumberland County Civic Center. "I've been in the business a long time," said F.A. Morrisette, manager of the Fine Arts Theater. "I never knew the man, but I felt he was one of my own. Sometimes the theater business isn't so good, but you could always count on one of his pictures to get you out of the red."

After New England, the concert tour was to have taken Elvis to Utica, New York, on August 19, nearby Syracuse on the 20th, Hartford, Connecticut, on the 21st, and the Nassau Coliseum in Uniondale, New York, on the 22nd. The tour then would have moved south to Lexington, Kentucky, and Roanoke, Virginia, on the 23rd and the 24th, with two stops in North Carolina—Fayetteville on the 25th and Asheville on the 26th—before winding up with concerts at the Mid-South Coliseum in Memphis on the 27th and 28th. Newspapers in those areas also gave the story of "what-might-have-been" extensive coverage. Later the cancelled concerts would produce other news. Some fans sought a memorial concert in lieu of the scheduled event. Thousands in each city refused to turn in their tickets for refunds, preferring to hold them as souvenirs or mementos or items of future value in the collectors' market. Some arena managers offered to tear off a corner of the ticket or in some other way invalidate it; others insisted on the complete ticket for a refund. The various state laws governing refunds came into play, some requiring money from a cancelled concert to be held in escrow for seven years. There were legal action and accounting nightmares for the local arena managements, promoters of the concerts, and the Presley estate—and more stories about Elvis for many months after he died.

To many journalists, it was incomprehensible that people of average or lower incomes would hold onto a fifteen- or twenty-five-dollar ticket to a concert that would not take place. But such behavior was not at all unusual on the part of Presley followers. The *Baltimore News-American* even found a dozen Europeans who had come from Paris to follow Elvis on his concert tour. Jean Marc Garguilo and his party were visiting Paul Dowling, a collector of Elvis memorabilia who lives in suburban Ruxton, Maryland, when they heard the news. Garguilo wept and said he felt as if his brother had died. Since 1968, when he met the singer in Las Vegas, the Frenchman had been bringing groups to the United States. Their Maryland host, who values his collection of Presley films and records in excess of $100,000, was showing them a film of the 1968 television special when they heard the news.

Other newspapers also located a resident Superfan, someone in their community who was an inveterate concert- or movie-goer, a collector of pictures, records, and memorabilia, a person who had been profoundly affected by the singer's death. Cliff Pawul, a twenty three-year-old native of Cleveland who packs automobile parts for a living, told *The Plain Dealer* he felt he had lost a brother. Just two weeks earlier, he had completed the full set of records—one hundred four singles and ninety-eight albums. Pawul had become a fan in 1968 when he first heard, "If I Can Dream." Since then he had collected thousands of clippings which he kept stored in fifteen department store suit boxes. He also owned the full set of bubble gum cards with Elvis's pictures on them issued in 1956. *The Montgomery Advertiser* featured a story and picture of thirty-four-year-old Ginger Vance, who started collecting Elvis items twenty-two years earlier when the singer kissed her on the cheek and gave her a photograph. She had gone to Garrett Coliseum to see a Kitty Wells concert, and Elvis had opened the show. She had since attended fifteen other concerts and had seen each of his thirty-three films five or six times .

Jim Curtin of Darby, Pennsylvania, who calls himself "the original Elvis freak" had seen forty-eight live concerts and claimed to have shaken Elvis's hand on thirty-two different occasions. A guitar teacher and sometime Elvis imitator, he told Philadelphia's *Bulletin* he was thinking of working full-time to keep the memory alive. Curtin has a collection of five thousand Presley records, copies of all the movies, and an Elvis Presley Boulevard street sign stolen in Memphis. Philadelphia also housed a figure well-known in Presley circles, Paul Lichter. *The Inquirer* ran his picture and reported on telephone tie-ups in his suburban neighborhood. Lichter, who had once claimed to make thirty thousand dollars a month dealing in Elvis memorabilia, is the largest single retailer of Presley records and memorabilia. In addition he possesses a large personal collection of Presley items, including automobiles and clothing once owned by the superstar. Lichter later complained that the Philadelphia paper's mention of his Presley earnings was in poor taste. He was a fan first and a marketer second, he said.

Newsday reported reminiscenses all over Long Island. Dozens of members of the Long Island Rod and Custom Association assembled in a parking lot with their special cars and Elvis mementos. At Lynbrook, eight fans gathered at the the home of Richard Hess, a thirty-five-year-old businessman who had once headed a now-defunct fan club. "I know it sounds crazy," Hess said. "Here I am, a married man with two kids and a business. But to me he was the greatest man alive. He was my thing. My little world. It's all over now. I guess my adolescent period will pass and I'm going to have to grow up." His wife, Angela, added that they had attended a hundred Elvis concerts through the years and had visited Graceland twice. "He was our hobby," she said. "Other families are involved in things; he is what we shared. He was our excitement and our involvement."

The *St. Petersburg Times* also found a businessman who was distraught over the news from Memphis. Jim Shirah as a young man had become a disc jockey just so he could play Elvis's records on air. In 1968 he had spent two days at Graceland and, on leaving, had asked the entertainer for a souvenir. Presley had given him the jacket he wore in *Viva Las Vegas* along with two pair of boots and two yellow shirts he wore in *Roustabout.*

The lead local story in *The Atlanta Journal* was about Debbi Cox who had collected Elvis items since she was four years old. Last winter she had stood, slept, and shivered in line to get seats for his Atlanta concert. On the morning of the day Elvis died, she had received a luggage tag with the singer's picture on it in the mail, her latest fan club memento. "They can tear the Omni down," she told the reporter. "We don't need it anymore."

Most of the fans the various newspapers located were women whose interest in Elvis began with a school-girl crush and matured into long-distance feelings of love and friendship. Nellie Austin, a thirty-eight-year-old housewife living in Lake Norman, North Carolina, told *The Charlotte Observer* that she once skipped school to spend the day at a record shop listening to Elvis. She had kept a life-size photo of Elvis on the back of her bedroom door until her husband threatened jokingly to replace it with a *National Enquirer* picture of the overweight Presley. Mrs. Austin said most of her high school girlfriends who recently gathered for a twentieth reunion were not as fervent in their feelings for Elvis. But her eighteen-year-old daughter was now a fan. "As long as I kept Elvis on top, he kept me young," she said. "Now I'll just have to slip into middle age. It's like a part of our lives is gone without him."

In a story about the fans published in Rochester's *Democrat and Chronicle*, reporter Larry King noted that "seeing Elvis might not have been the most important thing in their lives, but it sure ranked in the top ten." He told of fans who sought to sit as close to the stage as possible at an Elvis concert in order to catch a scarf or to make contact with their eyes or hands. One example was Jo Schreiber, who waited in line from 4:00 a.m., seeking a close seat for a 1976 concert in Buffalo. She told the box office teller that she was getting married soon and it was her dream to have Elvis kiss her wedding veil. She got a seat in Row 8, and her veil went unkissed.

The media and the fans seemed to be recalling every detail of the singer's career and giving them local angles. Many papers found residents who had served in the Army in Texas or Germany with Elvis. "I always admired the man," Chester Thompson told the Philadelphia *Bulletin.* "He never wanted preferential treatment and was strictly a soldier—an A-1 soldier. He did everything everyone else did."

Thompson, a ward councilman from Darby Borough, served with Elvis in the 790th Military Police Battalion in Frankfurt in 1958-59. He marveled that Presley never voiced regrets about being in the Army, that the singer felt it was his "moral obligation to serve the country."

The *Arkansas Democrat* ran a story recalling Elvis the recruit getting his hair cut at Fort Chaffee. Another story was an interview with John Mawn, who had served as public information officer for the Third Armored Division in Germany. He had set up a press conference when Elvis's unit arrived in Europe, a gathering Mawn called "the biggest press conference since Eisenhower announced the end of World War II." New Orleans *Times-Picayune* reporter Joe Massa had been part of Mawn's public relations team. He was among nine recruits picked after basic training "to make sure the world got knowledge of the important things in the life of the world's most famous draftee." In a story for his paper, Massa recalled informing the world from Fort Hood one day that Elvis had a sore throat but would recover before the weekend. "That was big news in those days."

The many "when Elvis was here" stories that appeared all over the country provided an indicator of the convulsion of grief that followed the news of his death, for those thousands who had attended the concerts over the past twenty-two years remembered the occasions vividly.

Newspaper files were sources for memories of past local performances, but the articles reprinting earlier reviews usually contained qualifying comments. Many of the reviews—particularly those from the fifties —were hostile, and a disclaimer usually noted that the audience liked the show even if the critic did not. George Arthur of the *Seattle*

Post-Intelligencer said a check of his clipping files showed that each Elvis concert was "an event, something beyond a performance by a popular entertainer." John Wendeborn, critic of *The Oregonian*, recalled panning Elvis in 1970 and receiving more than one hundred highly negative letters as a result. Since then he had covered four other concerts and "become enamored" of Presley. "Anyone who can spend more than an hour onstage and only sing half that time and still have what it takes to sell a song to an audience has kingly virtue as far as music is concerned," he wrote.

A *Providence Journal* critic called Elvis's June 1976 concert "the single most spectacular event of the Bicentennial year." In the audience of twenty-seven thousand was one of Rhode Island's two congressmen, Representative Edward P. Beard. His comment: "I've been waiting since 1955 to see this guy." Presley's one-day stand in Providence earned him more than a quarter-million dollars.

Some recalled the singer's early years. Mac McCloskey told the *Courier-Post* in Cherry Hill, New Jersey, he had booked Presley into the Dancette Ballroom, a compact two-story club, where eight hundred teenagers turned out to see the cocky young singer in the midfifties. *The Times-Picayune* interviewed a nightclub owner who had turned away a young Elvis in 1956 "because he wasn't well known enough" to command the one-hundred-fifty-dollars-a-night fee he demanded. Mrs. Lois Brown said she hired the Everly Brothers instead at her Cadillac Club in New Orleans. She added that she later became a friend of Elvis—"one of the sweetest guys this side of heaven"—when he was in the city to film *King Creole*. *The Times-Picayune* also noted Elvis's first New Orleans appearance, at the Municipal Auditorium on August 12, 1956, at ticket prices of $1.05, $1.26, and $1.47.

Bruce Bornino, writing in *The Cleveland Press*, recalled the singer's six visits—all advance sellouts—from the first in November 1956, to the last in October 1976. The critic said of that final appearance that he had seen Elvis look better, but never sound better. "Even though he seemed to be going through the motions much of the time, Elvis didn't miss a note," said Bornino. "And he sang tough tunes like 'America the Beautiful,' 'I'm Hurt,' and 'How Great Thou Art.' His vocal range and control are unbelievable."

Over a period of twenty years, Elvis had played San Diego on five occasions. *The San Diego Union* recalled that in April 1956, the singer had autographed records at a local store and walked down the street unrecognized. Three months later he had to sneak into town under cover of darkness with a police escort for a concert at the Arena. That fall Police Chief A. E. Jansen had threatened to jail the singer if he ever returned and "gyrated" as he did. It was fourteen years before Elvis returned.

Patrick MacDonald, arts and entertainment editor of the *Seattle Times*, called the audience at the 1973 Elvis concert at the Seattle Arena the most interesting he had ever seen. He wrote: "If Norman Rockwell wanted models for a portrait of contemporary Americans—they were all there—young, old, rich, poor, black, white. It was quite amazing and refreshing and ample proof of Elvis' widespread popularity."

The Boston Herald-American featured a story describing New England as "Elvis Country," recounting an appearance the previous year in Augusta, Maine, where the Sheraton Inn had auctioned off for local charity the furnishings from the singer's room. His pillow case brought two hundred twenty-five dollars; a pair of handtowels, three hundred dollars; the bath mat, one hundred five dollars; and the bed sheet, ninety-six dollars. The paper also reported Elvis's declining a 1960 invitation to the Charity Field Day, sponsored by the mayor of Boston. Instead of just saying no, Elvis had sent a check for one thousand dollars to the scholarship fund for the handicapped.

Wayne Harada, entertainment editor of the *Honolulu Advertiser*, traced a special relationship between Hawaii and Elvis existing since November 1957, when four thousand fans met his boat and fifteen thousand turned out for his first concert. Another story noted the "quiet, very special place here in Hawaii by which he will be remembered—even though it is really a memorial to 1,102 other men." This was a reference to the Arizona Memorial at Pearl Harbor, for which Elvis provided a fundraising concert and the needed publicity to complete its construction. Elvis had visited the memorial on each of his frequent trips to Hawaii, but only a few Navy men knew; there was no publicity. On Wednesday, the Navy laid a wreath at the memorial in Elvis's memory.

5

Late-Night Reflections

The late-evening news special is a not-unusual device the television networks use to provide in-depth reports on significant events. Generally, such reports are reserved for some occurrence that justifies more than the two or three minutes available on the evening news shows.

Normally set to start at 11:30 p.m., eastern standard time, right after local news shows, the special ofttimes is a planned event such as election coverage, where the votes are coming in late. It also has been used to provide a vehicle for presenting unusual or voluminous film which the network might have available. Earthquakes, tornadoes, or other foreign or domestic disasters have sometimes been the subject of such programs.

But such specials are used sparingly. Network schedules are set weeks in advance, and a viewer expecting to see the *Tonight* show or a movie that is listed in *TV Guide* may not be happy to discover a news program instead. The only promotion available for the hastily scheduled special is an announcement on the evening news or just before station breaks during the evening.

At NBC, the decision to present a special on the death of Elvis came early. Gordon Manning, then chief of special events at the network, was alerted shortly after five o'clock when the news broke. He remembers the tight deadline as his staff hurriedly began to assemble an outline for the program. Even though it was mid-August, he was amazed to discover that none of his team was on vacation. Everyone was there and available to do the show—writers, editors, researchers, production crew.

Most fortunately for him, the major proponent of doing the special was David Brinkley, the *Nightly News* anchor. He insisted on staying around to anchor the special himself. A native of Wilmington, North Carolina, who had worked in Nashville and other Southern cities in his pre-television journalism career, Brinkley was an astute observer of the American scene. He was keenly aware of the social impact of the Presley phenomenon.

"The truth is that I never liked Presley's music," Brinkley said later, explaining his preference for traditional jazz and chamber music, "but I knew millions of others did and so I thought a special program was called for." The newsman used that thought as he opened the program from New York: "It didn't even matter a great deal whether you liked Elvis or not. He was a part of our lives."

Speaking with the style that has made his voice one of the most familiar in America, Brinkley noted that other people have meant a lot, but most of them do not make changes.

"Elvis Presley *changed* things." The emphasis was Brinkley's, as he read the script he had written and polished during the evening. "He changed the way then teenaged America *thought* about things ... about public entertainers and popular music and popular attitudes toward *living* and *behaving* and *dressing* and *talking*."

The program then featured a live report from Jackson Bain, speaking from a point near the gate of Graceland. Bain had left Washington earlier that afternoon enroute to Atlanta on another assignment. He had been paged at the Atlanta airport and told of Presley's death; within fifteen minutes he was on a flight to Memphis.

On arrival there, Bain went directly to the studios of WMC-TV, NBC's Memphis affiliate. By the time the network's Atlanta-based camera crew had arrived on a later flight, he had made arrangements for the network to share the station's technical facilities. These proved excellent, particularly a news van which the local station got permission to park directly in front of the Presley mansion's gate—sitting astride , the center line that divides the four-lane highway. Looking down at the crowd from a vantage point atop the van, NBC's cameras could record all vehicles and persons entering and leaving the mansion, feed the signal back to WMC's midtown studios, then on to New York by cable.

Bain's brief report was a live recap of events during the past six hours, including a tape clip of a preliminary autopsy report which the coroner had announced a few minutes earlier. Bain described the rapidly growing crowd and the uncertainty of funeral plans.

Back in New York, Brinkley then began reading an obituary as still pictures were shown on the screen. From the network's extensive photo file, Manning and his staff had compiled scenes from the entertainer's career—a young Elvis at the microphone, pictures from his Army days, movie clips from the famous wedding that broke so many young hearts. Calling on the affiliates that the network owned and operated in Cleveland, Chicago, Los Angeles, New York, and Washington, the production staff was able to locate a print of *Elvis on Tour* to round out the obituary. The staff also obtained scenes from *Loving You* and *Aloha from Hawaii*, the NBC special that had been broadcast worldwide via satellite in 1973, for use later in the program. Editing was done at the NBC studios in Burbank, California, with transmission on cue at appropriate times during the program originating from New York.

Brinkley noted that Presley became a national sensation after his 1956 appearances on the Ed Sullivan television show, but he added that "it's on radio where popular musicians live or die." Fame and wealth come if their records are played on the radio, he said. Television cannot provide that.

His comments served as an introduction for a spot by Brian Ross, an NBC reporter who provided the reaction of New York's disc jockeys to the news of Elvis's death. Ross was joined in a panel discussion about the man and his music by Norm N. Nite of WNBC Radio, Murray the K, one of the most successful early promoters of rock and roll, David Marsh of *Rolling Stone*, and Steve Dunleavy of the *New York Post*. Their dialogue focused on the change that had hit the music business when rock and roll replaced mainstream popular music as radio's staple ingredient, a change that coincided with the appearance of the 45-rpm record, the rise of television, and the appearance of teenagers with money.

Their conversation rambled, then turned to the singer's background and the new book, *Elvis: What Happened?*, which Dunleavy had co-authored with the three ex-bodyguards. The bearded Dunleavy, waving a cigar, talked about Elvis's lifestyle, the seclusion, his weight problem, the drugs. He described Presley as "a poor kid from the South ... a bad word, a nasty word, but one that is often used, 'white trash.'"

Brinkley later said the phrase made him wince, and Brian Ross subsequently told a colleague he felt "a cold chill shoot down my spine" when he heard the term. The newsmen knew the words were offensive to many persons, particularly the rural poor who revered Presley so much. The discussion ended, and a short segment on Presley's movie career was presented; then the show went back to the live cameras outside Graceland for a report from Jackson Bain on the mood in Memphis.

"There is something in the rock and roll dictionary called the 'Memphis Sound,'" said Bain. "A solid rhythm and blues kind of music with roots heavy into Southern gospel. Memphis was the town Elvis Presley adopted as he rose from truck driver to established star. And the town adopted him as well."

Bain described the crowd that had continued to build, and close-up cameras showed the incredulity and shock on the faces of those who kept asking reporters if the news was really true. He then closed by noting that many fans were turning to the only Elvis they really knew, "the soft, deep baritone on the records they loved." Film of a record store—open late—on New York's 49th Street then came up as Brinkley described the run on Presley records that had started around the country.

To close the program, Brinkley returned to the theme of change:

"Presley came along in the fifties when the pop music world was ready . . . impatient, in fact, for something to come along.

"The famous swing era of the big bands was dead or dying. Benny Goodman and Artie Shaw and Tommy Dorsey had about had their day. Count Basie and Duke Ellington carried on, but it was uphill.

"There was something called bop—hard, difficult, obscure music you couldn't dance to. They called it jazz, but it wasn't. There was Bill Haley and the Comets . . . Chuck Berry . . . Fats Domino . . . and Elvis. It was a new way of playing old music called rhythm and blues . . . formerly known as race and blues. Hot and stomping and sweaty and sexy. The audience for it was there, and the audience went crazy.

"It didn't just change pop music. It changed society. Elvis was out there in front of it. Until the day he died—today—he could still fill an auditorium or a ball park any time he wanted."

The original script indicated the program was running almost three minutes short, and Manning had planned a "talk-back," a split-screen conversation between Brinkley in New York and Bain in Memphis. The two reporters had discussed the idea and chatted about some shared experiences a half hour before air time, but the live segments had run long and by the time Brinkley neared the end of his prepared remarks, the show had run almost the entire half hour.

"He changed our lives, like it or not," Brinkley concluded, and photos of Elvis began to move on the screen as the familiar voice came up on the sound track singing "Love Me Tender."

At the same hour, ABC transmitted its own half-hour tribute, entitled "Elvis: Love Me Tender." Even though the two networks were offering treatments of the same news event, ABC's choice to anchor the show almost smacked of counter-programming. The contrast with the mature, urbane Brinkley could not have been greater as Geraldo Rivera, a hip, long-haired New Yorker with a flowing mustache, was tapped for the assignment. Yet the thirty-four-year-old newscaster opened the show with a similar theme, that Presley had "revolutionized the music business, and in one way or another he touched most of our lives."

No stranger to late-night television, Rivera had been host in 1974-75 for a short-lived variety/talk show, *Good Night, America,* with which ABC attempted to counter the enormous ratings of Johnny Carson and NBC's *Tonight* show. The son of a Puerto Rican father and a Jewish mother, the Brooklyn-born Rivera had been trained as a lawyer. He first became prominent and attracted the attention of TV executives as spokesman and attorney for a group of Puerto Rican militants in 1970. He was hired by WABC-TV, and after a brief stint of general assignment reporting, he got his big break with a series of hard-hitting reports on the inhuman conditions at a state institution for the mentally retarded, reports which resulted in legislation and administrative reform and won him almost every journalism award available for local reporting.

Rivera soon moved to the network and, after serving as late-night talk-show host, was named traveling correspondent for *Good Morning, America.* In mid-1977 he became a featured reporter on the *ABC Evening News,* emerging as one of the hottest personalities in what Marshall McLuhan terms the cool medium of television. He often involved himself totally in his stories, sounding indignant, even crying on camera, using the medium as a vehicle for social reform. He continued to collect awards for his work, building a reputation as the leading exponent of the new "personal journalism." But many of his colleagues disliked the passion he brought to their profession.

Rivera carried this philosophy to his role as anchor for the late-night Elvis special, and his affection for the entertainer showed as he narrated the program.

"When it happened, I was very, very sorry, because it was like the passing of an era," Rivera said two years later, recalling the momentous day. "As a landmark, Elvis was so important in a cultural sense, to adolescents especially. I reported what we knew. I remember feeling very pleased at that time, at least initially, that he was not just another drug overdose."

The decision to air a special on Elvis was made sometime during the network's initial transmission of the *ABC Evening News*, with the announcement coming before sign off rather than during the news segment on Presley. Rivera did not get the call to anchor the show until almost eight o'clock that night, and he remembers the scramble under way to come up with a script and visuals to fill the half-hour time slot:

"When we went on the air, we had five minutes written. We had twenty-five minutes that we had to wing. We didn't know what was going to come in or what wasn't."

The program used a lot of feeds, direct transmission of reports from around the country, starting with straight news film from Baptist Memorial Hospital in Memphis, where a hospital spokesman and an ambulance driver recounted the event. Chuck Berry was interviewed in St. Louis, recalling a time in Las Vegas when Elvis and Sammy Davis, Jr. had come to his show in the Hilton Lounge and "danced a little bit in the aisles." Then, from Palm Springs, California, Bing Crosby called Elvis a major part of our musical history, saying, "the things that he did during his career, the things that he created are really something important."

Rivera noted the tributes that were pouring in from the entertainment industry, reading statements from Ann-Margret and Cher Allman. He then introduced "television's music historian," Dick Clark, who spoke from Las Vegas. But Clark, whose afternoon program, *American Bandstand*, on ABC Television during the late fifties was a major factor in popularizing rock and roll, contributed little more than a brief anecdote about Elvis coming in to see his recent stage show and his opinion that the singer in recent years had lived like "a caged animal."

Then technical problems hit, and on a live broadcast there is little leeway for correcting them.

"At about fifteen minutes after, one of the feeds didn't come through," recalled Rivera. A montage of films had been assembled on the seventh floor and was rushed in instead, but the script that was to accompany their showing failed to arrive at the WABC studio where Rivera was to supply the voice-over.

Watching the monitor, Rivera began ad-libbing a history of the period: "This is *King Creole*, one of the many movies Elvis made ... There's his marriage to Priscilla ... Here's Colonel Tom Parker, his legendary manager ... That concert he had in Hawaii, I remember it was beamed by satellite to stations all across the world."

Rivera knew his commentary lacked originality, but he also knew that three minutes of total silence would never work as background for the action film clips.

There were two more feeds. Rona Barrett, the Hollywood gossip columnist who in 1968 first broke the news of Elvis's impending marriage, gave a long commentary from Los Angeles. She traced his career, mixing her remarks with memories of her personal encounters with the entertainer.

"And in the end," she concluded, "still lonely, still insecure about a career that was constantly changing, and still missing the warmth that only his mother could provide, Elvis Presley died, an enigma, hopefully in peace."

Then came a strange, short interview from Las Vegas with Elias Ghanem, a physician who had treated Presley through the years. Gail Westrup of KSHO, the Las Vegas ABC affiliate, asked about excessive drug use: "Absolutely not ... I've never known Elvis to take any hard drugs whatsoever. ..." Drug overdose: "It could be, but ... his father ... told me that it was a heart attack. ..." Suicide: "He is a very religious man and he wouldn't even think of suicide at all."

"And then we had nothing," Rivera recalls. The camera returned to him, its red light flicked on, and the producer stretched his hands apart, indicating there was time remaining on the show.

"I have, of course, my own memories of Elvis Presley," Rivera began, telling of getting his first suit of clothes at age ten when a salesman asked him the name of his favorite singer.

"And I had just seen Elvis on the original Ed Sullivan program— that was twenty-two years ago. And I heard him and I loved him but I didn't know how to pronounce his name. It was so funny. After all, for a boy from New York, who is named Elvis?"

Rivera acknowledges the lack of professionalism and the justifiable criticism he received for using the personal anecdote, but in defense he says, "It was totally ad-libbed. I had to say something. We had two or three minutes there. I had to think about what to say, and I had no idea what I was going to talk about."

The show closed with excerpts from several songs and a final comment from Rivera: "The king is dead. Long live the music. Long live the memory. Elvis Presley, we'll miss you. Good night. Thank you."

Then, just as NBC was doing on the opposite channel, Elvis's recording of "Love Me Tender" sounded in the background as the program credits rolled.

The two networks considered their specials highly successful pieces of work. The ratings were good: NBC recorded a thirty-two share and ABC, a thirty-four, in the New York market. In Los Angeles, NBC had a thirty and ABC, a whopping forty-five—unusually high for late-night television.

Working under tight deadlines and the added pressure of live programming, the specials had come off well. The only negative responses focused on the "white trash" comment by Dunleavy. NBC in New York received fifty telephone calls immediately following the program; each of the callers protested Dunleavy's remarks.

Watching NBC's network affiliate in Tupelo, Mississippi, was Harold Montgomery, a state legislator who came from the same, poor rural background as the Presleys. He watched WTWV with a mixed sense of grief and pride, mourning the loss of someone he knew and admired but feeling good that David Brinkley was saying such nice things about this boy from East Tupelo. Then, he recalled, Dunleavy's comments "hit me across the face like a cold wet rag." He knew there is a world of difference in being poor and being trash.

To proud Southerners, many of whom have known poverty, the distinction is basic. When the "white trash" description was mentioned to an elderly Tupelo resident, she snapped: "Why Elvis and his family weren't trash. His mama worked. They *all* worked." White trash carries overtones of shiftlessness, criminality, failure, and inability to cope with life. Moreover, money cannot rescue "trash," and such Southern literary characters as William Faulkner's Flem Snopes or Margaret Mitchell's overseer at Tara are typical examples. The Presley family was hardworking, God-fearing, and mannerly. Elvis kept those traits, and they formed the essence of his appeal: he had stirred deep emotions because he was very much a part of his environment.

Harold Montgomery sent a telegram to David Brinkley, demanding an apology, forwarding a copy of his protest to James O. Eastland, senior senator from Mississippi, president pro tempore of the United States Senate and chairman of its powerful Judiciary Committee. Brinkley responded with a personal letter, apologizing, but saying he could do nothing about an ad-libbed remark on a live program. Senator Eastland heard from Herbert S. Schlosser, president and chief executive officer of the network, reiterating the apology and expressing regret in a four-page letter.

"In spontaneous discussion of this kind," wrote Schlosser, "guests being interviewed will occasionally make statements which many people disagree with and which, of course, do not represent NBC's views. This was such an instance. While we share your aversion to this expression, we hope you would agree that Mr. Dunleavy used it apologetically with no intent to demean Mr. Presley, his remarkable career, or the feelings of affection that millions have for him."

Brinkley, too, got additional mail about the much-watched special and the remark by Dunleavy. "And for weeks afterward," he recalled, "I was attacked in the southern rural press since it was wrongly reported that I had used it myself, as I had not and would not."

The state representative from Tupelo accepted the apology and acknowledged that Brinkley had little control over the matter, but he still felt the network should have made some sort of retraction over the air. "Being that he was anchorman for the show," Montgomery said, "he should have taken responsibility for it."

Meanwhile, at CBS, news executives were not happy. Not only had the *Evening News* taken a bath in the ratings, but also the CBS late movie that aired the night before—while ABC and NBC were presenting their Elvis specials—drew only a seven share in New York and a six in Los Angeles.

Ironically, it was on CBS that Elvis had gotten his start on national television. The program was *Stage Show*, produced by Jackie Gleason as a lead-in for his popular Saturday night variety program. *Stage Show* starred the Dorsey brothers, Tommy and Jimmy, and their orchestra, and featured the June Taylor Dancers, a staple attraction on the Gleason show. Big name vocalists appeared each week, but the program was unable to counter the enormous ratings of Perry Como's program broadcast in the same time slot on NBC.

Sarah Vaughan was the top guest artist on January 28, 1956, with Elvis also featured. He sang "Blue Suede Shoes," Carl Perkin's number one song on *Billboard's* country chart, and "Heartbreak Hotel," which Elvis had recorded two weeks earlier for RCA. But only the most avid fans recall the appearance. The full orchestral accompaniment drowned out the nuances that Elvis gave the songs.

The shaking hips and overt sexuality attracted some comment and, no doubt, more viewers, as Elvis returned on February 4, 11, and 18, and on March 17 and 24. He sang two songs on each of the programs, but the ratings change was negligible. Como still dominated the time slot; *Stage Show* was a distant second, and Red Foley's *Ozark Jubilee* on ABC trailed far behind.

But the national television exposure, coupled with the upward movement of "Heartbreak Hotel" on the record charts, gained Elvis a screen test by Producer Hal Wallis of 20th Century Fox. In a roundabout way, the Hollywood trip led to Presley's next CBS appearances.

While he was on the West Coast, Elvis was booked onto Milton Berle's April 3 show on NBC and was invited to return for a guest shot on June 3. Again, there was no particular change in the ratings; Berle had one of TV's highest rated shows anyway.

However, Steve Allen was watching, and he felt that Elvis might be just the ingredient he needed to add some drawing power to his Sunday night NBC program, scheduled opposite the CBS variety show, Ed Sullivan's *Toast of the Town*. On July 1, Allen brought Elvis on stage in a tuxedo and directed him to stand perfectly still as he sang "Hound Dog" to a mournful-looking basset. The studio was filled with screaming girls, and NBC thoroughly publicized the Presley appearance. The ratings were large; for the first time, Ed Sullivan was beaten in the ratings.

The Sullivan show was a mish-mash of acts faintly reminiscent of vaudeville or benefit performances. One act followed another—an opera singer, a trained-dog act, a stand-up comic, tap dancers, a comedy sketch, or a ballet troupe. All tied together by Sullivan acting as master of ceremonies, the show somehow caught the public's fancy. Baseball stars, politicians, Hollywood celebrities, and nostalgia figures often took brief bows from the audience. The show literally was studded with stars because Sullivan always booked the big acts. Now Elvis was big and getting bigger.

Sullivan booked Elvis for three performances. The fee was the highest ever paid to a single performer—fifty thousand dollars, an amount that heightened interest in the show.

September 9, 1956—Sunday night at eight o'clock, eastern standard time—was a milestone of television history as millions of people gathered around their sets all over the country. A record 82.6 percent of the population was watching, compared with 78.6 percent that had watched a few weeks earlier as President Eisenhower accepted his party's nomination for a second term. Sullivan missed the show; he was home recuperating from an automobile accident. The program originated in New York, with actor Charles Laughton as host. Elvis performed from CBS studios in Hollywood.

Obviously nervous, the young singer called the appearance "probably the greatest honor I've ever had in my life." He sang, "Don't Be Cruel" and then recited an incredible one-minute bit of patter that endeared him to the audience and showed his growing knowledge of show-business promotion. He had just turned twenty, but already his ability to "work the audience" with his teasing, self-mocking sense of humor was evident. He introduced a "brand-new song, completely different from anything we've ever done," and said that it just happened to be the title song from his new movie and the title of "our new RCA Victor escape, er, release . . . 'Love Me Tender.' "

On the second half of the show, he sang "Teddy Bear" and, gasping for breath, thanked the audience. He looked into the camera and wished Sullivan well, then said he would see him in New York for his next appearance, on October 28. Then he jokingly introduced his final song: "Friends, as a great philosopher once said, 'You ain't nothing but a hound dog.' "

Ed Sullivan had a strict code defining family entertainment. His son-in-law, and executive producer of the shows, Robert Precht, said Elvis's movements violated those standards. "Those gyrations were too sexually suggestive," said Precht, "so he ordered the director to focus only above the waist." The decision simply added to the Presley mystique and fueled more publicity.

Although two decades had passed since Elvis had first appeared on CBS, the network possessed, at the time of his death, a most valuable commodity—films of Elvis's most recent concert tour, shot in the Midwest two months earlier. CBS had been unable to use any of the film on its initial news broadcasts and its lawyers still vetoed its use until specific approval could be obtained from Colonel Parker.

Everyone remembered the Sullivan show, but, even though CBS originated the programs, the Sullivan estate retained rights to all the material. The network had to secure rights from Robert Precht and retrieve the film from a Long Island warehouse.

Permission to use excerpts from movies was easier to obtain, but prints of specific films had to be located and the actual scenes pulled out. The problem of identifying the proper person to grant permission consumed much more time because Elvis made movies for many different studios.

Responding to reporters' queries, CBS announced it did not have enough material in its files to do a "quality treatment" of the star's life. But Wednesday morning, when the ratings of the Elvis tributes on the other two networks came in, CBS executives began to reconsider. Late in the afternoon, they decided to broadcast a special on Thursday. They assigned Joan Richman to produce the program.

"There wasn't any point to doing a crash thing of the kind you would do the night he died," Richman recalled. "Because you are doing it two days later, you want to add something to what has already been done, something a little more ... a more thoughtful kind of program."

And she succeeded, mostly because of the inspired casting of Charles Kuralt as the narrator for the show. Like Brinkley, Kuralt is a native of North Carolina, acutely aware of the cultural heritage that had shaped Presley's music. But he seemed, at first glance, an unlikely choice for the assignment. To most Americans, Kuralt was the purveyor of good news, an image he built during eight years of sending "postcards to Walter Cronkite," weekly four-minute pieces that closed the *CBS Evening News*. These bits of Americana, called "On the Road," are among the most widely known human interest segments in broadcast journalism.

But during his long career at CBS, Kuralt also had provided some of the network's finest reporting during times of national trauma. He was the anchor for network coverage of the assassinations of Robert Kennedy and Martin Luther King, Jr. He was the reporter assigned to cover the funerals of former Presidents Truman and Eisenhower.

"At CBS News, when you want to do that kind of a show, Charlie would almost always be your first choice," said Richman. "He's done a lot of that over the years, and he's so sensitive that he's quite wonderful at it.

"Also, in this case, we made a decision right at the beginning that we wanted to try to do some sort of sociological impact. And you couldn't think of a better guy to write the essay about the fifties."

Richman said it was pure luck that Kuralt was in New York and available for the assignment and not on the road somewhere. She and her crew started with the essay Kuralt wrote, and built the show around it.

"Try to remember, try to remember," Kuralt began his script. "1956 was the year Elvis Presley made his first national impact. Ike was in his glory and Grace was in her palace and all was right with the world—except that an Alabama preacher named Martin Luther King didn't think so."

Kuralt related his feeling that Elvis, like the hula hoop and Davey Crockett hats, would be a passing fad. The best adult ideas—the space effort and the Edsel—were failures, but Elvis, "this unlikely phenomenon of youth," succeeded gaudily. Kuralt ticked off the "grownup fads" that were popular at the time—jet planes, tail fins, instant coffee, power mowers, electric typewriters, and Princess phones—all bland and innocent "beside this boy with the curled lips and pulsing hips."

Biographical data was given, with a still photo montage of early scenes from Presley's life.

"In looking at his life," said Kuralt, "you have to start with the fact of his name. It was perfect for fame, giving him an instant idiosyncratic identity, like those other public figures of the 1950s—Adlai and Tallulah. You never heard anybody ask, 'Elvis who?'"

Ed Rabel, chief of the network's Atlanta bureau, on the scene in Memphis, reported from the front gate of Graceland, where he interviewed mourners and described the funeral as film of the procession and the cemetery rolled. Chris Kelley, another CBS reporter, described the carnival aspects of the day as he interviewed buyers and sellers of souvenirs, T-shirts, and pennants.

"If some events surrounding Presley's funeral seem somewhat unusual, even incongruous, perhaps irreverent," said Kelley, "it might have been because of how these people perceived Presley himself—a person, not unlike them, from a simple background, who managed to climb above the confines of little education and poverty to become a heroic figure. His mourners today smiled more than they cried."

Although CBS had dispatched camera crews around the country to get reactions from entertainers, the network used only two interviews on the special. In one, Pat Boone said he saw Elvis as a man living a fugitive kind of life, yearning to have normal relationships with people. In the other, Stevie Wonder noted the influence on Elvis's music by black performers and praised the singer's "mental capability" to judge people without looking at the color of their skin.

After all the problems involved with securing the film, the network used only a short grainy segment from the *Ed Sullivan Show*. Assuming that everyone remembered the event that four out of five Americans watched in 1956, Kuralt supplied no details, simply calling the appearance stormy.

An observation was provided, however, by Marlo Lewis, who had produced the original program. "Well we were electrified, and he was electrifying, I should say, by the very gyrations of his body. He had a call of the wild, a sexuality, a sensuality, a lasciviousness to his music, and it communicated immediately to the audience."

Sociologist Vance Packard commented that Elvis was one factor in reducing restraints on sexual mores. He said the way Presley presented himself in his songs gave those who watched him "permission to break loose from the inhibitions that they'd had."

All the talk about Elvis as symbol and his significance to American culture, noted Kuralt, almost obscures the point that the Presley legend began with the music. Charles Osgood presented a piece from a Broadway record store, interviewing *New York Times* critic John Rockwell and Jonathan Schwartz, a popular disc jockey of radio station WNEW. Osgood reported that the record store was sold out of Presley's music but the store itself was a reflection of how much music had changed since the heyday of Tin Pan Alley: "David Bowie, the Stones, the Band, the Kiss. The rock world, as we know it today, came into being when that explosive event occurred in the mid-1950s. Its name was Elvis Presley."

The program's interviews and comments were interwoven with music. CBS found a print of *Jailhouse Rock* at its New York station, and located a print of *Viva Las Vegas* in Hollywood. The special used clips of Elvis singing the title song from each film, and an excerpt from *Bye, Bye*

Birdie, the 1963 movie version of the Broadway musical inspired by Elvis's induction into the Army.

"In some cases," CBS Producer Richman recalled, "we just didn't have any pictures, so we used record album covers and records. We had instant, instant cooperation from RCA Records. They were the easiest people to deal with, so we had no problem clearing any record material."

One rare piece of film her researchers found was news footage of a young Charles Kuralt interviewing Elvis after his discharge from the Army in 1960:

KURALT: Elvis, you have some screaming fans out there. Do you still like screaming girls?

PRESLEY (laughing): If it wasn't for them, I'd—I'd have to re-up in the Army, sir, I tell you.

Returning to the present, Kuralt commented, "Well, it was all so long ago."

Kuralt closed the program with a comment on Presley's generosity and on reports of mourning all over Europe. "But it's hard to imagine Elvis Presley's success coming anywhere but here," said Kuralt. "He molded it out of so many American elements: country and blues and gospel and rock, a little Memphis, a little Vegas, a little arrogance, a little piety. . . . He was a truck driver's boy from Tupelo who got so rich he could give away Cadillacs. That's an American story. How could we ever have felt estranged from Elvis? He was a native son."

Two years after the program Joan Richman called her assignment to produce the special on Elvis one that anybody in her work loves to get. "And when you can do a little more than just what amounts to a long obit," she said, "it's a kind of pleasure."

Executives at CBS also were happy; the special gained the highest late-night ratings the network had attained all year—a forty-one percent share of the audience in New York, almost double the *Tonight* show's twenty-one on NBC.

6

Gathering in Memphis

Just as he had done in life, Elvis in death continued to sell newspapers. Editors, as well as the business offices concerned with the circulation of their products, were caught short by the tremendous outpouring of interest by hard-core fans and the general public.

In Jacksonville, the *Florida Times-Union* sold more papers than it did on November 23, 1963, when its headlines were about the assassination of John F. Kennedy. Across the country, at the *Seattle Post-Intelligencer*, the papers reporting details of Elvis's death sold ten thousand more copies than normal for the day, mainly through vending machines which the circulation department constantly rushed to refill.

Bob Hively, director of circulation for the two Memphis newspapers said the papers were outselling those that had reported the deaths of President Kennedy and Martin Luther King at a ratio of better than five to one. During the four-day period following Elvis's death, *The Commercial Appeal* sold three hundred twenty-three thousand additional copies. In Atlanta, sales of the *Constitution* and *Journal* were up by ninety-nine thousand over normal for the three days following August 16.

With headlines reading "The King/dies at 42" on its front pages Wednesday morning, *The Dallas Morning News* found its circulation jumping by ten thousand copies and quickly dispatched a staff reporter to Memphis. Dozens of other newspapers made similar decisions. While the wire services and local reporters were churning out more than enough copy to fill columns with news about Elvis, many editors felt this story needed one of their own reporters on the scene. The heavy interest clearly justified special coverage.

For some papers in the South and Midwest, it was a fairly inexpensive decision to send a reporter on a short trip to Memphis. For newspapers such as *The New York Times, The Washington Post*, or *The Los Angeles Times*, it is routine practice to dispatch reporters to major news events anywhere in the country or abroad. But staffing an entertainer's funeral outside major metropolitan areas was highly unusual. For newspapers such as the *San Francisco Examiner* to send a reporter such a long distance was unheard of.

News of Elvis's death particularly electrified editors of the *National Enquirer* as they read the bulletins coming into their headquarters building in Lantana, Florida, a sleepy town about ten miles up the coast from West Palm Beach. They knew this was the biggest story of the year. The newspaper's average reader is a thirty-nine-year-old housewife with a high-school education, married and living with a husband and two children. The paper sells heavily at checkout counters of supermarkets and drugstores where customers react to emotional headlines on topics of interest. With a national weekly circulation exceeded only by *TV Guide*, the *Enquirer* through the years had never found a subject that so fascinated middle America as Elvis. Editors there began to mobilize a quasi-military operation to make sure readers would get the "untold story" of the entertainer's death. Within hours, Associate Editor Tom Kuncl was on a chartered Cessna Citation jet for Memphis, accompanied by four reporters and a photographer. Other editors were making telephone calls, hiring free-lance writers in Memphis. One of the paper's stringers reportedly was at Graceland before the ambulance left carrying Elvis's body to the hospital.

The *National Enquirer* hit Memphis on a grand scale. Kuncl rented the top floor of an apartment building and ordered twenty-two telephones installed. Word went out that the newspaper had cash available for exclusive information. Nanci Albritten recalls that the paper offered her five hundred dollars for her short-hand notes from the medical examiner's press conference. Kuncl later told the *Miami Herald* that someone had offered to sell him the sheets off the ambulance stretcher. The establishment press was repelled by the aggressive approach of the newspaper as the *Enquirer*'s reporters fanned out, interviewing every

Presley contact they could find—his employees, hospital personnel, former girlfriends, anyone. They offered to buy "exclusive rights" to whatever story was being offered; then they had to make sure the source stayed bought.

No accurate count exists of the journalists who began arriving on Tuesday night and continued until Thursday morning. Most estimates place the number near two hundred fifty by the time the week was out. The journalists competed with fans for the available airline seats and rental cars, and the unavailable hotel rooms. Every flight arriving at Memphis International Airport on Wednesday was filled. Complex routing carried passengers through Chicago's O'Hare Airport or to Louisville, Nashville, Dallas, or Atlanta to make connections into Memphis. Delta Air Lines, the carrier with the most flights into the city, found that the passenger load on its seven flights from Detroit doubled. One woman called the airline from General Motors saying she had been selected as the office delegate to go to the funeral and take pictures. Delta added extra sections to its flights from Atlanta. Passengers filled the planes, many of them representatives of foreign media making connections from their bureaus in Washington or New York.

Free-lance photographers headed for Memphis in record numbers. Television network crews arrived from Atlanta, Chicago, and Dallas. The wire services assembled teams of photographers to move into the city and compile a pictorial record of the event. Later, they would be setting up processing facilities for both black and white and color photos to be transmitted through telephone company circuits to clients around the world. In addition to the cry for photographs, the newspapers, along with radio and television clients, were demanding more and more copy from AP and UPI. The wire services made detailed plans to meet those requests.

The AP's tiny Memphis office was a wreck. Files were scattered, and the floor was littered with aborted leads and false starts of stories interrupted by the constantly ringing telephones. Les Seago had finished filing the Presley obituary late Tuesday afternoon when Phil Cannon, a summer intern who had the day off, came in to help. Seago was cursing himself for sending Cannon to Graceland instead of keeping him in the office to help with the phones. In addition to the foreign calls and the flood of domestic queries, the cable between Hawaii and the West Coast was out of order, and a Honolulu radio station called a dozen times wanting updates. People on the islands felt a special love for Elvis. He had raised $62,000 in a 1961 Pearl Harbor concert to build the USS Arizona Memorial. His 1973 satellite live television concert *Aloha From Hawaii*, the first use of the Telstar, was seen by one and a half billion people in forty countries and raised $75,000 for the Kui Lee Cancer Fund of the University of Hawaii. And he had filmed three movies there—*Blue Hawaii*; *Girls, Girls, Girls*; and *Paradise—Hawaiian Style*—films the *Honolulu Advertiser* called the best advertising the state had ever received from Hollywood.

"That station was really a pain in the butt," said Seago later, "but what the hell, they were an AP member and I firmly believe in taking care of the members. So, if I had a couple of minutes, I'd read 'em the latest copy or give 'em a blow-by-blow description of what was going on.

"I was trying to do everything that had to get done, when suddenly I had a terrible pain in my lower abdomen. I thought, 'My God, I'm going to die right here—just like Elvis.' Then it hit me. 'I have got to pee.' That's what it was. I had been going nonstop, and I hadn't had a chance to pee."

During a fleeting moment when the two incoming lines were quiet, he picked up one phone and called the other. Then he laid the two receivers on the desk and hurried down the hall to the men's room.

Marian Fox, who was due to work that night, arrived. She had been delayed by a doctor's appointment in East Memphis, and she had been blissfully unaware of the developing story. She quickly joined in the phone answering and sidebar preparation giving Seago a chance to get to the press conference at Baptist Hospital.

The encounter with the medical personnel was almost like a routine story after the chaos of the past few hours. Seago had double-checked the spelling of "arrythmia" and had dictated his story directly to Nashville. As he left the hospital, he almost collided with a Channel 5 reporter he at first failed to recognize. Gone was the carefully groomed TV appearance; his tie was askew, his sleeves rolled up, and he looked as if he had slept in his clothes. Seago looked startled, then they both laughed as it dawned on the AP reporter that his appearance was the same. "My God, this has been a hell of a day," said Seago, "and we've finally lived through it. I think I'm going home, get a drink, and get a good night's sleep."

But when he got back to the office, Seago realized that he wasn't going home, not for a long, long time. Nancy Shipley, the state bureau chief, called from Nashville and said she wanted to talk about man-power. Seago demurred, assuring her that the situation was under con-trol. There were no problems, he said. She insisted; New York wanted to send someone in, and she felt he needed more help.

"I don't know what it was," Seago recalled, although he admits he was physically and emotionally drained from the double-shift ordeal. "It was my turf, my story. And, goddammit, I didn't want any hired gun coming in." Shipley assured him that he was in charge, the one who would decide who went where and who did what. She finally convinced him that the story was much bigger than he realized and that the work really was just beginning. "It really hadn't hit me how big a story we had," Seago continued. "You know, I first thought, well, okay, we got him dead and tomorrow we get up and we'll get the funeral, and we'll bury him the next day and that'll be it. But I suddenly realized, we're going to have a twenty-four-hour operation here."

Shipley told him that Harry Rosenthal, a top AP reporter, was com-ing in and probably someone from AP Radio. She said she was sending Eric Newhouse from Chattanooga, and wire service photographers were coming in from bureaus around the country.

Seago left the office about four that morning, and got home for a couple of hours sleep. By the time more help arrived, he was glad to see them.

Harry Rosenthal, one of the best general assignments reporters for the Associated Press, was no Elvis fan. His son, an AP reporter in San Francisco and something of a music expert, later asked why the wire ser-vice had picked the only reporter in the organization who didn't know who Elvis was. But the veteran reporter, whose assignments in the past had included coverage of the Watergate scandal, has juices that start flowing with certain stories. This was one of them.

As he prepared to leave his office in downtown Washington Tuesday afternoon, Rosenthal read the bulletin from Memphis moving on the teletype. He immediately thought of the reaction to the death of Rudolph Valentino; this was going to be a hell of a story, too. He quickly made a phone call.

"If you're looking for folks to go to Memphis," he told the executive editor in New York, "put me on the list."

Not much chance, came the reply. In the editor's opinion, Presley was a has-been, just somebody from another age. He really didn't think there would be much of a stir about his death.

"That was an incredible lapse in news judgment," Rosenthal recalled. "Two hours later they were calling me at home and telling me to head for the airport."

Another newsman who read the bulletin in Washington was Mark Knoller, a twenty-five-year-old Brooklyn-born reporter manning the editing desk for Associated Press Radio. Several radio stations had called the network headquarters, asking about rumors of a Presley illness, but a check with member stations in Memphis brought a "we're-looking-into-it" response.

Presley was a name Knoller remembered from childhood, a style of music that turned him off, a vulgar sound. As a youngster riding with his parents, he would reach out and turn off the radio whenever he heard an Elvis record.

"I just never found him that entertaining," said Knoller. "I could not understand the enormous mass attraction. Quite frankly, as a personal opinion, I found his style rather repulsive."

Then the death story moved.

Big deal, thought Knoller. Not a head of state, not a government official. Just an entertainer.

"But everybody else in the office, without exception, went 'holy shit.'" Knoller remembered. "Everyone saw the magnitude of the story before I did. Then I got carried away and joined in the effort. We started working the phones. The office scrambled. One person was calling the cops in Memphis. Another was calling the emergency medical service. Another, the hospital. We all jumped into action; all of us working."

Slowly, bits of information were coming into the office, from sources the staff were working on the phone and reports from member stations in Memphis. People across the street from Graceland said they had seen an ambulance come and go. A priest from a church near Baptist Hospital had answered the phone in the emergency room and told AP Radio what he had seen as they wheeled Presley into the hospital.

"I still did not see the magnitude of the story," Knoller continued. "I thought that our free-lancers or our member stations in the city could handle it adequately, but everybody else thought it was enormous. Management did too, so they said, 'Knoller, go home, pack a bag and get down there.'"

As he gathered up his notebooks, tape recorder and microphone, Knoller speculated with others in the newsroom about how important this story really was. What will lead the TV news tonight? he asked. In the great scheme of things, what is *really* important? Driving to the airport, Knoller was overwhelmed with the importance every radio station in Washington was placing on the Elvis story. Even WGMS, the classical music station that serves as AP Radio's outlet in the capital, reported Elvis's death as its lead story on the hourly newscasts. His initial cynicism about the story was also being tempered somewhat by the information that wireside—the print side of the organization—was sending Harry Rosenthal to Memphis. Knoller had been to Tennessee with Rosenthal once before on a big story, when James Earl Ray, convicted killer of Martin Luther King, Jr., had broken out of Brushy Mountain State Prison. Harry is one of the best writers in the whole AP organization, thought Knoller. It will be good to work with him again.

When the news hit the UPI regional office in Atlanta, photographer Jerry Shields rounded up two of his colleagues—Hugh Peralta and Russ Yoder—and the three of them began stowing cameras, lenses, film, and other equipment into travel cases, gearing up to head for Memphis. They knew that Elvis's funeral would be an extraordinary photo event. Only after they finished packing did they learn they could not get a flight to Memphis until the next morning.

In Nashville, Sam Parrish, the UPI photographer who usually covered Memphis events for the wire service, could not get a flight. He grabbed his equipment, threw it into the trunk of his new Ford LTD, and headed west. He later claimed he had made the two hundred twenty-mile drive in just over two hours. When he arrived at the UPI office in Memphis, his car would not quit idling after he turned off the ignition.

UPI also sent in more reporters. Paula Schwed, sister of Craig Schwed, came from the Nashville bureau, riding with Parrish. Robert Carey from Little Rock and Tom Madden from Jackson, Mississippi, joined her the next day.

"You don't get on a story bigger than that in a lifetime," said Carey, who likened the news coverage in Memphis to the atmosphere among journalists reporting a space shot: "There's a tent approach with a lot of information from several reporters passing through a deskman or rewrite man. Of course, the difference in a space shot is that you don't have the masses of people hanging around, weeping and wailing."

The grieving fans in front of Graceland were the focal point of the story during the early hours of Wednesday morning. On the *CBS Morning News*, Ed Rabel opened his report with film of a Memphis news vendor shouting "Extra, extra, read all about it." Rabel, the network's Atlanta bureau chief, who had arrived in Memphis the night before, observed that in times past such hawking of newspapers heralded some earth-shaking event like the outbreak of war. He interviewed a woman who said that Elvis was "just as close to me as my husband is." He asked a man why he was standing in front of Graceland. The reply: "I don't really know. I just feel that I want to be here. I don't have any particular reason, outside of the fact that—that I loved him, and I want to be here where—where the atmosphere is, where he was."

Rabel recapped the news of Elvis's death, citing police reports that "a drug overdose was not suspected," and showed a brief film clip of Dr. Francisco, the county medical examiner, saying, "The cause of death is cardiac arrythmia due to undetermined causes." His segment closed with a look at the crowds arriving to pay their last respects.

Hundreds of people, mostly from the South and Midwest, simply gathered up their children, got in their cars, and headed for Memphis when they heard the news that Elvis had died. They had packed no bags; most had made no plans beyond telling friends or neighbors to notify their employers that they had gone. The three Tripper brothers—Joe, who was forty; Charlie, thirty-three; and John, thirty—identified so strongly with Elvis that they had driven nonstop from Buffalo, New York, in twelve hours. "We came off the field yesterday evening when we heard he was dead," said Charlie, still wearing his softball uniform. "There was no question; we just stopped to get money for gas and took off. He was the man. He was it. We had tickets for a concert he was going to give next month. We figured, he didn't come to see us, so we came to see him."

Already a few hucksters were appearing, selling Elvis memorabilia to the grieving fans who had been drawn to Graceland. But one person strolled through the crowd handing out free mementos to a collage of arms and hands. Ron Wolfe, president of the Elvis Presley Photo Club of Jacksonville, Florida, was the donor, and his gifts were snapshots of the entertainer. "I was driving my car when I heard about it," he said. "I nearly wrecked. I stopped and just screamed 'no, no, no,' at the top of my lungs. Then I just kept driving on up here."

NBC's Jackson Bain was one of the first out-of-town reporters to arrive. His only frame of reference to the bizarre scene in front of the mansion was the 1962 Air France plane crash at Paris' Orly Airport which killed 130 people, most of them from Atlanta. He had known many of them as the parents of his high school classmates. He remembered the grief that engulfed his neighborhood. He recalled particularly a scene at Lenox Square on the Sunday morning after the tragedy—an old black woman sitting on the curb, reading the names of the dead from a newspaper and lamenting, "Oh Lord, everybody knows somebody, don't they?"

Whether the old woman had known any of the victims of the crash or not, her grief was real. And to Bain, the people in the steadily growing crowd at Graceland were suffering a genuine personal loss. Death had snatched a part of their lives away.

"It's fascinating when you cover a story like that," Bain said later. "It's just incredible to observe the reactions of people to the death of a star."

Bain had broadcast one report on NBC's late-night special and another that morning on the *Today* program. He had interviewed a variety of fans, but mostly he was checking rumors. Although no announcement had been made (indeed, no one was making any announcements about anything), it was fair to guess that the funeral services would center around the mansion. The body had been at Memphis Funeral Home all night and a hearse would carry the dead singer to Graceland later in the day.

"What we were facing when we first got there," said Bain, "was that nothing was happening. Nothing was getting out about the death or anything else that was not tightly, tightly controlled by the entourage. There was a lot of noise about whether they were going to let anyone in. Finally they said they were going to let reporters in. Then they said no reporters, just the fans. We saw our story go dribbling down the drain."

To cover any eventuality, a young woman who was working at WMC-TV as a summer intern was standing in the crowd near the gate. She had no microphone, no notebook. If anyone inquired, she was just a fan.

Bain began to make frequent sorties from the news van, seeking sources of information. Late in the morning he made his way through the crowd and up to the gate to see if the taciturn guard had anything to say. Through the gate he saw a familiar face.

Anybody inside was a friend of mine, thought Bain, as the man inside ordered the guard to admit him. His patron was Eddie Fadal from Waco, Texas, where Bain had worked a decade earlier as a television newsman on the local station. They had been in Rotary Club together and Bain vaguely remembered that Fadal had a reputation around town, even in those days, for promoting Elvis.

Fadal, one of those rare persons who had slipped in and out of the Presley entourage for the better part of two decades, had arrived at Graceland a few hours earlier. A former radio announcer and theater manager, Fadal had first met Elvis in Dallas during the early barnstorming days when the entertainer was a big attraction in the South and Southwest but unknown to the rest of the nation. Later, when Elvis was drafted and sent to Fort Hood, the Fadal home in Waco became a weekend retreat whenever the singer/soldier could get a three-day pass. Through the years, there were visits, phone calls, and gifts exchanged.

Fadal had flown in that morning and taken a taxi to a point as close to Graceland as he could get. He found the scene "just like Mardi Gras in New Orleans, just wall-to-wall people" as he moved toward the house with his overnight bag. When he reached the gate he found a stranger on duty; but when Fadal said, "I was a friend of Elvis's and I've come for the funeral," he was waved through. He walked up the circular drive to the house he had visited many times. Fadal had been there when Elvis's mother died August 14, 1958, and he had served as a pallbearer three weeks later when the singer's favorite cousin, Junior Smith, died.

Inside the house he nodded to several acquaintances. Off to one side he saw Vernon Presley, the singer's father, looking very bad. He and the older man embraced; he offered condolences and asked what he could do to help.

"Just look around, Eddie," replied Vernon. "You've been with us through this before. Whatever you want to."

The inside of the house was chaotic, but the scene down at the gate was worse, thought Fadal. With Uncle Vester and the regular crew in mourning, the strangers at the gate really did not know the relatives or others who ought to be admitted. Maybe he could help there. He also thought he could help the media, answer some questions, add a little order to the scene.

"So I helped in that part," recalled Fadal. "When anybody came up and said they were invited guests or they needed to be there, those people that were on the gate would come up to me. And then I'd go and talk with them and see if they were bona fide, because I know all of his friends and all of his relatives and all around."

When he saw the familiar face from the past, Fadal invited Bain in and they sat in the gatehouse for a half hour, reminiscing as Southerners do. Then they went up to the house.

"When you get there, it's like you've been transported to some foreign galaxy," Bain recalled later. "I've never seen anything like it. The people involved were some of the strangest people I've ever seen in my life. If there were a monastery, high on a mountaintop in Greece, you could understand the kind of feelings—something in the air—just inside the gates of Graceland mansion.

"It was created by the people inside, the hangers-on, the ones running the show. And Presley was as much a prisoner of all that as he was the 'benefactor-hyphen-creator' of it. And it was even worse after his death."

To Bain, the dominant mood mixed with grief inside Graceland was fear. Those inside the mansion clearly were apprehensive that the growing crowd of people outside the walls might decide to storm the gates and tear the place apart. One of the bodyguards had told Fadal they would "have to keep 'em back somehow—we'll fire on 'em." And Bain—aware of Elvis's fascination with handguns—assumed there was an arsenal inside Graceland that these nervous associates would not hesitate to use if the crowd got out of control. Later, he saw a teenager who had sneaked into the grounds beaten senseless and tossed over the wall.

"I've never seen such violence," Bain said. "They were ready to do damage to people."

A fear of the media also was evident inside Graceland, a foreboding that the swarms of reporters and cameramen could incite a crowd explosion. Looking back on the event, Bain thought that their fears that some reporter would discover the extensive use of drugs by the entourage heightened their anxiety.

After a quick tour of Graceland's main floor, Bain watched as attendants overlaid the red carpeting in the front entranceway with a white covering. He left just as attendants from the funeral home wheeled the coffin bearing Presley's body into place.

7

The Tears of August

Outside the mansion, Mark Knoller and Harry Rosenthal had joined the growing crowd of journalists. Unable to get a direct flight, they had stayed overnight at a motel near the Atlanta airport. Arriving in Memphis Wednesday morning they went immediately to the Memphis AP office to get directions to Graceland.

Already Knoller had filed a couple of "sceners" describing the flags at half-staff throughout the city and motorists driving with their lights on to show their respect for the dead singer. He interviewed several of the mourning fans and arranged with a real estate office across the street from the mansion to use the telephone. Just before noon, he heard the sirens coming down the highway from the city. He soon saw the flashing yellow lights of the escort vehicles, then the white Cadillac hearse came into view.

"You could see it coming," Knoller recalled, "because the police cleared a path. And it had a police escort. Now I had traveled with Presidents and could understand the purpose of giving a presidential candidate a police escort, but here you had a dead individual. I mean, who's going to molest him? I just couldn't understand the outpouring. It was just bizarre to my eyes."

Many of the fans massed in front of the gate missed seeing the arrival of the hearse, which turned into a side entrance to the grounds.

Some of them had been waiting for more than twenty hours to pay their respects.

The sky was overcast and the temperature was in the nineties as word spread through the crowd that Vernon Presley had decided to permit the fans to come in and say good-bye. The doors would be open to the public at three o'clock that afternoon. Before that, however, there would be time for family and associates. And just before the public was admitted, the press would get its chance to view the body.

An area had been roped off for the media just inside the wall to the left of the main gate. Eddie Fadal said it looked like a hog-pen, but large trees shaded the area, and the reporters could observe all the comings and goings, with a clear view up the drive to the front door of the house. When Fadal or others known to be associated with Presley came down from the mansion, dozens of microphones would be thrust forward by those seeking information. But there was no official family spokesman, and the reporters were restricted to interviewing mourners and each other and sharing what little information they had. The schedule set two hours of public viewing and a private funeral service the next day in the house. Burial would be at Forest Hill Cemetery, about four miles north toward the city, near the grave of Elvis's mother.

Every few minutes screams of panic pierced the overheated air as someone else in the crowd passed out. The crowd near the gate was so dense that the victims could not fall down. The cry of "Medic, over here" was heard constantly, and an improvised first-aid station, manned by volunteers, was set up along the wall across the driveway from the press area. Several reporters compared the scene to a battlefield with the wounded lying on the closely cropped grass.

The crowd itself became the subject of commentary. "They seemed to come from all ranks of society," said John Filiatreau of Louisville's *The Courier Journal.* "There is no one characteristic that set them apart. Some were well-dressed, others in work clothes. Some were obviously grief-stricken; for others there seemed to be something of the camaraderie of a wake. It was a classless crowd of all ages." To Pete Hamill of the *New York Daily News,* they "were almost all working people; people who drove trucks and worked in gas stations and spent their youth in roadside taverns, listening to tales of their heartbreak hotel." William Thomas wrote in *The Commercial Appeal* that the majority of the mourners were not the beautiful people, but the plain and ordinary. UPI's Bob Carey said Thomas's description was the most perceptive thought expressed in all the millions of words that poured out of Memphis that week. The people gathered in front of Graceland were "authentic, like Elvis's style and music," wrote Carey. "These were his people. And they were all there at the end, as they should be, all the old high school and Army buddies, all the cousins with the double Christian names, all the aunts and uncles in their freshly pressed best who cried real tears."

William Thomas said the magic of Elvis attracted the huge crowds, but then he asked the question: "What kind of magic was that and how did it work and how had it gotten all these people out there, where he was lying dead, and what was it about him that had always attracted them, thousands of them, and made them do things they ordinarily wouldn't do like holler and stamp their feet and swoon and get very emotional whenever they saw him or heard him or thought about him doing the things that he did?" Thomas concluded that there were as many different answers as there were people—and there were a lot of people.

Mrs. Nancy Hunter of Plano, Texas, a thirty-five-year-old mother of four, said she had never done anything like it before, but when she heard that the casket would be open for public viewing, she felt she had to go to Memphis. Interviewed by Marilyn Schwartz of *The Dallas Morning News*, Mrs. Hunter said she made her decision at eleven that morning and got a seat on American Airlines's twelve-forty-five flight out of Dallas. "I had to fly first class," she added, "but I didn't care. I knew this would be my last chance to be close to Elvis."

Several Texas women brought their teenage daughters. Mrs. Frank Gregory of Dallas told Schwartz that she was thirteen, her daughter Jean's age, when she fell in love with Elvis. "I brought her with me because I hope she will catch some of the mood here. She's got to, because after tomorrow, there is no more Elvis. There is no more King. I want her to love him like I do."

Other reporters also searched for fans from their newspaper's circulation area. Reporter Kathleen Begley and photographer John H. White of the *Chicago Daily News* found many from the Midwest. Kathy Steagall of New London, Wisconsin, told Begley she first reconciled herself to the idea that she could not afford the trip on the salary of her schoolteacher husband. But in the twenty-four hours after hearing the news, the thirty-four-year-old housewife could not eat or sleep or concentrate on her husband or their six children. Finally, she drew three hundred dollars out of savings and got on an airplane for the first time in her life. "Elvis was such a wonderful person," she said. "I just had to see him one more time."

Vince Staten of the *Dayton Daily News* said the stories the fans told were variations on one theme: they had come to pay tribute. "These were people," he wrote, "who had never been asked to articulate a thought in their lives. Now suddenly they were shoved before microphones, linked to the world, and asked the hardest question of all: Why?" For Staten, they could tell what and when, but few could say exactly why they had come. Molly Ivins of *The New York Times* also asked why. The answer she got most often was, "Because we love him."

Ivins assumes her editor sent her to Memphis after *The New York Times* got its reports of street sales on Wednesday morning. "Nobody ever told me that," she said. "That's just my own reading, because I know that when I reported for work that morning, no one ever told me, 'You're going to Memphis today to cover the funeral.' They didn't tell me until at least noon, and I think it was later than that. And I began one of those frantic flights, you know, where you go charging out to the airport, no toothbrush, no nothing."

Ivins's first experience in Memphis introduced her to the attitudes of the man in the street and to the strange mood of the city, a certain zaniness, an unreality that would confront all out-of-town reporters as they tried to separate the commercialism and the carnival aspects of the event from the sense of tragedy that hit so many people so suddenly. It was about four o'clock, Memphis time, and hard on deadline when Ivins arrived at the airport: "I grab a cab and I say to the guy, 'Graceland, I'm in a hurry'—you know, great *Front Page* style. He says very knowingly, 'You know, it was such a shame that Elvis had to die when we had the Shriners in town.'"

This was the first inkling Ivins had that a big convention had taken over the city—a boon to the local economy and to those like the cabdriver whose livelihoods are linked to tourism. The convention was important, too, to the Shriners and to the burn victims and hospitals their activities support, but little noticed by the news media.

"You know," the cabdriver continued, "it's the first time in years we've had all the hotel rooms full. Elvis was such a thoughtful fellow, I know he would have put it off if he could have."

When she got to the mansion, Ivins began listening and watching the huge crowd of fans, as well as her fellow journalists. In an essay she wrote later, she noted that some of the observers seemed condescending or embarrassed by the open displays of sentimentality, mawkishness, and love that were evident there. "Mr. Presley's fans," she wrote, "saw nothing to be ashamed of in glorying in their sorrow. They were not offended by an instant commercialization of their grief, by the T-shirts reading 'Elvis Presley, In Memory, 1935-1977' that were on sale for $5 in front of Mr. Presley's mansion." In her opinion there were some who had come to Memphis just to be there, to see or be seen, without caring. But, for the most part, the city was awash with genuine emotion. "It is too easy to dismiss it as tasteless," she concluded. "It is not required that love be in impeccable taste."

But reporters continued to search for the real reason for the scene at Graceland, and the grieving fans kept trying to explain. Over and over, people repeated stories of Elvis's generosity. There was the time he came out of a Cadillac showroom and saw a young couple admiring his car. Do you like it? inquired Elvis. Very much, they replied. Well, that one's mine, but go in there and pick out one just like it and tell them to send the bill to me.

"It was just remarkable," said AP Radio's Knoller. "I had no way of checking out whether these stories were true, but everybody thought they were. Somehow the public—the masses—had grasped onto him, and they just loved him like a member of the family."

Thousands of human interest stories came from the crowd—the unique associations, the first school-girl crush, the pleasure his music brought them, the love that poured forth through their grief—a magnificent lode for the reporters to mine. But there was an unpleasantness to the scene as well, a shabbiness to the crush of people, perspiring in sweltering heat for up to three days, with little food and water and no chance to sleep or change clothes. Jackson Bain remembered the cloying smell, "a mixture of human body odor and Woolworth's perfume that would hit you like a soft brick wall." The women so desperately wanted to see Elvis, said Jerry Schwartz of the *Atlanta Constitution,* that they refused to relieve the "obvious physical torture and apparent psychological humiliation" that was being thrust upon them. John Keasler expressed it most succinctly in his lead in the *Miami News:* "Sorrow doesn't listen to logic."

When it came time for the press to view the body, the reporters were searched twice for hidden cameras. Tie clasps and belt buckles were checked. The family wanted no pictures taken inside.

Reporters were led single file from the press area to the front door of the mansion. Each person got a two-second glimpse of the corpse reposing in the copper casket. When they returned to the roped-off area and began to compare notes, several of the reporters realized that they really had not noticed any details. They began asking questions: Was that tie white or light blue? Did he have a ring on his finger? Was there a handkerchief in the pocket of his suit? The AP's Rosenthal suggested three or four of them go through again, each assigned to check specific details. Since the straggling line of mourning fans was now passing by the press area, it was easy for reporters to break into the line for a second trip up to the house.

Grumbling and shouts of protest broke out from those further back, but as the group approached the front door, total silence descended except for an occasional choking sob. Six or seven steps into the house, mourners saw the open casket with Elvis, his face puffy and pale, dressed in a white suit, a light blue shirt, and a white tie. His black hair was brushed back off the forehead and his eyes were closed. A white sheet covered the red carpeting in the alcove where the casket stood. No one was permitted to linger. The *Miami News*'s Keasler commented: "Whatever had made him look so eternally young in life was gone."

Most of the mourners were weeping as they emerged from the house. Some were unsteady on their feet as they stumbled the hundred yards back to the front gate. The press interviewed many as they passed the vantage point.

"I had never seen anything like it," Knoller said. "They were speechless, so grief-stricken so as not to be able to form a grammatical sentence. Some were able to give heart-rending descriptions of just how they felt viewing the body of this entertainer who meant so much to them and their lives.

"I was really impressed with the genuine feeling that was being demonstrated there. I did get the feeling at times that there were among members of the crowd people who got caught up in it and then found themselves competing with each other to see who was more grief stricken. But I think that, by and large, the feeling was most sincere and genuine."

The few seconds each of the mourners spent inside Graceland profoundly affected all of them, said Bob Greene of the *Chicago Sun-Times*. "Men, women, and children left the casket as if they had been punched in the stomach." Greene, also shaken by the experience, sat on the grass and thought about himself and about Elvis, who he had been and what he had become. He finally realized that his deadline was near, and he had to get back downtown to *The Commercial Appeal* office, where he had borrowed a desk and typewriter. Just getting through the gate proved a major task. Greene said he thought the surging crowd might knock him to the ground as he inched his way against the stream trying to get into the grounds. Only after he reached the jam of traffic on Elvis Presley Boulevard did he realize that he had no transportation. He had hitched a ride with a local reporter who had long since departed.

Greene saw a long, black Cadillac in the midst of the stalled traffic and recognized the driver as one of the few blacks who had been standing in the line at Graceland. Identifying himself as a reporter, he asked for a ride downtown. "Get in," said the driver. His name was A. J. Smith and he told Greene he had been hired to drive Elvis to the airport to begin the now-cancelled concert tour. "I had to be here today," said Smith. "I had to see the body. It seemed important to me." Greene later wrote a column about his ride in Elvis's limousine.

Henry Mitchell of *The Washington Post* had taken a taxi to Graceland and he, too, found himself without transportation back to the city. So he started walking, becoming, as he said, "one of the thousands, some coming, some going." He finally got a ride with Cordell Hull Sloan, a retired lawyer who farmed on the other side of the county. As they rode through the rush-hour traffic, Sloan told the reporter he disagreed with the frequent comments about Elvis dying young. "I don't think it's how long a man lives, but what he does with his time," he said. "Elvis made his mark." Mitchell later tried to sum up his perception of the feelings of many of the local residents, the non-fans like the farmer-lawyer, who went out to Graceland: "It was more that it was a great local event, yet he had not come in the way he would if an oil refinery had blown up. He had a sense of, you know, that a death had occurred, something significant. The attitude was one of respect."

At the Memphis bureau of UPI, Nanci Albritten got a call from Jack Warner in Atlanta, saying that Paula Schwed had not mentioned any flowers in the report she had phoned in from Graceland.

Albritten had just talked with the person at Memphis Funeral Home who had dressed the corpse for burial. He had given her a descrip-

tion of the clothing, the colors, material, style, and he had told her there
was a spray of roses on the casket.

"Goddamnit, we don't have any mention of the roses on the casket in
the copy," said Warner.

"Well, I just talked to the man who put them there," replied Albritten.

"Call him back," said Warner. "Confirm that there are roses on that
casket."

Grumbling to herself over the task, Albritten called her contact at
the funeral home. He told her he was talking to a colleague at the mansion on another line. He told the associate to go look at the casket and
tell him if there were still roses on it.

"And there were," said Albritten later. "And that's where we came
up with our lead about 'a rose-sprayed casket.' It's really funny how you
have to get into that kind of detail."

While few reporters bothered to mention the roses on the coffin,
practically everyone noted the massive array of flowers that were
banked along the front of the mansion. Every blossom available in
Memphis was sold by midday Wednesday, and additional flowers were
flown in from California, Colorado, and Illinois. It was the biggest day in
history for FTD, the Floral Telegraph Delivery association which links
the nation's florists into a national network. The Detroit-based organization dispatched two of its employees, Carole Freeman and Bud Lapenski,
to assist local florists and to answer queries from reporters. They said
there were two thousand one hundred fifty floral arrangements in all.
The average cost was twenty-one dollars and seventy-five cents.

Such figures were among the few hard facts the writers in Memphis
got, even though reporters have become used to being spoon-fed such
details when covering a story. Relatively unimportant by themselves,
these are the kinds of specific details, attributed to reliable sources, that
help round out stories and give them an added ring of authenticity.

By four o'clock the floral deliveries became so numerous that the
trucks carrying them were turned away from the mansion and the drivers were told to take them directly to the cemetery. The next morning,
more than a hundred vans transferred the mass of flowers from Graceland to the mausoleum—floral stars of blue, white, orange and green;
musical notes and lightning bolts; dozens of Bibles, sculpted from white
blossoms; many crosses and crowns, and at least fifty guitars. But also
among the commercial styrofoam-backed sprays there were Coke bottles

filled with daisies. Anita Coughlin, owner of a shop located directly across the street from Graceland, said hundreds of youngsters as well as grandmothers bought single roses or carnations to leave at the mansion. Jerry Schwartz of the *Atlanta Constitution* saw a nineteen-year-old Memphis woman hang a bouquet of red, yellow, and blue plastic roses high on the iron gate. He called the scene in front of Elvis's home "very much in the spirit of his life—emotional, a bit gaudy and distinctly Southern."

The situation at Graceland began to get messy when a police lieutenant announced through a megaphone shortly before five o'clock that the gates would close in ten minutes. A roar of disappointment came from the crowd; thousands were still waiting in line. The masses of mourners were pushing and shoving, pinning people against the partially opened gate. A hasty decision was reached to extend the viewing for another hour and a half, but it was clear that many fans would be disappointed.

Exactly how many people walked past the open casket will never be known. Memphis police are notorious for their inability to give accurate crowd estimates, and their guess that those outside the gates numbered sixty to eighty thousand was grossly exaggerated. The AP's Rosenthal timed the procession as it passed the press area, noting the number of persons passing each minute. There was no way that thirty thousand people, moving at a slow pace, single-file, up the driveway, could have seen the body in the time provided. But such estimates, accompanied by photographs of the mass of humanity in front of the gate with the music notes, were printed in newspapers around the world.

Finally, at six-thirty, six officers gathered at each side of the gate and forced it closed. Other policemen restrained individuals who doggedly tried to slip through. Then motorcycles moved in, clearing the crowd. Groans and shouts of "No, no" arose, and Mark Knoller felt the situation was becoming dangerous. "I was distressed about it," he recalled, "but it made a fantastic story: 'They closed the gates and an angry crowd'—and it was angry. There were some people there who I felt were just onlookers and were able to take advantage and be a little rowdy, but I also think that there was a genuine feeling from most that if they didn't see Elvis now, they're going to lose their chance."

The crowd dispersed, but soon it became obvious that many people were not going to leave. On this last evening their dead hero would spend in his home, they would keep a vigil outside the gates.

The television networks continued prominent play of the news from Memphis on Wednesday night. The closing of the gates and the cries from the crowd were the few seconds of film footage that producers dream of, but the event came too late for the early evening news shows. Bain on NBC and Rabel on CBS both used announcements of the funeral plans and the crowds lined up to view the body as their reports. ABC, yet to make its major leap forward in the ratings and still ranking at the bottom among the national networks, had to rely on newsfilm supplied by its Memphis affiliate, WHBQ-TV. Network reporter Charles Murphy did not arrive from Dallas until late Wednesday.

Radio, too, continued its massive coverage. Mark Knoller recalled that each time he filed a report, the desk would ask for more. The Black Radio Network told *Billboard* it labored indefatigably to put together news feeds about the man, the artists he influenced, and those who influenced him. The wire services were bombarded by their radio clients, begging for more copy. Stations in Memphis were reporting from Graceland and playing the music—from singles, albums, special performances, anything they could find. Many of the fans maintaining the vigil listened on their transistor radios as the music provided a constant complementary sound to the noise of helicopters whirring overhead and the frequent sirens of ambulances or police vehicles. Memphis's top-ranked WMPS presented an all-day chronological special on Elvis's career, starting with the Sun recordings of "That's All Right (Mama)" and "Blue Moon of Kentucky" and moving forward to tracks from "Moody Blue." But by the time the gates closed at Graceland, the station had reached only 1960 in the huge Presley catalogue.

In Washington, D.C., Tom Gaugher began his regular morning stint at ten o'clock on WMAL, and it became a five-hour Elvis special. The Memphis-born disc jockey did not plan it that way; he simply gathered up everything the station had on Presley and added his personal recollections of growing up in Elvis's home town. He told of the time Elvis appeared at a high school chapel program and afterwards found his white Cadillac covered with lipstick. He played tracks from interviews that Elvis had done early in his career. And he played lots of music. Early in the show the program manager gave Gaugher "a lot of flack" about the format and asked if he wasn't giving too much time to someone who was, after all, "just a singer." But the criticism abated as calls inundated the station with messages saying "Do more" and "Isn't this great," even volunteering their own recollections of Elvis. Management discovered that the callers were not teeny-boppers but the mature adult audience the station was targeting, the audience that had made WMAL the station with the highest ratings in the Washington market.

"Every radio station thinks its audience is super-sophisticated," Gaugher noted, "and this automatically means they can't like Elvis Presley. But it's not true. What we found out was that these were our hard-core listeners, this forty-plus—actually forty-six-point-whatever— median age we have in our listeners. They all like Presley."

When Gaugher's stint finished at 2 p.m., the listeners would not let the program end. The Elvis tribute continued into Ed Walker's program of nostalgia music that followed.

At WHN in New York, the station brought in extra people to man the telephones and to help prepare broadcast material on Presley. A twenty-four hour station with studios on Park Avenue, WHN bills itself as the most-listened-to country music station in the world; audience measurement samples show it averages one and a half million listeners a day, and surveys show Elvis—before and after his death—is the listeners' favorite artist. "You know people are tuning to you because this is where they hear the Elvis music," said Ed Salamon, the station's program director. "Sure they see it on television, but this is where they're still hearing the music, here at the radio station." To Salamon, Elvis's death was a major event in the lives of WHN's listeners comparable to the blackout or major elections or a transit strike. "In fact," he recalled, "when the Pope visited [in 1979], people were saying, 'Gee, nothing this big has happened on the radio station since the time Elvis died.'" WHN sent its music director, Pam Green, to Memphis to locate fans from the New York area and tape their comments for broadcast. She arrived just as the gates were closing at Graceland.

"I can't see how anything I can ever go through will ever top seeing those people," Green said. "I got my microphone out right away and caught some really old ladies off guard. They were crying and everything, but one of them told me, 'I never thought Elvis would die before I died.' And she said, 'I've always been meaning to go to one of his concerts.'"

Green's reservation for a rental car was cancelled by the time she got to Memphis, and she wound up spending the night in front of Graceland, easily locating fans from New York, New Jersey, and Connecticut and recording interviews. A family living nearby offered to let her use their telephone so that she could feed the voices back for broadcast on WHN's hourly news programs.

Many other out-of-town journalists also faced the choice of continuing the vigil at Graceland or—if they had transportation—making a long commute to Senatobia, Mississippi, or Forrest City, Arkansas, towns some forty to sixty miles away where motel vacancies were reported. Lynn Rosellini of *The Washington Star* was embarrassed at the experience of "showing up on the doorstep" of a friend she hadn't talked to in years and had been intending to call. "They had a guest room," she said, "and I sat down in their kitchen till four in the morning typing my story. They were very understanding." Susan White had turned her Memphis house over to the UPI contingent, and one of the AP photographers slept on a couch at Les Seago's home under the watchful eye of Seago's suspicious dog. Nanci Albritten recalls a *Time* reporter—a friend of her husband's—staying at their home. Henry Mitchell of *The Washington Post*, who had spent most of his adult life as a Memphis journalist before heading east a decade earlier, probably snared the most unusual accommodations. Trading on his local connections, he prevailed on the cautious management of the Parkview Hotel to rent him a room for a few days. Once a prestigious residential hotel, the Parkview now was a retirement home operated by the Presbyterian Church. Some of those attending the Shriners's convention offered to double up to make rooms available for journalists, important Presley business associates, or the fans who had descended on the city. But the demand for lodging continued to be acute.

In the best of times communication among independent reporters, each seeking his or her own story, is difficult. But for those who got the word, the Memphis Chamber of Commerce had arranged for the visiting journalists to rent rooms in a high-rise dormitory at Memphis State University. The organization's communications manager, Ed Dunn, had foreseen the media interest that Elvis's death would cause, and—like the businessmen the Chamber represents—he was concerned about the image of the city. Since Mr. Crump's death, Memphis had not quite been able to get everything together. Its once-vaunted reputation for good race relations had vanished with the 1968 King assassination, and *Time* magazine had called the city "a decaying backwater river town." Memphis was one of the few large Southern cities that had failed to share in the boom of the seventies. Now, thought Dunn, the world's media were arriving and sixteen thousand Shriners were in town. If the "buckle of the Sunbelt" remained slightly tarnished, at least someone could assist in providing amenities for the press. Besides securing lodging, Dunn arranged for a downtown press room, with tables, chairs, typewriters, and telephones. The giant Holiday Inn chain, headquartered in Memphis, offered three cars with drivers to help with transportation. The transit authority supplied buses to ferry reporters between Graceland and the cemetery. For late arrivals, particularly for the foreign press, the arrangements were a godsend. Dunn said the press room resembled a mini-United Nations, with reporters from Spain, Japan, Portugal, England, France, Mexico, Australia, Germany, and Switzerland. Members of the local chapter of the Public Relations Society of America took turns staffing the office, answering questions, and giving directions.

"All through this, the family did not want any contact with the press," said Dunn. "Our concern the whole time was that this thing not be allowed to become a three-ring circus. And it could have if there had been nobody to step in and make some attempt to coordinate, to assist these people."

The Chamber's efforts gained newsmen access to the cemetery in an area near the mausoleum. The family originally planned to exclude all media from the cemetery. Dunn was able to arrange for a pool interview with Joe Esposito, Elvis's road manager and the closest thing to an official spokesman for the Presley organization. Esposito finally agreed to talk with representatives of the two wire services after the public viewing ended. He gave Harry Rosenthal and Robert Carey a few details about plans for the funeral, but both reporters felt the inverview was unproductive.

"We were really asking what was happening inside the house," Rosenthal recalled. "People were reporting folks there that weren't anywhere near Memphis. And with that kind of thing—if somebody is reporting it, and you're not reporting it, you have to explain why. So everybody was picking up from everybody else. We didn't do this. I might have said there were reports so-and-so was there. But if I didn't see them, I didn't write them."

One of the celebrity visitors arrived shortly after Carey and Rosenthal had gone back downtown to brief some two dozen reporters on their meeting with Esposito. Caroline Kennedy, daughter of the late President, threaded her way up to the gate and was talking with the guard when Eddie Fadal saw her. "I don't understand it to this day," says Fadal. "She was totally unescorted. They were giving her a hard time at the gate, but I recognized her and told her to come on in and go on up to the house."

Word of her visit spread to the media, but many reporters said she was accompanied by her mother, Jacqueline Onassis. Other reports—not true but widely circulated—said that John Wayne and Burt Reynolds were at Graceland. Undisclosed at the time was information that Caroline Kennedy was working for the *New York Daily News*, and she had talked her way into Graceland not as a friend but as a reporter. She missed her paper's deadline, however, and later sold her story to *Rolling Stone*. While she apparently was the only reporter to get inside the house the night before the funeral, her article added nothing new. Albin Krebs, writing later in *The Times*, observed that her story contained only one quote from Priscilla Presley: "Would you like a Coke or a 7-Up?"

Except for the hundreds of people milling around and the cars parked along both sides of the highway for miles in both directions, the atmosphere was relatively calm at Graceland in the post-midnight hours. Police left Elvis Presley Boulevard open, although the constant traffic moved slowly as curious motorists looked at the crowds and the mansion on the hill with its windows lighted.

Television producer Lane Venardos remembers the vivid scene he encountered as his cab drove slowly past Graceland about two o'clock. "I couldn't believe it," he said. "It was a remarkable blend of so many different kinds of people." Venardos had been sent to Memphis to serve as the "cutting producer" for items CBS planned to use in its special that night and pieces for regular news broadcasts the rest of the week. He had been called off his regular assignment as Washington producer of the *CBS Evening News* just before broadcast time on Wednesday and ordered to drop what he was doing.

The highly unusual maneuver of dispatching a producer from a regular daily broadcast to cover the third day of an out-of-town event was another indication of CBS having to play catch-up on a very important story. But Venardos is among the best in his craft of taking late-breaking materials and making them into usable segments in time to get on a broadcast. Grabbing a commercial flight to Nashville, then a charter on to Memphis, he had directed a cabdriver to go past Graceland so that at least he could say he had seen the place. Then he went downtown to the studios of WREG-TV, the CBS affiliate.

"The amount of material to be waded through was enormous," Venardos recalled. "I saw all the material there was to see coming in on tape or live feed. With three crews of our own and the local crews covering the same event, you end up having the same thing shot from two or three different angles, plus you are out doing reaction interviews with the crowds, for example. Then you end up coming back with fifty or sixty minutes of interviews—you know, 'Why are you here?' and 'Where are you from?' and 'What do you think?' kinds of things."

For most of the reporters, photographers, and broadcast personnel, the vigil at Graceland now settled into a routine. It was a difficult story to cover, but the journalists were now more or less acclimated to the scene. Most of them had interviewed fans and captured the mood of the place, but there were only so many ways that fans could explain their presence and what Elvis meant to them. The pageant that the media had been watching for two days was coming to an end. The final act—the funeral service and interment—was a few hours away. The ceremony would be private, but thousands of onlookers would be massed at the home and at the cemetery and along the four-mile route linking the two sites. Photographers and cameramen had mapped out the route, noting vantage points for recording the procession. Reporters had staked out telephones and assembled names of persons who would attend the service and could supply details afterward. But on the night before the funeral, most of the journalists at last felt caught up, and now they had a chance to relax and get some sleep.

The UPI team decided not to come into the bureau until eight o'clock the next morning. Susan White got home shortly before three o'clock, and had been asleep for some forty-five minutes when the Atlanta desk called with the message, "Something terrible has happened at Graceland." Still asleep, White mumbled, "No, that was two days ago." There was no mistake, her caller insisted, a hit-and-run accident had occurred in front of the Presley mansion.

"So I went racing back to the bureau again," she recalled. "That started what was obviously the longest day of my life."

Police had cleared the Graceland side of the highway. The crowd of about a thousand people was concentrated in the parking lot across the street. But in the pre-dawn hours the tight control that had been the order of the day earlier had been relaxed, and the crowd had edged onto the roadway. Officers with flashlights slowed the few cars that passed by, but one vehicle driving south, turned around, and headed back at a high speed. The car struck two nineteen-year-olds from Monroe, Louisiana—Alice Hovatar and Joanne Johnson—killing them instantly. A third bystander, Tammy Baiter, a seventeen-year-old fan from Saint Clair, Missouri, was injured critically, suffering multiple fractures of the pelvis. The driver of the vehicle, Treatise Wheeler, was arrested and charged with second-degree murder and drunken driving.

Tom Madden, who had come to Memphis from the UPI office in Jackson, Mississippi, was the only wire service reporter on the scene. The only wire service photographer on hand was David Tenenbaum, usually based with the AP in Springfield, Illinois. He made a dramatic photo of the aftermath of the tragedy—bystanders kneeling over the injured, bleeding, unconscious Tammy Baiter as her sister, Mrs. Dianne Steele, stood over her, shouting, "My God, let her be alive." Tenenbaum phoned his eyewitness account of the accident to the AP in Nashville and gave an audio report to AP Radio.

Les Seago also had just fallen asleep when he got a call telling him to get out to Graceland. Although the bodies had been removed and AP had the story, there was fear that the accident might touch off some racial altercation since the driver of the car was black. All was quiet, however, when Seago reached the scene. It was his first trip there and the scene made a profound impression on him.

"There were hundreds of people out there who had spent all night, just staring at that big white house," he said later. "I don't think there were more than one or two Shelby County cars in the area. All of 'em were from out of town. But one girl in particular caught my eye. She looked like she might have been sixteen, but she swore up and down that she was twenty. She was skinny, with stringy blond hair, and she was holding this baby who was possibly two to three months old. And here it was six o'clock in the morning. The baby was so tired, so sick and hungry, and it had cried so much that it couldn't cry anymore; it could just— snuffle is the only term I can think of, just sort of whimper."

The woman told Seago she had driven down from Beloit, Wisconsin, in a 1965 Volkswagen when she heard the radio report that Elvis was dead. She said she called her husband at work and told him she was going to see Elvis one last time. When Seago asked her husband's reaction, she said, "He told me not to go. He told me if I went, that he wouldn't be there when I got back. But I love Elvis more than I could love my husband." The reporter's reaction was one of anger, an urge to shake her, to slap some sense into her. "Understand that I am not an Elvis Presley fan and never will be," Seago explained, "but I found it a little bit distressing, I guess, that people would act like that. And there were dozens like her. I guess I just don't understand the Presley mystique."

8

The Final Farewell

The crowd began building again shortly after dawn on Thursday. People were now more orderly; there was no urgency as there had been the day before when most of the people felt this was their last chance to see Elvis. The feeling now was one of resignation. They would stand quietly as the funeral procession passed through the gates: Elvis would leave Graceland for the last time. For the regulars in the press corps, those reporters and photographers who had been around for more than twenty-four hours, the day represented the last chapter of the many reports they had filed from Memphis. But for others in the media, this was their first—and maybe their only—chance to get a story on Elvis. They had just arrived in Memphis and there was an air of desperation about them.

"It was like every man for himself," recalled Lynn Rosellini of *The Washington Star*. "There was this horrible crush of reporters—foreign reporters and reporters from all over the country. In Washington everybody kind of knows each other, and if you don't, you at least have a common set of rules like at the press conferences and things. But the worst instincts seemed to be coming out; I mean, people were pushing and shoving. The competition was unlike anything I had ever seen."

Rosellini had been aboard a plane delayed by mechanical trouble at National Airport the previous day, a plane filled with Elvis fans who became hysterical at the thought of missing the funeral. She finally took another flight, but arrived in Memphis too late to view the body or record the dramatic scenes in a story for her paper. In an effort to recoup, she had arrived at Graceland early on Thursday and posted herself on the curb near the gate. An hour or so later a tall cameraman moved in front of her, pushing her back so she couldn't see. She countered by jamming a ball-point pen into his back. An argument ensued; he stood there defiantly for a while, then moved off. "I'd never done anything like that before in my life," Rosellini said. "It's a silly little story, but it just indicates the competition among the reporters who were down there."

Long before two o'clock, the scheduled time for the services, those who had been invited to the funeral began to arrive, threading their way through the crowd, into the grounds, and up the driveway to the house. They included little-known relatives and friends from the area, as well as important business associates—executives from RCA, Hollywood studios, and the Las Vegas Hilton—but most were unknown to the press and to the crowd. Actor George Hamilton, actress Ann-Margret and her actor-husband Roger Smith, and guitarist Chet Atkins were among the few recognizable celebrities on hand. Joe Esposito said that dozens of others had called, wanting to attend, but they had been told just to send condolences; the house could not hold any more guests.

Art Harris of the *San Francisco Examiner* remembers the scene "like one of those old TV movies that will always be there." He had arrived during the night and gathered information about the hit-and-run accident. After he made his way through three police lines and into the press area, he realized that the media had to rely on what the police were telling them. "There really wasn't a whole lot you could see," he said. "You were jockeying and straining against the ropes like cattle at an auction, just to get a glimpse of who was moving in or who was coming down the driveway. But the story was really not what was happening up there, but what was going on in the hearts and minds of the masses."

In 1975 Harris had written what he thought was a tongue-in-cheek piece on an Elvis fan club parade, an article that provoked dozens of threatening phone calls and angry letters from outraged women who saw no humor in his writing. He sensed then that the reaction to Elvis could reach almost religious proportions, so he was prepared for the sea of emotion he saw in front of Graceland. Other late arrivals were not. "Some were kind of cynical about it," Harris recalled. "Some reporters—

I mean, that's what we are. You can't buy into mass fervor, although it's really impossible not to be somewhat affected by it."

The three Memphis network affiliates stationed live television cameras outside Graceland and along the route of the procession to the cemetery, but cameras were barred from the service itself. Only CBS tried on its evening newscasts to depict the scene inside the house. Artist Ham Embree, whose work usually involves courtrooms from which cameras are excluded, sketched details of the funeral service from descriptions given him by some of those in attendance. The casket was moved into the music room at the south end of the mansion, and some two hundred people crowded inside or in the adjoining hallways. Leading the service was Reverend C. W. Bradley, a Church of Christ minister who was called shortly after midnight on Tuesday and asked to help plan the service. He was pastor of the church that Vernon's wife, Dee Presley, the singer's stepmother, attended, and he had visited with the family many times through the years. Assisting was the Reverend Rex Humbard, the television evangelist from Akron, Ohio, who later revealed in an interview with the *Akron Beacon-Journal* that he had prayed with a weeping Elvis and counseled him a few months earlier in Las Vegas. The two ministers made brief remarks and J. D. Sumner and the Stamps Quartet sang gospel songs. The songs, Vernon said, were his son's favorites, opening with "How Great Thou Art," the hymn that Elvis himself recorded and included in most of his concert appearances.

The service was scheduled to last a half hour, but it stretched to ninety minutes because, as Joe Esposito told the *Press-Scimitar*, "everyone wanted to say goodby to Elvis." The resulting delay threw already-hectic media schedules into further confusion. A photographer for *The Commercial Appeal* was aboard WMC radio's traffic helicopter hovering above Elvis Presley Boulevard, planning an aerial photograph of the procession to the cemetery—a white hearse and seventeen white limousines. The helicopter began to run low on fuel, however, and the pilot decided to return to the airport. "Dammit," yelled Photo Editor Robert Williams into the phone, "tell him to set down in an Exxon station."

Most Memphis radio stations observed two minutes of silence at the hour the funeral services began. They reported from the scene as frequently as they could, but the shortage of telephones was a major disadvantage. Getting from the press area in front of Graceland to the phones in the commercial strip across the street was extremely difficult, and reporters were reluctant to chance missing the buses that would take them to the cemetery.

UPI's Craig Schwed brought his bicycle with him to Graceland, and he was able to follow the four-mile procession with relative ease. Nanci Albritten arrived at the cemetery earlier in the morning and gave a complete description of the scene to the Atlanta desk. AP reporters Harry Rosenthal and Eric Newhouse also paid an early morning visit to Forest Hill and located what was apparently the only phone on the premises. They found it in a small laboratory building adjoining a chapel in the cemetery, a room most often used for final preparations prior to services that would be conducted at graveside. The reporters gave the attendant some money, guaranteeing their exclusive rights to the phone after the entombment.

The Commercial Appeal arranged for reporter William Thomas to pose as an employee of the Memphis Funeral Home. Dressed in a dark suit, he would not carry a notebook or a camera, just observe the scene inside the mausoleum. Nothing in his story the next morning revealed his sources or the role that he had played. In a copyrighted report, Thomas wrote that the journey for Elvis "ended at exactly 4:30 p.m. Thursday when the rock and roll star's body was entombed in a gray marble crypt 9 feet long and 27 inches high at Forest Hill Cemetery Midtown." He described the coffin being wheeled into the crypt room of Corridor Z and lifted into place. "Then, led by Elvis' white haired father, Vernon, the family filed into the crypt and one by one touched or kissed the coffin. Mr. Presley, wearing a black pinstripe suit, stood for an extended moment with his hand on his son's coffin. He had to be supported when he left."

Thomas also described what happened after the family left: Five workmen entered with their tools and sealed the crypt with a double slab of concrete and marble. Before they had finished their task, people who had entered the cemetery from the rear began pressing against the heavy steel doors.

"If Elvis Presley was, as proclaimed, the King of Rock 'n' Roll, then his funeral was truly majestic," said Mark Knoller on his voice report for AP Radio. "Some 2,200 floral arrangements completely blanketed the landscaped lawn in front of the large mausoleum into which the pallbearers slowly brought Presley's coffin. Presley was entombed in a six-crypt family room of the Forest Hill Cemetery Mausoleum which is situated just a few hundred yards from where his mother is buried. The public was barred from the cemetery and the press was kept at a distance."

Knoller ran to file the report from the phone his wireside colleagues had secured, while the print reporters waited for the procession to leave. He finally located the building and was dialing his office when he noticed the body of an old lady on a nearby slab. "While I'm there filing my report," Knoller recounted later, "two guys come in, slip her into this blue velvet burial gown, pick her up, one at the heels, the other at the head—she's stiff as a board—and load her into a coffin. I had never seen anything like that. That upset me more than anything I had seen the preceding day."

For most of the media, the day had been a hurry-up-and-wait situation. But an enterprising reporter always could use the idle moments to talk with the fans, still the best source of stories. As Eric Newhouse of the AP was waiting in the press area outside the mausoleum, he struck up a conversation with two women from Bridgeton, New Jersey, and produced one of the most unusual sidebars to come out of the day's activities.

The two women—Pat Christian and Dana Miletta—had, like so many others, dropped everything and headed for Memphis when they heard that Elvis had died. Unable to get a hotel room, they simply wandered around the city, then tried to get into the cemetery early in the morning. Refused admission at the main entrance, they climbed over a fence in the rear. The women told the AP reporter they saw the floral trucks "so we snuck up and started telling them where to put the arrangements. Everyone thought we worked there." For hours they worked, even riding out to reclaim souvenirs they had left with a newfound friend and returning, hidden in a florist's van. Their luck almost ran out when they tried to infiltrate the press corps in order to get closer to the mausoleum. "When the press was let in, we just walked in with them," said Pat Christian. "I noticed that everyone was carrying a pad, so I got my notebook out, too. They checked everyone else's credentials, but they were so used to seeing us that they just nodded us in."

As the tomb was sealed in late afternoon, the reporters boarded the buses for the trip downtown or made arrangements to get to telephones or typewriters and work on inserts and updates and to record their impressions of the day.

"In half an hour it was over," wrote Fred Girard of the *Detroit News.* "The celebrities (including Caroline Kennedy) had seen and been seen;

the ladies and gentlemen of the press had clambered down from their gravestone vantage points and stampeded out, with only a carpet of cigaret butts, paper wads and film boxes to mark their passing.

"Elvis Presley had been laid to rest."

For the local wire service personnel, the physical and emotional strain had reached a peak. Susan White counted her time: Since UPI had called her in Nashville with the news of Elvis's death seventy-two hours earlier, she had gotten exactly seven hours of sleep. Robert Shaw, the AP's correspondent in Jackson, Mississippi, arrived in Memphis with a message for Les Seago: "I'm supposed to tell you to get your ass home and not to come back until you've gotten a good day's sleep." Seago does not remember going home, but he does remember his wife preparing a steak and serving it to him in bed late Friday afternoon.

Reflections and analyses had to be written after the funeral, but one final news event remained to be covered. Vernon Presley announced that he wanted the flowers that covered the front lawn of the mausoleum to go to the fans. The distribution would be on Friday morning, and the members of the city's association of florists volunteered to help. Some three hundred fans slept outside the cemetery gates on Thursday night to be sure to get these final mementos. Ralph Davis, general superintendent at Forest Hill, estimated that fifty thousand people passed through the cemetery during the day. Lynn Doyle, president of the Professional Florists Association of Memphis, told reporters that an additional four hundred arrangements were delivered on Friday, bringing the total to more than thirty-five hundred.

The gifts of flowers gave late-arriving members of the media another angle and a second-day story. And for those writers and photographers who had been in Memphis since Tuesday, the distribution of the flowers was a colorful focus for wrapping up the varied events of the week. Visuals were there for the television cameras, and the crews could take their time in filming because broadcast deadlines were hours away. Shortly after noon, all the flowers were gone, and people were asking for the ribbons and the styrofoam—anything that was left. Harry Rosenthal of the AP was startled when he heard a man shout, "Hey Elvis, come here." The voice belonged to Paul MacLeod of Holly Springs, Mississippi, who was calling his four-year-old son, Elvis Aaron MacLeod. The man had grease-slicked hair and he was wearing silver sunglasses, a white jacket, and a black shirt. "I'd like to be like Elvis in every way," he told the reporter. "Why I even named my son after Elvis instead of naming him after myself."

At the end, the media focus once more was on the fans, some sobbing and hysterical, but most of them quietly and reverently approaching the tomb to receive a remembrance of their sad pilgrimage to Memphis. As Jackson Bain noted in his report for the *NBC Nightly News*, the trip to the cemetery was for many of the fans the closest they had come to the body of the singer.

9

Roots of the Legend

Elvis's popularity spans the globe, but for the most part Elvis stayed close to home, close to his past. His retinue of hangers-on, the boys always surrounding him, became more understandable to anyone who listened to them—they sounded like his past, they were reminders of where he had come from, benchmarks in his surreal existence as a world idol.

Elvis never forgot his own roots—and in the end his roots embraced him. Peggy Duggan of the *Nashville Banner*, who grew up in Memphis, wrote, "He was the nice boy from a small town who became a rich and famous star—and stayed a nice boy. That's how we remember him." The small town was Tupelo, Mississippi, where Elvis was born and where he lived until he was thirteen.

Tupelo got the news like everyone else—in a sudden rush that tied up communications and media for days.

The voice of Rex Allen, Jr., singing his current hit "Don't Say Goodbye," was just fading out, when disc jockey Asa Thompson swung his chair around to his microphone at the studio-transmitter just north of Tupelo and said: "The time is twenty-six minutes past four o'clock." Then he took a deep breath and added: "Ladies and gentlemen, WELO News has just received word that Elvis Presley has died in a Memphis hospital. Other details are not available, but WELO has learned that singer Elvis Presley has died in Baptist Hospital in Memphis, Tennessee. Stay tuned to WELO; we'll have further details later."

Tupelo is in the northeast corner of Mississippi, not far from the Tennessee line, and a few people had seen the news bulletin earlier on WHBQ-TV from Memphis. Telephone traffic already was heavy when the announcement officially came to the town of Elvis's birth. The media in Tupelo—three radio stations, a television station, a daily newspaper, and a weekly—were inundated with callers seeking confirmation.

"I've thought about this a lot of times since then," *Daily Journal* Editor James Graham has recalled, "and I hope sincerely that I never, ever have to live through anything like that any more. I mean, there are certain events in your life that you just don't want to do over, and I can't even conceive of anything like that big. But it just stood us and this town on its ear. That's what it amounted to."

Before Elvis came to prominence, Tupelo's claim to fame had been a massive tornado that ripped through the area in 1936, leaving two hundred dead and hundreds of others injured and homeless. The town rebuilt, but to the wealthy Midwesterners who made the town a rest stop as they drove to Florida in the forties and fifties, Tupelo looked like a typical Mississippi county seat—"unprepossessing," said Kenneth Holditch, an English professor at the University of New Orleans, who was born there. Although a Confederate monument stands near the courthouse, Tupelo wasn't incorporated until after the Civil War. For a town in the Deep South, this was "tantamount to being born out of wedlock," Holditch added. But Tupelo prospered, becoming the first municipality to contract for electricity with the Tennessee Valley Authority and the first school system in Mississippi to desegregate its schools voluntarily. Although the nation's interstate highway system passed the town by, it had become a major manufacturing and retail center and was selected an "All American City" in 1968 by *Look* magazine and the National League of Cities. With a 1970 population just over twenty thousand, Tupelo supported two major shopping malls and manufacturing plants drawing workers from sixty miles away. Its daily newspaper, fat with advertising, had a circulation of 34,782, unusually high for a city so small.

Tupelo acknowledged its most famous child early—but the city never was sure what to do about him. Elvis sang on WELO's "Black and White Jamboree" when he was twelve-years-old, and a few weeks later he won second place in a children's talent contest at the Mississippi-

Alabama Fair and Dairy Show. After the Presleys moved to Memphis, the family made occasional visits to see friends and relatives. Elvis took part in several country music shows that played high school gyms and National Guard armories in the area, and he drew a local following with his early Sun recordings. But it wasn't until he was picked to headline the grandstand show at the Fair that Elvis really came home to the people of Tupelo.

The agricultural exposition with its accompanying carnival midway was one of the fall highlights in Northeast Mississippi. The annual week-long event attracted more than a hundred thousand people and was almost as important to Mississippians as the official state fair in Jackson. Organizers of the Tupelo fair had booked Presley more than a year in advance, and his appearance there was one of those small-town commitments the singer still had to keep. By the time the date for the event rolled around, Elvis was a national celebrity because of his appearances on television. He arrived in Tupelo, riding the wave of fame from his first appearance two weeks earlier on the *Ed Sullivan Show.* Governor J. P. Coleman was on hand to extend an official welcome to the native son who had made good.

"I was in that crowd picture," recalled Nathan Duncan, editor of the *Lee County News.* Everyone in Tupelo would recognize the picture he meant—a sea of screaming teenagers reaching over the footlights towards the young singer in the white shoes and the black pants and shirt. Elvis's mother and father were there, and the contrasting image of the doting parents and the swivel-hipped rock singer became fixed in the public's mind, adding to the Presley lore. To cap the gala homecoming, Elvis announced that he would donate ten thousand dollars from his two appearances to the city for a park in East Tupelo, the part of town where he had been born, an area literally on the wrong side of the railroad tracks.

The city acquired the land for the park, and the two-room house, ten feet wide and thirty feet long, where Elvis was born, became its center-piece. The East Tupelo Garden Club took on maintenance of the house as its project, outfitting it with Depression-era furnishings. Grandiose plans for a youth center and a guitar-shaped swimming pool were announced, but somewhere along the way, the plans were changed. A youth center finally went up in the late sixties, along with a standard swimming pool, but the park fell into disrepair. Eddie Fadal, Elvis's Waco, Texas, friend, remembers a late-afternoon trip to Tupelo in 1959, when they found the sign identifying the "Birthplace of Elvis Presley" fallen, and the area overgrown with weeds. Nevertheless, a steady stream of Elvis fans, including many foreign visitors, kept turning up to see the place. East Tupelo became East Heights, then Elvis Presley Heights, much to the chagrin of some of the local residents. New suburban developments sprouted nearby in pastures and cotton fields. Yet most of the city's people were only vaguely aware of the birthplace. It was just there.

"People in Tupelo generally have not been overly fond of Elvis," Nathan Duncan recalled, searching for a precise reason. "After that first big show and all, they kind of just ignored him, just drug their feet on building a park. It's kind of like the way they treated William Faulkner over in Oxford. He was famous worldwide, but he was not so famous at home. I guess that happens to a lot of famous people."

But that all changed when Elvis died.

"All of a sudden," said James Graham, "the hottest place in the world was Elvis's birthplace out there, which we couldn't get any support for at all before. While he was living, well, who cared where he was born? It was just that shotgun house and everything out there, and people just started coming in from everywhere."

Like many others in Tupelo, Graham had not thought much about Presley in recent years. Elvis's voice was heard on juke boxes and on radio and his latest record was at the top of the country charts, but his music had always been there, almost like piped-in Muzak. For a long time there had been no new movies or television specials. In past years, reports occurred of night-time visits to Tupelo, and people would hear about them and call the newspaper. The singer once brought his daughter Lisa down to see the place where he was born.

"I think my particular problem was," said Graham, "like half the people in the world, we knew Elvis was out there, but we really didn't know or had lost touch with just how ingrained he was in the people."

The Tuesday night that Elvis died, the staff of the *Daily Journal* found time between the maddening barrage of telephone calls to gather materials on its "local angle" of the Presley story. The paper reported the sudden increase in the number of visitors at the birthplace. On the front page was a photo of Steve Meggison, a nineteen-year-old youth who had hammered an eightpenny nail into the top of the front door of the house, hung an arrangement of white flowers and greenery from the spike, then driven away in his pickup truck. "It was just something I wanted to do," he said. The paper led with the UPI story from Memphis and featured an unflattering picture of Elvis taken on his last concert tour. The edition became a collector's item. Bannered across its front page was the headline, "The King Is Dead."

"The next day," Graham continued, "about half the world decided to come to Tupelo, and I don't know where the other half went— Memphis, I suppose. And then they switched." For its second-day coverage, the *NBC Nightly News* featured a story on the birthplace, interviewing Mrs. J. C. Grimes, Elvis's grade-school teacher, and Mrs. Billy Boyd, curator of the birthplace. Other reporters followed, particularly after the funeral in Memphis. "I remember going out to the birthplace that Friday," said Graham, "and there were hundreds of people out there. I suspect that half of them were media."

On Thursday, half an hour before the funeral services were to begin in Memphis, about five hundred people gathered on a rise behind the birthplace for a memorial service organized by the Tupelo Ministerial Association. A dozen floral arrangements joined the single wreath placed there earlier. The service was brief, so that it would conclude by two o'clock. There were prayers and a reading from a passage of Scripture. Tupelo policeman Larry Montgomery sang two Presley favorites, "Love Me Tender" and "Precious Memories." Mayor Clyde Whitaker then read from a resolution the Board of Aldermen had adopted a few hours after Presley's death, proclaiming an official period of mourning and designating each January 8, the singer's birthday, as "Elvis Presley Day" in Tupelo. "Elvis Presley's career stands alone," said the mayor. "His accomplishments will be unsurpassed for their monumental impact on our culture." Lines of people formed to sign a register, later forwarded to the Presley family. Michael Kerr, *Daily Journal* city editor, said the little house on what used to be Old Saltillo Road probably hadn't seen so much activity since its interior was restored six years earlier.

On the day of Elvis's funeral, State Highway Commissioner Bobby Richardson said he would ask the legislature to rename that portion of U.S. Highway 78 that runs through Mississippi between Alabama and Tennessee the Elvis Presley Memorial Highway, and the three banks in Tupelo—the Bank of Mississippi, First Citizens National Bank, and the Peoples Bank and Trust Company—announced they would accept funds for construction of a suitable memorial to the singer. The East Heights Garden Club made the first contribution, nine hundred dollars.

In the following months, much debate took place in Tupelo about the proper approach. Many argued for a museum, but opponents pointed out the town did not have enough memorabilia even to begin such a venture. Some suggested a theme park. Mrs. Boyd, the guiding spirit behind efforts to keep the Presley birthplace intact through the years, resigned from the Garden Club; her explanation: "internal politics." She established the "Elvis—Tupelo Favorite Son—Gift Shop" on the newly renamed Elvis Presley Highway about three blocks from the birthplace.

While the city fathers debated what kind of memorial would be appropriate, the fund continued to grow, supported mainly by contributions from the thousands of visitors who streamed through the house and donations by fan clubs throughout the world. Finally, the mayor and Board of Aldermen approved the idea of a memorial chapel, a proposal put forth by Jannelle McComb, a bookkeeper for a local tobacco distributor, who was a poet and a longtime friend of Elvis and his family.

McComb has recalled that the idea came from Elvis one night not long after the town renovated the birthplace. She and her husband were visiting Graceland, and she had brought pictures of the house. The entertainer laughed, joking about the contrast between the shack no bigger than a railroad caboose and his Memphis mansion. He was immensely proud of his accomplishments, yet in some ways humble, McComb reminisced.

"I asked him if he knew who gave him his talent," McComb said. "And he said, 'Oh, yes,' and pointed up in the sky. And I said, 'Well, this brings me to something: If we ever did anything in your memory in Tupelo, what would you like?' And for a moment he stopped, and he said, 'Why don't you build a chapel so my fans can go and meditate and reflect on their own lives and know that no matter what station they reach in life, if they place their talent in the hands of God, he can bless it and they can make a contribution to the world?'"

McComb told other stories about people Elvis inspired, people who had risen from poverty to succeed in various occupations. Relating the story of the chapel, she took on an almost religious fervor. "I don't care what station you reach in life," she said, "there is something about where your mother gave birth that has to have an effect on you. Elvis never said an unkind word about Tupelo. There's got to be something about the place where it all began. And this is what we feel—that on fifteen acres you couldn't do a memorial without including God."

The mayor appointed a Memorial Commission and named McComb as its chairman. The city backed a loan of one hundred thousand dollars for construction of the building, poured the sidewalks, and contributed

other excavation services. Vernon Presley, the singer's father, blessed
the project and gave the family Bible for use in the chapel. Colonel
Parker, Presley's long-time manager, helped to raise funds. The original
bids came in at a quarter-million dollars, and the city scaled the plans
down to a smaller structure.

The result is a modern structure of twelve hundred square feet with
a redwood exterior. A large stained-glass window donated by Mrs. R. L.
Laukoff, a Memphis artisan, dominates one wall. Fifteen other stained-
glass windows, twelve benches, and other interior furnishings, crafted
from native oak, were donated by fan clubs and Presley associates. A
single clear window in the one-room building gives a view to the outside.
The window frames the birthplace, which is located to the northwest less
than a hundred feet away from the chapel. Ground was broken on January 8, 1979, and the building was dedicated on August 17, 1979, just two
years and a day after Elvis died. About four thousand people attended
the ceremonies, including Mississippi Governor Cliff Finch, four
hundred fans from England, and one hundred from Canada.

For Janelle McComb, the most difficult task was explaining to the
fans why there was no picture of Elvis hanging in the chapel. Acutely
aware of the religious feelings the singer stirred in so many people, she
went to great pains to point out that the building is a chapel to God. She
concluded that if a hundred thousand people were to visit Tupelo's
Presley Park and only one stopped to meditate on his or her own life,
then the memorial would prove its worth.

McComb's confidence that building the chapel was the right thing
for Tupelo to do was unhesitating and most of the city leaders and
business people gave the project their endorsement. The comment of a
Tupelo housewife active in the city's cultural activities typified the
awakening of the establishment to Presley's impact on the world. A few
years younger than Elvis, she had danced to his music, but she had never
thought much about the singer one way or another. "But then one day
you're downtown and you see two Greyhound buses with 'Elvis Presley
Fan Club of Japan' on the sides," she said, "and all these Japanese ladies
are in the stores shopping—well, it does give you pause for thought."

It is not surprising that Tupelo erected a memorial to Presley. What
is surprising is how many people thought it strange to build a religious
chapel as a memorial for Elvis Presley. A close look at the roots of Elvis
Presley's music and background make the meaning of the chapel appropriate. The influence of God, or God's music, on the young Presley

parallels the more often cited influence of Southern black rhythm and blues. Moreover, many observers often misunderstand Presley's relationship to blacks and their music. Some papers tried to explain the dual influence of religion and black music upon Presley, but most addressed it in an offhand way, if at all, concentrating on what Presley had become rather than on where he came from.

The Washington Post was one which delved into past influences in an editorial on the singer:

> Coming from a Mississippi background whose favorite music was white country blues, Elvis—it will not do, even in his obituary, to call him "Mr. Presley"—happened upon the commercial scene in the mid-1950s just as white music was being integrated, if you will, with the earthier, angrier black music of rhythm and blues and a touch of gospel. Not so coincidentally, white America was in the throes of its crisis of integration with black America. Elvis Presley became the leading practitioner of the new style, especially in the South, where at his death this week flags flew at half-staff.

And the *Chicago Sun-Times* gave a nod in the direction of the past in its editorial:

> A little gospel and, yes, a little blues. Elvis Presley, dead at 42, had his beginning in potent Southern music; it's only fitting for his ending, too.

Many people, however, failed to see any religious influence on Presley. Gary Deeb, radio-TV critic for the *Chicago Tribune*, recalled daily lectures from Sister Mary Helena at St. Margaret's School in Buffalo, New York, on the evils of the hip-swiveling Elvis. He had tried to convince her she was wrong, even sharing with her Elvis's recording of "How Great Thou Art." "It didn't do any good," Deeb said. "The record had a southern-revival flavor, and it turned out that Sister Mary Helena didn't care much for Protestants either."

But William Steif, Scripps-Howard correspondent, had been a young San Francisco reporter in 1956 following Presley on a series of one-night stands through Texas. Presley told him then: "God gave me my voice. I never danced vulgar in my life. I've just been jigglin' . . . I know this: All good things come from God. You don't have to go to church to know right from wrong. Sure, church helps, but you can be a Christian so long as you have a Christian heart."

Many believed that whatever influence black music had on Presley, he had long ago left it behind. The *Oregon Journal* summed up this view:

Pop music critics would say that once he left the confines of blue collar Memphis, he abandoned an authentic Southern brand of musical expression which owes much to black heritage, and traded it for the gaudy and garish showmanship that has been his trademark and that of musical groups who followed him the past two decades.

And *Billboard* reported, "Black record customers saw Presley as a kind of black stepchild. Even as the general market saw him as a modified country/rock singer, many blacks regarded him as a modified blues singer." Even so, some observers noted, "There was a kind of odd pride among blacks about Presley because in the minds of many he was the first white artist to openly acknowledge that his popularity stemmed directly from his association with black music."

Few blacks attended Elvis's funeral. Photos of the mourners outside the Graceland gates show seas of white faces with only an occasional black. This was not new. The media had always focused on the white teenagers whose outbursts of ecstasy were an Elvis trademark.

The picture of a white Elvis with only white fans comes from two perceptions. First is that Elvis himself was racist, a charge leveled, for instance, by protest activist Abbie Hoffman in *Crawdaddy*'s November 1977 postmortem on Elvis. The second perception is that blacks did not like Elvis. Richard Cohen, writing in *The Washington Post* a week after Elvis's death, accepted without question the idea of a caller who suggested that blacks, by and large, disliked the singer. He repeated the recurring rumor that Elvis once said that blacks could do nothing but shine his shoes and buy his records.

Both observations are wrong. The truth goes much deeper. Much of Presley's appeal came because he carried his past with him—his family and friends, his polite ways, his generosity, his Southerness, and his music roots, white and black.

"When this young fellow Elvis passed," said Memphis's oldest active black minister, "it was a saddening thing. It was like the clouds themselves wept." The grief of Dr. W. Herbert Brewster, grandson of a Georgia slave, gospel songwriter, unrelenting civil rights activist, political power broker, and minister of the East Trigg Baptist Church, was common among many in the black community, but it was not as visible.

"He had a great following among blacks, but you didn't see it," explained singer James Brown. "You know why? He was white and they were black. And they were never allowed to be his followers. You think a black girl could run up and kiss Elvis? That's what I'm talking about.

There's a line there. Elvis was accepted among everybody. The system wouldn't let us be together."

Brown, "Soul Brother No. 1," walked the streets during the civil rights revolution of the fifties and the sixties urging young blacks to stay in school. Brown's best known song became an anthem among blacks: "Say it Loud: I'm Black and I'm Proud." On stage, performing before mostly black audiences, he attracted the same emotional adulation Elvis stirred among white audiences.

Brown and Presley were friends for many years. "It was always Elvis and James," said Brown. "We were as close as me and anybody could be." They met early in their careers at a Hollywood party. Presley and Brown, both teetotalers, wound up together at a piano singing "Old Blind Barnabas" and other gospel songs. They discussed their music and its similarities and their common roots in Southern rural poverty. Later Elvis sought the James Brown band as a back-up for a recording session, but Colonel Parker vetoed the idea.

Brown was at his home in Augusta, Georgia, when he heard that Elvis had died. "That's a day that I'll remember," he said later. "I lost a whole lot that day personally. The country lost a lot; it hurt the music world tremendously."

Brown chartered a plane and flew into Memphis on Wednesday and spent several hours at Graceland. He did not stay for the funeral, however, saying simply, "I remembered Otis." He was referring to Otis Redding, a black singer who had made it big in Memphis as a recording artist for Stax Records. Shortly after Redding's recording "Sittin' on the Dock of the Bay" shot to the top of the charts, he was killed in a plane crash, and his funeral in Macon, Georgia, turned into a personality parade. A stream of political and musical luminaries distracted mourners from their grief. Brown did not want to be a part of that sort of scene again.

Elvis's friendship with Governor George Wallace of Alabama was widely publicized and better known than his friendship with James Brown. This, coupled with the following that Elvis enjoyed among working class whites in the forefront of opposition to integration, added to the false impression that he was, at heart, a white racist, or at least sympathetic to that point of view. But Elvis was completely apolitical, never a part of the show-business cycle of fundraisers and endorsements, never a participant, like Brown, in the civil rights revolution, the great social movement which paralleled Presley's career and periodically sent his home town of Memphis into social convulsions. Notwithstanding his reputation for contributing to many causes, he never gave money to any political candidate or movement on either side of the integration question—or any other political issue.

The politician to whom he was closest—former sheriff and now mayor of Shelby County, William Morris—traveled with Elvis and shared his friendship for years. Elvis gave him a Mercedes, but only after he left office as sheriff and long before he was again a candidate for mayor.

"They say that one time Elvis said, 'A black can't do nothing but shine my shoes,'" James Brown has observed. "He never said nothing like that. He never said that."

Speaking from a different perspective, Representative Harold Ford, the Congressman from Memphis, also has discredited the idea that Elvis sympathized with ideas of white supremacy: "While his fans, the vast majority, were white, he was beyond racism."

Not only was Elvis not a racist, but furthermore, according to Eldridge Cleaver, an ultra-militant black leader of the sixties, the singer was a key factor in the social revolution of that decade.

"So Elvis Presley," wrote Cleaver in his autobiography, *Soul on Ice*, "came strumming a weird guitar and wagging his tail across the continent, ripping off fame and fortune as he scrunched his way, and like a latter-day Johnny Appleseed, sowing seeds of a new rhythm and style in the white souls of the white youth of America whose inner hunger and need was no longer satisfied with the antiseptic white shoes and whiter songs of Pat Boone. 'You can do anything,' sang Elvis in Pat Boone's white shoes, 'but don't you step on my Blue Suede Shoes!'"

Cleaver likened the barriers between blacks and whites to a racial Maginot Line. Presley, and others, he wrote, "dared to do in the light of day what America had long been doing in the sneak thief anonymity of night—consorted on a human level with the blacks."

Mary Jenkins and Nancy Rooks, who served as cook and maid to the entertainer for more than a decade, shared in the largess of their employer, receiving many gifts, including automobiles, just as the white employees did.

Interviewed by Memphis television personality Marge Thrasher, Jenkins matter-of-factly mentioned "the year everybody got Pontiacs" and told about going to the Pontiac dealer to pick out the model she wanted. She recalled Presley calling from Los Angeles and telling her to "catch the first thing smokin'" to come out to cook for him at his house in Bel-Air. Provided with a car, she refused to drive on the Los Angeles freeways, so Elvis hired her a chauffeur at one hundred dollars a week to pick her up, take her to work, and take her home. Jenkins participated in the ground-breaking ceremonies of the Tupelo chapel and donated funds for a kneeling bench. Elvis had once donated money for a pew in her church in Memphis.

"Elvis used to slip around and catch old black folks that he'd known all his life," said James Brown. "He'd pay their rent for a year, and so many good things. They said he didn't like blacks, but this is a lie. The man had a legitimate affection for people."

Charitable organizations, black and white, benefited from Elvis's generosity, but to the Memphis black community, Presley had a low profile said Congressman Ford. "I was the only black, outside of those who worked for him, at the funeral," said Ford. "I don't know why I was invited. I never met him personally."

But Ford knew his music. "When I was a kid, I remember 'Blue Suede Shoes' and all those records," he recalled. "Blacks accepted his music. My sister bought it because we liked it; we identified with it; we could relate to it. At the same time blacks were trying to introduce soul into pop music and country, I think it was Presley who really focused the nation, and the nation accepted it. Prior to that it was just the blues."

Rufus Thomas, an entertainer and Memphis disc jockey who broadcast mainly for the black community, gave Elvis his first regular exposure on black radio. He admits his early feelings towards Presley and his music were ambivalent, attitudes shared by many black musicians who felt that the sounds of rock and roll were the property of blacks. While he knew that black teenage girls were buying Elvis records and requesting that his songs be played, the station for which he worked in effect banned white performers.

Thomas was a disc jockey for WDIA in Memphis. The station was a 50,000-watt outlet which had become one of the nation's most successful black-oriented broadcasters, partly because of its strong involvement with the Memphis black community, subsidizing day-care centers and softball teams and other activities with funds supplied by a series of concerts called Goodwill Reviews. In December 1956, at the Goodwill Review at Ellis Auditorium, Elvis did a walk-on and effectively changed the station's black-only policy.

"Never in your life have you seen such a surge of black faces converging on that stage," Thomas recalled in an interview with public television station WKNO-TV. "In a lifetime, I know of only one other person who could have that kind of magnetism. And that was Dr. Martin Luther King.

"I was probably the first black deejay to play his music on a regular basis," added Thomas, who went back to the station and started playing Elvis's records. Like many other black entertainers, Thomas thinks Elvis was the one who opened the door for black artists to white audiences.

Another was "Little Richard" Penneman, who when interviewed by *Rolling Stone,* had this to say:

> Like, see, when Elvis came out and a lot of black groups would say, "Elvis cannot do so and so and so, shoo shoo shoo [huffs and grumbles]." And I'd say, "Shut up, shut up." Let me tell you this—when I came out they wasn't playing no black artists on no Top 40 stations, I was the first to get played on the Top 40 stations—but it took people like Elvis and Pat Boone, Gene Vincent to open the door for this kind of music, and I thank God for Elvis Presley. I thank God for Elvis Presley. I thank the Lord for sending Elvis to open the door so I could walk down the road, you understand?

The music market of the fifties was as segregated as most of the rest of American life. But changes were in the offing. In 1949, *Billboard* stopped using the term "race music," referring instead to "rhythm and blues." With Memphis radio, too, racial barriers were beginning to fall. In the years following World War II, most of the city's stations offered some black programming, usually religious. The Fisk College Singers and the Jubilaires were Sunday morning fixtures on WREC. In 1951, however, WDIA—which had provided live broadcasts from the city's largest white church, Bellevue Baptist—switched to all-black programming, showcasing such artists as Joe Hill Lewis, Gatemouth Moore, and B.B. King. KWEM presented Howlin' Wolf, along with its Hayloft Jamboree and the Circle H. Cowboys. At its Chisca Hotel studios, WHBQ introduced a completely different style of programming, a late-night show called "Red, Hot and Blue." The show featured a white disc jockey named Dewey Phillips playing black rhythm and blues. His style was country, yet he was an early prototype of the screaming deejay, whooping, hollering, and dropping strange voices and phrases ("Anybody want to buy a duck?") into his patter. He would urge his listeners—the black and white teenagers—to patronize the sponsors and "Tell 'em Phillips sentcha!"

A few weeks after the historic 1954 Supreme Court decision on school desegregation, Elvis cut his first record, and Dewey Phillips played the demonstration copy of "That's All Right (Mama)" on his show. The reaction of the audience was so immediate and so ecstatic that Phillips played the song and its flip side, "Blue Moon of Kentucky," over and over and brought Elvis in for an interview.

"I don't know nothing about being interviewed, Mr. Phillips," said Elvis.

"Just don't say nothing dirty," replied Phillips, who drew from the young truck driver/singer the information that he had recently graduated from Humes, a white high school in North Memphis.

"I wanted to get that out," Phillips said later, "because a lot of people listening thought he was colored."

But the listeners wanted the song. Even before copies were available, Sun Records had orders for seven thousand records. Presley's career was on its way.

The small Sun Record company was founded by Sam Phillips (no relation to the deejay), a sound engineer with an incredible feel for the music of the region. He provided a recording studio for many of the black artists who brought their country sound into the city from small towns throughout the Midsouth. The studio itself was an acoustical rarity, bringing to recordings a natural resonance still sought, but seldom matched, today.

"That's All Right (Mama)" was recorded as the flip side of "Blue Moon of Kentucky," a bluegrass standard by Bill Monroe. Backed-up by Bill Black on guitar and Scotty Moore on bass, Elvis gave the country classic an upbeat rendition, and while "fooling around," he had launched into "That's All Right," a song by black artist "Big Boy" Arthur Cruddup. Sam Phillips, manning the controls at Sun Records, was amazed that a shy white kid like Elvis would even have heard of Cruddup, who was a favorite of his own.

Phillips had founded Sun Records primarily as a vehicle to record the variety of black artists who came into Memphis bringing from the surrounding countryside their authentic blues styles. According to legend, he had been listening and looking, too, "for a white man who had the Negro sound and the Negro feel." He found it in Elvis Presley.

Some critics have said Elvis stole the music of blacks. Columnist Richard Cohen, quoting indignant, if anonymous, black musicians, made that claim. So did musicologist Alan Lomax. Lomax felt Presley expropriated black music just as white composer Daniel Emmett had done a century earlier when he wrote "Dixie," and just as white musicians did when they performed in black-face minstrels. Bill Haley and the Comets, a white group, preceded Elvis in rock'n'roll. But so did black artists Chuck Berry and Little Richard Penneman.

Elvis's use of black music, however, is not like that of Steven Foster; nor is it like Columbia-educated Pat Boone's cleaned up version of "Ain't That a Shame," or the other so-called "cover" versions of rhythm and blues tunes rerecorded during this period in bland forms more acceptable to white audiences. Nor is Elvis's use of black music purely black. Elvis's rendition of "That's All Right" is a youthful, exuberant song different from Arthur Cruddup's blues, just as his "Blue Moon of Kentucky" bears scant resemblance to the Bill Monroe waltz.

Before Elvis, big band sounds dominated the radio market with their dance forms and the national focus on popular music settled on the sounds of Tin Pan Alley and the sexually safe lyrics of Broadway. Elvis borrowed from the two largest segments of minority music—rhythm and blues from the blacks and country music from the poor whites—and fused them with gospel to make his own music. He was not the first to produce a rock 'n' roll sound. With the possible exceptions of some of his early Sun recordings such as "Mystery Train," and later flashes like "Suspicious Minds," he was not rock's best singer. But he was the most successful, and the most durable.

In the mid-1950s President Dwight D. Eisenhower presided over the United States with a complacent hand. Perry Como was the leading pop singer. *My Fair Lady* reigned on Broadway, and Davey Crockett in the popular hero market. World War II changed the world but at that time few people knew how much.

The music industry, too, pulled away from old patterns after the war as new recording centers emerged outside of New York. Music historian H. F. Mooney notes that in the post-war era Louisville, Kentucky, produced "Slow Poke"; Nashville, Tennessee, recorded the "Tennessee Waltz" with Patti Page, "Big Bad John" with Jimmy Dean, "Cold, Cold Heart," "Jumbalaya," and "Your Cheatin' Heart" with Hank Williams, and "Bird Dog" with the Everly Brothers; Philadelphia, Pennsylvania, brought forth "Rock Around the Clock" and "A Whole Lot of Shakin' Going On"; and Chapel Hill, North Carolina, and Portland, Oregon, and others dipped their toes into the national recording market.

In 1954 the top hit was still Kitty Kallen's "Little Things Mean a Lot." Her predecessors in the Number One slot were Perry Como, Jo Stafford, Doris Day, and Eddie Fisher. But three years earlier Cleveland disc jockey Alan Freed already had coined the term "rock and roll." And

1954 saw, too, the appearance of Bill Haley's "Rock Around the Clock" and a Number One hit called "Sh-Boom." This latter song, put out by the Crew Cuts on Mercury was a "cover" disk strongly influenced by an original recording by the Chords on the Cat label. Some think that despite its nonsense love-song lyrics the song signifies the first explosion of a hydrogen bomb (sh-boom), announced by President Eisenhower February 2, 1954.

Tracking similar cultural rumblings, Presley gained national recognition with his own music by 1955. By 1956 he held the two top hit songs in the country: "Don't Be Cruel" and "Heartbreak Hotel." Music from Memphis in the mid-1950s was part of an explosion, and it owed much to the city itself.

Memphis is a Southern city, yet it postponed the turbulence of the 1950s and 1960s when the full force of the nation's civil rights commitments was striking all around it.

Black citizens there, accounting for forty percent of the population, voted and shared in the spoils of office, although in a paternalistic way. Good schools, paved streets, and other amenities existed in the black neighborhoods, and blacks had equal access to the segregated public housing. For Southern blacks in the years surrounding World War II, Memphis was a good place to live.

This anomaly was part of the legacy of Edward Hull Crump, one of many Mississippians who, like Elvis, had decided to make Memphis his home. For the first half of this century, Crump offered the city's poor the "bread and circuses" of parades, Christmas baskets, and athletic contests among top Negro high school athletes in exchange for their votes, and ruled as a benevolent dictator who dominated the city's lifestyle.

Crump came to Memphis in 1894 from Holly Springs, a small town of antebellum homes and Confederate graves located half-way between Memphis and Tupelo. In 1909 he was elected mayor and during the next four decades filled a variety of posts, winning elections twenty-five times without a defeat. His hand-picked candidates held almost every local office, and his ability to deliver the huge bloc of votes from Shelby County made him the most powerful political figure in Tennessee.

"There was a depressing, a chilling effect on any sort of self-government," recalled Memphis attorney Lucius Burch, Jr. "When Crump died [in 1954], there was a whole generation of Memphians with no experi-

ence in self-government whatever. A lot of people didn't know their way
to the courthouse."

Yet Crump gave Memphis an image of stability, cleanliness, low
taxes, and reduced crime, and what many perceived as the most honest
and efficient municipal government ever to appear on the American
scene.

This was the city that Elvis's father Vernon saw as his ticket out of
small-town Mississippi poverty. One day in 1948, he packed the family's
belongings in a 1939 Plymouth and drove his wife Gladys and thirteen-
year-old Elvis one hundred ten miles to the north on Highway 78.

"We were broke, man, broke, and we left Tupelo overnight," Elvis recalled years later. "We just headed to Memphis. Things had to be better."

Lacking a major commercial center, Mississippi for generations
watched its people migrate to the major cities just outside its borders:
Memphis, New Orleans, or Mobile. For those in the northern half of the
state—the flat, black-soiled, flood-plain of the Delta on the west along
the Mississippi river, where Negro populations exceeded eighty percent
in some counties; and the mostly-white, red-clay hill country of the Ap-
palachia foothills on the east, the poorest counties in the poorest state in
the Union—Memphis was the magnet. The people read *The Commercial
Appeal* and listened to Memphis radio stations. The city was the shopping mart, banking center, and entertainment hub for the rich. For the
poor it seemed to offer the hopes and dreams that things might get better.

At first the Presleys were no better off than they had been in
Tupelo. They lived in one room, sharing a bath with three other families,
cooking on a hot plate. Within a year, however, they moved into a
federally funded public housing project and occupied a two-bedroom
apartment with bath and kitchen in Lauderdale Courts near downtown
Memphis. After working at odd jobs, Vernon became a laborer for a
paint company and Gladys found a job as a waitress. Elvis enrolled in the
seventh grade of nearby L.C. Humes High School and began to explore
the city that he would call home for the next three decades.

Memphis, despite the calm of the Crump era, had a violent heritage.
Laid out in 1819 by Andrew Jackson and two companions, the city soon
became a "tough and uninviting place overrun by the scum of the river."
During the War Between the States, it fell early to Union forces,
suffered a bitter reconstruction, and was almost annihilated by a yellow
fever epidemic in 1878. But it made a miraculous recovery, building industry based on cotton and lumber. By 1900 it was the second largest

city in the South, its population of one hundred thousand exceeded only by New Orleans. With this rapid growth came crime and corruption. By the 1920s, Memphis was known as the "murder capital" of the nation.

The thousands of rural poor, white and black, who poured into the city brought their music with them. The most talented was W. C. Handy, universally recognized as the "father of the blues." He began composing his melodies while he was playing piano in Pee-Wee's Saloon, a dive on Beale Street, the legendary thoroughfare of pawn shops, pool halls, whore houses, and cheap cafes that ran from the river into the heart of the black communities.

Handy's early music paralleled the rise of Crump's political machine. One song he wrote, which was heard often on the city's street corners as the Mississippian began his first term as mayor and opened his drive to bring organization to the chaotic rivertown, evoked some of the atmosphere of the era. "Mr. Crump don't 'low no easy-riders here," wrote Handy in the opening line of the tune that became the "Memphis Blues." Speaking to the many who were attracted by the carefree Saturday night glamor of the city, his lyrics vowed to "barrel-house anyhow" and let Crump worry about the image of vice and corruption. The song brought Handy no revenue; he sold away the rights to a New York publisher for fifty dollars. But his creation was the first blues song, a new American art form Handy said was inspired by a local band he heard playing in nearby Cleveland, Mississippi. "Those country black boys taught me something that could not possibly be learned from books."

After teaching and traveling with a minstrel troupe, Handy had come to Memphis from Florence, Alabama, and organized a band. He earned great financial success and international acclaim with "St. Louis Blues," but it was the lyrics of the earlier song, sometimes called "Mr. Crump's Blues," that were rediscovered three decades later when the nation's media began to discover the unique one-man government that had changed the image of the city on the river.

By the time the Presleys arrived in Memphis, Mr. Crump had made good on the lyrics of the "Memphis Blues." The city was cleaned up—literally. Year after year, Memphis won the trophy of the National Municipal League in the clean-up, paint-up, fix-up competition. In 1940, as the city attracted what was to become the nation's largest inland naval installation, Crump passed the word, and police ran the city's legendary assortment of pimps and prostitutes out of town.

But the river town heritage of gambling, bad women, hard work, and violence lived in the city's music. Reflecting later, James "Son" Thomas, a black blues singer from Leland, Mississippi, noted: "The younger people, they can't understand the blues because they never did the hard work for low pay. The blues is set back in slavery, how people used to sing to get a good feeling. Maybe they weren't allowed to talk, but they could sing and singing would make 'em feel better."

One young person who did understand, or at least adapted the blues idiom, was Elvis, who frequented Beale Street often during his high school days.

Now mostly destroyed by urban renewal, the street was just a block from the famous Peabody Hotel, a gathering place for the region's plantation society, and from its lobby, said novelist and critic Stark Young, the Mississippi Delta began. At the intersection of Main and Beale stood the city's largest theater, the Malco, for white patrons, with a balcony for the blacks.

Between Second and Third streets is Handy's Park, a graveled half-block area where a life-sized bronzed statue of the composer stands. Handy's music sometimes is piped from nearby speakers.

Blues singer B. B. King, who had a radio program on Memphis radio station WDIA at the time, remembers meeting Elvis on Beale Street soon after the singer graduated from Humes High. He recalls him "hanging around," listening to the music—"the blind man on the corner," that W.C. Handy wrote about, a jug band playing for some coins from passersby, or the sounds emanating from the black cafes near Lansky Brothers Clothing Store. It was at Lansky's that Elvis bought the pegged pants, pink flared shirts, and other garments that complemented the sideburns and the image he had begun to affect. When Elvis died, Bernard and Guy Lansky bought a full page ad in *The Commercial Appeal* in memoriam:

> It was just twenty-three years ago we first met you. We noticed you, staring in our shop windows, just looking . . . looking. You were so young, . . . friendly, mannerly . . . and oh, so, sure of your future. We became good friends, and for the rest of our lives we shall have the lasting memory of your friendship.

The debt rock and roll owes to the blues is self-evident. But blues was not the only music Presley heard. The most segregated institution in the South—then as now—was the churches. Yet even there some mingling of blacks and whites occurred, particularly at funerals and weddings, although the basis might be a master-servant relationship: the black nurse attending the wedding of the now-grown-up little girl who used to be her charge, or the white family joining the mourners at the last rites for their long-time maid or family retainer. An exchange of music sometimes also took place with black choirs—usually singing spirituals—invited to white churches.

"There was no integration at the time," recalled Dr. Brewster, the minister at East Trigg Baptist Church in Memphis. "Nobody spoke of it; nobody thought about it."

But at East Trigg Baptist Church on Sunday nights in the fifties, lots of white people joined the black congregation. There were musicians such as the Blackwood Brothers—whose group Elvis at one time hoped to join—medical students from the University of Tennessee, or other young people bored with the more staid offerings of their own churches.

They heard the "Old Camp Meeting of the Air" broadcast over WHBQ—a spectacular gospel choir led by Dr. Brewster. Brewster himself carries a reputation as a magnificent songwriter, producing some of the most brilliant lyrics in gospel music. He is famous for his pageant plays, many centered on civil rights themes, and for songs which carried Queen C. Anderson, the choir's lead singer, Mahalia Jackson, and Clara Ward to national fame. Brewster's songs include "I'm Leaning and Depending on the Lord," "Move On Up a Little Higher," "Just Over the Hill," "I'm Getting Nearer My Home," "These Are They," "How I Got Over," and "Surely God Is Able."

The young people of Memphis heard the radio program and they came, reminisced Dr. Brewster, speaking with a cadence in his voice which for decades had carried him through songs and sermons and moved countless worshipers to commit their lives to God. "They came as the old Biblical quote says, from Dan to Beersheba, particularly the young people who were in the colleges here; they came from the medical school; they came to be in the big camp meeting that night ... And in that crowd was this young fellow Elvis. He enjoyed it to the highest; he liked the rhythm that we put into it. ...

"He hadn't gotten popular then. He hadn't started singing. He was driving a truck ... But he would get here as early as he could, get right up in front, and sometimes come back here. A bunch of them would get back here in the office before I could get out, and they were sitting on the floor with whatever they were wearing, and we just downed every kind of mark or line of demarcation and said we'll all just be people, happy people, praising the Lord ... And he enjoyed that so much.

"He didn't join any choir . . . Some of them sang in the choir; he sang in the congregation. He had a good voice.

"And afterward, we met again over there when we were trying out with Sam Phillips—when he was starting out over there at Marshall and Union. He had us [the choir] come over there to do an audition or two. And as we were coming out, Elvis was going in. And shortly after that, he began to get popular, and more and more his guitar began to ring all over the earth."

The gospel music Elvis heard at Brewster's church was a special breed. Coming to Memphis in the twenties, Brewster felt the full force of the music of Handy and other musicians on Beale Street. Some musicologists say Brewster's music was the first to combine blues and waltz forms with gospel, producing what one commentator called "irresistible rhythms," sometimes heightened with blues riffs and verbal repetition.

Brewster chuckled as he explained: "I had discovered—even though I had been on a committee to arrange a lot of church music, hymns and anthems—I discovered what my old granddad told me: 'If you want to catch fish, you have to bait the hook with the kind of bait that the fish like.' So I pepped up my music and—before that time, I had that kind of suavity that didn't allow people to be so loud. And yet the young people seemed to grow sleepy and tired and so on, and so I prayed over it, and I pepped my music up, and I put a beat in it.

"At any rate, there is a kind of connection between the old blues and the spirituals and the people who were happy-go-lucky that didn't belong to the church. They teed off on the other kind of music, and I claimed that all of the music is God's music, that whatever Satan has he took it; he stole it. And I said we ought to recapture it. We'll take some of it back.

"The song that I had written, they had stepped it up and put a beat in it so that I hardly knew it when I heard it. And so, I said I'm going to strike back at this and get a body of young people to sing." And he did, including Elvis.

Most of Elvis's exposure to the blues probably came after his family moved to Memphis, but gospel music—white and black—had been a part of his musical surroundings since childhood.

In Tupelo, a classmate recalled that Elvis rushed home after school to listen to Sister Rosetta Tharpe on WELO radio. This was one of the few black music programs the station broadcast. The station played Sister Tharpe's records each afternoon Monday through Friday. The joyous, shouting music clearly impressed Elvis, recalled Billy Welch, a psychiatrist at Mississippi State Hospital in Jackson, who lived near the Presleys as a youth.

The joyous tone of the gospel sound is one of its essential components. It resembles the cocky, brash, exuberant sound of early rock far more than the heavier and more sophisticated emotions of the blues. Gospel also shares with rock its beat, its drama, its demand for honesty of emotion, and its emphasis on participation. In this emphasis on participation, both gospel and rock differ from jazz, where both performers and audiences view the music as an art and stay more aloof from each other.

Gospel music comes in great variety—soloists, quartets, choirs, jazz and blues offshoots, duets. In the words of the fans, gospel singers don't "do their own thing," but they do "work out their soul's salvation"; congregations don't "freak out," but they will let a song "get all over them."

Gospel was something the poor of the South shared; the styles differed only in degree. Elvis was raised on gospel music in his neighborhood Assembly of God Church in East Tupelo. The decade of the forties, Elvis's formative years, produced at least a dozen prolific songwriters in the golden era of gospel. This was a time when pop veered between Broadway and Tin Pan Alley, country music was still in its rococo period, and rhythm and blues had fallen into a rut. But in the poor neighborhoods of the country, music—gospel music—flourished.

Hovie Lister, leader of the Statesmen Gospel Quartet, recalled playing in Memphis once a month at Ellis Auditorium when Elvis was finishing high school. "He used to come around to the stage door, because he couldn't afford a ticket, and we'd let him in the stage door. He was such a likeable little guy, we were naturally inclined to like him. Well, he'd come by so often, he knew every song by memory. He'd stand in the wings and sing along with us while we were singing on stage." He still came after he was famous.

He returned, too, to East Tupelo, standing outside to listen to gospel music shows at Lawhon Gym (pronounced Lawhorn) a few blocks away from his birthplace and at the Auto Race Track up the road toward Belden.

Despite the heavy, and often overlooked, role of gospel in shaping any music from this area, the music that dominated the taste of poor whites in the Midsouth was country or hillbilly. "Country and western ain't nothing but the white man's blues," said James Brown. Country is also durable. The young Elvis harbored a strong ambition to play at the Grand Ole Opry in Nashville, and long after he had surpassed any performers there, Elvis was to return often to his roots in country music.

In this sense of his own past and in his loyalty to the city of Memphis, Elvis's feelings resemble William Faulkner's description of why he, Faulkner, always returned home:

> You have seen a country wagon come into town, with a hound dog under the wagon. It stops on the Square and the folks get out, but that hound dog never gets very far from that wagon. He might be cajoled or scared out for a short distance, but first thing you know he has scuttled back under the wagon; maybe growls at you a little. Well, that's me.

Over the years, Elvis's manager, Colonel Parker, made a conscious effort to provide the nation's country music radio stations with Elvis records. The stations reciprocated. If the country deejays heard something by Elvis they liked, they would play it—a simple arrangement not available to most artists, who must convince the station the song is worth the air time.

Colonel Parker and the Presley business organization tightly restricted the use of Elvis's name or likeness to promote any product or cause. The only radio station ever permitted to use Elvis's name and image in its advertising is the big country station in New York, WHN, indicating the close ties between Elvis fans and country music fans.

"Country music fans are more loyal," said Pam Green, music director of WHN, in explaining Elvis's continuing popularity on country music stations two years after his death. "The whole idea with country is, you don't want to label anything, you want to let your listeners tell you whether they want to hear it or whether they like it. You try not to put a label on anything. That's what Elvis's music is."

This does not mean just anything qualifies as country music. In the fifties, an Elvis performance failed dismally at the Grand Ole Opry, and the Opry management even tried to delete Presley from *Billboard*'s country charts. The dust is still flying from the performance there of James Brown in 1979. But country music had a strong claim on the young Elvis.

Early in his career Elvis billed himself as "the Hill Billy Cat." Even earlier he had performed on the WELO's "Black and White Jamboree" where Mississippi Slim led the billing. Mississippi Slim was a country singer and radio personality and the feature of a one-hour country music show that was broadcast from the Lee County Court House in Tupelo. The "Black and White" title had no racial connotations, but instead referred to the show's sponsor, the Black and White Store, a sort of early day K-Mart characterized by checkerboard black and white tiles all across the front. Charlie Boren, announcer at WELO from 1945 to 1955, remembers young Elvis appearing on the Jamboree even before winning a prize for singing at the Fair. He feels that the lively Mississippi Slim (real name Carbell Lee Ausborn) influenced the young Elvis. "I really think he did. Slim didn't sing just straight country. He sang a little boogie-type stuff, you know, that the other stars didn't sing." Boren recalls another time that he got Elvis, Johnny Cash, Carl Perkins, "and one other group" to appear on a show for a total fee of only six hundred dollars.

In the fifties, Memphis provided fertile soil for all of these music roots and nurtured them in the slow, drowsy air of the Mississippi River. Elvis Presley absorbed these forces, synthesized them, and then added something of his own—a personal quality which set him and his music apart.

It was not that Presley did anything radically different. Since the war, white country singers had borrowed freely from the black material. Even Presley's clothes were not that unusual compared to some of the garish outfits of country and western singers. But Presley took the music further than it had gone before. He freed country music from its plodding rhythms; and he made blues a defiant medium as well as one of emotional release.

The Commercial Appeal's columnist, Paul Coppock, writing of the close ties between Presley and Memphis, reminded his readers that the reaction to Elvis's music came long before anyone saw him wiggle his hips. The Memphis teenagers who besieged Sam Phillips to play Elvis's first record again and again had no idea what he looked like. Nor did many others in the Midsouth who first heard his records and then came to see him in person.

Some journalists, like Richard Maschal of the Knight News Service, felt that the unique Presley impact was due to the "attitude Presley brought to a song—to get right inside the words, and if a song was low-down, make you feel low-down; if a song was happy, he could ride that feeling, too." Maschal attributed this ability to Elvis's blues background. Getting the feeling of the song is an essential part of the blues. In the words of one blues musician: "Trying to make a living and satisfy people, keep a-moving and going from place to place trying to find something better, that's what the blues is made up from. There was nothing you could do about it but sing a sad song about the way your feelings felt."

Dr. Brewster has provided a similar view of Presley's music from a different musical perspective: "When this young fellow sang those [gospel] songs, his voice seemed to have gained a new melody. It was something about it that was most spiritual; it was something about it that was heart warming and had a meaningfulness. He personalized it and made it his own testimony, and that of itself is one of the highest points, I think, in his impact on gospel songs, on gospel singing. He also made it stick because of his friendliness, his good-heartedness, his lavish extravagance in giving things to people—irrespective of color, race, and creed."

This emotional release had been a characteristic of the working classes, and blues, gospel, country, and rock came from the common people. Beginning with Plato, aristocratic standing always has been associated with passive contemplation. Como, Crosby, Sinatra all seem to derive their musical inspiration from "fine arts," from "high class" or "good" music, observes musicologist Carl Belz. Their music is pleasant, orderly, and arranged with correct musical structure. With rhythm and blues, and later with rock and roll, the music is styled around how it feels as much as how it sounds. It is a gut response rather than one of intellect and good taste.

As Senator S. I. Hayakawa put it, the working class gratify themselves without making it a cosmic issue. And, when post-World War II middle class rebels who repudiated middle class culture embraced the emotional release of rock music, it not only altered the tone of American popular music, but also did far more.

In *Walden*, Henry David Thoreau warned: "Even music may be intoxicating. Such apparently slight causes destroyed Greece and Rome, and will destroy England and America." Sources as venerable as Plato support this idea. "The introduction of a new kind of music must be shunned as imperiling the whole state," the philosopher wrote, "since styles of music are never disturbed without affecting the most important political institutions." And in 1704, Scottish nationalist Andrew Fletcher took a more pragmatic view in a long statement commonly condensed into a paraphrase: "Let me write the songs of a people, and you can write their laws."

The South always has been particularly suited for the self-expressive and emotional form of singing Presley produced. There these characteristics were not confined to the lower classes.

William Faulkner, too, addressed the personalization of art in a 1933 unpublished, 1,000-word essay on writers and the South:

> Because it is himself that the Southerner is writing about, not about his environment; who has, figuratively speaking, taken the artist in him in one hand and his milieu in the other and thrust the one into the other like a clawing and spitting cat into a croker sack. And he writes.

Ironically, Faulkner predicted that this trait would preclude a Southern contribution to music:

> We have never got, and probably will never get, anywhere with music or the plastic forms. We need to talk, to tell, since oratory is our heritage.

But country music, gospel, blues, early rock—all these talk as they sing; all tell a story along with the feeling and the rhythm. None may be what Faulkner referred to as music, but all are compatible with their Southern heritage.

In *Place in Fiction* Eudora Welty carries the link between art and its place of origin further:

> It seems that the art that speaks most clearly, explicitly, directly, and passionately from its place of origin will remain the longest understood. It is through place that we put out roots, wherever birth, chance, fate, or our traveling selves set us down, but where those roots reach toward—whether in America, England, or Timbuktu—is the deep and running vein, eternal and consistent and everywhere purely itself—that feeds and is fed by the human understanding. The challenge ... today, I think, is not to disown any part of our heritage. Whatever our theme..., it is old and tired. Whatever our place, it has been visited by the stranger, it will never be new again. It is only the vision that can be new; but that is enough.

Heritage is extremely important in the South. Where someone came from is important there. "Memory believes before knowing remembers," Faulkner wrote. Elvis "was a youngster that had been touched first, I think, in his childhood there in Tupelo," said Dr. Brewster, "There was something in the area of Tupelo."

10

Interpreting the Myth

While fans may have had trouble articulating exactly what Elvis had meant to them, the nation's pundits did not. Millions of words of analysis churned out from the nation's critics, commentators, and editorial writers as they attempted to explain the meaning of Elvis Presley.

At *The Commercial Appeal*, editorial writer Guy Northrop had a sense of *deja vu* late Tuesday afternoon as he sat down to write an editorial on the death of his city's best-known resident. That morning his newspaper published a brief editorial, "He'll Be Missed," and the lead sentence said: "Memphis music won't seem quite the same again." The piece was about Dr. Thomas Ferguson, director of Memphis State bands who was leaving to take up a post at Arizona State University. Now only a few moments were left to compose an editorial about the nation's ultimate musical personality.

As a longtime employee of the newspaper, Northrop had watched Elvis's career with the detached view of the average Memphis journalist, bemused at the reaction the singer provoked, amazed at the continued interest. He also was the newspaper's art critic, however, and his avocation gave him a different perspective on the singer's passing. Northrop wrote:

Elvis. The man-boy's name stood alone. On a marquee it conveyed more than a million flamboyant words of promotional copy. Elvis Presley, an American cultural phenomenon who will never be fully understood, was too many things to be categorized in words. He was feeling, emotion, sexuality. He was at least a part of the "American dream."

The editorial focused on Presley as native son, "a boy-made-good in the tough world of entertainment," who always returned home to Memphis to the love of family and the comfort of friends. "He was an asset to Memphis in more ways than fame," Northrop wrote. "A tourist attraction, yes. But also a symbol. His rock and roll style, his easy physical grace, his modulated drawl, his glance of recognition as he passed you on the street, made him fit the surroundings. If he was proud to tell others that he was from Memphis, Memphis was proud to have him claim it as home."

The *Memphis Press-Scimitar* also praised the "awkward country boy" who became "a good, well-behaved citizen." The paper's editorial writer turned to the files and quoted at length from a letter written by a Pittsburgh girl in 1957. The fan explained the appeal of Elvis in terms of the electricity of his voice, looks, and personality combined with his devastating smile, sweetness, sideburns, and Southern accent.

The *Daily Journal* in Tupelo, Mississippi, also recalled "the young man who lived here for the first thirteen years of his life," emphasizing Elvis's music and his generosity. But the editorial writer noted too the entertainer's lack of a normal lifestyle: "His remark, 'I'm here, but how do I get back?' says much for those of us who have no trouble going unnoticed in a crowd." It was one of the few editorials that did not try to explain Elvis in terms of youth and change. "He was the symbol of an age," said the editorial in the *Detroit Free Press*, "of a time in American life when there were few heroes, when many of the country's youth had lost their innocence on the far-off battlefields of Pork Chop Hill and Heartbreak Ridge."

Similar views were voiced in Shreveport, Louisiana, where Elvis had first really caught on as a performer as a regular with KWTH radio's *Louisiana Hayride*. There *The Times* editorial writer conceded his inability to fit Elvis into the youth revolution of the fifties and sixties: "He was not one to sing songs designed for social change in the manner of the '60s folk singers, yet the very fact of his performances seemed to bring on changes. His greatest effect may well have been that ongoing image of youth—an image that made us almost believe we could all just keep on being young together." Yet Jeff Lyon, writing in the *Chicago Tribune*, declared that Elvis really was singing folk music for the "chafing young," as much as Woody Guthrie was singing for the dustbowl farmer or Huddie Ledbetter for the Delta black. Said Lyon:

> Our parents, their own youths scarred by Depression and World War, had sought to spare us pain. They placed us, cloyed and pampered, inside their airless vision of the perfect world, a world of shopping plazas and ranch houses and summer camp and twinburgers and cars on one's sixteenth birthday and fat allowances.
> There was something missing in this life of endless comfort, and we sensed it. Later we would come to recognize this unease as disgust with false values. Back then, we only knew we wanted to taste the forbidden grit of life.
> Elvis Presley, with his sensuous sneer and his hard edges and his wiggling, rolling rhythms, gave it to us.

The Philadelphia *Bulletin* also called Presley a folk hero, "a generation's music maker—its weaver of dreams," and *The San Diego Union* went to great lengths trying to interpret the heroism of Presley. He was not an anti-hero, said its editorial writer, nor a hero in the sense of Churchill or Lou Gehrig or Lindberg. "In Presley, rather, were evident good feelings and benevolence, if also sensuality. Presley was supremely a man of the times."

Taking a more cautious view, the *Dayton Daily News* editorial about Elvis was headlined, "A man of his times' limitations," and the writer concluded that the singer's "real impact came from the collective mood of his time, and probably not even he understood the psychic chemistry of his success." In Cleveland, *The Plain Dealer* said Presley had the wits and talent to change with the times, traits that secure his niche in the cultural history of the country.

But defining culture or good taste proved troublesome for many critics. *The Hartford Courant*, in a generally favorable editorial, said Elvis never advanced what is called "culture." Frank Gagnard, a columnist for the New Orleans *Times-Picayune*, said cultural snobbery probably deprived the elite of the "most popular and most representative voice" of the time. "There was something solid, maybe even respectable, in that voice that singled it out from the crowd and suggested that it was a safe one to attend," wrote Gagnard. "Anyone who didn't respond to his music just wasn't receptive to music as a popular art form." In 1967, conductor Skitch Henderson told the *Memphis Press-Scimitar* that Elvis had become "the Beethoven of the school" in his musical field. He said the entertainer proved his talent by hanging on. "You can't quarrel with longevity," he added. "The public is a severe critic." A decade later, as the tributes poured in following Presley's death, Richard Maschal, music critic for the Knight Newspapers, echoed that sentiment, saying, "The truth seems plain—in his own place and his own time, he was a great musician."

Lynn Van Matre, rock critic of the *Chicago Tribune*, noted in a page one article that Elvis's crown had been askew in recent years. "But," said Van Matre, "his impact on popular music was like a kick in the head from a blue suede shoe, and he remains one of the seminal figures in the sound called rock 'n' roll." John Carroll of the *San Francisco Examiner* said it was "probably only luck" that carried Elvis to the heights of American commercial music, "but he did it, and that's what's important." Cliff Radel of *The Cincinnati Enquirer* praised the singer's vocal presence, the sense of urgency in his voice "that only youth or a youthful person can generate."

Many entertainers ranging across the spectrum of the pop music world offered meaningful comments on the news of Elvis's death. Bing Crosby said that what Presley "did and created" was a part of music history, "and it's something wonderful that he's left behind." Peter Frampton called the singer "one of the greatest entertainers and one of the most influential forces" of the century. Muddy Waters, the blues stylist, called Elvis a "joint in the music structure," and noted that "when the king moves out," everybody feels it. On Broadway, the regular cast of the hit musical *Beatlemania* chose not to go on, and the show was altered to include a brief tribute to Elvis. The audience stopped the show when cast replacements dedicated the song "Yesterday" to Presley. At a concert by the rock group Kiss in San Francisco's Cow Palace, guitarist Paul Stanley dedicated the last song to Elvis, smashed his guitar on the stage, and handed it cordially to a fan. James Kelton, who reviewed the show for the *San Francisco Examiner*, said, "It was a spirited gesture and a meaningful one on the night of Presley's death." Carl Wilson of the Beach Boys said Presley's voice influenced the entire group. "His music was the only thing that was exclusively ours," Wilson added. "His wasn't my mom and dad's music. His voice was a total miracle, a true miracle in the music business." The singer whose comments received the most press coverage was probably Pat Boone, the college-educated Tennessee contemporary of Presley's. In a series of interviews,

Boone, whose clean-cut image contrasted to the more primitive early Elvis, praised his friend and rival, lamenting the isolation that had been forced on him. He observed that Elvis had died young like James Dean and suggested that may be the best way for the public to remember him. "No one can imagine an old Elvis," said Boone, returning to the theme of youth that so many commentators used. "We're definitely grownups now," said Paul Simon. "If he's dead then we can't be kids anymore. It's a very unpleasant and unhappy time for me." The thirty-three-year-old city editor of *The Des Moines Register*, Laurence M. Paul, also wrote about Elvis and growing old. "You've outlived something," said Paul. "You've outlived an institution that was your youth."

"His was no small career," said *The Washington Post*. "Elvis gave pleasure and a measure of self-worth to a great many people who were, by reason of their region or class or age, in transition." Robert Hilburn wrote in *The Los Angeles Times* that Elvis's legacy will continue "as long as rock 'n' roll is played." Arthur Wick, writing in the *Seattle Post-Intelligencer*, said the records remain and "that voice—the pure gospel baritone that could soar inexplicably into a weeping soprano—no one will ever use that voice again." And *The Des Moines Register* said in an editorial that his celebrity was the product of "raw genius."

Not all the comments were so favorable.

Entertainer and musician Steve Allen, interviewed about the state of American television by *U.S. News & World Report*, casually observed that Elvis's songs were the worst that any established singer ever recorded. "The fact that someone with so little ability became the most popular singer in history says something significant about our cultural standards," said Allen. The interview produced more letters than the magazine had ever received on any subject other than a political issue such as inflation, socialized medicine, or the ethics of lawyers. A full page of letters was printed in a subsequent issue; all of the writers reacted angrily to Allen's comments on Elvis, none mentioned his observations on music or TV. The *Tulsa World*, while conceding in an editorial that Elvis had that "undefinable something" that had brought success, called him a mediocre singer and noted that there were scores of better musicians and that almost anyone was a better actor. Columnist John L. Wasserman of the *San Francisco Chronicle* called Presley "extraordinarily untalented." He said Elvis's singing ability was only adequate and he was only an amatuer musician who could not write a lyric, compose a melody, or act. "All he could do was reach people," said Wasserman, "and that was obviously enough. Elvis, whatever else may be said about him, was an experience."

The most devastating comments about Elvis probably came from Mike Royko, the widely syndicated columnist for the *Chicago Sun-Times.* "I think what Presley's success really proves," wrote Royko, "is that the majority of Americans—while fine, decent people—have lousy taste in music." The columnist expressed amazement at the phenomenal press coverage the singer's death received, contending that Elvis had pulled off "an enormous con." Said Royko: "He not only promoted a limited talent into a vast fortune, but he established a myth that his music and career were of great importance in the development of modern western civilization." The next day Royko wrote a more serious column about death, saying he had covered public reaction to many well-known persons in the fourteen years since the assassination of John Kennedy. "But nothing has equaled the present national grief." Negative criticism also came from the *Deseret News,* the Salt Lake City daily owned by the Mormon Church. In an editorial, the paper listed the many changes that Elvis had wrought in American music and entertainment tastes and concluded: "In the saga of Elvis Presley, there is something profoundly sad because of what it says about this country and some of its values. Some mourning is definitely in order."

The Washington Star also noted the newsprint and television time expended on Elvis and speculated on the cause. The editorial writer quoted from the analysis by rock critic John Rockwell in *The New York Times* that Presley was "as much a metaphor as a maker of music." The *Star's* writer warned of a danger in overindulgence in social metaphors but agreed that Rockwell might be onto something in explaining such phenomena: "Like mythic figures in a minor key, they apparently mirror and reflect so many elements of a time and circumstance that the response to them has a quality that extends beyond the merely rational. They simply are."

Also writing of time and mirrors was Thomas Willis, music critic of the *Chicago Tribune.* In a long analysis asking "Why Elvis?," he contended that like other superstars in the electronic age, the entertainer succeeded because he was "a sign of the times, a signal of things to come, and an atavistic symbol of what each of his admirers deeply felt or desired." Elvis captured the nation's youth and they remained loyal through the years, said Willis, because "everything he did acted as a mirror to them. By his applause and tears, each admirer was repeating silently, 'I, I, I.' "

A common theme resounding through most rock criticism of the seventies was that Elvis had done his best work at Sun Records. There his style was more natural and the raw talent came through, uninhibited by the full orchestration and the back-up groups and the mechanical gimmicks technicians added to his music when he moved to RCA Records. Self-styled spokesmen of the radical youth culture denigrated his military service and the wealth and the glamor of Hollywood and Las Vegas—factors, they said, that destroyed his leadership of the revolution he had touched off. Abbie Hoffman, a refugee from the protest wars of the sixties, provided such commentary in an essay entitled "Too Soon the Hero," published in *Crawdaddy.* "It's hard to stay a rebel," he wrote, "once you've sucked at the golden cow; harder still if you're a poor boy from Mississippi." But this line of reasoning was rebutted by several editorial writers. The *Denver Post*, which called Elvis the "first superstar of the television age," said critics who accused Elvis of selling out missed the point: "The essential cry of the American rebel has never been for destruction but for a piece of the action." And the Portland *Oregonian* summed up: "He lived long enough to see his revolution become an establishment, even respectable, a fate not necessarily worse than death."

If evidence were needed of the singer's accession to the establishment, these editorial outpourings, even those from the hostile critics, provided it. The political establishment was quick to add its tributes. "Elvis Presley's career stands alone," the Board of Aldermen of Tupelo, Mississippi, said in an official proclamation adopted at its regular meeting a few hours after Elvis died: "His accomplishments will be unsurpassed for their monumental impact on our culture." In Nashville, delegates to a state constitutional convention paused in their deliberations to read a resolution of praise: "Few men in the history of the world have been allowed by the Creator to make such a dramatic contribution to the world of music and to the music of the world."

The governors of Tennessee, Mississippi, and Alabama ordered flags to be flown at half-staff. "Elvis set the pace for two decades of Americans," said Tennessee Governor Ray Blanton, "changing not only our music but the style of our lives." In California, Governor Jerry Brown praised Presley as a man who had made a "significant impact on the culture and consciousness of America." Brown, who was thirty-nine when Elvis died, had been a teenager when the singer emerged on the national musical scene. "I like his music," he said. "I spent a lot of time at the 'Heartbreak Hotel' and I used to have a pair of blue suede shoes."

Another lawmaker from the Presley generation was Congresswoman Pat Schroeder of Colorado, who shared the sense of loss with the distressed fans who were calling her district office in Denver. "I grew up with Elvis," she recalled, "the all-night slumber parties, the twenty-four-hour-a-day Elvis music on the radio. I really saw him as a transitional figure. His independence and his throwing out the lower lip, the surliness, I think kind of led to the Vietnam generation, although I'm not sure he would appreciate my saying that. I think he unleashed a lot of things."

When Congress returned to Washington in September, Schroeder placed in the *Congressional Record* an unsigned article entitled "Blue Suede Shoes" that had appeared in *The New Yorker*. The piece, written by free-lance writer Stan Mieses, was a tribute to Elvis as one who "imperfectly, understood the nature of his integrity and his cool." The writer lamented that he had seen nothing on television or in the newspapers about how cool Elvis was. "I saw a television newscast about Elvis and it made me mad," he wrote, "because the newsman who conducted it was exactly the kind of nineteen-fifties guy—full of false inflection and false authority—who was completely blown away by Elvis."

Schroeder said she thought the piece "kind of said it all" and that she was impressed that the piece had been in *The New Yorker*. "The thing that amazed me about Elvis was that he made it fighting the establishment," she said. "I think kids going through that adolescent period really related to that. That was my generation, and I certainly did. And then he became establishment—I mean, he wanted to become establishment, but he never really made it, and that may have been what killed him."

Mrs. Dolores Flores of Seattle, acting under the little-used clause of the Constitution which gives citizens the right to petition their government, filed a petition asking the Congress to declare January 8 as National Elvis Presley Day.

Senator Howard Baker of Tennessee paid a tribute in the *Congressional Record,* and other political leaders joined in lauding Elvis. Alabama Governor George C. Wallace hailed the singer as "one of the greatest entertainers of my lifetime." At the request of a constituent from the Bronx, Representative Mario Biaggi of New York introduced a resolution asking the Department of the Interior to designate Graceland as a National Historic Landmark. Governor James R. Thompson of Illinois later would proclaim August 16 as Elvis Presley Memorial Day in honor of one who "revolutionized a new era in music, bringing countless hours of musical entertainment to the world."

Editorial comments continued to pour forth. For every comment on his music, there were references to Presley's role in changing lifestyles and unleashing the sexual revolution. "Oozing sexuality and redneck chic, he became a superstar," wrote Marc Schogol in *The Philadelphia Inquirer*. "The Elvis Presley of 1956 was a lean, mean, whip-like young man, whose greasy hair, sideburns, white pants, purple shirts and all-around low-rent, drugstore-hood appearance set teenage America on fire." A highly negative appraisal by Lester Bangs on the front page of the *Village Voice* credited Elvis with bringing "overt blatant vulgar sexual frenzy to the popular arts in America."

The Commercial Appeal's James McDaniel said Elvis may have been a major factor in precipitating the women's liberation movement that began emerging in the late sixties. "I think he was the first person to have that kind of impact on feminism, on emerging equal rights, because he kind of freed women to express opinions about sex and other things." McDaniel acknowledged that Sinatra excited bobby-soxers, but that was a simple adulation compared to the almost worship that Elvis inspired. Raymond Browne, professor of popular culture at Ohio's Bowling Green State University, agrees. Elvis opened doors for the women of the country, says Browne. They rode with him, even though they may not have known it. Before Elvis, they had never been as free to express opinions. But there was raw sex appeal as well, adds Browne. "When Elvis came along, with his sweat and his shirt open, exposing his nipples and all of this—well, it made women get terribly excited. The truth of the matter is, that Elvis's pants were filled, and the women knew it. And I think, as much as anything else, this is what heralded his success."

Los Angeles radio reporter Barbara Esensten told her listeners about Elvis's impact on her teenage view of sex in the taboo-ridden fifties. Her mother, prodded into explaining her opposition to the singer, finally told Esensten that he looked as if he were trying to get women excited. "He is," the daughter admitted, and the two women looked at each other and laughed. "I can't help but believe," said the reporter, "that in many different ways Elvis Presley freed up a lot of folks." Columnist Emmett Watson of the *Seattle Post-Intelligencer* expressed a similar thought as he quoted a "Southern-born lady in her late thirties" who said that Elvis brought sex out of the closets, back seats, and rear doors. The *St. Louis Post-Dispatch* asked Richard C. Nikeson, a psychology professor at St. Louis University, to explain Presley to its readers. "He was sexier than Sinatra," Nikeson said. "There was a great deal more emotion, a great deal more heat, in his delivery. It got to be fashionable to almost faint when watching him." Many writers slipped into the comments on sexuality by recalling Elvis's appearance on Ed Sullivan's *Toast of the Town* in 1956, when the television cameras focused only above the waist.

The *Honolulu Star-Bulletin* credited him with unleashing the new attitudes toward sex, but the Hawaii paper said the revolution roared past and Elvis "became more of a symbol of old values than of new." The debate over Elvis's role in the nation's cultural mores was meaningless, Mike Clary said in a front page essay in the *Akron Beacon-Journal*. He recalled hearing "Heartbreak Hotel" when he was an eighth-grader in Cuyahoga Falls, and to people of his generation such analysis was a waste of time. "We like him because he was real," said Clary, "because when we danced in the gym to the throb of 'Hound Dog' and 'Don't Be Cruel,' it felt good."

Sports Editor Billy Reed, in an essay in *The Courier-Journal*, said Elvis deserved his place in history, although he would leave it to the historians and sociologists to explain the meaning of it all. "This doesn't mean that Presley's importance should be made larger in death than it was in life," said Reed. "He didn't cure anybody's cancer or invent the atom bomb or fly to the moon. But he did something very important. He brought an infinite amount of happiness, pleasure and excitement into a lot of ordinary, workaday lives." Other sports writers brought their talents to the news pages in efforts to explain the Presley phenomena. David Israel of *The Washington Star* questioned the notion that America's legends always died too soon. Is it not possible, he asked, that they died at just the right time? "They died as we should remember them— young and productive . . . living well is more important than living long." Israel said Elvis was not comfortable with evolution. As the years went by, his world had not changed, his friends, his songs, and his fans were the same; but he could not stay the same. "Elvis Presley could no longer sneer and mean it," wrote Israel. "It was time to freeze the legend."

Bob Schildgen, a professor of English and journalism at Merritt College, said Elvis had much to sneer about. In an essay in *The Los Angeles Times*, Schildgen hailed Presley for infusing mainstream songs with the wail of the white underdog. Perhaps Elvis's "grandest sneer of all" was flaunting his wealth with a vengeance by giving away automobiles and expensive rings to friends and strangers alike, instead of endowing hospital wings or building art galleries or taking tax deductions like the "old money" people do. "This is something middle-class liberals and middle-class leftists can't really comprehend," said Schildgen. "They want their heroes to be austere, to abnegate, to practice the cult of lowered expectations—and they can't stand something like Elvis'—or Ali's—Cadillacs. What they don't understand is that if you ain't never had nothin', it's damn hard to abnegate—and anyway, I doubt whether any of these refined souls ever told Elvis that his display of wealth was 'vulgar.'"

Schildgen called Presley another in the "great American tradition of modern Orpheuses getting wasted for art's sake." His was only one of the many literary allusions writers used. Pete Hamill, writing in the *New York Daily News*, called Elvis a "hillbilly Faust" who had made a pact with success because he had seen too many people living their lives out in obscurity. Andrea Karchmer, a former Memphian living in New York, said Elvis embodied the "tough/gentile, earthy sensuality of Southern manhood that Tennessee Williams poeticized." In a letter to *The Commercial Appeal*'s entertainment editor, she called Presley "the 'sweet bird of youth' who made it." John Anders opened his column in *The Dallas Morning News* with the lines from Walt Whitman's "When Lilacs Last in the Dooryard Bloom'd":

> O powerful western fallen star!
> O shades of night—O moody, tearful night!
> O great star disappeared . . .

"The question that keeps hitting me," Anders wrote in a highly personal tribute, "the thing I don't understand is simply this: Why does it hurt so much?" Anders discussed his lack of interest in the singer in recent years, Elvis's turning forty and getting fat, the singer's ability to spoof himself. "We loved him anyway for reasons that need not be examined too closely," the columnist concluded. "Elvis simply was Elvis—a rare, splendid piece of indefinable energy who came to us for a short while and provided us with a special joy in being alive."

Besides the flood of words in the printed media, the nation's editorial cartoonists also were busy, providing commentary and illustrating the events in Memphis. *The Commercial Appeal*'s Bill Garner drew a simple pair of very large blue suede shoes—empty. In Louisville, *The Courier-Journal*'s Hugh Haynie drew the RCA trademark dog listening to the bell of a Victrola, with a tear running down its cheek. The same concept was used in the *St. Petersburg Times*.

Mike Peters in the *Dayton Daily News* depicted a shrieking gaggle of winged, teenaged angels wearing skirts, sweaters, and sneakers as they looked out through the pearly gates screaming "Elvis!" An elderly, bewildered St. Peter, standing at his book, looked apprehensive as they awaited the new arrival. A celestial theme also inspired Jacob Burck in the *Chicago Sun-Times*, who showed a winged Elvis, with a puzzled look on his face trying to figure out how to play a harp. And Calvin Grondahl in the *Deseret News* in Salt Lake City showed a heavenly orchestra of harp-playing angels, startled by the white-robed Elvis playing a guitar with a loud "Twang."

Charles Brooks, in a *Birmingham News* cartoon captioned "Imprint," sketched a globe covered with people looking to the heavens where music notes among the stars spell out Elvis.

In *The Atlanta Journal,* Lou Ericson's cartoon showed a group of teenagers standing around crying and consoling each other in front of a building captioned Heartbreak Hotel with a funeral wreath on the door. Sandy Campbell in *The Tennessean* in Nashville also showed a Heartbreak Hotel with a line of mourners waiting to check in at the registration desk.

At week's end, Wayne Stayskal in the *Chicago Tribune* showed a group of warehouse hoods looking at a map and saying, "Forget that truckload of cigarets we were going to hijack. I heard that a shipment of Elvis Presley records is coming through about midnight."

Two western cartoonists came up with amazingly similar ideas. Each showed a guitar with a broken string which had coiled into script and spelled out the singer's name. Karl Hubenthal of the *Los Angeles Herald-Examiner* included a wavering music note that dotted the "i" in Elvis, and captioned his work "The Song is Ended." Reg Manning in the Phoenix *Arizona Republic* drew a heart-shaped guitar, "the hearts of world's rock 'n' roll fans." J. Morin in the *Richmond Times-Dispatch* also showed a single guitar. The instrument was propped against a wall with a crown, slightly askew, hanging from it. Nearby was an unplugged microphone.

The most poignant cartoon of the week came from the pen of Draper Hill of the *Detroit News.* He depicted a stunned middle-aged couple looking at a photo of Elvis and the dates, 1935-1977, on a TV screen, as their teenaged son sprawled on the floor with his record albums of the Kiss and Alice Cooper. Hill captioned his cartoon, "Passages."

One cannot help wondering what Elvis would have thought of all the comments being made about him.

Columnist Bob Greene of the *Chicago Sun-Times* said it was a shame the singer was not around to hear "the sober extolling and glorification."

"Elvis would have laughed," said Greene. "And then sneered that sneer."

11

The President Himself

FOR IMMEDIATE RELEASE   August 17, 1977

            Office of the White House Press Secretary

                        THE WHITE HOUSE

The following is the President's statement on the death of
Elvis Presley:

    Elvis Presley's death deprives our country of a part of
itself. He was unique; and irreplaceable. More than twenty
years ago he burst upon the scene with an impact that was
unprecedented and will probably never be equaled. His music
and his personality, fusing the styles of white country and
black rhythm and blues, permanently changed the face of American
popular culture. His following was immense and he was a symbol
to people the world over, of the vitality, rebelliousness, and
good humor of his country.
                            #   #   #

It is not unusual for local leaders to comment on the death of a well-known citizen, particularly when that person has attained international fame. Nor is it unusual for members of Congress to laud well-known persons in the *Congressional Record*. But it is something a bit apart for the President of the United States to make a formal statement on someone's death.

Even the prolific Lyndon Johnson marked the passing of only fifty-five persons during the five years of his presidency. They included statesmen and politicians like Bernard Baruch and Adlai Stevenson, heroes of past wars like Sergeant Alvin York or General Douglas MacArthur, journalists or literary figures like John Steinbeck, Edward R. Murrow, and Henry Luce. Distinguished citizens such as Helen Keller and the Reverend Martin Luther King, Jr., were added to the list. But neither entertainers nor popular singers were praised in Johnson's official statements. Other chief executives were even more sparing in their comments on the deaths of the nation's prominent citizens.

Why, then, did President Jimmy Carter decide to take official note of the passing of Elvis Presley? Why was the statement so well written, striking chords in the hearts of the singer's fans and showing more than a superficial understanding of the Elvis phenomenon? And, why, with a few notable exceptions, was the statement reported simply as a matter of course—as a natural and appropriate event—throughout the world?

The Carter White House had no set procedure for issuing statements on the death of famous persons; Press Secretary Jody Powell usually decided that a tribute was needed and sent a request to one of the presidential speechwriters. When the news of Elvis's death came over the wire, Powell's assistant, Rex Granum, called Jerry Doolittle with the assignment. The speechwriter responded without enthusiasm and drafted a eulogy he said was designed "to kill the whole idea" of issuing a statement.

"I thought the death of Elvis Presley was the least significant event of the century," said Doolittle. "We couldn't go around putting out statements on every pop singer and entertainer. Groucho Marx [who died a few days after Presley] was eminently more worthy."

Doolittle wrote:

> Elvis Presley left his mark on the music of an entire nation. His popularity came so early and so suddenly that it seemed likely to be brief. And yet he kept his hold on his tens of millions of fans until premature death cut short his career today. For years to come, those fans will be singing the songs he popularized. His untimely passing leaves a void in the world of popular music.
>
> Elvis Presley was drafted into the service of his country as a young man at the height of his extraordinary fame and popularity. From being an idol to the millions, he became an Army truckdriver. And yet he served without complaint until he was free to resume his career. This, too, we should not forget.

Doolittle handed the draft to Rex Granum shortly before six o'clock that evening in the White House barbershop. Granum did not think it was very appropriate, and he quickly cut the paragraph about military service. A short time later, the entire statement was rejected. "I was alone in not thinking the White House should memorialize the passing of Elvis Presley," said Doolittle, admitting his "abysmally bad" political judgment.

Speechwriter Griffin Smith, who came to the White House after publishing the highly successful *Texas Monthly* magazine, agreed that political considerations were involved. "For Jimmy Carter to have ignored the death of Elvis Presley would have been for him to turn his back on some of the people who elected him. This obviously was not just a plain old 'croaker.'"

The intensity of feeling among Elvis fans is legendary, and they demanded, as Doolittle phrased it, "assurance that the President cared about the death of their hero." Soon after the news of Presley's death began flashing around the country, callers jammed the White House switchboard wanting a day of mourning, a national holiday, an official declaration—something. Some spokesmen for the singer's fans ascribe the President's statement solely to political considerations, a direct response to the intense telephone traffic. But the truth seems to go beyond such simple explanations.

Although the White House did not issue a statement until Wednesday morning, the order from the press office came too quickly after the first news bulletin to be just a switchboard response. Moreover, others in the White House were reacting to the news. Griffin Smith, who learned of Elvis's death from a friend's telephone call about four-thirty, shared the news with fellow speechwriter Hendrick 'Rick' Hertzberg. Hertzberg immediately said a presidential statement was called for. Like others throughout the country, they began to reminisce about Elvis, and Smith loaned his colleague a copy of Greil Marcus's *Mystery Train*, a respected book on the history of rock music that draws its title from an early Elvis recording. Hertzberg read the chapter on Presley to help collect his thoughts. Then, not knowing the press office had already assigned the task to someone else, he prepared a statement on his own. With a few minor changes, his draft became the official tribute which the President issued the next morning.

In many ways Hertzberg seemed a strange choice to draft the Presley statement. Thirty-three years of age, Hertzberg was described by *Newsweek* as "an archetypal child of the 60s." Born to New York socialists, his father a labor figure and his mother a professor, he shared little in background or philosophy with the entertainer. Hertzberg was educated at Harvard, spent two years as a Naval officer, and worked at the San Francisco bureau of *Newsweek* and *The New Yorker* before joining the Carter administration. He wore wire-rimmed glasses and rode a bicycle to the White House—a far cry from the Southern, blue-collar, big-car world of Elvis.

But Hertzberg was not unsuited to the task. At *Newsweek* he covered the emerging rock movement. He attended Elvis's first-ever New York appearance in Madison Square Garden in June 1972, and he wrote about it for the "Talk of the Town" section of *The New Yorker*:

> He looked like an apparition, and this was appropriate, because he had been a figure of fantasy for seventeen years. As the performance went on, it became impossible to avoid the conclusion that he is a consummate professional. . . .
> Throughout, Elvis remained a certain ironic distance from it all . . . But he manifestly enjoyed the audiences's enjoyment, even as he indicated with a smile here and a gesture there that it all had less to do with him than with their idea of him.

Now, at the news of Presley's death, Hertzberg echoed the words of Southerner Rex Granum when he said a presidential statement "seemed natural—seemed the thing to do." Searching for a further explanation of why he prepared the statement, Hertzberg finally concluded, "I really *wanted* to do it." This was what Hertzberg wrote:

> Elvis Presley's death deprives our country of a part of itself. He was unique; *he was* irreplaceable. More than twenty years ago, he burst upon the scene with an impact that was unprecedented and will probably never be equaled *again*. His music and his personality, fusing the styles of white country and black rhythm and blues, permanently changed the face of American popular culture. His following was immense, *yet he never took himself or his myth too seriously.* And he was a symbol, *not just to his fellow Americans, but* to people the world over, of the vitality, rebelliousness, and good humor of his country.

Except for the few portions in italics, the statement stood. The editing and the statement peculiarly fit both the President and Elvis. "Carter is a very good editor," said Hertzberg. "He has a good eye for cutting out the crap, and he likes to get down to brass tacks rather than try to move his audience by emotional rhetoric. That may be a reaction to the traditional Southern demagoguery. It's the downside of his sincerity; he doesn't like to fake it. The idea of giving a speech that raises the emotions seems to rub him the wrong way."

President Carter may shun emotional appeals in speeches, but he certainly understood the very emotional impact of the music of Elvis Presley, and he saw the music as a generally positive force. The statement he issued was one of the few to note the importance of humor in Presley's appeal.

When Elvis appeared in a 1973 concert at the Omni in Atlanta, those in the audience included then-Governor Carter and his wife. Accompanying them was Wanda Lewis, a member of the governor's staff and an avid Elvis fan. At intermission they visited with the entertainer backstage, where he posed for pictures and autographed their ticket stubs. The visit was short, but Carter invited Elvis to come over to the governor's mansion to play tennis. Lewis was astounded at Elvis's vivacity. "I'd always heard he was very shy," she recalled, "but he was really friendly and just talked up a storm."

Presley generally remained aloof from politics; it was an avenue of power he rarely exercised. He once paid a secret visit to President Richard Nixon, volunteering his services for undercover work in law enforcement. And a few weeks before he died, Elvis called President Carter on behalf of a friend.

Security officials in Memphis learned that Elvis had been attempting to telephone the President for several days, only to be rebuffed by White House aides reacting incredulously to a voice saying, "This is Elvis Presley; I'd like to speak to President Carter." An FBI agent passed the information to W. J. Michael Cody, United States attorney for West Tennessee and the highest ranking Carter appointee in Memphis. Cody called fellow Memphian Landrum Butler, a special assistant for political affairs at the White House, and told him that Elvis was trying to call the President. Within a few hours, Cody got a call from Chip Carter, the President's son, seeking more information.

Cody explained that he had no idea why Presley was calling, but he urged that the entertainer be put through, if the President could find time. Elvis was a figure of enormous influence in the Midsouth. If word was passed that the President would not talk with him, it could do the Democrats considerable harm.

A few days later Chip Carter again telephoned Cody. Here is the way Cody recalled the conversation:

Carter:Mike, this is Chip. I just thought you'd like to know that Dad talked with Elvis.

Cody: Oh, I'm glad to hear it.

Carter: Don't you want to know what they talked about?
Cody: Well, I am curious. But if it's private—
Carter: Well, Dad thinks you ought to know.

Young Carter then told the attorney that Presley had asked the President to intercede in behalf of George Klein, whose trial on a charge of mail fraud was pending in Federal District Court in Memphis. Klein, a one-time disc jockey, was one of Elvis's closest friends. They had attended Humes High School together, and Klein was to serve as a pallbearer at Elvis's funeral. Later, Vernon Presley, the singer's father, appeared as a character witness when Klein was brought to trial in December 1977. The jury found him guilty, and he served a sentence of sixty days in the Shelby County Jail.

Although the telephone call was embarrassing to the Justice Department, the President did not fault the entertainer for the indiscretion.

The Carter eulogy to Presley raised a few eyebrows; those critics who reacted with amazement at the wide-ranging media outpouring also questioned the propriety of a presidential tribute to the entertainer. But they were few in number. For those who understood the pervasiveness of music in the American South, with the religious background and the black/white milieu that developed it, a statement from the Southern-born President was proper and inevitable.

Not only were there the Southern roots, the affinity of place, that linked the entertainer and the President, but Carter also sensed the feeling of humanity that Presley and his music engendered among the great masses of working-class America. Carter had appealed to the same people in his campaign for the White House as he called for a "government as good as its people" and emphasized the importance of his family—his wife, his mother, his children, his brother and sisters. Like Elvis, he was most comfortable with people from home, the key White House staff and the advisers who came to be known as the "Georgia Mafia."

Carter also genuinely liked the music. At a fundraising event in October 1979 at Ford's Theatre in Washington, he called country music "as universal as tears and as personal as a baby's smile," reminding his audience that this was the music he had grown up with in Plains, Georgia. "Country music," he said, "is about all kinds of experiences—sad times and bad times, wasted lives, dashed dreams, the dirty dog that took advantage of you. But it also celebrates the good and the permanent times, home and family, faith and trust, love that lasts for a lifetime and sometimes, I admit, love that lasts just for one good time."

A decade older than Elvis, Carter was the first president who was too young to serve in World War II, the first President of the nuclear generation. Rock has been bound up in the nuclear age since its beginning, and candidate Carter, through his ties with Phil Walden of Capricorn Records, was the first presidential candidate to use rock groups in his campaign. He was the first, as Griffin Smith put it, "to appeal to our generation on its own terms." There was really never a question that President Carter would issue an official statement when Elvis died.

Partly because of the timing of its release, the presidential statement on Wednesday morning did not attract extensive media attention in the United States. In most overseas newspapers, however, it drew large headlines and editorial comment. Indeed, a major West German newspaper said the Carter statement showed the strength of the American democracy, for no German head of state could have commented on a pop singer and remained in office.

12

The World Joins In

Even before he had moved the story on the wire, Les Seago at the AP desk in Memphis was astounded to receive a call from a London paper requesting confirmation of Elvis's death. Those people must have a communication system all their own, he thought.

The rest of the world was not quite as quick as this British reporter—but it did not lag far behind. Before the day ended, the South Central Bell Telephone Company in Memphis called in extra operators to handle the long distance calls. "We have received calls from all over the world—Japan, Europe, Australia," reported Elaine Shaupe, a Bell assistant manager in Memphis. "People were calling to express their loss. Their loss and heaven's gain." Many didn't know whom to call in Memphis—they just called Memphis. But others called the Memphis Funeral Home asking where to send flowers. Calls to the funeral home came not only from all fifty states but also from places as far away as Guam and South Africa.

Marcus Eliason, an AP newsman in Tel Aviv who grew up in Rhodesia, illustrates the worldwide impact of Presley. "When I left Rhodesia and moved to Israel at the age of 16," he says, "my greatest fear was that I would lose contact with Elvis. If Rhodesia was remote, I reasoned, what was the embattled Middle East?

"My fears were unfounded. The first thing I saw from the Tel Aviv bus station was a slogan in tall Hebrew letters daubed on a tenement wall. Fifteen years later, it is still there. It says: 'Long Live Elvis.' "

Newspapers around the world gave the story prominent play. Presley's death made front pages, often with banner headlines and photos, in Switzerland, Israel, Mexico, Brazil, Denmark, Belgium, Hong Kong, Indonesia, Singapore, Thailand, Australia, New Zealand, and Canada.

Even countries which officially disapproved of Presley's music — notably Moslem countries — provided strong coverage. In northern Africa, authorities considered rock music indecent. But news agencies in Morocco, Tunisia, and Algeria printed long obituaries they usually reserved for political leaders. Elvis's popularity in the Islamic world continued after his death. More than two years later, as American hostages remained captive in the United States embassy in Teheran and Iranian mobs gathered in front of the embassy to vent their rage against the American government, reporters found street vendors a few blocks away selling Elvis tapes. Bogden Kominowski, a singer and actor who played the title role in the London musical, *Elvis*, recalled the day an Arab prince hired the theater's dress circle for himself and his entourage. "He bought fifteen thousands pounds worth of flowers for the foyer," said Kominowski, "and paid the actresses to kiss him as he walked in. I thought it was a joke; there were bloody flowers everywhere! After that, he hired the theater for the day. Dressing himself in an Elvis Presley catsuit, he had a camera crew film him singing Presley songs on stage."

Communist countries reported the news, although not to the extent the free world did, accompanied by varying degrees of commentary. In Moscow, *Izvestia* characterized Presley as a victim of the greedy American system: "Enterprising businessmen transformed Presley into the idol of rock and roll, putting his talent and renown to work in the service of profits." *Izvestia* echoed the theme outlined a few weeks earlier in the Soviet Literary Gazette (*Literaturnaya Gazeta*) which pictured Presley as a lonely man consumed by capitalism. The *Komsomolskaya Pravda* in Moscow, the voice of the Young Communist League, went even further. The journal viewed rock music as a tool of mass control, not of revolution: "He helped the 'powers that be' hammer young people's heads with rock so that there would be no time for thoughts about justice and injustice." *Pravda* and Radio Moscow gave short, factual statements that

Presley had died, but avoided making any comment—good or bad—on the situation.

Presley had been the object of some adulation in Communist Europe for years. Even during the dark days of the fifties, a black market flourished in Elvis records in Poland. Later, while never officially approving rock music, the government tolerated it. Polish papers carried short articles on Elvis's death, and Radio Warsaw broadcast a special show of an hour of Presley's music.

Even the state recording company in the Soviet Union, Melodiya, issued some Presley songs on its international pop compilation, "*Estradnaya Orbita*" ("Variety Orbit"), which includes Presley singing "Careless" and "True Love." No albums officially released in the Soviet Union feature Elvis alone, but *Billboard* called the new album, "a minor Soviet memorial."

The news of Elvis's death set off a frantic scramble at the Voice of America, which broadcast the news behind the Iron Curtain a full day before Radio Moscow reported it. At the Voice of America studios in Washington, the staff of the Russian section were broadcasting "Night Owl," a wrap-up of news and features airing from midnight to one o'clock in Moscow. A technician with no knowledge of Russian, bored with the studio activity, watched a television set in the control room while setting the dials and monitoring sound levels. "About half way through the show, he saw the news bulletin," recalled Tamara Dombrofski, who has been broadcasting American pop music to the Soviet Union for VOA since 1970. "The folks in the studio called me; I grabbed the *Rock Biographical Encyclopedia* and a handful of Elvis records. I literally wrote on the run and got copy to the control room." A ten-minute "bulletin" went on the air without the approval that the agency's regulations require. The news department was still waiting for a second confirmation of the news.

Dombrofski was reacting to the knowledge that Presley cut across ideological, cultural, and religious lines—that he had played a good-will role between America and other places around the world. Eudora Welty two decades earlier articulated why this might be so:

> Mutual understanding in the world being nearly always, as now, at a low ebb, it is comforting to remember that it is through art that one country can nearly always speak reliably to another, if the other can hear at all.

Art, though, is never the voice of a country; it is an even more precious thing, the voice of the individual, doing its best to speak, not comfort of any sort, indeed, but truth.

The impact of Presley's voice was evident even from the treatment accorded to copies of the Memphis newspapers that the State Department forwarded abroad after Presley's death. They were gems, doled out with care. Jack Harrod of the United States Information Agency, cultural affairs officer in Moscow in August of 1977, got six copies. He shared them with the AP and UPI bureaus. Peter Bezshehowzi, Harrod's counterpart in Cracow, Poland, got forty copies to distribute to media, jazz clubs, and others.

Louis Lerner, the United States ambassador to Norway, offered a backdrop explaining why such strong press reaction occurred all over the world: "One of the things I've realized in the job I have now—and this is a terribly important thing which enough people simply don't realize—and that is that America is known not by its military and not by its diplomats, but by its popular culture." Lerner lived by this lesson. The ambassador's residence in Oslo, a palatial Russian-style building on extensive, well-tended grounds, was filled with Lerner's personal collection of pop art. He arranged receptions for Kris Kristofferson, Rita Coolidge, Alex Haley, jazz pianist Keith Jarrett, Dizzy Gillespie, the Chicago Blues Band, and dozens of other American artists. He felt strongly that if he, as a diplomat, could identify himself with American popular culture, he would have a much better chance of succeeding as an ambassador. His unorthodox approach to his job—including conversing in Norwegian—ruffled feathers of some, but it also got him extensive and unanimously favorable press coverage throughout Norway. Lerner regretted not placing a register for condolences at the embassy when Presley died, for he recalled "Christ is coming"-style headlines throughout Scandinavia that week. It was the same in other countries.

"*Vier Dinge hat Amerika der Welt gegeben*" ("four things has America given the world"), exclaimed the largest daily in Zurich, Switzerland, "*Baseball, Mickey Mouse, Coca-Cola und Elvis.*" The head of Belgium's Elvis Fan Club, Francoise Geyser, said, "It is as if I had lost my brother; I cried all night." In Brussels, fans gathered at record stores and wept.

The Daily Nation in Nairobi, Kenya, reported, "Elvis Presley turned out to be no false idol. He was a superstar. He was an innovator. He was the stuff of which history is made." West Germany's conservative

Frankfurter Allgemeine Zeitung said, "His fame is so secure that we need not worry about his legend." The *Ilta Sanomat* in Helsinki noted Presley's revolutionary impact: "He aroused youth all over the world into a united resistance to the old norms."

A Dutch newspaper embraced that spirit of rebellion: "He twisted, he shouted, he panted and sweated. At last there was somebody who smashed down the hammer and yelled out to the older generation: You made a mess of it and now it's our turn." Dutch composer-producer Eddy Owwens, who performs under the name Danny Mirror, recorded a tribute called, "I Remember Elvis Presley." It sold ten thousand copies in one day.

In Sri Lanka, the *Ceylon Daily News* hit upon Presley's inescapability: "More people cared to . . . or were forced to listen to him than to any other modern singer."

In Johannesburg, South Africa, Elvis crossed the color line. "From Naboomspruit to Johannesburg's Lower Houghton," said the *Rand Daily Mail*, "black, white, young and old mourned Elvis the Pelvis, the truck driver who became a legend." The newspaper ran four photos of fans—a black, a white, a black, and a white—with the captions, "very upset . . . distressed . . . cut up . . . very sad," running underneath.

Danish television produced a one-hour memorial and Dan Turrell and Edmondt Jensen produced a play based on the words of American protest folk singer-composer, Phil Ochs, who said, "The only possibility in the United States for a humane society would be a revolution with Elvis Presley as leader."

Elvis never performed abroad, never made the triumphal foreign concert tour that would have been a publicist's dream. His one trip to Europe was his hitch in the Army, to Northern Germany, where he was stationed near Frankfurt-am-Main. His military tour generated much publicity among the German people, most of it favorable. His records sold well; his movies—with or without the German subtitles—were hits; and to many of his fans there, he was like a native son. The German press treated the news of his death with a mixture of sensational syntax and detached analysis.

The tabloid *Bild*, which is published simultaneously in eight major population centers, devoted a quarter of its August 18 front page to the headlines from Memphis. The bold captions leaped from the pages, proclaiming *"Sein Todeskampf"* ("His Death Struggle") and *"Brustkorb geoffnet-Herzmassage"* ("Chest opened—heartmassage"). *Bild*, with a circulation close to five million, is part of the Alex Springer group, Europe's largest newspaper publisher, and its pull at the emotions of the German people was never stronger than in its Elvis coverage. "*14.30 Uhr: Letzter Atemzug—aus!*" completed the headlines—"2:30 p.m.: His last breath—out!" The article continued in the same vein, describing the futile efforts of doctors who took the singer's heart in their hands and pumped it in an effort to revive him.

In Cologne, the *Express* proclaimed in bold, underlined type, "*Elvis Presley/tot! Erstickt!*" ("Elvis Presley/dead! Struck down!"), and the story was bordered in black. Another tabloid often read on the subways warned of "a suicidal wave following the death of Elvis." Using stories filed by their own news service in New York, the *Abendzeitung* in Munich focused on the "*Massenhysterie*" ("mass hysteria") among Presley's fans expected as the psychological result of his death.

More so than in most other countries, the entertainer's physical condition at the time of his death was a focus of the German press. *Bild* laid the cause of death at the door of pills, drugs, and overeating. The *Kolnische Runschau* said Elvis was a down-and-out type at forty-two and that "his stomach was a virtual drugstore."

The nation's two major weekly news magazines—*Stern* and *Der Spiegel*, each with circulations of more than a million—reiterated the singer's physical problems. *Stern* took a softer approach, featuring a personal profile written by Udo Lindenberg, a German rock star. Lindenberg described the devastating lifestyle that Elvis faced. "As a rock'n' roller," wrote Lindenberg, "you can become a superstar, but you cannot grow old." The more caustic *Der Spiegel*, famous for its muckraking investigative reports, pictured the grieving fans in Memphis and captioned with quotes from two of them: "The King will live on in our hearts" and "don't tell us he was fat." A long, interpretive article in *Der Spiegel* noted that the mourners in Memphis were grieving for an image that was no longer real and that was somewhat superficial and flashy when it did exist.

Three of West Germany's most influential dailies saw Presley in a more favorable light. The prestigious *Frankfurter Allgemeine-Zeitung* noted the tremendous vacuum left by his death and called Presley's impact greater than that of many figures of the establishment. Hamburg's *Die Welt* said Elvis's optimism became a lifestyle that would be his legacy. And the *Suddeutsche Zeitung* in Munich reminisced about "*das bisschen Mehr,*" that little piece more, that special something that set Elvis apart from all the others.

In the rathskellers and the discos of West Germany, only Presley music was played, and the nation's radio stations provided many hours of his records and tributes to the singer. *Musik Joker,* a popular weekly, printed one hundred eighty thousand copies of its editions on September 5, a special issue about Elvis that included an article exploring the black music roots of the Presley sound. Near the end of the year, A.R.D., the state television network, produced a fifty-minute documentary, "Elvis, Time After," which focused on the booming Presley market and the American capacity for not letting grief get in the way of making money.

Europe got the word of Presley's death at ten-forty-five Tuesday evening from disc jockey Tony Prince on Radio Luxembourg. As soon as the announcement came, the station cancelled its commercials to broadcast four continuous hours of Presley's records, mixing the music with live calls from fans. The special programming cost Radio Luxembourg at least seventeen thousand dollars in lost revenue, but the station had reason to give special play to Elvis. One of continental Europe's four commercial radio stations—and the only one not broadcasting solely in French for French audiences—Radio Luxembourg set up operation May 31, 1931. In the last quarter-century, however, it had loaded its programming heavily with the popular music of post-war youth. With long-wave, medium-wave, FM, and short-wave transmitters and a potential capacity of one million watts, the station enjoyed audiences in Great Britain and throughout most of Europe on boths sides of the Iron Curtain. Surrounded by France, Belgium, and Germany, the independent Duchy of Luxembourg is ideally situated for the international programming which is its trademark. The station broadcasts in French, German, English, Dutch, and schedules some national programming. Radio Luxembourg also does special broadcasts for the Italian, Spanish, Portuguese, and Serbo-Croatian workers in the area. Its loyal following among the post-war youth, however, stems from the fact that until the advent of the "pirate" radio stations in the sixties, it was the only station where they could hear Elvis Presley and other rock stars. Not until 1967, for instance, did the British Broadcasting Corporation dedicate part of the broadcast time of Radio 247, the "light programme" frequency, for popular music.

Other media were not so closely tied to the history of the rock movement. Nevertheless, many of them gave special play to the Presley story.

Listeners had no trouble after Elvis's death finding his music being broadcast on stations throughout Europe and in other places around the world. In Israel, the news came first in a bulletin on the Army's radio station. Government radio played Elvis songs frequently during the day. Places as divergent as Santiago, Chile, and Manila, in the Philippines, responded similarly. Santiago stations played Elvis music for several hours, and, in Manila, pop station DWIA played Presley records thirty minutes a night for a month after his death.

In Rio de Janeiro, an American passenger heard the news over a taxicab radio. At first he thought that there was some error or that he had misunderstood the announcer's Portuguese. Joachim Jean Aberbach, owner of a posh Manhattan art gallery, became quite ill when he arrived at the home of his host and learned that the announcement was true. Aberbach and his family own more than half the copyrights to Presley's music. He had met Elvis many times and he was distressed that the funeral was held so quickly that he was unable to get to Memphis for the services.

"I never do anything in life which is strictly a business investment," Aberbach said later, contending that his purchase of the copyrights and his expertise in the world of fine art had nothing to do with his reaction to Elvis's performances. "If there is no creative element involved, it doesn't interest me regardless of the earning potential.

"I always love Elvis's music," he said. "I found it exciting, and although I knew the sources, I consider it to be unique. The uniqueness came through his interpretation."

In Thailand, while several local papers splashed big Elvis headlines, the English-language *Bangkok Post* reported that "people from all walks of life in Bangkok expressed shock yesterday over the sudden death of Elvis Presley" and newspaper and radio offices were "inundated with phone calls seeking confirmation of his untimely death." Lek Wongsawang, a Bangkok disc jockey, played Elvis records forty-two hours a week on four stations. From the time of Presley's death until November 15, 1977, Wongsawang played nothing but Elvis; then he cut it to Wednesdays and Saturdays on the four stations for ten hours a week. The disc jockey also sold twenty-three thousand copies of an Elvis biography he had written.

Continued demand for Elvis's music appeared throughout portions of the Far East. Before the year ended, the Mandarin Hotel in Singapore had produced special Elvis shows, rock and roll dance competitions, and a performer—Wilson David—billed as Singapore's answer to Elvis. In Indonesia, a serial of Elvis articles appeared on the front pages of the newspaper *Suara Karya* in Jakarta. In Malaysia, the Regent Hotel in Kuala Lumpur showed an Elvis movie every day during an "Elvis week."

One common response among foreign groups was the sending of condolences to their American counterparts. The Chilean Artists' Union sent its counterpart in the United States a sympathy telegram, and Ken Gupwell, an employee of a Massey-Ferguson plant in England, cabled Massey-Ferguson's export department in Des Moines, Iowa: "We are terribly stunned here, as is the whole nation. We join you in a very distressed emotion."

Canada and Mexico, neighbors to the north and south of the United States, for many years have felt the impact of American culture—including Elvis Presley. Even before his death, more Elvis records were sold per capita in Quebec than in any other place in the world. Major Canadian newspapers reported massive sales of records in Canada when Elvis died. But Kay Parley, a Saskatoon, Saskatchewan, psychologist, decried the news interest in record sales. She had taped recorded articles from the international fan club *Elvis Monthly* for possible radio broadcast, and a local television crew came to her house to interview the person who apparently was the city's most prominent fan. "Why the emotional reaction to the funeral?" they asked. Parley replied, "People have always made a symbol of this boy, but speaking for the fans, we feel as if we have a personal relationship with Elvis. Everybody has him in their primary group; he's part of the family. Dozens have told me that he is husband or brother or son or father to them . . . or friend . . . most of them say friend. And for some reason Elvis was able to project a kind of warmth and empathy in his music that made us, the fans, feel that he also cared about us."

Parley later described the interview this way: "They only gave me about forty seconds, so I couldn't say much, but I said what I felt. When the interview came on the TV news that evening the interviewer followed it with the comment, 'That statement may sound crazy to a lot of us.' (The media men hadn't changed their attitude, not even then!) Then he went on to talk about how the music stores in Saskatoon had sold out every Elvis record within hours at the announcement of his death. They were more interested in talking about that than in anything I might have said about interpersonal relationships with Elvis!"

Two hundred twenty-seven Canadians flew a chartered plane from

Montreal to the funeral. Montreal station CKVL arranged the charter and sent Johnny Farago, a rock singer who produced many Presley records in French, on the trip to Memphis. The Toronto *Globe and Mail* described the entourage as "mostly good-looking people in their 30s and 40s. Intelligent-looking, scrubbed and well-dressed, overwhelmingly French-speaking." Elvis never performed in Montreal. The Catholic Church banned him in the Montreal diocese during his 1957 Canadian tour; but Elvis passed through there on his way to his performances in Ottawa, and thousands mobbed Windsor Station as they tried to board the train.

That polarity of condemnation and adoration continued. Dennis Braithwaite sounded a sour note in the *Toronto Star*. He proposed a farewell to the "foolish, hysterical and more than a little vicious era of rock and roll," and took a swipe at President Carter's statement on Presley and at the extensive media coverage in the United States and in Toronto. Braithwaite clearly wanted to "move on."

A less visceral reaction came from Toronto's *Globe and Mail*. Bart Testa, Toronto rock writer, provided an analysis of Elvis and American culture entitled, "Elvis died an artifact of supreme importance." He opened with a quote from W.J. Cash, historian of the American South, a quote that could have applied to Elvis:

> To lie on his back for days and weeks storing power as the air he breathes stores power under the hot sun of August, and then to explode, as the air explodes in the thunderstorm in a violent outburst of emotion—in such a fashion would he make life not only tolerable, but infinitely sweet.

Testa went to the heart of the new explosion, now twenty years old, in American culture:

> With gestures and a persona of unerring, even stupifying power, Elvis Presley may very well have epitomized all that is worst and much that is splendid about American culture. His was the monumental arrogance that accompanies, but never fails to nullify America's incredibly heroic naivete. The self-made man is something of a bore. But a self-made king, now that is something else entirely. And for the last decade Presley was nothing short of America's populist king. Emerson may have dreamed of an American sun king, a fantasy of the artistic soul, but Elvis embodied that dream in epic style flinging his raiments with a vulgar but magnificent sweep that defied even the largest expactations.

In describing why the explosion was so powerful, Testa claimed Presley
was far more than something for teenagers:

> But it was more. He exploded with sexual power across "Hound Dog"
> and then lapsed into sweet pleading with "Love Me Tender" to show
> subliminally as well as obviously that the senses and the sentiments could
> reach fusion without a snigger, a unique accomplishment in American pop
> culture.

Far below the southern border, in Mexico City, radio stations broadcast special programs and newspapers printed many stories about
Presley—but they sometimes included subtle and not-so-subtle references to Presley and rock as an outside, almost unwelcome culture. *El
Dia* carried a full page cartoon *"El Rock en la cultura...colonial."* The
paper traced the marketing of rock and roll, its association with drugs,
and the hysteria over Presley's death. It compared all this with the tiny
coverage given a development *"verdaderamente importante para la cultura de Mexico"* ("truly important for the culture of Mexico")—a national plan to promote indigenous languages and revitalize the unique
and varied cultures of the nation.

The tabloid *La Prensa*, one of the Mexican capital's most heavily circulated newspapers, published Presley stories accompanied by
numerous pictures but also emphasized quotations and views of local
rock stars such as César Costa.

Farther to the south, where American culture perhaps was more a
choice than a constant presence, coverage was less ambivalent and
emphasized directly the Presley impact. In Santiago, Chile, there was
reported incredulity among the local artistic community: *"Consternación
en el ambiente artístico chileno el deceso del popular cantante nor-
teamericano."* Radio stations repeated the news over and over. The popular *El Tiempo* in Bogotá, Colombia, printed the UPI wire story headlined
"El Gato de la Montana" ("The Hill Billy Cat"). Córdoba, Argentina, explored the drug rumors side by side with a story on the *"Hombre
generoso"* ("Generous man"). In Rio de Janeiro, Brazil, the *Jornal do
Brasil* dedicated a full page to Presley and quoted its own leading rock
star, Roberto Carlos, "Elvis is dead but his music will live forever." Similar treatment was accorded Presley in *La Prensa* in Lima, Peru.

On the other side of the globe, New Zealand joined in the world reaction. In Wellington, the *Evening Post* reported local mourning as record
stores around town placed flowers and wreaths in their windows. Local
radio stations played special Elvis programs and one, Radio 2ZB, inter-

viewed people at WHBQ in Memphis. The *Evening Post* also ran an editorial asserting that Elvis, unlike many others, fully deserved the appellation "Superstar" and said that Elvis's "clean-cut qualities" contributed to the affection his fans felt for him. "Behind all the mystique ... was a man who was ... unbelievably friendly and unaffected."

In Auckland, *The New Zealand Herald* homed in on a writer who had served in the military in the Southern United States during the fifties. He gave an outsider's view of the early Presley phenomenon:

> Morning, noon and night it was country and western at top volume—mostly from stations so small the cost of their ever present Coca-Cola machines exceeded their music budgets.
> Then came Elvis from Memphis, and the decibels became even more deafening, if that was possible. ...
> The irony was that the sons of Dixie, not previously noted for rapport with the black man, were falling head over heels for a white man who—more than any other—would bring the gut beat of black music into the mainstream.

Few, if any, nations in the world traditionally have felt a greater affection for the United States than Australia. The Australian reaction to Presley mirrored that sentiment. Minutes after the news was broadcast, sobbing women inundated radio stations' switchboards requesting favorite Elvis songs and asking where to send flowers. They complained about broadcasts devoted to discussion of such matters as the national budget; call-in shows had difficulty coping with sometime hysterical callers.

Australia probably was the first foreign country to erect a permanent monument to the late entertainer. On November 26, 1977, the Victoria Elvis Presley Fan Club in Melbourne dedicated a stone structure with "ELVIS" emblazoned across the top, "In gratitude from the millions to whom you gave so much."

Media coverage was extensive. The government broadcasting agency, the ABC (Australian Broadcasting Commission) produced a special, television channels showed Elvis films, and radio stations broadcast his music and memorials to him. Some radio stations established direct lines to American commentators and disc jockeys. Australia has a wide range of both government and commercial broadcasting. The country also has many daily papers with large circulations, usually regionally based. And it is the home base of tabloid magnate Rupert Murdoch. Murdoch owns *The Australian*, published simultaneously in Sydney, Melbourne, Perth, and Brisbane, and one of the few Australian papers which can claim a national circulation, although not the largest in numbers. *The Australian* called Elvis "a 24 carat, solid-state star." But it headlined "Lone Death for Presley" and "Fans Give Elvis a Shoving Farewell," referring to the crowds outside the Graceland gates.

The nation's popular press went all out on the Presley story. The *Sun* reported selling an extra twenty-nine thousand copies of the paper announcing Elvis's death. The *Daily Mirror* solicited comments on the entertainer from its readers and reported: "One of the greatest responses to a competition staged by the Daily Mirror—that's the verdict for our Tribute to Elvis contest. We received more than twenty-one thousand entries." The Sydney paper, *Sunday*, invited its readers to participate in a seance where a psychic, Mr. John, would try to contact Elvis. Although only six persons could participate, over seven thousand applied.

"The King was the first white boy to put sex into rock and roll," observed the liberal weekly, *Nation Review.* "He was the white punk and it didn't matter how hard Colonel Parker, Hollywood, the army and Las Vegas tried to turn him into the all-time charismatic entertainer. It was the curling lip, the tilting pelvis and the sneaky sideburns that unleashed all those libidos, and that's what most of us will remember."

In *The National Times*, a respected weekly news magazine, Craig McGregor called Elvis "a prisoner of his own fame," and chided publicists and commentators who were more concerned with image than reality and who ignored the fact that Elvis was "a hell of a good singer." McGregor denounced the process that had turned the rebel into a commercial product. "Presley is one of the macabre success stories of our time," he wrote. "He is a chilling example of what happens to a genuinely creative artist who gets caught up in the commercial machine, turned into something salable, and then has every ounce of originality pumped out of him until he becomes a husk of his former self."

Some Australians developed unusual themes in their efforts to explain Elvis's appeal. One, for instance, compared Presley with a primitive sacrificial figure called a corn king. According to Bob Connell, sociology professor at the University of New South Wales, the corn king was raised from nothing by his fellows, reigned for a year, and then was killed, guaranteeing a good harvest and serving as a ritual reminder of the cycle of birth, death, and regeneration. Professor Connell characterized Presley as a modern corn king, although he conceded that it was not the public which killed him. In support of his thesis, Connell pointed to the unusual emotion Presley's death touched off, which, he said, indicated "that he was more than just an entertainer, that it has some form of symbolic significance."

Another writer explored the theme of what, or who, controlled the Elvis phenomenon. In "The King who marched to a colonel's tune,"*Australian* New York correspondent John Raedler looked at Elvis and his manager, Colonel Tom Parker. Locally *The Australian* discovered a grandmother in her fifties who was a member of the Australian Elvis fan club and the former Donald Leslie McNulty, who had legally changed his name to Elvis after he saw the movie *G. I. Blues.*

The Sydney Morning Herald, on the other hand, was one of the few newspapers which, after covering the sobbing fans and the funeral chaos, proceeded to an analysis not of Elvis's impact on the world but of the impact of Memphis on Elvis. In "Memphis Bids Farewell to its 'Good old boy,'" staff correspondent Richard MacKenzie wrote:

> Elvis Presley, who died this week aged 42, was buried here yesterday in the town he never really left.
> In spite of his millions and his popularity, he was always thought of by locals in this Southern city as "a good old boy."
> He was, they say, a person who never forgot his roots, and who always remembered the poverty-stricken background from which he emerged to become the most popular entertainer of the century.
> The important fact here about the King of Rock and Roll is not that he was adored throughout the world, but he always considered Memphis his home.
> In this Bible-belt region, one has reached the pinnacle when one moves to Memphis where the pace of life is that much slower and the worries seem fewer but still "it's the city."

In Brisbane, a special local event added to the story. As Elvis lay dead in Memphis, Radio 4IP auctioned a wood-mounted gold LP "Blue Hawaii" for fifteen hundred dollars. Originally acquired from RCA for use in an Elvis competition, the station decided when Elvis died that "Rather than capitalize on his death, we would auction it for the Autistic Children's Fund."

The ties between Australia and the United States are strong. Besides a common language, both countries originally were new territories with vast space, have few direct neighbors, and grew out of a pioneer heritage. An affinity of mood and media coverage was natural. However, countries sometimes at odds with the United States—Sweden and France—offer an illustrative comparison.

In Sweden, where things American frequently evoke ambivalent reactions, the media decided with near unanimity that Elvis's death was the week's biggest news story. With English a common second language, particularly among those under forty, and with the nation's high literacy rate, relative affluence, and heavy sales of records and movie tickets, Sweden's people knew Elvis well.

After his death Stockholm's TV-2 scheduled screenings of several Elvis movies. The Swedish capital's big afternoon daily *Expressen* headlined its Wednesday editions: "*ELVIS DOG—sjuk, ensam och rädd*" ("ELVIS DIED—sick, alone and afraid"). The large type, along with a photograph, took up the entire front page of the tabloid-sized paper. On page six was a banner headline about rumors concerning Elvis's death and two subheads: "Doctors Say Heart Attack" and "Police Say Drugs."

Expressen did far more than report the death. Hans Fridlund, under a headline which translates: "The Saga of Elvis: Sex and Millions," called Presley's life one of the twentieth century's *"mest guld kantade"* ("most golden stories"). His lengthy article traced the career and concluded that during the seventies Elvis had become, more and more, "rock's grand old man." Sten Berglind, a columnist and long-time Elvis fan who later wrote a best-selling Swedish biography of the entertainer, wrote a detailed analysis of his music. Under a headline, "A Terrible Shock," the leading Scandinavian musicians discussed Elvis's influence on their lives.

The competing *Aftonbladet*, which like *Expressen*, circulates nationwide, headlined, "Elvis Dead After Heart Attack," in the largest possible type. A black border surrounded the entire front page. Calling Presley "the biggest teenage idol ever," the newspaper asked, "What did Elvis mean for you?" One-paragraph replies and photographs of some two dozen respondents were printed, much like the inquiring photographer feature once common in many newspapers in the United States. The feature included wire service reports of comments by well-known American entertainers (Cher, Hank Snow, Carl Wilson of the Beach Boys, Ann-Margret), Swedish rock stars (Svenne Hedlund, Little Gerhard, Leif 'Burken' Bjorklund), and ordinary citizens. Most were favorable, but Pavel Ramel, a fifty-five-year-old Stockholm artist and poet, commented, "I never liked Elvis ... He has never meant anything to me." And Carmenzita Almo, thirty-six years of age, said: "I always thought he

was a slob" (*"slibbig"*). She said she preferred "a cute blond named Tommy Steele."

Most replies resembled comments that appeared the next day when
Aftonbladet ran an entire page of letters to the editor praising Elvis. The
newspaper's custom is to identify the occupations of the writers, who included several students, a shopgirl, a seamstress, a salesman, a factory
worker, several housewives, two hospital orderlies, several secretaries, a
pensioner, and a retail store supervisor. The letters expressed grief ("it
hurt when he died"), praise ("there was never anyone greater"), identity
("we had the same type of childhood"), but mostly the fans wrote about
feelings of shared experiences through his music and his movies. One
writer had seen Elvis perform in Las Vegas; another recalled the importance of Elvis in giving teenagers a sense of identity. A thirty-year-old
factory worker from Malmo, a city in the South near Denmark, said
membership in the fan club had changed his entire life. "I was personally
rather reserved," he wrote, "but the activity ... helped bring out other
parts of myself. It gave me pen friends around the world. Thanks to Elvis
and the fan clubs, I evolved into the person I am today."

That same feeling of identity with Elvis, shared by many of
Sweden's population, was analyzed in depth in an *Aftonbladet* article by
Sven Lindberg. He recounted what Elvis meant to those growing up in
Stockholm's working-class suburb of Hökarangen during the fifties. He
described Elvis as *"polaren,"* a word that has no direct English
equivalent, meaning more than a friend, possibly akin to the American
idiom, "soul brother." Elvis served, wrote Lindberg, as a role model for
the Hokarangen youth who turned to motorcycles, gangs, and rock
music—ideas from America—as release from the boredom of factory
life. In spite of his "big pile of money," he remained one of the guys. With
some sort of talent or ability, one could dream and be like Elvis. If you
succeeded, you got respect for yourself and money for you and your
friends. And you could get away from the completely empty and
meaningless lives everyone else accepted.

Lindberg recalled that at one time he had looked up to Elvis and
wanted to be like him. "Today," he concluded, "I still look at him with a
friend's love," even though Elvis had landed on "that damned carousel"
of fame, liquor, drugs, and sex. "The bastards at the top used him and
drove him to an early death. He has been robbed and cheated. His life

will be revenged. So long Elvis. You did what most of us would have done. And that makes me sort of cry."

This theme of Elvis as victim of the American system received even harsher treatment in other parts of the Swedish press, but several writers also criticized the Swedish establishment for failing to give Elvis his due or for failure to appreciate Elvis's contributions earlier.

The most prominent example was a weekend think-piece in *Expressen*, by Sten Berglind, asking why Program 3, the state radio network that features pop music, had played no Elvis records on the day of his death. "Were they afraid?" he asked. He also questioned the mayors and ministers who were making favorable comments now that Elvis was dead and reminded his readers of their attitudes in the fifties toward "this vulgar country singer."

Berglind used a stream-of-consciousness style in his article, *"Vagen Till Memphis"* ("On the way to Memphis"). Using the first person, he described a drive along suburban highways catching images of the past in the flashing lights of passing cars and nearby towns. He was particularly incensed by the recurring question, "Why do you like Elvis?" His reply:

"I wonder what they think you should answer. You usually answer that Elvis did everything better than all the stupid jerks; that instead of all the pop and punk and all that stuff, it's just blaha-blaha; that Mick Jagger could never sing 'Jailhouse Rock'; something like that.

"If you try to explain what it's all about, what it's really all about, there's really no point in ever trying. You either know as you hear it or you just don't get it and you're never going to." Later, in a book on Elvis written along these same lines, Berglind lamented, "Now they will put Elvis in the parlor and make culture out of him."

New Day, the nation's Communist weekly, printed a full page essay by music critic Tommy Rander, who called Elvis the epitome of the American dream, a career that combined marketing, economics, and talent. But his emphasis was on Elvis as "the dark side" of the American dream, one who had done everything by the time he was twenty-five: "Nothing new happened, just the same, same old past. Meaninglessness, emptiness, escape, death."

The shift of Western economic and political power from Europe after World War II also affected the sources of film, music, fashion, radio, and television. During the fifties, these ideas and patterns of life originated almost exclusively in North America, wrote Rander, and Elvis was the symbol of the change. Presley discovered nothing new, but he was the right person at the right time in history—the first rock singer who was young, handsome, and backed with the millions of a major record company. And he happened to be good.

Rander called Elvis's early records "incredibly well done," a quality he attributed to the environment from which the singer sprang—the people's music of country, blues, and gospel. Then Elvis was placed in "the flat and stupid so-called culture" of Hollywood, sent to the Army, and remodeled into a family entertainer. With few exceptions, all music got artistically worse in the sixties, but there was no economic decline, wrote Rander, because record buyers increased. Even today, he added, rock music is used simply as a tranquilizer or a sports-hall spectacle, a flight from reality instead of a message to the world.

The critic contended that, whatever medical conclusions were reached in Memphis, Elvis died of boredom and the pain of nothing to do. He suggested that Elvis should have gone back to driving a truck. By so doing, he would have felt better and his music would have improved as well.

The whole society never really accepted rock music, Rander concluded, because when it is played right, it is too vulgar. "Any music that is called vulgar," he said, "is always worth investigating."

In France, logic and language sometimes dominate reporting more than facts. The details of an event may not be so important there as its meaning. The only "facts" presented may be those in the headline, and the only unpardonable sin is to be tedious. Thus the French reporter entwines the reader in his story and conveys the news by making the reader conceive the event in his or her own mind. Nowhere is this style more evident than in the reporting of an emotional event such as the death of a popular hero.

The dominant Parisian afternoon daily, *Le Monde*, is one of the few consistently profitable French papers. With a steady circulation of about half a million, many of them professionals, government officials, and intellectuals, *Le Monde* rarely prints photos. This, plus its tightly packed columns, makes it appear almost totally gray in color even from a short distance away. It is not written to catch the eye but to hold the mind with endless twists of argument.

The death of Elvis Presley, however, rated a picture. After a first-page story on "*La Mort D'Elvis Presley: Le Demon du rock,*" an inside page displayed a cartoon illustration. Some criticize *Le Monde* for a "leftist bias," and the cartoon flattered neither Elvis nor his fans. It showed a crowd of persons waving money and rushing toward a funeral hearse. The corpse, surrounded by American dollars, had risen from its coffin (labeled "*Le Mythe*") and was selling records.

While *Le Monde* was more direct than most, it was not alone in remarking on the role of money and capitalism in the life and image of Elvis Presley. Before World War II, much of the French press was owned, controlled, or supported by industries or wealthy patriarchs either as a hobby or a special interest. In 1977, *L'Aurore*, with a circulation in Paris of more than a quarter of a million, was owned by Marcel Boussac, octogenarian, cotton magnate, and the last of the old newspaper patriarchs. *L'Aurore*, pro-Western and anti-Communist, called Elvis Presley *"L'idole qui venait du show"* ("The idol created by show business").

Two popular French papers focused not on the role of capitalism but on the role of drugs in Elvis's death. *Le Parisien*, one of the few Paris dailies with a large circulation outside the capital, published a story entitled *"Les Medicaments Amaigrissants"* ("Diet Pills"), concluding in red-inked, title-size type: *"Ont-ils tue le roi du rock?"* ("Did they kill the King of Rock?") Along the left side of the story was a picture of the lean and lithe Presley of the fifties. On the right side was a picture of the older, heavier Presley of the seventies.

Meanwhile, *France-Soir*, which used dazzling picture and headline layouts even before World War II, splashed its front page with two photographs of Elvis and five separate headlines. Three of them dealt directly with Elvis's failing health: First came *"Elvis Presley est mort— pour avoir voulu maigrir"* ("Elvis Presley is dead—trying to lose weight"). Following this was *"Foudroyé à 42 ans parce que son coeur n'a pas tenu"* ("Struck down at 42 because his heart gave out"). Beneath the pictures came *"Entre l'Elvis des années et celui de son dernier recital a Las Vegas, des millions de disques, et des kilos en plus"* ("Between the Elvis of years ago and the one of his last concert in Las Vegas, millions of records and many added pounds"). The inside stories continued the theme. An analysis by Marie-Claude Dubin said, in effect, that "the drugs to lose weight could have killed him." A French specialist in cures for obesity was consulted for the story.

Le Figaro, the respected moderate-conservative Parisian daily published since 1828, decided to praise the King as well as to bury him. A

homecoming triumph greets Elvis at the Mississippi-Alabama Fair and Dairy Show in
pelo, Mississippi, in 1956.

The off-duty soldier in the home he rented in Killeen, Texas, while stationed at Fort Hood.

Photo courtesy of Eddie Fadal

A young Elvis of happier times, browsing in a Memphis record store, where his albums were the pacesetters for the new rock and roll market.

Jimmy and Rosalyn Carter join the entertainer backstage at the Omni, in Atlanta, 1973.

Elvis in a familiar pose, the photo selected by *The Commercial Appeal* for Page One of its editions on the morning after he died

Cameramen vie with grieving fans for position outside the famous gates in front of Graceland, where the entertainer's body lay in repose.

The copper coffin with the body of Elvis Presley is borne past thousands of floral tributes into the mausoleum in Forest Hill Cemetery.

Photo by The Commercial Appeal

Photo by Ken Davidson

Photo by Larry J. Coyne, *Memphis Press-Scimitar*

The Elvis Presley Memorial Chapel and the entertainer's birthplace in Tupelo, Mississippi.

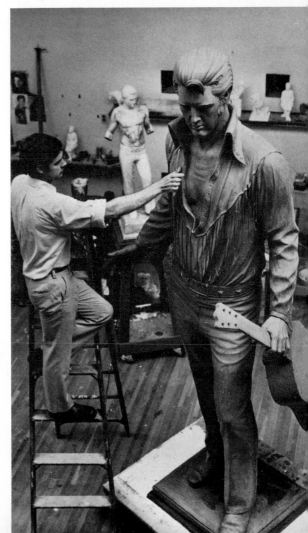

Sculptor Eric Parks and a model of the statue of Elvis planned for a park downtown Memphis.

Photo by Ray Lustig, *The Washington Sta*

commentary by Jean de Wachhausen concludes:

> The electric guitars are still. The death of Elvis Presley cannot be just a banal, historic moment where an idol got too old too quickly, used up by an easy life, ravaged by success. Rather, he has left behind the profiled image of a grand king, lost, alone, plunged into the days that were too long amidst his souvenirs and who, if he had stayed, would surely have been recognized as one of the greatest singers of his generation.
>
> Kings never die, and even though he was only called a king, he has done nothing more than cross over beyond the footlights.

The French press historically has been sectarian and opinionated. In 1946 there were twenty-eight Parisian dailies with a circulation of five million, and one hundred seventy-five provincial papers with a circulation of nine million. They reflected the fragmentation of French society. By 1980 there were less than half as many papers, and circulation was down to three million in Paris and a little more than seven million in the provinces. Most of the old media fiefdoms have disappeared, and new, more modern ones took their place in paris and the provinces. But some aspects of the general style of the French press remained, and most of the French papers conveyed a definite viewpoint on Presley. They viewed his life and the money surrounding him with some distaste; they probed with alarm his worsening health; or they praised him. Only the extensive extreme-left French press seemed at a loss about how to judge him. Clearly they were torn between condemnation of his patriotism and capitalism and admiration for the simple fact that he had revolutionized the world. Some examples of their comments illustrate this ambivalence.

Liberation wrote:

> Elvis is stll the symbol of rock despite the torrents of fluff that he didn't prevent from enveloping him. Moreover, America will profit very quickly from her hero. And, consciously or not, she will make use of his image to seduce millions of young people all over the world, especially the Far East. Moreover, consecrating this fact, Warhol will choose him as one of the symbols of America, with Marilyn Monroe, the Coke bottle and the tin of Campbell's soup. Elvis—man/object? Was rock only a pretext, like the films for Marilyn? Could he have existed on his own? Or only by simple exposure by the media?

Rouge commented:

> How not to recall that, like so many girls and boys my age, I had been a fan set free by the King. How to explain to younger pals who listened with

amazement, yesterday, to our passion for this bloated, warped singer? Before becoming the first big product of American "show biz," before giving us honeyed melodies, Elvis *was* rock and roll.

And *Le Matin* paid homage:

> The rock phenomenon that we've known for 20 years owes it all to him. The politicizing of American campuses during the '60s got its start among lax American youth made plastic and receptive by attitudes he made popular. Elvis Presley—loving and respectful son, solidly "establishment," who became, in the final years of his career, the idol of happy families—had incontestably "paved the road" for many rebels that the whole world knows today.

The granddaddy of the French left press, *L'Humanité*, the official Communist paper in Paris since 1904, with a daily circulation of more than two hundred thousand, faced the same problem. Its Sunday magazine *Humanité Dimanche* carried a story in its cultural section with a fantastic drawing of Elvis, in boxing shorts, kneeling before an altar surrounded by Hollywood make-up lights. But the report is largely autobiographical, depicting the impact of Elvis on French youth. The writer, Jean Rouah, recalled the sense of loss and undirected anger youth felt at the death of James Dean, and the revival of spirit with the introduction of Bill Haley. "We had just arrived at our youth," he says, "but we had no god. Then he arrived. His name was Elvis Presley." He recounts the inadequacy of the music adults sang, which was pretty, and said they loved life and everything about it. Instead, Elvis's music became a "liberator of the heart." By dressing to look like Elvis, "You could steal from an idol a little bit of his prestige and be loved in his place." Then came the dancing, where the cadence "liberated our bodies."

When Elvis entered the military, "in the USA a general was President; in France, a general had taken power; all was in order."

Time passed. The war in Algeria ended. Elvis arrived in films with short hair which convinced mothers their daughters were safe. And, "our prince slept," through the Beatles, the Stones, and Bob Dylan, whom the author calls "nothing more than braggarts."

In 1968, wrote Rouah, "History grabbed us by the ears." American youth confronted Vietnam, and Elvis returned—but changed. With his dried-up hair and white suit, the singer was "a hippy of luxury. America was drowning in Watergate and Vietnam," he said, "but Elvis sang 'American Trilogy.' "

13

The Special Case of Britain

He never came. Almost every citizen of England who had heard of Elvis Presley knew that.

England is headquarters for the thirty-five thousand member International Elvis Fan Club. British fans have easily been among the most dedicated and fervent in the world. From 1956 to his death, Elvis's songs had registered on the British charts of top songs for one thousand weeks. Fifty songs had made the top ten; sixteen songs had been number one. Even the Beatles surpassed Elvis in only one category by having a total of seventeen number one songs. But Elvis never performed in Britain. Persistent rumors that, at the time of his death, Elvis had been actively planning to come to England only imbedded his loss deeper in the British mind.

More than a year after Elvis's death, people gathered at the American Church in London, a small church on Tottenham Court Road near the British Museum, to listen to Elvis recordings of Christmas carols, offer a few prayers, hear a few remarks, and take up a collection for charity in Elvis's name. Afterward, in an interview, the church pastor, the Reverend Warren L. Danskin, like many educated people, seemed at pains to explain why he was involved in his second Elvis worship service.

"A group of fans came to me and asked," he said, "and their grief was real."

The grief and the sense of loss in England were real—so real that the BBC interrupted its evening programming to announce Elvis's death, an honor usually accorded only to heads of state; so real that *The Times* accorded Elvis front page coverage two days running, an extensive obituary, several features, and an editorial.

From the beginning, the impact of Elvis upon Britain was somewhat different from his role in American society and music. While the United States was booming, post-war Britain in the mid-fifties still struggled to recover.

British commercial television broadcast programs depicting this new America to viewers in the United Kingdom beginning in 1955. ITV brought *Dragnet, Highway Patrol*, and many other programs of that era to the British small screen. Television showed American youngsters parking their own cars in the school yard. Magazines used as ballast on ships arrived with advertisements for all kinds of luxuries rich Americans could buy.

When Elvis Presley burst upon the scene he was, to England, "the arrival of the American dream." That, at least, was the opinion of Todd Slaughter, secretary of the International Elvis Presley Fan Club. He probably was right on target.

Elvis was a "rags to riches" success story—proof that someone from a poor family could succeed in the post-war world. He was free. His vibrant, irreverent music broke through the silent, mushroom-clouded threats of the increasingly tense Cold War era—proof that people could still enjoy life in the nuclear age. He was young, new, and different—a voice for those whose memories of "The War" already were distant childhood images. He was rebellious—a tangible symbol that no one needed to accept the world on its own terms but on whatever terms the listener chose. These qualities stirred deep, responsive chords in young Britons in the mid-fifties. Explaining why those chords vibrated for so long and with such resonance is difficult.

Much of Elvis's impact probably came from the joyous release his early records conveyed; all else may have been relatively superfluous. His initial impact alone would have been enough to enshrine him for an entire generation.

Zigzag, a tabloid for young British rock fans, still felt Presley's impact even though its first article on him was an obituary long removed from those "dim and distant days" when Elvis first made his mark: "*Zigzag's* only eight years old and Elvis hasn't had anything to do with rock 'n'roll for well over a decade, so we've never carried an article on him," explained the paper's editors. "But 20 years ago he was going through worse shit from parents then the so-called Punk Bands are now."

Elvis was never a fake. Over time his songs became more respectable and less rebellious, but his music came from his knees, his personality, and his heart whether he was singing "That's All Right (Mama)" or "How Great Thou Art."

Taking a more sociological view, as England assumed a lesser role in the post-war world, and America's power increased, Elvis's music was a way to take part in the new world order and in the new American power. This situation lasted for a decade, when the Beatles put England back in the lead in popular music. But the Beatles came, made their mark, and disbanded. Elvis remained, through it all. When Elvis died, John Lennon recalled that he was their inspiration, the one who started the unkempt quartet on its road to fame.

The reaction in Britain to Elvis's death not only was deep and genuine, but enhanced by a "natural media event." While American press focused on the details of the funeral, British media could report both the events in Memphis as well as local reaction. Several memorial services were conducted in Britain. Perhaps the largest was at Christ Church in Cockfosters, a working-class neighborhood at the northeast end of the Piccadilly line of the London underground. Mrs. Caroline Zetland, secretary of the North London branch of the fan club, had mentioned the service on television the night before. So many came that a second service was scheduled later. "Memphis and Cockfosters were as one yesterday— united in grief," reported Frances Kenley in *The Guardian.* Later, other services would take place, such as the ones at the American Church in central London and a Christmas tribute to Elvis at St. Johns Church, Peckham, which filled the sanctuary and produced a contribution to the Elvis Presley Heart Fund at St. Thomas's Hospital in London.

In August 1977, the local story was stretched out through the weekend because of a major event for Presley fans. Each year the International Fan Club organized a convention where members mingled with fellow Elvis fans, watched old Elvis movies, and generally entertained themselves. In 1977 the annual convention was scheduled to take place in Nottingham on August 20, the very weekend after Elvis died. The anticipated joyous event turned into a wake.

Elvis wore a ring with a lightning flash and the letters "TCB" imprinted upon it. It meant "Taking Care of Business—in a flash." The letters "TCE"—Taking Care of Elvis—with a lightning flash jolting the "C" out of line is the symbol of the "Official Elvis Presley Fan Club World Wide." This organization has existed for twenty-four years. Todd Slaughter, head of the club since August 16, 1967, *exactly* ten years before Elvis's death, described it this way in a hastily compiled biography published by the *Daily Mirror* shortly after Presley's death:

> The Official Elvis Presley Fan Club of Great Britain and the Commonwealth is the world's largest Presley fan club. With a membership figure in excess of 12,000 the club recently celebrated its 21st Birthday.
>
> Each new member receives a membership card, an introductory letter and a fan club magazine packed with news and pictures about Elvis Presley, the fan club, its activities, special offers, and members' services. Magazines are despatched to members at regular two-monthly intervals. A comprehensive branch leader network operates throughout the UK, and during the year local branch secretaries stage regular get-togethers, parties, coach outings to fan club events and film specials.
>
> The British Fan Club has an active travel service. In recent years members have been taken to Belgium, Holland, France, Germany and Luxembourg for winter-break mini holiday promotions. The annual USA charter—a two week inclusive tour of the United States including Presley in concert—usually visits Nashville, Memphis, Tupelo, Las Vegas, Hollywood, Los Angeles and San Francisco.
>
> Nearer to home, the fan club organises film shows in major UK centres, and in the summer each year there's the Elvis Convention. Attracting over 2,000 fans, this special show is organised in aid of the Guide Dogs for the Blind Association.

The club was founded by Albert Hand. He began with a small magazine called *Elvis Monthly*, devoted totally to Elvis, with almost all the articles contributed by readers, and still readily found on British newsstands in 1980.

Hand wanted to sell Elvis records, but to do so he had to buy a retail outlet. With a partner, he began to operate a chiefly mail-order service housed in the back half of a sporting goods store in Heanor, Derbyshire. Its modest housing is deceptive. The mail-order business has been brisk, not only from regular sales but also because the club staff would try to find a copy of any Elvis record a fan might want.

The Heanor shop has sold mostly records and books. Down the road, a shop in the more accessible city of Leicester has peddled bric-a-brac and souvenirs. From the Heanor shop also comes the T.C.E. official fan club magazine. A two pound subscription makes any fan a member.

Members of the fan club range "from a dustman to a member of the national symphony," and it has grown. At the time of Elvis's death, Slaughter estimated membership at twelve thousand. In August 1979, he said it was thirty-five thousand. Slaughter, an engineer by training, had to devote full time to the fan club, with at least one assistant.

Clearly, the shock of Elvis's death and the publicity the fan club received from the British media which flocked to interview the local Elvis authority, Todd Slaughter, moved a substantial number of British citizens to perpetuate Elvis's role in their lives through membership in the club. A surprising number are not simply perpetuating an old influence, however. In 1979, Slaughter estimated that sixty percent of the club's new subscribers were under the age of sixteen. The majority of the rest were over twenty-five. Only the group between those ages, caught up in newer popular styles, was missing.

Whatever their ages, they gathered at the Palais de Danse, Nottingham, on the weekend of August 20, 1977. One thousand tickets were sold out a month before the gathering and those who had them attended. Those who did not listened to Elvis music piped outside. The film, *Love Me Tender*, a melodrama of life after the War Between the States, was one of the scheduled attractions. But Elvis dies in it, and the film was not shown because the convention leaders feared the effect of seeing Elvis die on the screen might have been catastrophic for the grieving fans. Ambulances and first aid squads already were busy, treating at least eighteen people soon after the meeting began. Some fans had not eaten since Elvis died. Most were in somber attire, but one sobbing woman had stitched the words, "Elvis Still Lives," in sequins on her blouse.

The biggest applause at the convention came after Slaughter read a message from highly popular British disc jockey Jimmy Saville attacking the "load of crap in the press this week," referring to reports that drug abuse contributed to Elvis's death.

Roy Hollingsworth tried to capture the spirit at Nottingham in an article in *Melody Maker:*

> When we got there the Palais looked all askew and adrift. The neon was out and there was nothing to celebrate. But there were loads of people all around ...
> Most of them were dusty and stale and full of dandruff. It seemed as though they had nowhere to go anymore.
> Elvis was dead. And loads of these miners and technicians and fitters, and just honest fellas who'd built and modeled their whole existence on

Presley, were dead, too.

But he wasn't . . .

Leslie Priestly and Dennis Raymond are big, tough-looking Teds from Southhampton way who look like they had raw meat and whiskey for breakfast. But Les, in a curiously strange voice for a big fella, says, "I was all choked up. He gave me life. But I'll carry on because he ain't dead. God don't die."

Hollingsworth likened the event to "seeing the remnants of Napoleon's all-conquering army coming home from Moscow, knowing that it had all gone wrong. These troops suddenly had nothing to do." Nothing, that is, except mourn and answer questions from the press. "The press are all here asking ridiculous questions, which they always do," said Hollingsworth, "and these people of this defeated army still somehow have the balls to answer them."

Later, the members of the fan club would find plenty to do. They would continue their gatherings. About twenty-five hundred attend the annual conventions. And several hundred each year take a memorial trip—to visit the grave in Memphis and the birthplace in Tupelo, then tour through Disney World, Washington, D.C., New Orleans, or other American attractions. Admiration for Presley is only a common meeting ground for fan club members, who enjoy a lively social life in the club. Todd Slaughter attempted to explain this in the September 1977 issue of *Elvis Monthly*:

> To me personally, the greatest thing about Elvis was his world-wide influence amongst his fans—an influence that seems to have fostered and cemented thousands of friendships. I have never failed to wonder at the atmosphere of goodwill which prevailed wherever his admirers gathered . . . To me and to the charities which have benefitted from this spirit of goodwill and brotherhood, this is the most wonderful thing about Elvis, transcending even his unchallenged lead in the world of entertainment and his talents which have brought pleasure to millions of people throughout the world.

But in those first hectic days after the singer's death, dealing with the press consumed much of the club's time—especially that of its head, Todd Slaughter. "When I arrived in Nottingham on Saturday," Slaughter said, "I was met by some sixty newspaper reporters, photographers, and film crews from the BBC, ITV, and Belgian television. I had previously put off the American CBS, ABC, and NBC networks, plus a team which had just arrived from Brazil. But Canadian radio was already set up to record the highlights."

Some press reports remark that television and radio were barred from the Nottingham meeting in order to protect the privacy of the grieving fans. Actually, Todd Slaughter would have welcomed the media. But the Palais is owned by Eric Morely's Mecca Properties, sponsors of the Miss World Contest, and it was the policy of the owners which barred the press. Journalists were admitted if they had tickets. Radio came in through the back door. The TV crews lined up across the road. It was one more episode in twenty-four-hour coverage that had descended on Slaughter moments after news of Elvis's death reached the United Kingdom.

The first bulletin came at 9:29 p.m. in London, just as Reginald Bosanque was ending his half-hour late evening news broadcast on ITV, the independent commercial television network that links the non-BBC stations for special programming.

London was undergoing one of the worst thunderstorms in a long time. Raising his hand to the ear-piece and pausing momentarily, Bosanque announced "I have just been informed that Mr. Elvis Presley has died in Memphis, Tennessee." It was barely thirty minutes after the official announcement had been made at Baptist Memorial Hospital in Memphis. Some in England already knew the news, and one called Todd Slaughter moments before. The General Post Office worked to keep phone lines open to Slaughter's home as calls began pouring in from all over the world.

By three-thirty the next morning, a crew of the Independent Broadcasting Authority set up shop in Slaughter's living room. At six o'clock he was interviewed by the BBC in Leicester, then in Birmingham, then by ATV satellite to Brazil.

Slaughter's first BBC interview, by Nigel Rees, appeared on the *Today* show, where Presley's death was the lead story.

"The King is dead and there is no one who could possibly replace Elvis Presley as the king of rock and roll," said Rees. "A show biz superstar, a carefully contrived legend, a gift to the impressionists—but how and why did he achieve his unique position?" Rees also lamented Presley's failure to appear in Britain and interviewed Paul Gambacini, a popular disc jockey.

The next day, the BBC was back in Leicester for further explanation of the wake. Gambacini said, "It isn't that Elvis Presley died this week that seems unbelievable. It's that Elvis Presley *could* die."

BBC radio logs indicate that fifty-seven separate news spots on Presley were broadcast the next four days, including local reaction throughout the United Kingdom as well as feeds from correspondents in the United States.

But while the BBC, like other media, was desperately searching for any and all Presley material to fill air time, Radio 1 refused to play "My Way" because its lyrics imply death ("... as I approach the final curtain.") A new single, "Unchained Melody" backed by "Softly As I Leave You" also was shunned by British RCA and broadcasters.

Gambicini's weekly show, *Rock On*, featured a full tribute to Presley on Friday. He distinguished between Presley and other popular singers: "There have been other singers in this country who enjoyed as much fame as Elvis... certainly Sinatra, most definitely Crosby, perhaps Jolson. The *Guinness Book of World Records* even claims that Crosby has outsold Elvis. But those other singers were products of eras that were already under way. Presley was the catalyst who brought an entire era into being. It was nice that Bing and Frank existed. It was necessary that Elvis Presley existed for the youth revolution to sweep America and the world."

Beginning on October 9, Radio 1 also broadcast a thirteen-part series, *The Elvis Presley Story*, written by Jerry Hopkins and narrated by Wink Martindale. Thames television aired a tribute on August 17. Foreshadowing the durability of the Elvis phenomenon which continued for years after his death, the BBC ran twelve Elvis movies during the Christmas season, showing the films every morning December 22 to January 4 except Christmas and New Year's Eve. A notice in *Elvis Monthly* reminded fans to write and thank the BBC for this scheduling.

The lofty London *Times*, whose learned pages led a nation and lent a certain social standing to its readers since 1785, kept a respectable distance from the grief and shock of the Elvis fans. Although the editors of *The Times* gave front page space and substantial coverage to the event, it was not the leading story. On August 17, a large picture featured President Tito of Yugoslavia visiting Moscow and the largest headline concerned industrial actions disrupting flights at London's huge Heathrow airport.

Like other elite papers such as *The New York Times*, the stories referred to *Mr.* Elvis Presley as the King of rock and roll *music*, a correctness of style that would seem redundant in the popular press. *The Times*, too, seemed unsure whether to acknowledge this "Mr. Presley," but upheld its reputation for thorough reporting by giving the story full play.

On August 17, *The Times* devoted about ten inches of front page space to Presley, relying on its correspondent in New York, Michael Leapman. In addition, it awarded Presley an obituary almost two full columns long. The Leapman story, headlined "Elvis Presley dies in hospital, aged 42," was mundane, recalling the early days—the nickname "Elvis the Pelvis," the greased hair, sideburns, and sneer, and limiting the reports of the more recent events in Elvis's life to his health problems. The obituary was straightforward both in its acknowledgement of Presley as significant and in its clear distaste for the man, his music, and his revolution. The paper identified Presley's recordings of "Blue Suede Shoes," "Hound Dog," and "Heartbreak Hotel" as establishing rock and roll's "otherwise fitful claim to be a 20th century art form." *The Times* said that the details concerning Presley are "irrelevant in the immensity of his legend." The paper termed the American preoccupation in the fifties with teenagers a scandal, saying that Elvis was the "embodiment of its rebellion and uncleanliness." *The Times* story recognized, however, the importance of Memphis, Tennessee, as a meeting ground for vital musical cultures and Elvis as the one who blended them and touched off a social explosion. The obituary traced his career and his resumption of command of the rock field by the time he was forty-years-old. Finally, it noted the impact that Elvis's failure to come to Britain had on the nation: "That he never visited England was felt by many to be a betrayal of his most faithful audience; to others it was part of his incalculable fascination." The column concluded: "Merely by innuendo, he is assured of his place in history."

Second day coverage in *The Times* began with what most non-American newspapers recognized as the most significant development—the statement on Presley made by the President of the United States. This appeared on page one, with updates from Michael Leapman on the masses gathering in Memphis and a Peter Godfrey interview with Todd Slaughter shunted to an inside page.

But *The Times* took one other significant step on August 18. It published a leading article (or editorial) on Presley. Entitled "A Singer of Social Significance," this exposition of the official views of *The Times* editors hewed closely to the lines of the obituary the day before, emphasizing the social revolution Presley helped to generate.

The Times' aloofness did not go unchallenged. A few days later, on August 20, the paper printed a letter from Tim Rice of Wardour Street which asked, "which popular singers do you consider superior? Or are you unwilling to admit that any popular singers have any merit what-soever?" True to form, *The Times* provided no further identification of the writer, although Tim Rice was imminently qualified to respond to the newspaper's comments. With composer Andrew Lloyd Webber, the thirty-three-year-old lyricist wrote the hit rock musical, *Jesus Christ Superstar*, and had just co-authored the *Guinness Book of British Hit Singles*, a 1977 work that documented Presley's appeal in England. "I am glad," Rice added in his letter, "that President Carter has also paid tribute to this extraordinary entertainer."

A voice spoke for the other side when Owen W. Jaques of Cornwall asserted it was "difficult to understand how the President of the United States of America can pay tribute to a man who caused many parents distress."

Perhaps the most meaningful statement came from Mrs. Joel Hurstfield of Hampstead. She wrote: "Sir, In 1956, the year when Elvis Presley's extraordinary talent burst upon the world, I started to teach in a large mixed comprehensive school in northwest London. I shall never forget the elderly senior mistress coming into the staff room one morning and saying sternly, 'I must speak to a boy called Elvis Presley because he has carved his name on every desk in the school.' "

The Times coverage continued for the third day when pictures and stories appeared concerning both the funeral in Memphis and the memorial service held in the London working class neighborhood of Cockfosters. The articles appeared on an inside page but received mention in the front page summary.

The Times was one of the few papers to note, even indirectly, the economic impact Presley had made on the popular music business over the years. A report in the paper's "Business Diary" on the 19th noted that Bloomsbury was hosting a four-day British Musical Instruments Trade Fair, and the *Music Trades International Daily* circulating there recognized the debt of popular music business to Presley under the heading "the death of a salesman." London's influential *Financial Times*, a possible forum for an article on the economic impact of Presley, did not publish August 5 through August 23, 1977, due to an industrial dispute, and made no mention of the event in a recap of recent news published August 26. *The Economist* in its August 20, 1977, issue, did note

Presley's passing in a boxed story, "The 1950s are dead." In an oblique reference to his economic impact, the story noted Presley's record sales, reputedly ahead of the Beatles, and Presley's staying power: "Rich, reclusive, he was plagued by overweight, but escaped burning himself out in his 20s as many who followed him were to do."

The Times ended its coverage of Elvis's death with a brief story on August 22 about sightseers around the grave and a picture a month later, of American sculptor Eric Parks and his model for a fifty-ton bronze statue of Presley to be set on a river bluff in Memphis.

By Sunday, the newspapers were writing about the deaths of two famous personalities as veteran comedian Groucho Marx had died on Friday, August 19. While the death of Groucho was more recent, commentary about Elvis dominated the coverage. *The Sunday Times*, with a circulation of 1.4 million, nearly five times that of its daily counterpart, carried a second page story on the Elvis meeting at Nottingham and a long Presley analysis in its 'Weekly Review." The stories clearly were aimed at a wider audience than that of the daily *Times*. A column was headlined "Elvis: A Prisoner of Fame." This was set off by an eleven-inch Presley photo captioned, "What must it have been like for him? Thomas McNamee describes the besieged life of the King of Rock and Roll." McNamee was an excellent choice for this detailed analysis. Born in 1947 in Memphis, he grew up within a mile of Presley's home. He wrote from his own experience about the impact Presley made in his own country, of the "raw, free, cocky" music which drew on "the incantatory potency of its deep black roots" at a time when "the Negroes were suddenly part of everything" and which "summoned up lush fantasies of teen-age sex." "The response," he said, "was quick and violent: wherever Elvis appeared, people just went crazy." McNamee chronicled Elvis through his 1968 comeback, but said the real Elvis was the singer who made popular culture dangerous in the fifties. "Elvis is dead," he concluded.

Interest in Elvis was not so dead, however, to prevent *The Sunday Times* from publishing a full color souvenir issue of its "Magazine" on September 11 featuring the singer, calling readers' attention to it with a photo and a note concerning the publication on the top corner of the front page. The special section included numerous pictures of the singer and a reprint, entitled "The King Is Dead: The Legend Lives," of a comprehensive 1977 *Rolling Stone* article on Presley by Peter Guralnick.

The Guardian and the *Daily Telegraph* also are leading London daily newspapers. Both covered the Presley story in their own style. Like

The Times, the *Telegraph* provided front page, but not lead, coverage to Presley's death on August 17. Unlike *The Times*, this Fleet Street product, with a circulation of 1.3 million, stressed both the rumors about a drug-related death and the religious heritage of Presley.

On that first day, the *Telegraph* relied on stories filed by its Washington, D.C., correspondent Stephen Barber, who was clearly out of his element in covering the event. The *Telegraph* front page story, "Elvis Presley dies of 'overdose'" and a special obituary, "Choirboy Who Made It to Las Vegas," are replete with inaccuracies and unchecked assumptions.

The page one story said that Presley was "25 when he launched a new style in country rock singing." By then the singer had been in and out of the Army, and, for some observers, the revolution had come and gone. Barber also said, "Presley did not smoke or drink or even drive a car"—a grossly inaccurate statement since Presley's love affair with large automobiles was almost as well known as his music. In the obituary, Barber did write about the importance of Presley's early exposure to religious music but incorrectly portrayed Presley as a member of a choir. The obituary ended with an epilogue prophetically noting that "The death of Elvis Presley ... is likely to extend the legend he built around himself during his lifetime."

By the second day, August 18, Barber returned to political matters (namely, Judge Johnson's nomination to head the F.B.I.), and the *Telegraph* assigned Ann Morrow to report on Presley directly from Memphis. The story assumed more prominence when a large picture in the top center of the front page showed fans at the gates of Graceland with the headline "U.S. mourns Presley the lost rebel," and the paper included on page three a survey of Soviet coverage of the death filed by Moscow correspondent Richard Beeston.

On August 19, the *Telegraph* ran another page one picture similarly placed, showing the Presley funeral. The end of the caption guided the reader to another picture and story on page thirteen.

In her stories on August 18 and 19, Ann Morrow depicted, with some sense of drama, the grief flowing in Memphis. "The great gates of a house in the heart of blues country opened yesterday and women who were prettier 20 years ago went in to see Elvis Presley lying in his coffin," she began. The headline accompanying the funeral story, "Hound-Dog Wreath with Guitar of Roses for Presley," referred to the most expensive floral arrangement at the funeral, costing three hundred dollars, according to the *Telegraph*. Morrow, like many reporters on the scene, relied on rumor to report who was in Memphis for the funeral and erroneously listed Mrs. Jacqueline Onassis as a visiting dignitary, accompanying her daughter Caroline.

On August 19, the *Telegraph* also printed a report about the second memorial service held at Cockfosters after fans had filled the first service.

The paper offered a detailed review of Presley in its Sunday edition. There, on the Arts page, Peter Clayton wrote about "The man who was yesterday":

> "Like perhaps half the people I met on Wednesday, they had all invested some part of their lives in Elvis Presley, and his sudden death had hit them with a sense of shock and loss utterly incomprehensible to anyone not belonging to certain favoured age groups. But if you can imagine Rudolph Valentino, Marilyn Monroe, James Dean, Mario Lanza, Judy Garland, and Bix Beiderbecke all combined into one corporate super-tragistar, you will at least get some idea of his hold on those to whom he belonged. What has died is the adolescence of an entire generation. It's the memory of several million people's first intimation of freedom that was in the white hearse. It's a greater loss than anyone of the wrong age can realise."

Coverage in *The Guardian* really began on the second day, with a page one picture and story headed "Much more than a hound dog," from Jonathan Steele in Memphis. The story had been carried the day before only as a last-minute inclusion in the news-in-brief column on the front page. The Steele story referred to an "ineffable" *New York Times* headline of August 17 which termed Presley an "Object of adult ire in the 50's," and called President Jimmy Carter, "the second best known white Southerner of the post-war period." But Steele made the same mistake as others who assumed that because Presley had been poor he was considered "white trash."

The Guardian gave the most extensive second day coverage of the establishment' London press. The Jonathan Steele article was supplemented by an extensive history and analysis on the Arts page by Robert Denselow that was also reprinted in the *Manchester Guardian Weekly* on August 28. Denselow claimed that only Presley and Marilyn Monroe of the post-war American entertainers had acquired "truly mythical status." As though it were proof of this, he noted that Andy Warhol's best known two-dimensional pop art posters pictured Presley and Monroe. "He deserves to be remembered," Denselow wrote, "not for his unhappy private life or his recent patchy output, but for those exhilarating and extraordinary years before 1958, and a talent that remains as enigmatic and unknown as the man because it was never fully tested."

Following up the Steele and Denselow articles, *The Guardian* sent Martin Walker to cover local fan clubs and carried a leader (an editorial) which expressed well *The Guardian*'s world view. It likened the goings-on in Memphis to "a Roman chronicle of the death of Germanicus." The revulsion which *The Times* clearly felt for Presley as an individual was focused in *The Guardian* on the system and on mankind: "Many of the stars who die young are stars driven to drugs and breakdowns by the weight of their own successes and their inability to sustain it. There is something profoundly repugnant in the juxtaposition, within twenty-four hours, of a sick and troubled Presley collapsing alone in his Tennessee mansion and the three-ring circus of grief that at once follows his end ... it is the chill side of the warm heart of show business—a bilious glimpse of the entrails of humanity."

The Guardian continued full coverage of these "entrails," however, with more stories from Steele in Memphis as well as front page coverage on August 19 of the Cockfosters service in an article headed "Crying in the Chapel for Elvis" written by Frances Kenley. Editors highlighted this account by using a different, heavier typeface for the entire story than for other articles on the page.

Clive James, a writer for *The Observer*, an independent weekly published since 1971, was as well aware of the emotional idolatry surrounding the Presley funeral as the editors of *The Guardian*. After a recap of events, he put a sharp edge on the matter, however, and a different twist to Elvis and sex:

> As I write, hysterical pilgrims to Elvis's deathbed are running each other over. At the prospect of such drooling idolatry there might seem to be a good case for saying that Elvis Presley was never anything but a manufactured event. But only someone who has never danced could think that. It has nothing to do with your age—just with whether or not you feel music through your knees. The first Elvis Presley records set standards which subsequent rock singers might approach in different ways but never surpass, since Elvis had expressed the rhythm of pure happiness, and there is nothing more pure than pure. The talk about his sexual explicitness is accurate but beside the point. He wasn't saying that dancing should be like sex. He was saying that sex was like dancing.

After a front page story on the local angle of the Nottingham convention, Dave Gelly tackled for *The Observer* the inevitable question "Why Elvis was the King." He wrote, "Little Richard was more frantic, Jerry Lee

Lewis more dangerous, Buddy Holly more vulnerably lovable, and Chuck Berry infinitely more talented, but Elvis was the King. The reason," Gelly believed, "probably has as much to do with social history and mass psychology as with music. The cry of 'That's not proper singing, just a disgusting noise' has been heard at regular ten-year intervals since the end of the First World War. It represents a fear that something bigger than music is under attack." Gelly credited Elvis with the greatest of These upheavals.

While *The Observer* and all the other more reputable papers commented on the Presley phenomenon and mass psychology, the British popular press lived it. Tabloids like the *Daily Express*, with a circulation of two and a half million and the *Daily Mirror* and Rupert Murdoch's *The Sun*, with circulations of almost four million each, fairly screamed the story, the emotion, the loss, at readers and passersby alike.

A six-inch headline "ELVIS IS DEAD" and a picture consumed the entire front page of the *Daily Express* on August 17. By August 18, the *Express* offered a souvenir pullout in the center, and the front page covered the "Billion Dollar Wake" in Memphis.

The Sun wrote of "Homage to the King! Women Weep for Elvis," and the *Daily Mirror* covered the "Siege of Grief." *The Sun*, too, had a special pull-out section—and a contest: Complete in 25 words or less "I will remember Elvis because . . ." The winner would receive a set of records valued at ten pounds. *The Sun* also offered a poster for fifty pence. Demand was so heavy that the paper included a free picture in its August 30 issue while asking for patience while it filled the poster orders.

All assigned reporters on the spot in Memphis. One, Brian Vine, wrote for the *Daily Express* about going to Presley's funeral in a bus escorted by police outriders from the city's force. He called the event "symbolic of the frenzied burial of the King of Rock."

Generally, the popular press did not dwell on the rumors about drugs involved in Presley's death. They emphasized reports about grieving fans, the funeral itself, and a recapping of Presley's life, stressing his loneliness and isolation. All used numerous pictures.

Presley always spoke best to the working classes, and nowhere is this quality more apparent than in the working class press in Britain. The British tabloid is aimed squarely at the nation's large industrial working class. Such papers do not carry as much weight in a society like America, where upwardly mobile people often prefer not to think of themselves as part of a lower class. In Britain, however, workers often are cheekily proud of their station and their political influence, and they welcome publications designed specifically for them.

Some might call this style of writing a disgrace to the news profession. *The New Musical Express* took the popular press to task in an August 27, 1977, article, "A Matter of Taste—Presley's Death: The Media Aftermath." It noted that *The Sun* was the first to sharpen its quill, reporting Presley "could not stop stuffing himself full of stodgy foods" and recounting the temper tantrums of "the lonely fattie." The *Mirror* was the first to publish so-called "world exclusives" including an "inside story" on the "Drug Yearning that Dragged Down a Legend." *The New Musical Express* reserved its harshest criticism for the Sunday editions when, "the school of journalism which is a far deeper shade of yellow than mere jaundice burst forth its bile in an unprecedented exhibition of ghoulish sensationalism." The *Sunday Mirror* reported on "Elvis—His Idea of a Night Out was a Tour of the Undertakers." *The News of the World* reported "He Knew He Didn't Have Long to Go." And the *Sunday People* hit the "top of the Muck-o-Meter" with "Elvis Was my Lover—by Diana Dors" plus "The Elvis I Knew Was No Junkie" by Jimmie Saville.

A Tom Stoppard character presented a different view of British popular newspapers. In the Stoppard play *Night and Day*, middle-aged reporter Jacob Milne defended the tabloid with which he formerly had worked:

> People think that rubbish-journalism is produced by men of discrimination who are vaguely ashamed of trucking to the lowest taste. But it's not. It's produced by people doing their best work ... I started out like that ... I felt part of a privileged group, inside society and yet outside it, with a license to scourge it and a duty to defend it, night and day, the street of adventure, the fourth estate. And the thing is—I was dead right. That's what it was, and I *was* part of it because it's indivisible. Junk journalism is the evidence of a society that has got at least one thing right, that there should be nobody with the power to dictate where responsible journalism begins.

Australian Rupert Murdoch is the world's premier example of popular journalism. He defends his style as one which "puts the reader above all else." To those who accuse him of pandering to the lowest common denominator, Murdoch retorts, "The lowest common denominator doesn't have 35 cents." To those who would call popular journalism trash, he counters that "a press that fails to interest its whole community is one that will ultimately become a house organ of the elite, engaged in an increasingly private conversation."

Some media observers believe that this is precisely what is happening in American journalism, where the media want to impress advertisers with an upscale audience of heavy spenders and where journalists themselves are affluent. Advertising may amount to only about a tenth of the income of a Murdoch enterprise.

Few erudite phrases appear in the British tabloids and almost no social commentary; they are more like a mixture of a family album and a soap opera.

In the *Telegraph*, Peter Grieg made one contribution to the understanding of Presley:

> "The great American writer Scott Fitzgerald capsuled it all when he said, 'The rich are different.' The very rich are very different. The many multi-millions which Elvis Presley earned throughout his incredible career meant that he could never lead a normal life ... or normal death."

And finally, *The Times* of London, at the end of 1977, gave recognition to the personal impact of Presley's death:

> "It was a year of deaths that recalled mortality with a shock to generations not yet used to thinking of themselves in the front line: Tony Crosland, Robert Lowell, Maria Callas, Elvis Presley."

14

Seeking the Image

The reaction to Elvis's death was so personal among his dedicated as well as his casual fans that any attempt to imitate or capitalize on the singer could go sour as an attempt to exploit—almost rob—his grave. Yet no show business personality inspired so many imitators as Elvis, and the number grew after he died.

These were not simply mimics adding Elvis to their routine of impersonations; many made their living giving concerts, dressed in sequined jumpsuits, banging on a guitar, and singing the songs that Elvis had made famous. Some replicated the familiar baritone voice. Others mastered the karate chop hand motions and the wiggle of the hips that were Presley trademarks. All told their audiences they were not imitating Presley: they were offering a tribute.

Fans turned out in droves to see performers, to remember the magic of Elvis, to compare and note that none was as good as the original. In Las Vegas, Alan Meyer came on stage at the Tropicana and said, "Hello, ladies and gentlemen, I'm Alan." He asked for a moment of silence for the man who had died that afternoon, saying, "This man meant more to me than anyone who ever lived." The house lights dimmed, and spotlights faded; only countless cigarettes glowed in the dark. Moments later, Alan returned in a fire-red jumpsuit and launched his act of Elvis

184

music. In Longview, Washington, fans bought every seat in the four-hundred seat ballroom of the New Monticello Hotel as Johnny Rusk, who had imitated Elvis for five years, began his show. The hotel manager told the Associated Press the phone lines "went crazy" with reservation seekers after the news that afternoon from Memphis. Jesse King went before a standing-room-only audience at Big Daddy's Lounge in Tampa, Florida, with the announcement: "I'm going to dedicate this performance to the king."

Rick Saucedo, a twenty-one-year-old performer who was probably the best of the imitators, cancelled his Tuesday night show at Orrie's of Wheaton, Illinois. He told the *Chicago Sun-Times* he sat up all night "thinking." He resumed his act that weekend and later, backed by the Jordanaires, the quartet that had accompanied Elvis on many of his hit records, brought his show to Broadway for a brief run.

During the months after Elvis's death, other imitators headlined memorial concerts or special attractions. A Washington, D.C., promoter booked Saucedo and three other impressionists into the Capital Centre for a three-hour birthday tribute in January 1979. Ten thousand people attended. Delegations from Elvis fan clubs bought blocs of tickets, and one group presented the arena management with a bronze plaque noting the dates of Elvis's three concerts there.

In Memphis, a special concert benefitted Tammy Baiter, the young girl injured by a hit-and-run driver outside Graceland on the night before Elvis's funeral. Thirty-five hundred people attended to hear imitator Bill Haney. "I never studied his moves or tried to do a real imitation," Haney said. "I'm doing a created illusion so people can get a taste of something similar to an Elvis performance."

In England, Jack Good and Ray Cooney worried about the reaction of fans as they set about producing a play based on Elvis's life and music. "I thought we were going to have to put the whole thing off when Presley died," said Cooney. "It would look as though we were jumping on the bandwagon." London's *Daily Express* leveled such a charge at the effort, but the British interest in Elvis was so high, the pair decided to go ahead.

They hit the jackpot. "It's fantastic," said Todd Slaughter, head of the British fan club. "The fans are going to be very happy that this has happened first in England." *The Times* published a glowing review and *The Sunday Times* a good one. The play, titled *Elvis*, won the *Evening Standard* Drama Award as the best London musical of 1977. In its first year, three hundred fifty thousand people saw the show, and it grossed one million pounds.

In the West End of London, world-renowned for its many theaters, playgoers can see the cream of English-language drama at reasonable prices—usually long before other cities offer them. Many different theaters play to Londoners, tourists, and shoppers from all over Britain, and to some two million foreign visitors a year. During the 1977-78 season, only one West End play advertised with a large, flashing neon sign. It was at the newly reopened Astoria Theater on Charing Cross Road, and the play was *Elvis.*

Opening November 28, 1977, the play was designed as a multi-media technical triumph, fashioned along the lines of Jack Good's *Beatlemania.* It told the Presley story through song, not dialogue—more than seventy songs in all—with a backdrop of news reels, clips from movies, slides, and blow-up photographs. Even balloons were released into the audience at one high point in the production. Enormous screens used in the show measured forty by twenty feet, the largest ever designed as permanent sets for a stage production. Twelve projectors gave front and back projections of still photographs, and two other projectors showed thirty minutes of such diverse film clips as Queen Mary and George V at their Silver Jubilee in 1935 (the year of Elvis's birth), the first moon landing, and Elvis in the Army. Onstage musicians and a sophisticated sound system reproduced diverse musical styles ranging from the early simple Elvis tunes to his complex Las Vegas productions.

The title role was portrayed by three actors appearing not in sequence but at appropriate points in the play. Frequently all three appeared on stage at the same time. Roughly parallelling the three decades spanned by the entertainer's life, the three actors portrayed the young singer of the Sun Record days, the Elvis of the first RCA records and the movies, and the entertainer from the Las Vegas years.

Ray Cooney was anxious to cast the play in Britain, "because the Americans say we won't find the talent here." The players changed over time, but the first three included Timothy Whitnall, just sixteen-years-old, as the young Elvis; Shakin' Stevens in the middle slot; and James (P.J.) Proby as the Vegas superstar. It was Whitnall's first venture on the stage; before the play, he did Elvis impressions only for family and friends. Like many others, Whitnall heard about auditions for the play during a Jack Good interview on the BBC's "Start the Week" program. In appearance, the young singer more closely resembled the young Ricky

Nelson, but he clearly conveyed the youthful exhuberant rebellion associated with Presley.

Shakin' Stevens, son of a Welsh miner, had been in the music field for several years as a singer with a local group, the Sunsets, which had enjoyed some success in the European rock'n'roll market. Stevens expertly aped the knee-flapping, toe-dancing gyrations of Presley.

Born in Houston, Texas, Proby had actually known Elvis in the late fifties. Known as P.J. Proby, he also had long-standing ties to Jack Good, beginning with Good's international television production *Shindig*. Good brought Proby to England.

The reviewer for *The Times* Irving Wardle had this to say of the three actors: "Of the three leads, Mr. Stevens has a driving rock style and a great flair of knee-splits and baseball-pitching climaxes. What he lacks is the insolence and danger of the original. Mr. Proby has all that, plus sheer authority and a command of Presley's falsetto swoops and vibrato. But for sheer evocation of why the fifties went wild over Presley, my vote goes to the guilelessly electrifying Mr. Whitnall."

Eleven hundred members of the official Elvis Presley Fan Club saw these actions when the club came en masse to a gala performance on February 11, 1978, complete with photographic events set aside for the press as the fan club arrived as well as during the final twenty minutes of the show when the club members themselves put on a show of dancing, celebration, and mourning.

Unfortunately, P.J. Proby, who, according to *The Sun*, had been shoveling muck at a Yorkshire farm for ten pounds a week before joining the show, proved unable to maintain the discipline and regimen of daily theatrical performance. On May 17, 1978, not quite six months after the play opened, Bogdan Kominowski, a New Zealand singing star who had been playing the title role in *Jesus Christ Superstar* at another West End theater, replaced Proby.

Elvis makes no attempt either to analyze Presley or even to record all of his life. It mentions neither Colonel Parker nor Elvis's former wife Priscilla. But their absence is inconsequential. Michael Billiut of *The Guardian* took the show to task for its lack of dialogue:

> But although the show is impressively staged, it would be five times as good if it were more than a songfest and filled out its pious tribute to Elvis with rather more concrete information.

Director Jack Good would disagree. The emphasis on simply experienc-
ing the music is deliberate. The show, Good said, is "an evocation of Elvis
through his music. ... It does not attempt to recreate the 'real Elvis' as
allegedly revealed in the current plethora of sensationalized memories of
various secretaries, self-proclaimed girl friends and former body-guards.
Rather the show is a celebration of Elvis as we know him through his
music—and perhaps for that reason, since music was at his heart's
core—it happens to tell us the essential truth about the man."

These sentiments are reflected in several media comments. Wardle
in *The Times* wrote:

> Jack Good's musical no more tells the story of Elvis Presley's career
> than *Triumph of the Will* recounts the history of the Nazi party, but it sells
> its subject with considerable flair, and amounts to a staggeringly effective
> show.

Michael Coveny, editor of *Plays and Players* noted:

> Although it is a stage extravaganza, it is beautifully angled dra-
> matically—one of the most wonderful musical evenings in the theater.

The *Financial Times* agreed that:

> The last thing that "Elvis" is, is a play, or any serious interpretation of
> the man, his place in social or musical history, or a moral tale. It is very
> akin to the television rock shows that Jack Good used to produce so well.

The *Daily Mail* called the play:

> ...refreshingly free of mawkish pretension. It tells the story without
> narrative, and faithfully recreates the memories in sound without trouble.

And Peter Clayton in the *Sunday Telegraph* called the show a "pop-
up edition of the legend." But he added:

> It is the second musical theatrical reproduction in quick succession to
> concern itself not with plot, subplot and often clumsy pretext for song, but
> with straight musical history, and in its own utterly different way it is
> quite as good as the first, "Bubbling Brown Sugar" [a musical about Fats
> Waller]. "Elvis" is all the things a rock'n'roll legend staged by Jack Good
> ought to be: breath-taking, dazzling and deafening. ...

But the play had its shortcomings—as any attempt to recreate so
charismatic a figure as Elvis must—and some critics quickly spotted the
failings.

John Barber in the *Daily Telegraph* noted the power of the play in
spite of its shortcomings. He called the show:

> Not so much a celebration as an exhumation of the recently deceased

Elvis Presley. ... The show does no more than animate the mood of his records—hysterical, half-drugged or stewed in a glutinous religiosity. Throughout, however, is felt the guiding hand of two experts of theatrical bravura—Jack Good and Ray Cooney. A butcher's shop of showbiz vulgarity, then? Undoubtedly. But they were dancing in the aisles, the most animated theater audience I have seen in years.

Victoria Radin of *The Observer* was more direct. She called the play a "white wash job" because it failed to note Presley's failings. "Also overlooked is the other side of his appeal," she wrote, "the quality of flaming, sneering, hip-swivelling, sheer sexiness which made him early on a figure of teenage adulation as well as grown-up outrage and which was certainly the primary source of his appeal."

In *The Sunday Times*, Derek Jewell said the production "dazzles rather than convinces," and his review raised the question of Elvis's contribution to music—catalyst or revolutionary? Jewell concluded that imitations could explain neither mystery.

The driving force behind the success of the West End play and other attempts to represent the Elvis phenomenon on the stages of a nightclub or a concert hall is highly complex. Those who lived through the era wanted to recall it and to pass it on to those who had not. Younger fans wanted to understand what created all the excitement in the first place.

Many sought the answers in Elvis's movies.

On the day after the entertainer died, Films, Incorporated, the world's largest distributor of sixteen-millimeter films, rolled up its biggest day in history. The company, based in surburban Chicago, rents mostly to college audiences and stocks half the films Presley made, those released by MGM. Their most requested title was *Jailhouse Rock*, a 1957 release. The company's catalogue offered a capsule review: "An ex-con with a big talent for singing becomes famous—and conceited."

Elvis's thirty-three films, which always drew large television audiences late at night or on Sunday afternoons, suddenly were in great demand, and television stations throughout the United States lucky enough to have a print on hand began scheduling changes. Newspapers gave full coverage to the announcements as part of the local news about Elvis reaction. Most of the films had received negative reviews when they first appeared, but all made money. The plots were simple; all offered lots of music. In many of them, the real purpose of the film was to create another record album—the soundtrack of the movie.

The Films, Inc., catalogue lists other Elvis movies as follows: *It Happened at the World's Fair* (1963)—"Our hero is a singing baby sitter";

Viva Las Vegas (1964)—"Band leader is chased by three luscious lovelies"; *Girl Happy* (1965)—"Elvis is a Florida chaperone"; *Harum Scarum* (1965)—"Karate plus music, Presley style, in a modern Arabian Nights story"; *Spinout* (1966)—"Our hero is a race car driver who romances sexy Ann-Margret"; *Double Trouble* (1967)—"Elvis is pursued by gals and crooks"; *Speedway* (1968)—"Lady IRS agent audits an auto racer and falls in love"; *Stay Away Joe* (1968)—"Elvis plays a half-breed who sings and romances"; *Live a Little, Love a Little* (1968)—"Elvis is a fashion photographer who sings"; *The Trouble with Girls* (1969)—"Elvis has his hands full with more romance than he bargained for."

Presley had shown flashes of a raw, natural acting ability, particularly in *King Creole*, his fourth film, completed just before he went into the Army. *New York Times* critic Harold Thompson was led to write of his performance: "As the lad himself might say, cut off my legs and call me Shorty! Elvis Presley can act." *Chicago Tribune* movie critic Gene Siskel said Elvis's films were "Southerns" as contrasted to the Westerns that became a film genre. He likened the movies to the films that have proven highly successful for Burt Reynolds—whether he was cast as a racing car driver, a speedboat operator, a cowboy, or a boxer, Elvis always played the "good old boy" of the American South.

Norman Taurog, who directed Elvis in nine films, called him a fine, light-comedy actor. "I was always proud of his work, even if I wasn't too proud of the scripts," Taurog said. "I think he could have been a good dramatic actor, too. His performance in *King Creole* proved that. But the powers at MGM and Colonel Parker always wanted him in lighter films surrounded by pretty girls."

Elvis had memorized the James Dean role in *Rebel Without a Cause*, and he wanted the chance to play a serious dramatic film role. Film makers offered him the male lead in *A Star Is Born* opposite Barbra Streisand, but his manager turned it down. Colonel Parker cared little about the scripts or the parts that Elvis played. Reportedly he once said: "We don't have approval on scripts, only money. Anyway, what's Elvis need? A couple of songs, a little story and some nice people around him."

Rentals on Presley films for the year preceding his death totalled almost $16,000 at Films, Inc. In the year beginning August 16, 1977, Elvis's films grossed $40,319 for the company. The biggest increase came from the documentary concert films, which basically show the star performing on stage, without the added baggage of a hackneyed script.

Elvis, That's the Way It Is, a 1970 film, follows him backstage and onstage for his Las Vegas show. *Elvis On Tour*, a split-screen documentary, records a 1972 tour of fifteen cities in fifteen nights.

Another documentary concert film was compiled by a television crew that followed the singer for two weeks in June, just two months before he died. CBS broadcast the film on October 3, 1977, and it became the definitive memorial special. Concerts were videotaped in Omaha, Nebraska, and Rapid City, South Dakota, and the resulting product gave the appearance of a single show. Elvis sang fourteen songs, interspersed with other segments made in Cincinnati and Indianapolis and at Graceland, showing airport activity, the band, the fans, and the Presley organization moving the tour from city to city. "He was performing extremely well," said Gary Smith, the show's producer. "He was singing the spirituals with so much more conviction than he was any other kind of music. I wonder now in retrospect whether he had some sense of perception about it."

To thousands of fans, Elvis never looked worse. He was paunchier than usual, even his face looked bloated. But he poured tremendous energy into the performance, and the camera caught the perspiration and the agony as he successfully hit the high notes of the gospel hymn, "How Great Thou Art." He offered an impromptu rendition of "My Way," a song that became a posthumous hit. "It was just like in the movies, but it was real," said Smith. "He just threw in 'My Way' one night, even admitting that he didn't know the lyrics and would we excuse him if he read it."

The end of the film showed Elvis getting into a limousine and riding away. His hand was at the window, waving a final farewell. Then, in a poignant moment, his father came on camera and expressed his appreciation for the messages of condolence the family had received. "It was a neighborly touch," said Canadian fan Kay Parley, "a recognition that we have thought of Elvis as one of the family and Vernon was returning the compliment—treating us as members of the family, or at least as friends. I realized that there were things in the show besides the concert and the music. Things that we will always remember. I wonder if CBS knows that?"

Other television specials followed. Lawrence Welk featured an hour of Elvis songs on his syndicated program. Several independent producers made documentaries; one of the most successful was *Elvis: Love Him Tender* produced by Frank Bloomer of Seattle and distributed by Hanna

Barberra Productions. And CBS broadcast a special on January 8, 1978, *Nashville Remembers Elvis on His Birthday*, a collection of musical numbers interspersed with comments by friends and associates. Carl Perkins, Roy Orbison, and Charlie Rich recalled the Sun Record days, Nancy Sinatra remembered high school in the fifties. The Jordanaires told of the concert tours and recording sessions. Many of the co-stars from his movies—Bill Bixby, Mary Ann Mobley, Stella Stevens, and Arthur O'Connell—talked about working with him. "Elvis was an actor like no other actor ever before, because he was so involved in it," said O'Connell, who played the singer's father in *Follow That Dream*. "Without ever taking a lesson, he knew more about acting than any actor I ever worked with. Elvis was very special. The public were not cheated when they walked into a theater to see him do something." The program ended with a clip of Elvis singing "My Way" and shaking hands from the stage. Then he said "Good night," and Jimmy Dean, host for the program, sang "Peace in the Valley."

Jerry Franklin at WKNO-TV, the Memphis public television station, produced one of the best memorial tributes. Using stills, interviews, and tape footage from Graceland at the time Elvis died, the program effectively portrayed Presley's life. John P. Bakke, professor of rhetoric and communications art at Memphis State University, discussed the importance of the singer, and moving remembrances came from the Rev. C.W. Bradley, the family friend who preached at Elvis's funeral; Bernard and Guy Lansky, who remembered the young kid at their Beale Street clothing store; and Rufus Thomas, the first black disc jockey to play Elvis's music. The recollections of Marion Keisker MacInnes recounting the day the young truck driver came into Memphis Recording Service to cut a record highlighted the program. Her reminiscence became the title of the show—"$3 One Side, $4 Two Sides, a Tribute to Elvis Presley." First broadcast in Memphis on September 4, 1977, the program was repeated but due to technical problems with the tape, the Public Broadcasting Service did not pick up the film.

The first non-documentary appeared on February 11, 1979, and it was a blockbuster. *Elvis* was the title of a three-hour, made-for-television motion picture broadcast as the *ABC Sunday Night Movie*. It got excellent reviews, and the young actor who played Elvis—Kurt Russell— was nominated for an Emmy as the best actor in a dramatic role. The film biography was produced by Dick Clark, viewed by some as the godfather of rock music since his days as host of the after-school *American*

Bandstand that gave national television exposure for the records of the fifties. Clark remembered the music, and the film is filled with the songs that Elvis popularized.

But, more important, the movie had a solid script by Anthony Lawrence and first-rate direction by John Carpenter. While slightly saccharine, the film with fair accuracy traced the young truck driver's rise to the pinnacle of the popular entertainment world. It opened in Las Vegas on July 26, 1969, as Elvis prepared for his first appearance in nine years before a live audience. Using flashbacks, *Elvis* showed the singer's boyhood in Tupelo and Memphis, his appearance at a high school variety show singing "Old Shep," the first trip to Sun Records, the one-night stands, and making it big on the *Ed Sullivan Show*. Other sequences showed his movie making and his being drafted into the Army, his meeting Priscilla, his marriage, and the adoring fans. There was the darker side as well—the death of the mother he adored, the strained relations in his marriage, his efforts to cope with success.

Shelley Winters gave a convincing performance as his mother. A new actress, Season Hubley, offered a credible Priscilla, and Bing Russell (father of Kurt Russell) played Vernon Presley. In a relatively minor role, Pat Hingle played the cigar-chomping Colonel Parker. But the movie is Kurt Russell's. Not an Elvis look-alike, he managed to capture the many moods of the entertainer thanks to rigorous coaching by Associate Producer Jim Ritz, a self-proclaimed Elvis fanatic and collector, who shared his films and tapes and recordings of everything Presley ever did. Charlie Hodge, who played back-up guitar for Presley for seventeen years, acted as technical advisor and played himself in the film. His remembrances gave the film added authenticity, and he worked with the screenwriter, contributing dialogue that sounded like Elvis and correcting factual errors. Larry Geller, who had been Elvis's hairdresser and confidante, provided details on the singer's spiritual life that rounded out the script. Geller contributed the strangest sequence in the film, Elvis conversing with his twin brother Jesse, who had been born dead.

Colonel Parker refused Dick Clark's request to use Elvis's recordings in the film, and Kurt Russell's singing was supplied by Ronnie MacDowell with uncanny accuracy. MacDowell had been a relatively unknown country singer when he recorded a tribute song, "The King Is Gone," two days after Presley's death. The song sold a million copies within a week.

An unusually high reaction to the ABC production immediately hit the studios. In New York and at affiliated stations in seven other cities, ABC Television received 438 phone calls praising the movie, commending it as a fitting tribute. Later, 232 letters arrived, most of them praising Kurt Russell's performance. "With the presentation's authenticity and tasteful appeal, I'm sure that Elvis himself would have approved," wrote one fan. A dozen negative letters were received, objecting to the "impersonation of a legend." Said one fan: "Let him rest in peace ... Please."

ABC network executives were convinced that Presley fans would like the movie, but they were elated when the general public and the critics responded so favorably. The network slotted *Elvis* in the crucial Sunday night time period in an all important "sweeps week," when the A. C. Nielsen Company and Arbitron conducted nationwide viewer surveys. CBS countered with a repeat showing of *Gone With the Wind* and moved up the starting time by an hour. NBC scheduled the first television showing of the award-winning film, *One Flew Over the Cuckoo's Nest.* When the samplings were tabulated, *Elvis* had won with a forty-one percent share of the audience to twenty-four for CBS and thirteen for NBC.

The television production later was condensed into a two-hour movie for theater release, winning rave reviews and setting box office records in Europe and Australia. The theater version was scheduled to appear later in the United States and to be made available for showings to campus audiences and fan clubs.

An entertaining movie, *Elvis* ends with the singer making his triumphant Las Vegas return, before the darker side of his life began to emerge, before he began to put on weight, and before he died. "Myth is perpetuated, embroidered, festooned," said Judy Flander in a review in *The Washington Star.* "The idol of the fifties is perfectly captured and carefully displayed under a glass bell, definitely removed from reality into folklore."

15

Buying a Memory

People will collect almost anything—string, stamps, bottle caps, matchbook covers, bugs. If there is enough of something to make a group, someone will collect it, for reasons ranging from the pleasure of a hobby to investment potential as a hedge against inflation.

Elvis collectors have gone about their business with a zeal that invites comment from the media. The Communist press in particular ascribed such activity to capitalistic greed and a desire to exploit the memory of the dead singer for profit. The American media have tended to focus more on the almost religious fervor of many Presley fans.

The most important measure of the marketing and collecting of Elvis Presley is his music, his record sales. Members of the press flooded Presley's label, RCA, with phone calls from the time the bulletin reporting his death moved on the wire. Two secretaries were the only employees in RCA Records's New York publicity department when the phones began to go berserk. For the next several hours, they tried to field messages, their plight worsened because RCA's Los Angeles office was referring all its calls to New York. When a reporter asked how many calls they received in the first hour, one of the women just laughed hysterically. The next day the company drafted other employees to help the public relations office and hired temporary help to cope with the telephones.

RCA gave little information to help the inquiring, and often beleaguered, reporters. They wanted biographies. But Colonel Parker opposed giving biographical details about Presley. That way, said Arthur Gold in the *Chicago Tribune*, the press always had to do its homework, and the Colonel didn't have to bother with updates.

The media wanted information on record sales. RCA could supply data on "platinum" and "gold" records, and some of the popular press such as *Variety* and *Billboard* estimated Elvis sales had reached some six hundred million singles and albums by 1977. But RCA never has officially disclosed the total volume of Presley sales. Colonel Parker does not want the company to release the information. This has put the RCA public affairs people in a difficult spot, since their business is to promote their record stars, not to turn away inquiries.

The Colonel has total control of Elvis's business matters in death as well as life. But does he have veto power over RCA's public affairs department?

"Veto power?" Herbert Helman, division vice-president at RCA Records, repeated the question. "Let's put it this way. He has influence. And if the Colonel says he sees no benefits to be derived from talking about Elvis's death and what occurred after it, so be it."

RCA has maintained this policy in the face of what must have been tempting reasons to violate it. Early in 1980, the *Guinness Book of Records* declared that Paul McCartney was the biggest-selling recording artist in history. Although knowledgeable people in the recording industry know the top slot should go to Presley, no one at RCA voiced a public objection.

The only statement the record company issued about Elvis after his death came from Lewis Couttolenc, president of RCA Records. It was a standard, canned expression of official grief:

> Elvis Presley was the greatest legend of the modern entertainment world. He ushered in the rock music era, forever changing the tastes of the music-loving public. The legend is lost to us. And all the hundreds of millions of people around the world whose lives were in some way touched by his music can only be greatly saddened by his death. We at RCA have been proud to be associated with this great artist the last 22 years.

RCA executives had other worries besides inquiring reporters. They could benefit enormously from the reaction to Presley's death—but they did not want deliberately to exploit the situation. Attending the dedication of the Presley chapel in Tupelo, RCA executive Joan Deary discussed the awkwardness of the situation and how the company handled it. "Everything—all advertising was pulled," she said. "All promotional activities were pulled, because the executives of our company felt we should not exploit the tragedy, which is what it was, a tragedy, but merely supply whatever records were being demanded, and do it that way. But everything had to be handled very dignified. ... The first record we put out after the concert album—which the Colonel wanted to get out because of the television show—but the first record we released was an inspirational type of record called 'He Walks Beside Me,' and, again, that was a presidential decision from our company. They wanted something dignified and in good taste."

RCA's only ads were full page memorials in *Billboard* and other trade publications. The page was all black with white letters saying "Elvis/1935-1977." In the lower corner was the RCA logo.

Despite the lack of direct information from RCA, the press pieced together a picture of massive production efforts and phenomenal record sales. RCA achieved its best year in history in 1977. Earnings rose to $247 million, a gain of 39 percent over 1976 operations, while sales grew by 10 percent to $5.9 billion. Contributing to that attractive report to shareholders were the sales of Elvis records.

In the past, people had always asked for a specific Elvis record; now they were buying *any* Elvis recording. Newspapers all over the world reported local record stores selling out their stock of Presley albums within hours—many to customers older than usual, to people who hadn't been in record stores for years, but who came in now, many white-faced and red-eyed.

But that was only the beginning. Steve Libman, vice-president and general manager of Southland Records, a major Atlanta distributor, said RCA booked about $1 million in orders for Elvis records on the day he died. The huge RCA pressing plant in Indianapolis, with a capacity of producing 250,000 albums a day, went on a three-shift, six-day-a-week schedule. All 50 Presley albums—the entire catalogue—were included in the catch-up activities. On Wednesday, August 17, the plant pressed 250,000 copies of the latest album "Moody Blue." Demand before the singer's death had been about 100,000 a week.

The market reaction was much the same in Germany. There, thousands of fans came into record shops—again many who had not done so for years—and started a boom in the record industry. RCA German Sales

Chief Harold Heilmann reported selling 500,000 albums in the week after Presley died—only because that was all he could supply. The same was true at Inelco in Holland, with 100,000 sold in three days. Electra in Sweden reported that with both fans and dealers swamping the company with calls, its switchboard almost broke down. The RCA Camden label, Pickwick, said the seven Presley albums in its catalog sold 250,000 copies in Britain in two days. From the other side of the world in Japan came similar reports. Only the military post exchanges seemed to miss the boat. The Dallas headquarters of the Army and Air Force Exchange Service, according to *Variety,* got only 35,000 additional albums for worldwide distribution.

In South Africa, a spokesman for Teal Records said, "The dealers are going quite frantic. If they carry on ordering at this rate our whole production could switch to Elvis." That was the case in Germany, where RCA Hamburg stepped up to day and night shifts. In the United States in the months after Elvis died, a standing joke circulated in the record industry: Don't release a record now because you can't get it pressed.

RCA not only operated its own facilities around the clock, it subcontracted every available outside pressing plant in the country. Although there were some other factors at play in the situation—a general upturn in the record business and European strikes hitting major record producers there—they were minor compared with the impact of Presley's death.

Industry veterans couldn't recall anything like it. By September 1, RCA still could not meet the demand. By October 1, six Presley albums were in the first half of *Billboard*'s "Top LPs and Tapes," and eight of the top sixteen spots in the "Hot Country LP" albums belonged to Elvis. By November, RCA's backorders reached into the next year. The *Memphis Press-Scimitar* quoted Nashville RCA executive Paul Randall saying the company sold eight million Elvis records in the first five days after he died. But *Billboard* calculated that the nation's pressing plants were shipping twenty million Elvis records a week. All figures are estimates; the true statistics are locked in corporate files.

Besides calling RCA when Elvis died, reporters in their search for background on the entertainer and his music sought out Colonel Tom Parker, Elvis's manager. Many newspapers published stories about "the man behind the legend," but all were rehashed from previous articles and anecdotes. During normal times the Colonel—the title and nickname stemmed from an honorary commission given him by the governor of Kentucky—always shunned the press, refusing all requests for interviews or comments. When Elvis died, he dropped from sight altogether. No journalist could find him; even CBS was hamstrung in its efforts to get his clearance to use certain films and tapes in news broadcasts. Later he was seen at the funeral, tieless and wearing a baseball cap. But he had no comments for the media.

Although out of the public eye on the day of Elvis's death, the Colonel was not idle. When he got the news, he was in Portland, Maine, making arrangements for the concert tour Elvis was to have begun the next day. He telephoned Felton Jarvis, Elvis's producer, who was in a Nashville airport hangar supervising the loading of sound equipment, and told him to unload the plane and head for Memphis. True to form, the Colonel volunteered no explanation. When Jarvis asked if something had happened to Vernon Presley, he was told that it was Elvis and "an act of God." Not until Jarvis got off the plane in Memphis did he learn the full story.

Parker and his organization also were busy making sure that the Presley company kept control of the marketing binge sure to ensue.

Elvis and Colonel Parker jointly had controlled Boxcar Enterprises, a Tennessee corporation which served as the vehicle for licensing commercial Elvis Presley rights. Their method was to sublicense to other companies for actual manufacture and sale, while Boxcar maintained general control and collected royalties.

The day Elvis died, Colonel Parker, acting on behalf of Boxcar, called in Harry Geissler, a Delaware entrepreneur. On the day of the funeral, Boxcar granted Geissler's company, Factors, Etc., Inc., the exclusive license to market the name and likeness of Elvis Presley. Vernon Presley announced the arrangement to the public the following week.

Before Elvis died, memorabilia was marketed largely through fan clubs and other avenues aimed chiefly at the loyal Elvis fans throughout the world. Paul Lichter of Philadelphia, who made thirty thousand dollars a month marketing Elvis records and memorabilia, and who got his start handing out leaflets at Presley concerts, is typical of the Elvis market of the 1970s. Also the shopping mall across from the Presley home contained a souvenir shop among other businesses to serve fans and tourists visiting Graceland.

But after Presley died, memorabilia sprouted everywhere. Presley marketers of varying tastes literally took over the Graceland shopping center—peddlers "spread like Kudzu"* as *The Commercial Appeal* put it. One by one, all the other businesses gave up and moved on as the crush of visitors to Graceland made it impossible for other shoppers to park nearby. Some peddlers offered T-shirts, jackets, tote bags, and posters; others sold key chains, ash trays, glasses, serving trays, and piggy banks; there were "TCB" bracelets, necklaces, photostats of Elvis's schoolboy report cards, and even his will. All sold well.

Established citizens of Memphis refer to them all as schlock shops, reflecting their judgment of the merchandise and their frustration that, for the present, that was all Memphis had to offer its Elvis fans and visitors.

The most vituperative comments came from *The Commercial Appeal*, which found the haste to make money on the Presley memory embarrassing. The paper itself had felt the full brunt of the crush and hysteria since the first morning when papers disappeared all over the city. Less than two weeks after Presley's death, Michael Grehl, editor of *The Commercial Appeal* had already had enough. In a special commentary entitled "Presley Memory Lives in Pocketbook Pandering" he wrote:

> Even the least interested know that Elvis Presley gave voice to a generation unable to articulate its aspirations and frustrations. The grateful generation, now middle-aged, rewarded him with what may be the most enduring adulation enjoyed by any entertainer. His appeal was to the relatively unsophisticated, and regrettably they now are easiest prey to the unprincipled and the fast buck artists.
>
> On a somewhat higher plane, there is a line of charities and institutions forming, all seeking to get money or holy relics through the posthumous blessing of the singer. Worthy causes, to be sure, but the scramble is unseemly. ...
>
> Since little Caroline Kennedy, daughter of the late President, lost so little time inveigling herself into the Presley home so that she could cast her well-bred eye over the decor in an account to be carried (and no doubt syndicated) by *Rolling Stone*, we can look for a flourishing trade in goods of the style she found at Graceland. The painting on black velveteen business should boom. ...
>
> Before the flowers were gone from Forest Hill Cemetery I personally turned away two persons who wished to collaborate with our newspaper in this newest form of "history." They were astonished that we saw no purpose in helping them cash in.
>
> All of us on the newspaper staff were embarrassed at the scalping of last week's editions and the fact that we have no control over it.

---

*Kudzu is a vine imported from Japan in the 1930s into the South because of its peculiar ability quickly to replenish nitrogen in overused soils. The vine also grows extremely rapidly, covering everything in its path: trees, telephone poles and—so the many stories go—even cows if they stand still too long.

But, as I said, you haven't seen anything yet.

When the Hollywood and TV paragons of pandering get their hooks into the Presley Story we may see a new record for profit. ... The plot lines are limitless and we undoubtedly shall see too many versions to sort out.

The mentality that unabashedly can offer Dirty Harry and douche commercials as family fare must literally be frenzied over the possibilities of the Presley life and death. ...

On the first anniversary, August 17, 1978, Bill Garner, *The Commercial Appeal* cartoonist, drew a blunt portrait. It showed a pig with a straw hat which said, "Hucksters" on it. The pig was selling Elvis T-shirts, ashtrays, plates, glasses. Nearby were books for sale, entitled, "I Knew Elvis." "I Knew Him Better," and "But I Know All the Other Stuff."

Down the road in Tupelo, quality control was better. The city drew a lower volume of visitors, and the single souvenir shop—on U.S. Highway 78 (now Elvis Aaron Presley Memorial Highway) near Elvis's birthplace—was operated by Mrs. Billy Boyd. She combined her souvenir shop with a museum display area of personal memorabilia that included two thousand newspaper clippings about Presley dating back to 1957. She knew the Presleys, and was there to talk to visitors. Her shop had a personal touch and a home feeling not found in other places.

Eventually a small shop was opened in the recreation center behind the Presley birthplace. The selection is not large—books, jackets, bumper stickers, plates, and other items carrying a photo of the birthplace or the words, "Tupelo, Birthplace of Elvis Presley." But the merchandise offered there would sell as well at the Kennedy Center in Washington, D.C., or at a museum shop featuring the King Tut exhibit, if the words were changed.

Memphis and Tupelo represented only the beginning. Tennessee's official tourist and convention literature highlights Graceland as a major attraction. Mississippi, at its welcome centers along major highways entering the state, provides free children's coloring books that include drawings of Elvis and the Tupelo birthplace. The leading attraction at Nashville's Country Music Hall of Fame is Elvis's gold Cadillac with the top cut away so its interior can be seen in a tilted mirror. Commemorative liquor decanters and specially bottled Elvis brands of wine have appeared in memory of the teetotaling Presley. Roadside stands invariably carry an Elvis likeness among their black velveteen paintings, and souvenir and mercantile shops of all kinds display ceramic statues, mirrored pictures, or other Elvis items. Many fans seem to take it in stride. But the media seem uncomfortable with the marketing of Presley, commenting only on its poor taste, if they comment at all.

Harry Geissler reached an easy truce in himself about marketing Presley, saying, "I've never told anybody I'm not in this for the money." Standing at the dedication of the chapel at Elvis's birthplace, Geissler explained, "If I could sell tickets, I'd sell them right now. That's my game. I respect the man and everything like that, ... but, you understand, if we didn't do that, we wouldn't have this thing here today."

Geissler's company—Factors, Etc., Inc.—specializes in the T-shirt heat transfer business—and in celebrity merchandising. Geissler recalled his biggest deal as the coon-skin hats of Davy Crockett. Even before the agreement with Parker, 1977 had been a banner year for him when success with Farrah Fawcett-Majors T-shirts provided him with cash to purchase merchandising licenses to *Star Wars*, *Rocky*, and, later, *Superman The Movie*.

Two years later when four hundred members of the British fan club came through Washington, D.C. in August of 1979, Geissler and his son Lee invited the group to Bear, Delaware, for the day to tour the T-shirt factory there. The offices are plush, and a small plant nearby combines designing, manufacturing, and shipping operations under one roof. The welcome mat was out—complete with British flags. Each fan received an Elvis tote bag containing an Elvis button, an Elvis keychain, and a Bear, Delaware, frisbee. Hot dogs, hamburgers, cool drinks, popcorn, and the like were on sale in the parking lot alongside three brightly colored tents featuring video tapes of Elvis in performance and filled with Elvis merchandise.

Guiding the group was the smiling, rotund Harry Geissler, who looks like a friendly bear, uses gold embossed bear paws on his stationery and on the doors of his limousines, and who never uses the hard sell. He seemed to be there just to make sure everyone was happy. The British fans toured the factory and offices, watched the shows, lined up to eat American junk food, appeared to have a marvelous time, and snapped up the merchanise until their tote bags overflowed. Especially popular were the Elvis records, pressed in every stripe and color imaginable.

Boxcar Enterprises probably had more in mind than a good merchandiser when it contacted Geissler. Factors prides itself on its vigorous control of its licenses and its willingness to make a total effort to stop bootlegging.

Among the three hundred actions the company initiated in its first two years as holder of the Elvis license, one went all the way to the Supreme Court. The defendants were Pro Arts, Inc., a competitor probably best known for its bathing suit poster of Farrah Fawcett-Majors, and Stop and Shop Companies, parent of Bradlees retail stores. An *Atlanta Journal* photographer had taken a photo of Presley in concert at the Omni. The paper published it after the singer died, superimposing the name "Elvis Presley" and the years "1935-1977." Pro Arts bought rights to the photo, got a copyright for it, added "In Memory" in bold white letters in one corner, blew the photo up, and began to market it three days after Presley's death.

In the courts, Pro Arts argued that it was not infringing on Factors's right to exploit the Presley name and likeness. Even if Factors did have exclusive rights in this area, the company claimed, these rights would not include a "memorial poster" commenting on a newsworthy event; and that

> our Constitution does not permit one who has lived an entire life in the limelight, projecting his image into every home and upon every consciousness in the nation, to one day withdraw his image from the artists and communicators—and consequently from their audiences—except upon payment of a tidy ransom.

Pro Arts presented itself as one of the artists and communicators and maintained that, like any other print medium, posters were protected by the First Amendment.

But the courts disagreed. The Federal District Court for Southern New York enjoined Pro Arts from manufacturing, selling, and distributing the posters. The Supreme Court left in effect a Second U.S. Circuit Court of Appeals ruling that Boxcar's exclusive right to exploit the Presley name and likeness, because exercised during Presley's life, survived his death and the right to transfer exclusively to Factors was legally binding.

A year later, however, the Sixth U.S. Circuit Court of Appeals took a different tack. The court ruled in a Memphis case that the heirs of famous people do not have the exclusive right to profit from the continuing fame of the deceased.

"There are strong reasons for declining to recognize the inheritability of the (exclusive marketing) right," argued the court. "How long would the 'property interest' last? In perpetuity? For a term of years? At what point does the right collide with the right of free expression guaranteed by the First Amendment? Does the right apply to elected officials, as well as to movie stars, singers and athletes?

"Does the right cover posters or engraved likenesses of, for example, Farrah Fawcett-Majors or Mahatma Gandhi, kitchen utensils ('Revere Ware'), insurance ('John Hancock'), electric utilities ('Edison'), a football stadium ('RFK'), a pastry ('Napoleon'), or the innumerable subdivisions and apartment complexes named after famous people?"

The court concluded, "Fame falls in the same category as reputation; it is an attribute from which others may benefit, but not own."

Factors predicted a flood of inferior merchandise. But the incident that sparked the suit was the effort to erect a statue of Presley near downtown Memphis.

Financing of a larger-than-life bronze statue by Eric Parks was to be through selling eight-inch pewter replicas of the statue for twenty-five dollars each. The Memphis Development Foundation, sponsor of the creation, is a nonprofit organization involving itself with preservation and restoration projects such as saving Memphis's oldest theater, the Orpheum, and revitalizing the downtown area. As writer Joe Mulherin described the situation for *Memphis* magazine, "In their haste to memorialize Elvis in 1977, the Foundation consulted with neither the Presley estate, which was still unsettled and wary of uncontrolled exploitation of its scion's recent demise, nor the City of Memphis, which was, in true municipal tradition, forming a committee to study the situation." By the end of 1979, however, the city and county mayors had lined up behind the movement to erect the statue, and, a few months later came the favorable court decision.

The city endorsement grew out of a long period of indecision during which Memphis officials and representatives of the Presley estates could never agree on a common plan to honor the city's most famous citizen. Memphis—established Memphis—always found it much easier to be a cradle of blues tradition than a birthplace of rock and roll. Although a vigorous effort was under way to honor Presley, each idea seemed to founder.

While the Memphis Development Foundation waged its court battle, the city discussed plans for acquiring Graceland as an Elvis museum. Sponsors of the plan felt that the estate asked too much and promised too little in return. City fathers could not commit themselves to large outlays of taxpayer money; executors of the estate had to be careful they did not give away too much.

The city missed a strong opportunity when Gray Line tours bought the building at Union and Marshall that had housed the old Sun Record studios where Elvis made his first recordings. Sam Phillips, who owns most of the original recording equipment, had been willing to participate in the restoration of the studio only with a nonprofit, noncommercial enterprise, but the city had been too slow in agreeing on a price with the owner.

Other ideas abounded, including a proposal for a high-rise glass pyramid overlooking the river and housing a talent exchange. Few such ideas ever got to a serious discussion stage.

Whatever one's views on all the memorabilia and memorializing— whether it is a necessary ingredient, as in Harry Geissler's view, a part of the scene, as many fans accept; or an abomination, as Michael Grehl feels—they were very and are very much in evidence after Presley's death. Even the media joined the parade.

The major networks produced special programs. Many newspapers went a step further and produced their own memorabilia in the form of special Elvis sections or supplements. Grehl's own paper, *The Commercial Appeal*, produced a special edition with its sister paper, the *Press-Scimitar*, although these papers forwarded all profits to charity.

Public interest simply demanded something tangible.

No accurate measurement exists of the speed at which news can travel in the modern age. Some events become etched in time for people who recall where they were when they heard about the Japanese attack on Pearl Harbor or the assassination of John F. Kennedy. Many fix the late afternoon of August 16, 1977, that way in their mind's eye; to them the news from Memphis was a personal tragedy of massive proportions. To others, the news of Elvis's passing was at most an item of fleeting interest. They did not like the music or appreciate the cultural impact of the man's life, but they knew that he had died. As Charles Kuralt noted on the night of the funeral, no one asked, "Elvis who?"

Some indicators are available to document the speed at which the news of Elvis's death traveled—telephone tie-ups, the massive response of radio, the pressure on the wire services, the homes using television that night. It was clearly not a normal August evening in the media world. The interest continued over the next few days as print media continued to get more demands from readers wanting more information about Presley.

Like many other newspapers, *The Courier Journal* in Louisville recorded huge sales of its Wednesday morning papers, and an unusual number of callers sought extra copies. Editors there decided to publish a supplement about Elvis for inclusion in its newspapers the following week, an edition timed to coincide with the opening of the Kentucky State Fair. Michael J. Davis, the managing editor, recalled making the decision at 4:30 p.m. on Wednesday, after Standard Gravure said it was possible. Normal deadline for a roto-magazine is weeks in advance of publication, but Standard Gravure—the nation's largest rotogravure printing plant—was nearby and was owned by the same family enterprise that controls the two Louisville newspapers.

Color deadlines were set for midnight Thursday, and all type was due six hours later. When editors made the decision to go ahead, the newspaper had no color transparencies, the film from which the color printing plates would be prepared. No stories were on hand, not even firm ideas for stories. But the Associated Press in New York came up with several pieces of art, including the portrait photo of Elvis that adorned the magazine cover. Dore Freeman, a private collector of Elvis photos at MGM in Culver City, California, offered other pictures, and staff members found a few more in the files. The newspaper sent a photographer to Memphis to provide daily coverage. His orders were to supply color photos for the magazine as well, particularly coverage of the funeral. Editors assigned the two *Courier Journal* reporters in Memphis to write stories for the special section. Standard Gravure, which publishes Sunday magazines for most of the nation's major newspapers, offered its regular clients copies of the supplement to include in their regular newspapers. Some bought it sight unseen. Eventually the Elvis section sold over 7.6 million copies in 44 cities.

The Courier Journal on Monday, August 22, recorded its largest circulation in history—385,000. Its usual daily distribution is 210,000. When the early or "bulldog" edition went on sale Sunday night, traffic jams around the building delayed departure of delivery trucks waiting to roll into southern Indiana and rural Kentucky. Some stores raised prices from the usual fifteen cents to a quarter. Bundles of papers left on street corners for newsboys were stolen. Some people fed fifteen cents into vending machines, then removed the entire supply.

Similar incidents occurred elsewhere. The *St. Louis Post-Dispatch* ran the section as part of its regular editions of August 27, increasing the normal Friday press run by 90,000. The paper ordered 370,000 copies of the supplement from Standard Gravure, but, before distribution began, its circulation department was receiving a call from the *Chicago Daily News* and *Sun-Times* requesting 100,000 copies to add to their diminished supplies. The *Post-Dispatch* switchboard operators began getting calls late Friday morning just as the afternoon paper's early edition hit the streets. Callers could not find copies of the paper and its supplement. One man bought 500 copies of the newspaper, but the most bizarre development occurred about two o'clock that afternoon as Charles Dunn was driving his van along Illinois Route 159 to deliver copies of the *Post-Dispatch* to customers in suburban Fairview Heights and Collinsville. He told police a black automobile forced him off the road, and a man wielding a baseball bat wrapped in black tape demanded 50 copies of the paper.

The Courier Journal's Davis said he felt they had put out a decent, quality product in less than 36 hours. "I know one thing," he added. "The Elvis Presley section helped get the *Courier* to people it will probably never reach again."

Most of the newspapers which bought the eight-page supplement with its seven stories and five pages of color used it for a single promotion, a gimmick to increase circulation for a given day, usually the last Sunday in August, traditionally a time of low circulation. But the two Atlanta newspapers used a different approach. The evening *Journal* and the morning *Constitution* offered the "Louisville Roto Magazine" to any reader who subscribed to either newspaper by paying for thirteen weeks in advance at a cost of $15.63. A full-page advertisement in the combined Sunday newspapers of August 20 featured a photo of Elvis taken at an Atlanta concert and the following copy: "Our home delivered subscribers read the heartbreaking news of Elvis Presley's death and all of the repercussions and consequences at their homes. Our presses printed over 40,000 extra copies for our newspaper racks. Hundreds found these were SOLD OUT! There is no substitute for in-depth newspaper coverage of stories large and small."

With the Louisville supplement included, the *Birmingham News* marked its highest circulation ever—95,000 above the normal 180,000. *The Des Moines Register* recognized the strong demand for copies and dispatched its circulation staff to guard vending machines after many papers were stolen. The newspaper's circulation manager in Dubuque reported people arriving in his office at 2:30 a.m., demanding the morning paper with its Elvis section.

In its search for photos, *The Courier Journal* editors had called *The Commercial Appeal* which was still reeling from its big local story. The Memphis newspaper's Sunday magazine, *Mid-South*, is published by Standard Gravure, and the company offered its Memphis client a special deal on the supplement about Elvis. But *The Commercial Appeal* declined. "When we realized what they were going to do," Managing Editor James McDaniel recalled, "we realized we were in a better position than they were. They had the volume, but we had the material." The Memphis newspaper operation recently had been computerized, and all the stories already published on Presley's death—the obituaries, the analyses, the features, the backgrounders, the multi-faceted sidebars—were being held on machine readable discs, available to call up and reprint.

Memphis Publishing Company decided to produce a special paper, in two sections of twelve pages each with no advertising. The company offered it by mail-order only at a price of fifty cents a copy. The front page of *The Commercial Appeal* section was identical to the paper's front page of August 17. On the front of the *Press-Scimitar* section was a blue box calling the special paper "A Tribute to Elvis" explaining that it contained reprints of all Presley pictures and stories, with as few changes as possible, that had been published during the five-day period. The day after the newspapers announced the publication, fourteen bags of mail arrived requesting it. The next day there were twenty, and the company hired forty extra employees to log the requests and type address labels.

"This was before we have even put the section together," said McDaniel. "I couldn't believe it. I went down there and they had mail everywhere in a room on the second floor. It was an incredible outpouring of interest."

When the special section was printed, the company erected a ceiling-high chain link fence inside the building to protect the papers from potential thieves. Every employee of the two papers received a copy of the souvenir section along with his or her paycheck and an option to buy ten more copies. Any additional copies had to be ordered by mail. A dealer for the Memphis Seven-Eleven stores ordered 25,000 copies and put them on sale for $1.25. A newspaper in Alabama bought 10,000 copies and resold them for $3.50 each. Scripps-Howard newspapers in other cities bought bulk orders. *The Cleveland Press* printed a photo of the lines around its building when the supplements went on sale there the first week in September. Three thousand copies were sold in the first hour; within three hours the entire supply of 5,000 was exhausted, and another 10,000 copies were ordered. After a press run of 1.7 million, Memphis Publishing Company stopped printing the special paper in March 1978. Even though the charge of 50 cents a copy was designed to cover production and postage, the company netted a profit of more than $25,000. The money was given to the United Fund.

Other newspapers also produced special sections, but none marketed them beyond their own circulation areas. The *New York Daily News*, which had sold an extra 110,000 copies of its editions reporting Elvis's death, sold an additional 75,000 copies of its Thursday morning paper which included a four-page pullout on the entertainer's life. *The Charlotte Observer* produced an eight-page supplement with a full-color photo of Elvis on its cover. The publication sold out and an additional 50,000 copies were printed. Hundreds of irate North Carolina subscribers reported their papers stolen from their front yards. The *Observer* had the largest press run in the newspaper's history—262,652 copies. (Circulation during the week is normally 170,000; on Sundays, 233,000). Publisher Rolfe Neill observed that the paper's readers obviously had "a great craving for information about a very popular entertainment figure and an instinctive yearning that only print can satisfy." Newspapers across South Carolina also set records. The *Spartanburg Herald* ran color on its front pages on Wednesday, Thursday, and Friday of the week Elvis died and sold 5,000 extra copies above its normal 50,000 each day. *The Greenville News* ran a color photo of Elvis across its front page on Wednesday and recorded 2,500 extra street sales. On Friday the paper published a twenty-five-cent tabloid on Elvis. Its initial printing of 7,500 sold out immediately; 10,000 more were published. The two newspapers in the state capital of Columbia—*The State* and *The Record*—reported 30 percent increases in newsstand sales. In Macon, Georgia, where the *News* normally sells 800-1,000 copies of its final afternoon edition from street racks, 18,000 were sold on Wednesday. The reason: a black and white photo of Elvis covered the entire front page.

The amazing newspaper statistics, particularly unusual for August's traditional slow sales, were not confined to the South. An eight-page tabloid section went into the *Chicago Tribune* on the Sunday after Elvis's death, promoted as a souvenir issue. An extra 40,000 copies of the paper were sold. "No reason alone can explain the public's reaction to Presley's death," *Tribune* Managing Editor Mike Argirion said later. "He was the first teen rebel. Without him rock'n'roll might have been just another passing phenomenon. If you can't understand it, I guess you are either too young to remember, or you became the parent of a kid who dressed like him."

The *Philadelphia Daily News* published a special pullout section and ordered a press run of 304,314 copies. The section was reprinted with an additional run of 250,000. Several newspapers devoted their weekend amusements and television sections to Elvis, printing many of the wire service feature articles and sidebars that had been transmitted during the week. The *News-American* in Baltimore was one; its "Zest" magazine featured a charcoal sketch of Elvis on the cover. Inside the eight-page tabloid were articles by its staff members, UPI, and the Knight-Ridder newspaper syndicate.

The *Shreveport Journal* devoted its weekend magazine "Showcase" to the singer. One of the articles profiled Frank Page, former master of ceremonies for *Louisiana Hayride*, the local radio show that gave Elvis a stage for his first employment as a performer on a fairly regular basis.

The *Daily Journal* in Tupelo, Mississippi, reported thousands of calls requesting its front page of Wednesday morning with the headline, "The King Is Dead." Special four-page copies of the paper including that page and other material from the Wednesday edition were sold, and the *Journal* editors dedicated the weekend "View" magazine to the singer who had been born in their city. Advertisements from local business firms, mostly in the form of memorials, doubled the normal size of the supplement to fifty-six pages. Unique local remembrances and rare early Elvis photos made the paper a collector's item and increased the circulation several thousand beyond its normal run of 36,000. The *Lee County News*, a Tupelo weekly, added an historical section on Elvis to its regular edition and printed 30,000 copies, 26,000 more than its normal press run.

Mona Sharpe, publisher of the *Lee County News*, wrote that Elvis was "more alive today than at any other time" because of the media reaction. "Never before have so many people tried to say so much about him at one time," she added. "People outside the media devote hours to remembering, listening and mourning, looking to the media to keep on triggering emotions."

One-shot specials were not limited to the daily newspapers. Fan magazines flooded newsstands with special tribute editions. Columnist

Liz Smith of the *New York Daily News* said that many of the special magazines resulted from rumors that Elvis was ill. Some publishers, she said, were convinced that the singer had cancer and had made all preparations except for last minute revisions and updating. Some magazines were on the presses within sixteen hours after the news flashed from Memphis. *Photoplay* produced a "treasury" of articles it had run through the years. Called "The Man! The Magic! The Music!" the publication of 128 pages sold for two dollars.

Rolling Stone, the leading journal covering rock music, made its September 22 edition an Elvis special, with twenty-two pages of stories and comment on all aspects of the Presley phenomena, and stories on the music and the beginnings of rock. Jerry Hopkins, who in 1970 wrote the only decent biography of the singer, wrote an article on Colonel Parker. The edition also included the much-publicized article by Caroline Kennedy. In an introductory note, the publisher said: "We pushed deadlines back and worked around the clock, never doubting for a minute that he was worth it. Elvis was the first King we ever had." *Crawdaddy* featured Elvis on its cover in November, with thirteen pages of articles and photographs, including a devastating profile of Paul Lichter, the Philadelphia record retailer who operates the Elvis Unique Record Club, Inc. with its membership of two hundred thousand. Writer Fred Schruers characterized him as the man who cried all the way to the bank in the days after Elvis died. There was a piece on media reaction and a loving reminiscence, "Down at the End of Lonely Street," by Robert Ward, and a not-so-affectionate piece by Abbie Hoffman. Most of the photographs were from the fifties and many of them were the work of *The Commercial Appeal's* photographer, Bob Williams, showing the younger, happier Elvis at ease in his hometown.

Country Music magazine assembled a special tribute issue which was published in December. Every copy placed on newsstands was sold, five times the normal. Its New York offices received thousands of requests for the issue, which featured a cover photo of the entertainer with the caption, "ELVIS—The King Remembered." The magazine included an "oral history of Elvis"—interviews with dozens of people who were close to the singer—by John Morthland, former editor of *Rolling Stone* and *Creem* magazine. Also included were interviews with producer Felton Jarvis and Sam Phillips; a personal memoir by Peter Guralnick, who wrote the rockabilly chapter of the *Rolling Stone Illustrated History of Rock and Roll*; a feature on life inside Graceland; an article on the enigma of Elvis, by Nick Tosches; and dozens of photographs supplied by John Reggero, a bacteriologist and Elvis fan who claimed to have in his collection every single Elvis record in existence. In a foreword, *Country Music* Editor Michael Bane wrote, "We've assembled the best people for this edition, because nothing but the best would do."

Major national weeklies gave full play to the story, some of it highly sensational. The *National Enquirer* with its army of reporters and its ready cash produced a best-selling issue. The last week in August its sales hit 6.7 million copies, mainly because of its cover picture—Elvis lying dead in his casket. Exactly who took "the last photo" or how much the paper paid for it—reportedly $75,000—the *Enquirer* is not telling. During the three days in Memphis, the paper had supplied tiny Minox cameras to several fans and instructed them to snap a picture as they passed Elvis's bier. The photo the paper published, however, was not taken during the public viewing in the alcove at Graceland, but somewhere else in the home or at the funeral home. Vernon Presley later charged in a *Good Housekeeping* article that "one of Elvis' own cousins" was responsible. The *National Enquirer's* big seller—its first to top six million in circulation—included a readable narrative of the discovery of Elvis's body and the events that followed, written in a somewhat heart-rending style. There were "exclusive" reports by the ambulance driver and by Ginger Alden, Elvis's girlfriend. The fee paid to Alden, the last person to see Elvis alive and the one who discovered the body, reportedly was cut when she talked to Lawrence Buser, a reporter for *The Commercial Appeal*, before the tabloid's publication. (Buser camped out at Alden's home and questioned her on the front porch as she returned from the funeral.) A week later the *Enquirer* scored again, with a front page picture showing "The Last Photo of Elvis Alive," a grainy Kodak Instamatic snapshot taken by a fan as the singer drove through the gate of Graceland at 12:28 on the morning he died. *The Star*, the top competitor for the checkout-counter market, countered with a serialization of the Dunleavy book, *Elvis: What Happened?* Owned by Rupert Murdoch who had financed publication of the book by the three bodyguards, *The Star* already had scheduled the series to begin in late August and had been promoting the book heavily prior to publication. Elvis's death moved up the schedule by one week. A third nationally distributed tabloid, the *Midnight Globe*, featured as its front page headline "Elvis: Last Words." But the caption was highly misleading; the article inside was about the singer's "last words to ex-wife Priscilla only two days before he died."

On the other hand, neither of the nation's major news magazines— *Time* and *Newsweek*—led with the Presley story or used it on the cover. Each did, however, devote four full-color pages to the death of the entertainer. A spokesman for *Time* listed three reasons the magazine did not use Elvis on the cover. First, the planned cover story on the "American Underclass" had been in the works for a long time. Second, by the time the magazine hit the streets the following Monday, the news would have lost its immediacy. (Nevertheless, some of the daily press were still publishing special sections then and even later). Third, he asserted that *Time*'s policy was to look forward, not back, observing that even after President Kennedy had been killed, the magazine's cover focused not on the fallen leader but on the new administration. Inside, *Time* headed its coverage, "Last Stop on the Mystery Train," a reference to the Presley recording which many believe to be his best—and perhaps the best rock song ever recorded.

Newsweek's explanations of why it did not feature Presley on the cover were similar. *Newsweek* splashed its cover with the continuing Washington story of the difficulties overtaking President Carter's friend and adviser, Bert Lance. General Editor Maureen Orth wrote the Presley obituary and Senior Editor Jack Kroll provided an analysis, calling Elvis the "Heartbreak Kid" and tracing the tragedies of his life from the death of his mother to his own demise "bloated by the American ambrosia—peanut butter, Pepsi, pills and success." Kroll said he would not sentimentalize the story, but "it's important to feel something for the man whose great contribution was feeling." Then he recalled the scene many Presley followers remembered best—Elvis's appearances on television that Sunday night in 1956. Kroll recounted the legendary tale of Ed Sullivan standing in the wings while the singer performed, and Sullivan muttering over and over to himself, "Son of a bitch ... son of a bitch!"

16

Epilogue

The media fascination with Elvis continues, fueled in part by developments regarding his death and the settlement of his estate. The will was probated, and its contents were revealed to the world. Elvis left all his possessions to his father, his grandmother, and his daughter, Lisa, with Lisa inheriting the shares of the older Presleys when they died.

More than a million people visited Forest Hill Cemetery in the month after Elvis was entombed. After an aborted attempt to steal the body, however, Vernon Presley obtained a zoning variance and permission to move the bodies of Elvis and his mother Gladys to the Meditation Garden near the south end of the mansion. The Tennessee State Department of Archives and History provided an historical marker for Graceland, and the family opened the grounds to visitors who came by the thousands to visit the graves. Parts of Elvis's first Cadillac were melted down and pressed into heart-shaped pendants and offered for sale. Memorial albums appeared. An entreprenuer tried to sell pieces of the marble crypt in which Elvis had been entombed. Madame Toussard's in London unveiled a three thousand dollar wax effigy of Elvis standing near Kojak, Marilyn Monroe, and the Royal Family. Many of the custom-designed luxury automobiles Elvis had owned toured the country as attractions for car dealers and other businesses.

On January 8, 1978, radio stations around the world marked Elvis's birthday—he would have been forty-three—and played his music continually.

While the media did not provide the concentrated coverage that Elvis's death and funeral evoked, the steady trickle of news indicated that these were items of interest to many people.

Then came August 16, 1978—the first anniversary of the entertainer's death.

Dozens of memorial events were scheduled in Memphis. The Memphian, the theater Elvis frequently rented for post-midnight showings for his friends, booked a festival of Presley films. Concerts were planned. Andy Warhol would be on hand to open an exhibition of his painting, "Elvis Forty-nine Times," at Brooks Memorial Art Gallery. The Circle G Ranch, property once owned by Elvis in nearby Mississippi, announced sunset memorial services at the base of a fifty-foot high concrete cross.

But a massive strike by its police and fire departments crippled the city. The National Guard was called out; a curfew imposed. Many of the events were cancelled. Thousands of Elvis fans showed up anyway, along with network television crews and reporters who descended on Memphis to report the labor unrest as well as the Elvis pilgrimage. In the midst of it all, a drunken electric company employee knocked out most of the city's power supply.

All the side events and peculiar happenings—as well as a spate of retrospective analysis and commentary—filled newspapers and television screens once again. An editorial writer for *The New York Times* asked: "Which will seem more absurd to students of our time, the nationwide flap in the 1950's that kept Elvis Presley's gyrating hips from being televised or the hysteria with which his fans this week commemorated the first anniversary of his death?" The irreverent NBC television program *Saturday Night Live* satirized the situation in Memphis, interviewing the city's mayor, gum-chewing young National Guardsmen in full-battle dress, and two visiting British housewives wearing sweaters with "Elvis" stitched in rhinestones across the front. Gary Trudeau's "Doonesbury" cartoon strip made light of a fan who had visited Memphis and stocked up on Elvis souvenirs of questionable taste.

Elvis's box-office drawing power was tapped once more at the Las Vegas Hilton, where a romanticized statue was dedicated in September 1978. The life-sized bronze of the entertainer by Carl Romanelli was placed in a glass case outside the newly dedicated "Elvis Presley Showroom," the giant dinner theater where Presley—and only Presley—never played to an empty seat. Barron Hilton, head of the hotel chain, and Priscilla Presley pulled a gold cord to unveil the statue, a moment that highlighted an "Always Elvis" festival produced by Vernon Presley and Colonel Parker. *Variety* called the event in the hotel's pavillion "a big hustle," featuring a multimedia production, accompanied by a memorabilia display of costumes and personal effects, along with souvenir booths. Representatives of RCA Records presented Vernon with fifteen gold and platinum records in recognition of Elvis's record sales in the year following his death. At the Hughes Executive Terminal of the Las Vegas Airport, fans could see Elvis's Convair 880 jet, the *Lisa Marie*, for a five-dollar admission fee.

Another year passed and *Elvis*, the ABC television movie, attracted top ratings and critical prise. Dozens of books about the singer appeared, written by fans, by his nurse, by his bodyguards. Then, Elvis's father, Vernon, died and was buried at Graceland next to his first wife and his only child. His will named Priscilla Presley, Elvis's former wife, as executrix of the estate.

Compared to the two previous years, in August 1979 Memphis was calm. There were memorial services. A fiberglass model of the proposed statue was exhibited. Memphis State University presented a series of seminars on the man and his music to mark the second anniversary of his death. In Tupelo, officials dedicated the memorial chapel.

On September 13, 1979, came the ABC television bombshell that drugs—not a heart attack—killed Elvis. A few days later, *The New York Times* published a front page story about the mystery surrounding the singer's death two years earlier. *People* magazine ran a story about ABC's investigation in Memphis and featured Elvis on its cover. Once more the nation's media responded in a ricochet fashion even though the rumors of drug problems had been there all along. A few months after Elvis died, *The Commercial Appeal* had copyrighted a story by Beth Tampke which said that the singer's body contained at least ten different drugs and that a private autopsy report by Baptist Hospital listed the cause of death as "polypharmacy."

Simultaneously with the airing of ABC's *20/20* investigative report, Tennessee's Board of Medical Examiners charged Dr. George Nichopoulos with "overprescribing" drugs. A sensational public hearing in January 1980, with television cameras present, revealed that

Nichopoulos had prescribed "almost ten thousand tablets of uppers, downers, tranquilizers and narcotics" for Elvis in the twenty months before his death. The board suspended his license for ninety days and placed him on three months probation. On May 16, 1980, a Shelby County grand jury returned a fourteen-count indictment against Nichopoulos, charging him with "unlawfully, willfully and feloniously dispensing" ten controlled drugs.

The news of drug usage, the darker side of the Presley persona, dominated much of the media coverage, but it failed to diminish the appeal of the entertainer. Radio stations continued to play his music, responding to requests of loyal fans. His records continued to sell. A new market of teenagers developed. January 8 and August 16—the anniversaries of his birth and his death—became standard entries in wire service day books, the calendars that remind media assignment editors of important impending events. And crowds continued to come to Graceland.

Rumors persist that other Elvis songs exist—rejected tapes from his many recording sessions. Even if future audiences are limited to hearing only the existing Presley catalogue, the potential market for more Elvis recordings is mind-boggling. New albums will be issued with new covers and new combinations of songs. Records can be pressed on different colors of vinyl. Technology permits the addition of new music to the Presley voice tracks—a disco beat or more strings or a heavier bass. And the Presley voice can be joined in duets by Dolly Parton, Jim Reeves, John Denver, or other RCA recording artists.

Like so many other historic structures in Memphis, the building at 495 Union Avenue that housed the two newspapers and the wire service bureaus has been torn down. The building that was the nerve center for the huge media event surrounding Elvis's death has been replaced by a modern, mirrored edifice with carpeted rooms and computer terminals that one veteran reporter said resembles an insurance office more than a newspaper plant.

Other changes had come to Memphis in the three years following Elvis's death, but the city's plans to memorialize its most famous citizen remained in the discussion stage. A downtown park at Main and Beale was designated as the site for the Eric Parks statue, but legal problems remained and the quarter million dollars the memorial will cost had not been raised. Concern also centered on the fate of the Presley home. There seemed no opposition to the city's acquiring Graceland for preservation as a museum and historic site, but an agreement never got off the ground. In May 1980, Mrs. Minnie Presley, Elvis's grandmother, died and was buried in the meditation garden. Her death left Lisa Marie Presley as the sole heiress to the estate. Lisa's mother indicated to friends there would be no change at Graceland, however, leading to speculation that the decision would be left to Elvis's daughter, who comes into her full inheritance when she is twenty-five-years-old.

"We don't know what sort of interest will be there in the future," said Memphis City Attorney Clifford Pierce, Jr. "The crowds may continue to come, or he may wind up like Rudolph Valentino with one rose on his grave."

The appeal of Presley will, for many, forever remain a mystery. But there no longer is any question of the worldwide strength that appeal has. This is reinforced by the fact that the media was, in many cases, slow to sense the magnitude of the impact when Presley died. One major television network did not lead with the story, and several large newspapers did not send reporters to Memphis until street sales figures started coming in the following morning. Reporter after reporter said they had expected a big story—but nothing like what they found.

Events in the social sphere are more difficult to fathom because they are rarely logical. Nor do they always follow an ordered sequence. Moreover, conflicting forces often work simultaneously to bring about the same event. But this is all in accordance with reality: In any sports activity, for example, the freedom of "giving one's all" works side by side with the limitations of human possibilities to produce an intense emotional exhilaration. No single theory explains Elvis Presley and the reaction to his death.

It was a little over a year from the time Elvis made his first recording until he had the number one pop song in the land and was the human focal point of a cultural revolution that upset all in its path despite the sermons and diatribes against it and against him.

Over the next two decades, rock stars came and went—usually rapidly. The demise of Elvis was pronounced many times. But it never occurred.

When he died, his death in itself became a social event. It was not the trauma of a murdered John Kennedy or Martin Luther King. But the grief was real, outspoken, and wide.

Colleges and universities rapidly insured some permanence of the Presley phenomenon. By 1980 at least two hundred college courses centered on Elvis, his music, or the sociology of the fifties. *The Southern*

Quarterly, a journal of the arts published by the University of Southern Mississippi, called its Fall 1979 issue, "Elvis: Images and Fancies." With an Andy Warhol painting on its cover, the publication featured a dozen essays examining various facets of the man and the myth including music, religion, Southern identity, and his international appeal. The Library of Congress had catalogued some forty-nine books about Elvis (including titles in German, Spanish, Swedish, Finnish, Danish, and Czech), and the British Library, twenty-three. There were even books and stories about Elvis printed in Braille, especially tailored for junior high school blind children.

Young musicians began to discover—and rediscover—Presley's music. Vicki Helms Carter, music director of the Broadway show *Eubie,* said she heard dozens of classically trained musicians voicing their respect for Elvis's musical ability and style. "People get snobbish and don't want to talk about how they really liked him," said Carter, a native of Tupelo who never met her hometown's most famous son. "But once you get them to start—classical pianists, opera singers, whatever—they'll tell you how much they admired his natural talent. He didn't spend hours studying voice like we do now and taking those little lessons where you stand in front of a mirror so you know how to smile."

In Memphis, Sam Phillips got permission from the Federal Communications Commission to change the call letters of his radio station to WLVS. Featuring all kinds of music, the station played one nostalgia song each hour, frequently an Elvis recording. In Washington, D.C., Representative Barbara Mikulski, who represents a predominantly blue-collar Baltimore district in Congress, introduced House Joint Resolution 488, in January 1980, "authorizing and requesting the President to issue a proclamation designating January 8, 1981, as Elvis Presley Day." Later, other members of Congress from North Carolina to California co-sponsored the resolution.

Since Presley's death, his fans keep turning up in the strangest places. At the Department of Justice in Washington, the chief of the organized crime section, David Margolis, hung an Elvis poster on his office wall. So did Edward P. Beard, member of Congress from Rhode Island. Queen Sirikit of Thailand is an Elvis fan. So is Brian Weber, the white worker who challenged Kaiser Aluminum's affirmative action promotion policies as reverse discrimination. Former British Prime Minister James Callahan, in Memphis to speak to a business group, insisted on visiting Graceland. Robert Mugabe, the Marxist theoretician

and holder of six university degrees who became Zimbabwe's first president after bloody Rhodesian civil war, likes to relax by listening to Elvis
records.

Elvis Presley offered something for almost everyone. He began as a
catalyst for the new worldwide youth movement—as something that
belonged exclusively to the youth who faced adulthood with the great
economic depression and global war behind them, the nuclear age ahead.
One wonders if anything after 1957 really made any difference. In a
sense it didn't. The fuse had been lit, and Elvis Presley would have remained the symbol of the youth movement no matter what else happened.

But other things did happen. In the midst of the low quality output
after his days in the Army, Elvis continued to move with his generation
as time went on and they, too, grew older. Like them, he moved from
rebellion into the mainstream of American life.

When pressed to explain why the President of the United States felt
it would be "right" and "natural" to put out a statement on the death of a
popular singer like Elvis, the speechwriter who penned the tribute suggested after some thought, "because he unified popular culture both
here and all around the world."

This probably comes nearer to the mark than anything. It applied in
the United States because of Presley's unique intermingling of popular
musical styles, yet it was also a thought presaged in the mid-seventies at
so unlikely a place as a meeting of the Council of Europe. Raymond
Fletcher, a member of the House of Commons from Derbyshire in the
Midlands of England, told the parliamentarians that Elvis had done
more to unite Europe than they. Cognizant of the theory that political
phenomena often begin as musical events, Fletcher observed that Elvis
arrived on the European scene just as young people there became aware
that something new was beginning to happen. In a Europe just beginning
to grope away from old hatreds, Presley had an extra significance as a
common focus for European youth that he did not even carry in his own
country.

When Elvis opened his second show in Las Vegas, he mimicked Dean
Martin. As the entertainer who sold more records than anyone in history, Elvis received only one "Grammy" award from the music industry—
for his album of gospel songs. His rendition of "How Great Thou Art," a
hymn featured at Billy Graham revival crusades, was the highlight of
most of his concerts. He took the songs of others and gave them his own

unique interpretation. In his final performance, Elvis sang "My Way," a song written for Frank Sinatra by Paul Anka, and made it a hit. Yet other entertainers never took an Elvis song and made the audience forget who sang it best.

Elvis offered country ballads and great hymns and soft lullabies and an undemanding patriotism; but he also never lost the capacity to convey the rebelliousness and the unremitting, driving rock beat that had been his first trademark.

In the Music Room at Graceland, among all the gold records and other tributes, hangs the entertainer's high school diploma. Friends say he was prouder of that simple, framed document than all the other awards. He was the first member of his family to finish high school.

This is the dichotomy—distinctly Southern—that arrests the imagination and holds the attention. It is the white boy who drew on black music without affectation; the catalyst for rebellion who never himself rebelled; the quintessentially polite youth who took no gaffe; the religious man who might backslide on Saturday night; the no-nonsense musician who laughed at himself and the myth he had become.

While the paradox of Elvis challenged the mind of an entire generation, the hearts of millions were won by the hero who never forgot his people and his roots. He was not just the poor boy who made it to the top. He symbolized the ultimate rebellion of all common folk against all forms of restraint: He showed it was possible not just to *be* somebody, but to do it "the American way"—to be somebody and to have a good time doing it.

Selected Editorials

The Asheville Citizen
Asheville, North Carolina, August 18, 1977

The King

When Elvis Presley made the scene in the middle 1950s, the music world did not quite know how to take him. More than one critic and performer looked down a long nose of contempt at the young gyrating singer from Memphis as a "flash in the pan."

They were wrong, of course, terribly wrong. Presley not only survived in a cut-throat business, he prevailed through the rock and roll era and the music revolution of the 1960s and 1970s. He took what many considered a small talent as a singer and spanned several fields of music—rock and roll, blues, middle of the road, and spiritual. This "flash in the pan" glowed with 45 Gold Records.

There was a magic about the man and his music that still defies comprehension. Perhaps as close as we can come to understanding the spell Elvis cast over people was that he, at base, was a sincere, natural man, whose sincerity and naturalness came through in his words and songs.

We will never forget a hot summer night in 1969 in a tough Southern town. The bus station restaurant was full of GIs, for it was the height of the Vietnam conflict. On the jukebox, Presley was singing about ghetto children, and the cynical, young soldiers were listening intently. He sent chill bumps up our spine. The sincerity was not manufactured by some Hollywood or Nashville publicity agent: it came from the soul and heart and mind of the man.

The ability to lift hearts, young and old, helps explain why Elvis Presley was "The King," and why his star will continue to soar even in death.

The Atlanta Constitution
Atlanta, Georgia, August 17, 1977

Elvis Presley

Elvis Presley was an American phenomenon.

He came out of obscurity—more precisely Tupelo, Miss.—and became one of the most famous popular entertainers of his era. He was loved by millions of fans—and was looked on condescendingly by many others—as he sang almost incomprehensible but highly rhythmic and driving lyrics to songs that were the early versions of rock 'n' roll. *Nothin' But a Houn' Dog, Don't Be Cruel, Heartbreak Hotel*—these were only a few of his many millions-seller records. Unlike most popular music, Elvis' records are still played by his admirers—and those admirers now include many who first dismissed him as a passing fad.

Elvis was well known and well loved here in Atlanta where he appeared often and to wildly enthusiastic crowds. He was an innovator in music, a stylesetter, a charismatic personality who spawned a host of imitators. His singing style had variety, strength and unlike most popular singers, remarkable staying power.

But, behind all the show business glitter that was an inevitable part of the career of a popular singer, Elvis had a strong vein of solid character. At the height of his fame he went into the Army when his country called and served the hitch without complaint. Later he made a long series of popular movies—and turned out to be a pretty fair actor.

Late yesterday the news came that Elvis Presley, 42, had died suddenly, unexpectedly. It was a shock. He was still a young man. He was still going strong in his career. His music was still as popular as ever. "I've got simple pleasures," Elvis, a modest man, once said. "You can't go beyond your limitations."

Elvis Presley gave a great deal of pleasure to a great many people. Whatever his limits may have been, he will be remembered for his remarkable talent.

The Atlanta Journal
Atlanta, Georgia, August 17, 1977

Death Of A Star

A lot of people feel a bit older and much sadder at the news of the death of Elvis Presley. Some of them grew up in the shadow of his stardom, and will find it hard to accept that he is gone so soon.

When he first burst upon the entertainment scene in the 1950s Elvis was a symbol of youthful rebellion. His hair was a little longer than standard, he was pioneering in popularizing rock-and-roll music which was controversial in itself, and there were his physical gyrations when he performed, gyrations which had to be censored in his first appearance on the Ed Sullivan show.

But the age of the early Elvis was an age of innocence compared with what was to come later. He never pushed drugs in his songs; whatever the truth about his private life, he never publicly paraded perversity or tried to influence others toward it. These things were in sharp contrast to the behavior of later idols of youth. And he quietly did his duty to his country when the call came.

In his many films, which were often more entertaining then sophisticated critics cared to admit, Presley usually portrayed an honorable, decent sort of fellow. If he got in trouble it wasn't because he was really bad, only misunderstood.

Through the years he remained one of the top attractions of the entertainment world. Near the end he retained popularity with those who had been young when he was, and was just as popular with some of their sons and daughters.

Though it is sad, it is also strangely appropriate that this idol of youth spent only a short time in the middle years of life and thus will remain forever young in the memory of most of his fans.

The Record
Bergen County, New Jersey, August 18, 1977

Elvis

Forget the swiveling hips that Ed Sullivan was afraid to show on the TV screen. Forget the excessive adulation that caused teen-aged fans to scream and faint at the mere sight of him. Forget the greasy hair, sideburns, pink Cadillacs, and the trivial, sentimental movies. Elvis Presley was an original, an authentic innovator of American popular music. With his untimely death this week, we have lost the man who—more than anyone else—created rock 'n'roll.

Many others helped pave the way. Little Richard, Chuck Berry, Jerry Lee Lewis, Bill Haley, the Drifters: All applied their talent and ambition to fuse together the two roots, rhythm-and-blues and country music, that came together as rock 'n' roll. But none did it as well as Elvis, and none did it on so grand a scale. In his songs and in his image, Elvis captured the essence of rock. His songs were simple, direct, and earthy. They were honest, yet full of vitality. In contrast to the bland and often pretentious popular music being churned out by Tin Pan Alley when he came on the scene in the mid-Fifties, Elvis's material was full of passion and exuberance.

He was primarily a performer, seldom writing the songs he made famous. But as a performer he had no peer. His deep, rich voice could growl out a number, in the words of rock critic Greil Marcus, with "an ease and an intensity that has no parallel in American music. ... He cooked up a sound all his own: hot, fierce, overbearing, full of energy and desire, a sound to jump right out of the jukebox."

He became the focus of an aggressive, tough, youth-oriented music that redefined popular forms. His image, like his music, was simultaneously arrogant and innocent, raucous and sweet. He perfected the image of the rocker as working-class rebel that later stars, from John Lennon and Bob Dylan to Bruce Springsteen, could only imitate.

His later career, unfortunately, was only a dull echo of his formative days. An overweight Elvis would croon for the nightclub crowd in Las Vegas, but, with occasional exceptions, he had lost the fire on which he had once thrived. Perhaps it isn't possible for creators of this rebellious and passionate young music to sustain an extended career; perhaps respectability and success blunted Presley's early passion; maybe he had simply said what he had to say.

It doesn't matter. His contribution is there to be heard, again and again, in his early recordings. Elvis Presley rose from obscurity and transformed American popular music. It's as simple as that, one of those rare cases where the legend is actually matched by the deed.

The Daily Herald
Biloxi-Gulfport, Mississippi, August 18, 1977
From Tupelo to "Heartbreak Hotel"

The hearts of three decades of teenagers are heavy today. Mississippians sustain a unique loss, not limited to the claim that he was a native son of Tupelo.

Many long time Coast residents remember their acquaintance with Elvis Presley before his fame had spread nationally. He performed, with two other musicians, at the old Biloxi Community Center, later destroyed by fire, for $150 a night and at Keesler AFB and other places.

On his frequent visits to the Coast in those yearling days, he often gave impromptu performances at Sie's Place in Biloxi and he could be seen at numerous spots along the Beach. Even then, his generosity, his appreciation for his fans and his sense of contact with everyday people was evident.

A heart attack snuffed out his life in middle age (42) while Presley maintained his reign in the tumultuous music business for 20 years.

They still love him tender in Tupelo where Presley was born in a two-room shotgun house on January 8, 1935. His hometown and thousands of other people were touched by his unexpected generosity over the years. He shared his success. Those who know around Tupelo tell the stories about how Presley had given secret donations for charities and spent thousands of dollars for food baskets. He gave Cadillacs to security guards and just plain strangers.

He strode into Jackson in May 1975 for a benefit performance to raise funds for homeless victims of a McComb toranado. He left a $108,000 check behind.

We knew less and less of Elvis the Pelvis in his middle-aged years. Hungry gossip columnists changed it to Elvis the Paunch. He lived like a king in his multi-million dollar Memphis mansion named Graceland. His managers shrewdly shielded Presley in Howard Hughes-like seclusion, creating only that much more demand from teenage fans. Many were born after his national debut in 1956 on the Ed Sullivan Show. Parents were revolted by his gyrations, his black leather and motorcycle image. His fans made him more than a rock'n'roll star—they made him a symbol of teenage rebellion that gave birth to the Beatles years later. But the Beatles are has-beens. Presley was still king at death. His performances were sold out just as fast in 1977 as in 1957.

The slicked-back hair and T-shirt image he cast on the American public in the mid-1950's fit the times. It mirrored his poor childhood in Mississippi. His rebel stage attitude that alarmed America's parents could be changed as fast as his stage clothes. After all, it was a $4 birthday recording that Presley made for his mother that skyrocketed the truck-driving high school graduate into a 19-year-old teenage heart throb. A stint in the Army smoothed some of his rough edges and Presley changed into an all-American boy-next-door at the dawn of the '60s. The leather image of the '50s gave way to satins and silks and sequins of the '70s, but the magic was still the same.

The Presley legend after death will become larger than the King himself in life. Elvis is one Mississippian who won't be forgotten.

His music was an odd mix. It wasn't rock. It wasn't pop. It wasn't country and western. But there's an awful lot of Mississippi and Memphis and the southern country life mixed in those 250 million albums.

The Birmingham News

Birmingham, Alabama, August 18, 1977

King of Rock'N Roll

Elvis Presley, singing idol of the 50s, had aged since "Hound Dog," and "All Shook Up." His hips didn't swivel as they had 20 years ago. He had gained lots of weight.

But the magic in his voice was the same early this year when he performed at the Birmingham-Jefferson County Civic Center Coliseum. Teenagers didn't swoon, but the over-30s, those who had been teens when Elvis started out, cheered and whistled and gave the King of Rock'N Roll a standing ovation.

Many memories are tied to the music and lyrics of Elvis' songs—to what was, back then, a "new" sound. "Elvis the Pelvis" sneered fathers as they forbade daughters from attending a concert, and as mothers collected albums with such memorable soulful sounds as "Love Me Tender."

The tall, skinny, hip-swinging kid from Tupelo, Miss., opened pop music to innovation and changed the performing style of singers and instrumentalists. Today's big stage with musicians scattered over it, floating spotlights and mixture of country, western, blues and back-country revival hymns are spin-offs from the style of Elvis Presley.

Elvis had the magnetic quality of a star and the down-to-earth sincerity of the boy next door. He is dead at 42, but his musical legacy will last, on and on.

The Idaho Statesman

Boise, Idaho, August 19, 1977

So Long, Elvis

That he will be missed is an exercise in understatement. Between yearbook pictures with scribbled missives and corny love notes, Elvis' portrait is missing, but we all know that he belonged. He was an important classmate and made growing up a lot less painful than most locker partners.

And he was unorthodox. Even his death was unorthodox. Some rock 'n' roll stars found musical immortality with a drug overdose. Elvis did it differently.

He changed things.

With him, big bands gave way to single low-slung guitars, twitching lips and swiveling hips. His lyrics were perhaps less inspired than the pop that was sung before him, but his delivery made things happen. That he could sing "Heartbreak Hotel" and "Jailhouse Rock," keep every bone in his body in perpetual motion and still not pass out from exhaustion is some kind of showbiz landmark.

The music was white and bluesy—a paradox in the Beale Street days of Memphis.

The top 100 hits of the late '50s are saturated with Elvis' songs. Some will become standards. They were titles that changed our cotton pickin' ideas of the South. Every song he sang, whether it was about the ghetto, the jailhouse or God, was deeply rooted in middle- and lower-class Southern life. Not until the mid-'60s did Elvis get political with some of his songs.

Parents watched his TV specials with one eye open for curiosity, the other closed for dignity.

A Rolling Stone writer said that without Elvis, we'd look different today: our clothes, our hair, our dance, our style. Without Elvis, our music would sound different. That his impact was more cultural than artful is a foregone conclusion.

He's really not dead after all.

The Boston Globe
Boston, Massachusetts, August 18, 1977

The Elvis legend

Elvis Presley's life was an American life. The Horatio Alger story of a $35-a-week truck driver who made millions. The sneering rebel rejected, then embraced by the mainstream. The young man who willingly sacrificed a bit of his career to serve his country. The craftily marketed "star." The conspicuous consumption. The equally conspicuous generosity. The enduring tension between the demands of celebrity and the desire for privacy. And, underpinning it all, a unique and legitimate talent.

In recent years, as the changing styles and substance of rock flashed by, Elvis seemed increasingly an icon from an earlier age. He evinced neither a social conscience nor a social antipathy. In an age of wiry stars, he had a problem with his weight. With jeans and body shirts the uniforms of the day, his gold lame suits and high shirt collars seemed as outdated as high-button shoes. In an age when stars led lives of quiet ostentation, Elvis's Memphis mansion with its regiment of hangers-on and its motorpool of Cadillacs seemed unfashionable, even gauche. And in a time when the Beatles had long since "done it in the road," Elvis's modest pelvic rolls were tame indeed. Like other fading stars of the entertainment arts, Elvis seemed to become almost a parody of himself.

But if pop music passed Elvis by, it traveled on the course he had set. With his DA haircut, his low-slung pants, his undulations, his driving rhythms, his curled upper lip, Elvis led a revolt against the Tin Pan Alley music of the Fifties. Thousands of screaming and adulating fans joined the cause. And it triumphed.

Others sharpened the rock revolt, made its sexual appeal even more overt, added to both the substance of the lyrics and the subtlety of the music, allied it with the broader cultural and political ferment of the time.

With his rebellious pose and his driving style, Elvis had an effect on each succeeding phase. As the song said, rock 'n roll is here to stay—at least its influence is. And with it will remain the legend and legacy of Elvis.

Buffalo Evening News
Buffalo, New York, August 17, 1977

Elvis

There never has been anybody like Elvis Presley. There have been superstars before and hysterical audiences before, but Elvis created his own particular style of magic when before an audience. A generation ago when he was skyrocketing to stardom, it was popular for those over 30 (those who had swooned over Sinatra or Johnny Ray) to sneer at Elvis and his young fans, but he was undeniably a great performer who had a phenomenal effect on an audience.

Elvis was a Mississippi boy who grew up on the wrong side of the tracks at a time when the "big band" era was ending and rock 'n'roll was beginning. He became the undisputed king of the new beat with such songs as "You Ain't Nothing But a Hound Dog," but also displayed another side in slow, expressive songs such as "Love Me Tender."

His death at only 42 years of age is especially tragic since he was a youth star who was still in mid-career. He will be mourned and missed by millions throughout the world, including countless admirers in Buffalo, where he was planning another visit this fall.

The Charleston Gazette
Charleston, West Virginia, August 18, 1977

Presley Kept People Appeal

More than any other peoples, Americans make heroes of entertainers, invariably fuzzing the line between performance and reality.

As a result, entertainers themselves also fuzz the line, adopting personalities suited to savored roles. Thus did John Wayne come to be spokesman for the he-man school of political thought with his performances becoming a secondary pursuit.

Nor was Elvis Presley merely a performer blessed with a pleasing voice. He was the ultimate Good Ol' Boy, not in the perjorative sense but in the sense of a man who could communicate amiably with those millions of Americans who do not sit in corporate offices.

There was a comfortable-as-an-old-shoe magnetism in Presley's appeal to a huge and largely blue-collar constituency. He was a motion picture star but was never "Hollywood." He lived in a palace but never let himself or anyone else forget he had been a truck driver.

Presley is survived by other American heroes. But John Wayne and Frank Sinatra—as John L. Lewis and Harry Truman did—have outlived, almost, their own fame. It is a cruel truth that he who dies at the heights is most venerated and best remembered.

The Charlotte Observer
Charlotte, North Carolina, August 17, 1977

Elvis Rocked The Music World

People who knew Elvis Presley only through his movies and later albums can only imagine the revolution he brought to the music world.

He gave musical propriety a quick flip of the hip, knocking its restrictions aside to clear the way for a new vitality in form and performance of popular music. On stage, he let the music move him with a roguish abandon that caused TV moguls to ban below-the-navel shots of his performance.

An Elvis Presley cannot be a private person; he is the prisoner of his fame. But he appeared to bear it well, with little of the public pettiness of some superstars.

There will be other stars, but not another Elvis Presley. He was the most exciting performer of his generation.

The Chattanooga Times
Chattanooga, Tennessee, August 19, 1977

Passing of an Idol

At 42, Elvis Presley was 20 years away from the dawning of the rock-'n-roll era of which he was the main architect and became the chief idol. In cutting two-score million-copy records and appearing in numerous low-budget movies, he made millions. No one seems to know quite how many. In quixotic bursts of generosity, he gave away huge sums. No one stopped to tote up the sum. But quite apparently, there was plenty left.

He was a man of many contradictions. He lived the supercharged life of a superstar, but he never severed the ties which bound him to kinspeople with whom he had emerged from a Mississippi dirt-farm background. Fans mobbed him wherever he went, but he retired when he could to his Memphis home in isolation from the public. His first marriage reputedly was a stormy one and some associates said he depended heavily upon "pep pills" to mould his moods; another close friend, however, characterized him as basically a religious person. One of his greatest hits was an album of "old time" hymns.

The Russians said not long ago that Elvis Presley was an example of how capitalism uses a person up and casts him aside, friendless and in rags. Some discard, some rags! He had just launched a whole new series of tours which promised to establish the fact his popularity had extended into a second generation.

A heart attack ended his life Tuesday, leaving unanswered the question of whether he had attained or could ever reach that stage of life which most persons regard as one of contentment and satisfaction.

Chicago Daily News
Chicago, Illinois, August 18, 1977

Era passes with Elvis

Elvis Presley, dead. Whether his first gyrations and passionate renditions titillated you as a teen or repulsed you as an adult, they simply don't seem to have erupted that long ago for the rock 'n' roll king, now, to be gone, at the age of 42.

Yes, the mind runs through the social turmoil, the political protests and the lifestyle changes of more recent years and tells you that the "care-free good old days" of the '50s are indeed long gone. But the periodic reappearance of Elvis had created a comforting bond to which the emotions could cling and that eclipsed the passage of decades.

As inevitably noted upon his most recent performances, the idol had not escaped age. He was beginning to bald. He had acquired a paunch. His bumps and grinds were more subdued. But unlike some other idols, lesser ones to be sure, of his heyday, he didn't try to update his act or affectations. No torn T-shirts and bluejeans for him; he stuck to his star-spangled duds. No songs of protest or rebellion; just the plaintive ballads and upbeat rockers. He wasn't the Elvis of old, but he didn't magnify the slippage with what would have been a futile and embarrassing grab for the contemporary audience. The once frenzied teenager could easily return to the joys of past adolescence. And the once repulsed adult who may have grown even more repulsed by some of today's pop stars could smile at the innocuousness of it all.

A revolutionary figure in the evolution of music is dead. The one true tie to a time fondly recalled and increasingly imitated has been broken.

Chicago Sun-Times
Chicago, Illinois, August 18, 1977

Elvis: time for blues

A little gospel and, yes, a little blues.

Elvis Presley, dead at 42, had his beginning in potent Southern music; it's only fitting for his ending, too.

A new generation grew up with his rock and roll, idolized him, fed on his energy. He knew what he had, and he shook it. He curled his lip, and thousands screamed.

He held some in a 20-year spell of sequins, tight pants and throaty ballads. On stage and film and records, he was on a sensual attack—wiggling and sneering and playing the bedroom-eyed baritone "punk."

But in private, he retreated from swagger to insecurity—behind bodyguards and high fences and the impersonality of expensive, impulsive gifts to strangers. Some say he retreated to heavy, heavy drugs.

If he was indeed the "lonely little kid" from Tupelo, Miss., as a bodyguard has said, then this man the world knew on a first-name basis never knew himself well enough. Or perhaps he knew and did not like.

Decades as "The King" affected him. The body failed the test of his reign. Apparently the spirit flagged, too. Then the energy—and thus so much of the talent.

At least the legend lives.

Chicago Tribune

Chicago, Illinois, August 18, 1977

Elvis Presley

The death of Elvis Presley at 42 reminds us of a lot of things. It reminds us that a meagerly educated former truck driver from a little Mississippi town could have more influence on the popular culture and popular music of America and of foreign lands than politicians and conservatory musicians.

It reminds us that we are a society of incredibly upward mibility, where cultural democracy instead of cultural czars determines who shall be successful and influential. On his way to riches, Mr. Presley turned off most parents while turning on a whole generation of children to a new, hard-driving sound that influenced the more "refined" artists of song who followed. Britain's Beatles and America's own Bob Dylan, for example, stepped grandly onto an international stage that Elvis had set.

Like many entertainers, Mr. Presley did not live a conventionally model life. He wasn't able to handle his wealth and stardom particularly well; his habits may have helped to shorten his life.

His success was achieved not so much by the technical quality of his voice as by the explosive quality of his presence. It was a passionate, gyrating, frankly sexual presence, half sweet young working-class boy, half menacing, greasy-haired, leather-jacketed punk. It scared adults, excited young girls, and enabled him to outdraw President Eisenhower on television.

Still, his influence should be seen in perspective. He no more caused the so-called sexual revolution than he did the rift between the generations. The society would undoubtedly have changed, as societies always do, without him.

But the sheer volume of his work—45 records that each sold one million or more copies and 31 motion pictures—refutes any notion that he wasn't somebody special in the nation's popular consciousness.

The Plain Dealer

Cleveland, Ohio, August 18, 1977

Elvis Aron Presley

It is impossible to imagine the compilation of any history of American culture, and particularly American popular music during the late 1950s and early 1960s, that would not include a discussion of the late Elvis Aron Presley.

To an extraordinary degree, Presley became synonymous with the uniquely American musical phenomenon known as rock-and-roll. He was its pre-eminent practitioner.

A generation of Americans grew up listening and dancing to the combination country and blues styles that characterized rock-and-roll. Most of them were fans of the sharecropper's son from Tupelo, Miss.

Whatever the moral debates that raged over Presley's sensuous delivery, most Americans came to see him as a decent and kindly individual who uncomplainingly served in the armed forces at the height of his fame and dissipated chunks of his fortune buying Cadillacs for his family and friends.

He wore his wealth and fame with courtesy and dignity if not always with the greatest wisdom. And unlike many popular music stars, Presley had the wits and talent to change with the times, a fact that permitted him to amass new fans and fortunes for two decades.

His niche in the cultural history of his country is secure and it is entirely fitting that his untimely passing is mourned by millions.

The Cleveland Press

Cleveland, Ohio, August 17, 1977

Elvis, the king, is dead

It hardly seems possible that Elvis Presley, the king of American rock and roll, is dead at the age of 42.

With the exception of Frank Sinatra, it is difficult to think of another entertainer who shot to stardom so fast and stayed at the top of the heap for so long.

There never was anything subtle about Presley's approach to music. His style was sensual, suggestive and appealed to something basic and visceral in his millions of fans.

Born in a two-room house in Tupelo, Miss., he was already a show business legend in his early 20's and by the age of 30 was the highest paid performer in the history of show business.

Anyone who grew up in the early 1950's heard his early hits like "Hound Dog" and "Blue Suede Shoes" constantly blaring from jukeboxes and radios. Bluenoses found his delivery so blatantly suggestive that in his early appearances on TV the camera would show him only from the waist up, hiding the grinding Elvis' pelvis.

In the last few years he appeared bloated, still encased in the skin-tight pants that were his trademark. If he was no longer svelte, that in no way diminished his appeal, as his last successful appearance at the Coliseum here demonstrated.

There was evidence that Presley had turned to drugs, but this apparently played no part in his death, ascribed to a heart attack. Elvis Presley was an original and millions will mourn the untimely death of the man who truly was King of American rock and roll.

The State

Columbia, South Carolina, August 20, 1977

Elvis Presley

The untimely death of the King of Rock-and-Roll, Elvis Presley, has taken on the appearance of a national tragedy, and that it is for legions of his devoted fans.

The spontaneous and unabashed outpouring of affection by people of all ages across the social strata of America is a cultural phenomenon, reflected in the media's heavy coverage of his death.

Indeed, Elvis Presley was a phenomenon, a rare and significant individual from whom Americans for two decades drew an infusion of new cultural blood. His arrival on the entertainment scene in the mid-1950s marked the beginning of a new era in music, lifestyles, modes of dress and appearances, and youthful departure from adult-established standards of behavior.

There is a paradox. Presley's hip-swinging, sexy performances—his style—were carefully calculated to excite his audiences, as were the lyrics and the beat of his music. Yet, in news stories about his life there is much evidence of a gentle and generous man, sensitive to his friends and family, and an absence of the raunchy stories often associated with superstars.

The personal traits were not lost on his fans. It has been his human qualities of which they speak now, not the performance, not the entertainer, not his style and music—those remain on film, tapes and records. It is the person of Elvis Presley for which they grieve.

However one may have related or reacted to Elvis Presley, his death invokes a genuine American legend. He has touched the hearts of many, and, with his singular impact on our culture, he influenced the lives of all.

The Dallas Morning News
Dallas, Texas, August 18, 1977

King Elvis

From the acres of newsprint, the oceans of words expended on his passing, one might have supposed Elvis Presley to be a president or a king. And perhaps in fact he was. If the popular music of the '50s, '60s and '70s can be said to have had a monarch, that monarch was Elvis. No other performer of his generation—not even, surely, the Beatles—made so many scream with delight, nor stayed so long at the top.

What was it about Elvis? Was it stage presence, animal magnetism, sex appeal, musical style? Maybe it was all of them, bunched together in an exotic, intoxicating bouquet.

Of course Presley was not everyone's cup of tea. He was blamed more than any otner rock 'n' roller for the demise of "good music," and in the '50s his gyrations stirred national debate. But in retrospect, it is hard not to like him. He was no sullen lump of conceits and neuroses—like so many rock stars—nor was his an angry voice of protest. He was fundamentally a good old boy from Mississippi who wanted no more than to do what he did best—entertain.

Dayton Daily News
Dayton, Ohio, August 18, 1977

A man of his times' limitations

Elvis dead at 42? That seems as improbable as his life—or his lives.

The shy, benevolent man never seemed quite whole, not even as the living legend that made him a virtual recluse except when he stormed into his concerts.

Some say his impact on music will keep his name alive for many centuries. This is a majestic epitaph; it's not true, but it doesn't detract from his accomplishments to acknowledge that. His real impact came from the collective mood of his time, and probably not even he understood the psychic chemistry of his success.

Just as Rudolph Valentino is hard for this generation to understand as an emotional experience of different times, so Elvis was hard for 1950s parents to understand. But to many of the young, he expressed a new musical thrust—a combination of country, popular and blues music blended with a raw, straight-forward force.

Thus Elvis grew into more than a person. He was a man who also was a production, a popular expression. He played the role— which became an ambience for its era— and became enormously rich by it.

But he never seemed to be freed by it. The humility and frenzied fans were a curious combination. He cherished privacy, a close circle of friends and seemed bemused by the furore. He had cars, women, bejeweled clothes—anything material that he wanted—but he knew the real limits of the image created by the needs of the public, and he was both trapped and nourished by that image, that collective mindset.

Because he was so popular, and in his way contributed so much to others' enjoyment, those who liked him assumed—or at least hoped—that he was happy. But it is hard to avoid the nagging feeling that he wasn't. In that, too, he exemplified something of our times, limits of the outward glory we have arranged for others in order that we might share it through them, hoping we will touch something more, something deeper, something lasting.

Dead at 42.

The Denver Post
Denver, Colorado, August 18, 1977
Suddenly we feel older

It's one of those moments that makes a whole generation suddenly feel older. Elvis Presley is dead in Memphis at age 42 of a heart ailment.

To his fans, it seems incomprehensible. Not that a singer could die—but that an era could slide by so quickly.

The vividness of the memories defies their decades-old label. Close your eyes for just a moment and it's 1956 again, with that lanky rebel staring at you in the halftones of the Ed Sullivan show; writhing with raw uncontrolled energy to "You ain't nothing but a houn' dog..."

Though they seem tame by the antics of today's rock stars, the gyrations of the "The Pelvis" were deemed so potent that the cameras were discreetly focused above his waist. But the motions wouldn't stay censored, and were mimicked by a generation defiantly roaring "Keep off my blue suede shoes!"

Not that all the young were Elvis fans. But his presence was so dominating that even his detractors ended up incorporating parts of him in their self-definitions, as part of what they weren't if not as part of what they were.

There had been phenomena before, like Frank Sinatra. But Elvis was the first super-star of the television age, when such personalities acquired unprecedented impact. Later, he would lose his menacing image as the rock culture of the drug-drenched '60s consumed many of its brightest stars in tragic deaths.

Critics then accused the mellowed Elvis of "selling out." They missed the point. The essential cry of the American rebel has never been for destruction but for a piece of the action.

Elvis' share was larger than most, but he was generous about sharing it, as those who remember his car-gift spree in Denver know. And his fans were carving out their own modest but comfortable niches of America themselves- and he kept his broad appeal.

He told us, after all, "I don't want to be your tiger, cuz' tigers play too rough...just want to be your teddy bear."

And he made the transition, from raw tiger of youthful rebellion to lovable teddy bear of a still lively and vital but more mature following.

And now he is gone, departed in the prime of life. But he left his epitaph in "Hound Dog." For those who loved him, Elvis Presley was high class—and that was no line.

The Des Moines Register
Des Moines, Iowa, August 18, 1977
He Shocked and Influenced

It began with Elvis.

Other artists had captured elements of the sound and beat of rock and roll before him. But it was the kid from Memphis who blended gospel, "hillbilly" and rhythm and blues into the musical tidal wave which would eventually—after leaping the Atlantic and bouncing back with The Beatles—sweep all popular music before it.

Elvis Presley was a legend when he died Tuesday at 42, apparently of a heart attack. In his first decade he was so big he could maintain multi-million dollar incomes from records and B-caliber movies without the hassle of concerts.

In recent years, record sales had not been so phenomenal. But lines—and prices—for concerts were.

Television and radio networks preempted regular programs for tributes Tuesday night. The story of his rocket to fame and two decades of super-idol status were told and retold.

The retelling cannot convey to those who did not share it the magnitude of the shock waves Presley set off in middle-class homes in the late 1950s. He was an intruder, threatening and even repulsive. He looked like the "hoods" at high school. The music was low-class in character. His pelvic grinding and overt sexuality boggled the mind.

But the music was his own. In 22 years it didn't change much. Neither did he. The music was overshadowed by the phenomenon of his celebrity. The celebrity, however, was less the product of ballyhoo than his raw genius.

Detroit Free Press
Detroit, Michigan, August 18, 1977

Elvis: Symbol of an Age

Elvis Presley was far more than the pulsating pasha of rock 'n' roll that was his popular image. He was the symbol of an age, of a time in American life when there were few heroes, when many of the country's youth had lost their innocence on the far-off battlefields of Pork Chop Hill and Heartbreak Ridge.

Elvis filled a need for hundreds of thousands of young Americans they couldn't express in words. More than any other figure in their youthful lives, Elvis was theirs—someone to emulate, to identify with, to adore.

And he proved to be an enduring figure. When he entered his forties, and began to put on weight, his fans—many of them now happily married and with children of their own—loved him just the same.

He was said to be a sex figure, a swiveling chimera of good times, loose morals, and the free and easy life. But that was only the facade. Beneath there lay a person of warmth, of generosity, of indominable spirit.

He was the one and only Elvis. Let that be his grandest epitaph.

Fort Worth Star-Telegram
Fort Worth, Texas, August 18, 1977

Elvis

Forty-two is a tender age for anyone to confront death.

The early age added to the shock Americans felt at news that Elvis Presley had died. It by no means accounted for the sense of loss felt so sincerely by so many.

Numerical years don't measure the timeless impact that Elvis (his fame was such that a surname was unnecessary) had on American life.

He was a bridge between generations, a controversial but talented individual who not only charmed his own '50s generation but who changed the very fabric of America's musical tastes.

His style—gyrating hips, long sideburns and music such as "You Ain't Nothing But a Hound Dog"—infuriated some, but his fans were vocal and loyal.

Even in the first year in his climb to lasting fame—1956—Elvis filled the 7,000 seats in Fort Worth's North Side Coliseum.

Nearly 20 years later a scheduled one-nighter in the 14,000-seat Tarrant County Convention Center stretched into four nights due to sellouts.

The former truck driver, Tupelo, Miss.-born, recorded his first hit, "Blue Moon of Kentucky," in 1955. His rise to fame was rapid.

His popularity zoomed as each of the million-sellers came—more than 30 gold records in all.

Then came the ultimate compliment in that age, an appearance on the Ed Sullivan Show, where fears about his sexuality caused him to be shown only from the waist up. Regardless, the show was watched on a single network by more people than saw President Eisenhower make his acceptance speech on three networks.

He appeared in about 25 movies during his career.

Elvis, considered by some in those early years to be a flash-in-the-pan, launched and secured the rock 'n' roll era and made a lasting impact on Americana much greater than his 42 years might suggest.

His mother knew his secret. She once told him:

"You're puttin' too much into your singing. Keep that up, you won't live to be 30."

He will be missed.

Greensboro Daily News

Greensboro, North Carolina, August 17, 1977

Elvis

The king is dead.

It seems only yesterday that this jaunty sideburned singer swivel-hipped his way to stardom on the Ed Sullivan show. They filmed him only from the waist up, but that was provocation enough. Teenagers screamed, and so rock 'n' roll was officially born.

Elvis' music, like his person, was passionate. It plucked heart strings and stirred emotions. He was a crooner who projected blues with a streak of country. He didn't just sing into microphones, he seduced them.

Elvis energized a whole generation, down to the last duck-tail. His was the early music of rebellion. People be-bopped when he strutted, sighed when he joined the Army, envied his opulence and marveled at his endurance. He was emulated and imitated, but never equaled.

Success eventually took its toll on Elvis, as it has other rock stars. He became reclusive and overweight. He was only 42 when he died.

Because of Elvis, to paraphrase the song, rock 'n' roll is here to stay. But now that he is gone, it will never be the same.

The Greenville News

Greenville, South Carolina, August 18, 1977

Elvis

A classified advertisement in The Greenville News-Greenville Piedmont of last Sunday said the advertiser wanted to buy 3 "Elvis" tickets to the Asheville concert.

That pretty well shows the pulling power of the king of rock-and-roll, the guy who made popular a new song and dance style and possibly a new lifestyle back in the 1950's.

Elvis won't be in Asheville. He died Tuesday and a whole generation was shocked by his passing at age 42.

Seems like only yesterday when Elvis the Pelvis began twitching, banging his guitar and singing and sneering on stage to set the young girls wild. He also set off a new thing in the world of entertainment.

Many entertainers of today acknowledge artistic descent from him.

The news columns and air-waves are full of stories about Elvis and personal accounts from some of his multitude of admirers. Many try to explain his appeal to and hold over so many people for so long a time. Perhaps he caught a mood of change and was able to express it before others could grasp the fact that the mood of the young was in a state of flux.

You can start a hot argument over whether Elvis was a good or a bad influence. But there is no room to argue the fact of his enormous influence through his hold on a whole generation. Now Elvis is dead—and nobody asks, "Elvis Who?"

The Hartford Courant

Hartford, Connecticut, August 18, 1977

The King Is Dead

It would have been impossible, 20 years ago, to imagine that Elvis Presley would be mourned by "wholesome" Americans, "family" people.

For Mr. Presley was perceived to be a rebel. With his slick black hair and plunging sideburns, turned-up collar, permanent sneer and, most of all, his famed wiggling pelvis, he was just what parents warned their children against.

But at his death, he was remembered for his virtues. He believed in God, attended church and recorded much religious music. He called his elders "sir" and "ma'am," adored his parents, and served honorably in the Army. He neither drank nor smoked.

Mr. Presley's impact on American popular music was great, although it was felt most in the mid-1950s when he was just gaining popularity. He gave white teenagers the same type of music that black "rhythm-and-blues" performers had been exhibiting to black audiences. The result was rock and roll, which author Mark Crispin Miller called "the great domestic annoyance of the 1950s."

Neither a songwriter nor an especially adept instrumentalist, Mr. Presley was best known for his singing style. On the fast songs—the rockers—he shut his eyes, gyrated his hips, and belted out the tunes. On the slow ones—the rollers—he hunched over the microphone, stared at the audience with heavy-lidded eyes, and crooned in a low voice. Either way, the effect was astonishing and he spawned an entire genration of popular singers.

But when he joined the Army in 1958, his days as a mu:ical innovator were over. Emerging two years later without the

grease, the sideburns or the cocky swagger, he settled comfortably into stardom.

He married, then divorced, a woman he met in Germany, and they had a daughter, now 9. All the time, he put out a constant stream of movies and records, and passed into middle age with his fans.

When Mr. Presley appeared in Hartford last year, the sellout crowd at the Hartford Civic Center was enthusiastic but subdued in comparison to other pop music audiences. It was a largely adult crowd, which had gone from bobby sox to pantyhose as their hero had traded his blue jeans and Army fatigues for a glittering white Las Vegas-style suit.

For 20 years, Mr. Presley was known as the King of Rock and Roll. Through the fads and fancies of the 1960s and 1970s, he kept a powerful grip on the throne; the Hartford show held in 1976 sold out in six and a half hours.

Now, at 42, the King is dead. And though it can hardly be said that Mr. Presley advanced what is called "culture," it is only fitting that his title be retired.

The Honolulu Advertiser
Honolulu, Hawaii, August 17, 1977

Elvis

Elvis Presley was several things to the American people in a career that spanned three decades.

When he first came on the scene in the mid-1950s, he was a national phenomenon, a pop hero with the kind of screaming teen-age fans Frank Sinatra brought forth in the early 1940s.

Many considered his gyrations morally shocking. Parents often saw his brash black-leather stage image as a threat.

And in a sense Presley may be seen in retrospect sociologically as a kind of early warning for adults of the kind of culture shock that awaited them in the 1960s and early '70s. Some viewed him in later years with nostalgia.

But there was more to Elvis Presley than animal image and public outrage. For he was an unlikely pioneer in the revolution that has taken place in popular music.

Critics were harsh when he first appeared. But today many credit him with

popularizing the synthesis of black blues and white country music that became rock-and-roll.

In the process, he inspired or stimulated many young musicians including several teen-agers growing up in Liverpool who were to become the Beatles.

Some older adults will still regard that a dubious contribution to American music. But there is no doubt Presley is appreciated by millions more people today as a major figure in popular music, and a kind of Sun-King star who lived in an older image.

Singer Pat Boone, a friend whose early smooth style was the antithesis of Presley, said yesterday, "No one can imagine an old Elvis."

Yet the man who died at age 42 in Memphis was a different figure. The onetime "threat" to American morals was more of a recluse living in a mansion. The "King of Rock" most often played the Las

Vegas circuit where he was acclaimed more by middle-aged fans than teen-agers who have other heroes.

Presley was, by most accounts, a man with his share of faults and weaknesses. But there was a generous side seen in gifts he gave friends and strangers. We at The Advertiser remember him kindly for appearing free at a benefit here that led to the building of the U.S.S. Arizona Memorial.

And, despite his success, the mansions, the cars, etc., there was a certain modesty, such as when he once said:

"My daddy invest my monies, Colonel Parker manages my show-business career. And I mind my own business. I've got simple pleasures. You can't go beyond your limitations."

For a time, Elvis Presley broke the limitations of popular music and opened the way for changes still under way. That is not a modest achievement.

Honolulu Star-Bulletin
Honolulu, Hawaii, August 17, 1977

Elvis Presley

Elvis Presley, dead at 42, is perhaps as good a milestone as any by which to measure the scope of the sexual revolution.

Twenty years ago Presley's swiveling hips were so daring, television's directors showed him only from the waist up when he appeared on the toprated Ed Sullivan Show.

In two decades Presley, though still relatively young chronologically, came to seem old and almost sedate. He was one of those who unleashed the sexual revolution.

Then it roared past him, and he became more of a symbol of old values than of new.

The Indianapolis Star
Indianapolis, Indiana, August 18, 1977

First In An Era

Elvis Presley came out of nowhere some 20 years ago and struck the spark of a new era in American popular music—the era of "rock 'n roll."

A new style of music is often controversial, and that's perhaps the mildest thing that could be said of Presley's innovation. It included not only a new kind of musical rhythm and structure but also an accompaniment of body gyration that made him and television adversaries for most of his now foreshortened career.

But if ever there was a performer of these times who could afford to be indifferent to TV it was Elvis Presley. He had something for which a lot of Americans, mostly among the relatively young, were ready. His new style took hold like the wildfire that has been devastating West Coast forests and brushlands, and was similarly unpredictable and uncontainable.

He was the first performer to make a phonograph album that sold a million copies after the industry began officially certifying such million-sellers as "gold records." In all he made 30 of them. He appeared in more than a score of movies; he had a huge fan club with chapters in seven countries; the style he set is still a potent force on the musical scene.

When word of his death at the age of 42 flashed across the nation Tuesday, it would have been mighty hard to find an American of any but tender age who would have asked, "Who's he?"

The Knoxville Journal
Knoxville, Tennessee, August 18, 1977

The King

Elvis Presley was a man out of time.

He suggestively gyrated on stage a decade or more before the faceless rock music groups with funny names made animated and bizarre performances the standard. Somehow in the process, Elvis became tame. An act once considered too shocking for television almost overnight became a welcome reminder of an age of stability.

Others before him had caused audiences to swoon; he sent them into a frenzy. That, too, became subdued by comparison with the subsequent atmosphere of the rock concerts.

Other singers had captured popular attention. None, however, had sold so many records. Elvis' first million-copy record was followed by more than 40 more which topped that magic mark.

Elvis was the heart-throb of that gigantic mass of American "war babies" which reached the teenage years in the 1950s. His appeal lingered through subsequent generations, in a career which spanned more than 20 years. But Elvis did not change much. The world around him did.

That stint in the Army, chided by some at the time as merely another publicity gimmick, in retrospect earned him an "All-American Boy" status as entertainers who came on the scene in the 1960s and early 1970s dodged the draft, fled to Canada and joined in the antiwar protests.

Throughout it all there was a thread of pure modern Americana—a country boy who made it big, not through clear talent, but with a swashbuckling style that even in the beginning captivated the emerging protest against convention.

The trauma of his untimely death cannot be minimized. Elvis Presley was one of the few remaining links with those "happy days" of the 50s—the days before the country's stature, moral standards, lifestyle, resources and grasp on the future started coming unglued.

Lexington Herald
Lexington, Kentucky, August 17, 1977

Requiem for the Rock-and-Roll King

He was a greasy-haired, butt-wiggling superstar.

He was a leather-jacketed, sexy-throated sensation. He was the Cadillac-crazy creator of a cultural phenomenon that swept the world. He was Tupelo, Mississippi's most famous son.

He was a genius of popular music.

Elvis—that was all the name he ever needed—is dead at 42. This was a special tragedy for Lexington. Next Tuesday night he was to sweep into town for a packed concert that would send thousands and thousands of his fanatically-loyal followers into fits of ecstasy.

When Elvis appeared it was more than just a concert: It was a ritual renewal of faith in the hillbilly, gospel and rhythm-and-blues roots that fuel an ever-more-complex musical idiom. Elvis helped invent that idiom, and at his concerts he kept that first, pure musical flame alive.

In his last years he was a shy, reclusive hermit in a Memphis mansion. Much of the world forgot the power of his fame. It saw only a washed-up, overweight star of B-grade movies. But now it remembers.

Legions of middle-aged men and women remember. They remember and mourn an era long past and the man that symbolized it—ponytails, ducktails, bobby-sox, tee shirts—and Elvis.

He was the king of rock and roll.

Arkansas Democrat
Little Rock, Arkansas, August 18, 1977

The passing of Presley

Superstars who become legends in their own time have that unnerving habit of dying as dramatically as they have lived. The Will Rogerses, the Marilyns, the James Deans come to mind. And now Elvis Presley, the King of Rock, has proved no exception. He died Tuesday in his beloved Memphis of an apparent heart attack at age 42.

What was there about this Mississippi-born truck driver that let him, in 20 brief years, sing and gyrate his way into emerging, more than any one other person as the symbol of an era of bubble gum, grease and Cold War? And why, at Elvis' death, do millions worldwide mourn his passing, including many who until now have never counted themselves among the card-carrying "Elvis fans"?

Well, because John Donne was right. When a man dies who somehow has touched us all, it diminishes each of us. A small part of our being, a portion of our past, somehow is subtracted. A part of what we have been in our own lives perishes with the death of the greatest among us.

Some will doubt or even deny Elvis' "greatness." But we think his greatness surpasses in scope the man himself—even transcends his emergent role as the idol of teenagers. Elvis' greatness was best seen in his mature years, not in his third-rate acting (although his 31 motion pictures grossed him millions), but in his evolution as a capital-P Performer, a showman who could first dazzle, then capture, vast audiences and hold them in the palm of his hand.

In many ways Elvis WAS the '50s—that too-brief era of relief between the revelation of the Bomb and the catapulting of the nation into a series of migraine headaches with names that now are commonplace to us: inflation, Vietnam, energy crises and Watergate.

Now, not just the '50s, but the symbol of the '50s—the King—is dead. And those of us who mourn the one must almost surely mourn the other as well.

The Courier-Journal
Louisville, Kentucky, August 18, 1977

Across the generation gaps, a corner of our hearts

Several generation gaps probably will come and go before students of both music and sociology quit debating what Elvis Presley meant to the youth of the 1950s. But they may never penetrate the roadblock pointed out by his admirers: Those who have to ask will never fully understand.

Generation gaps, at least in our era, are most clearly mapped by popular music. Popular singers mark our social history just as wars and economic upheavals form the landmarks of political history. More permanent music carries conscious ties to the past. The appeal of non-singing movie and TV stars, who because of economic pressures must please broader audiences, usually is less fragile.

But the Presley performances, like those of stars of other eras, were a generation's own. Few parents in the '50s could share the enthusiasm of their children for this noisy and even vulgar phenomenon, just as *their* parents had wondered about the skinny fellow with the Adam's apple, Frank Sinatra; and *their* parents about jazz. That's part of why Elvis' music—and Elvis himself—were treasured by those who felt he represented a very special and private period in their lives.

In time, most of Elvis' detractors came to acknowledge that the bespangled Mississippian wasn't the devil himself, or even his viceroy. It became increasingly clear that he was an enormously talented young man who gave color to a generally drab era by defying the conventions of age and thus raising the spirits of youth.

Small wonder that his once-youthful admirers, even as they became middle-aged parents themselves, never surrendered that small corner of their hearts in which they kept alive the time when life was more thrilling. Elvis is gone, and so suddenly at 42. But what he represented, because it cut across all the generation gaps, will never die.

The Commercial Appeal
Memphis, Tennessee, August 17, 1977

Elvis Presley

ELVIS. The man-boy's name stood alone. On a marquee it conveyed more than a million flamboyant words of promotional copy.

Elvis Presley, an American cultural phenomenon who will never be fully understood, was too many things to be categorized in words.

He was feeling, emotion, sexuality. He was at least a part of the "American dream."

He came in the guise of singer and musician. And he set a style that shook the world of "pop" music, stood it on its head, radicalized it, and left a trail of imitators, copiers and apprentices.

Is it safe to say that had it not been for Elvis there would not have been the Beatles? Had there not been Elvis the stage might never have seen a show like "Jesus Christ Superstar." Had there not been an Elvis there might never have been a Nashville Sound or a Memphis Sound. Had there not been an Elvis, millions of bobby-sox fantasies might have been denied.

Yes, and had there not been an Elvis there would not have been the years of pilgrimages from all over the world to a shrine on a Whitehaven hill called Graceland.

Memphis always saw Elvis as a son, a boy-made-good in the tough world of entertainment, a success that defied convention. He came out of a mold that the youth of the 1950s comprehended, he communicated, he gave dignity and respect to the pubescent girl or boy who was frightened of growing up, unsure of being loved, afraid of acting natural.

Cults are not unusual, although they always disturb the staid world. Elvis was clutched to hearts in the same way as Valentino, Gable, Sinatra. He was Andy Hardy with slick hair and a Gable grin. He was Al Jolson in white-face, Bing Crosby in the New World, Gene Autry without need of a horse.

He was the entertainer who magnetized the nerve system of the young and to touch him was to be sanctified.

He had what is essential to any successful entertainer—a trusting, fervently loyal audience. He could be loved because he seemed lovable. And a generation of fans grew older with Elvis, each of them faithful in the way of the good wife, the good friend. Age did not dim either the reality of the human Elvis or the mystique of show-biz mythology.

Memphis will not soon forget this illustrious citizen, dead now at 42, even as thousands of fans from teens to middle-age had awaited the chance to attend yet another personal appearance by Elvis on tour and at home.

Elvis Presley could not escape the isolation that is forced on the cult figure. But he rejected total immersion in the world of Hollywood, Las Vegas and tinsel-wealth.

He could not help but reflect openly his love of family, his comfort with old friends, his preference for the environment in which he grew up.

Sometimes he was just another Humes High School kid grown up to big-car status. If he preferred karate to golf, that was part of his special personality. If he kept late hours, he also kept the peace.

His generosity was as much a legend as his career.

From the beginning of his ascent he turned back to help those who remained in the humble state from which he rose.

He was an asset to Memphis in more ways than fame. A tourist attraction, yes. But also a symbol. His rock and roll style, his easy physical grace, his modulated drawl, his glance of recognition as he passed you on the street, made him fit the surroundings.

If he was proud to tell others that he was from Memphis, Memphis was proud to have him claim it as home.

Memphis Press-Scimitar

Memphis, Tennessee, August 17, 1977

Elvis Presley

Just a quarter-century ago, no one had ever head of Elvis Presley, save his classmates at Humes High School. They knew him as an ordinary, awkward country boy, moved here recently with his parents from Tupelo, Miss.

Yesterday, when Presley died, he was probably the world's best known entertainer. His records sold in the millions. His motion pictures were shown in theaters all over the world. His public performances were always sell-outs.

It was a good life the country boy built for himself—a glamorous life. He had everything anyone could want. Money, friends, and legions of worshipful admirers.

Yet the Presley candle that had glowed so brilliantly burned out just 22 years after he made his first record in Memphis.

But the big question remains: What was the Presley secret, what ingredient of life did he possess that was denied to others?

For the answer, we turn to a *Press-Scimitar* clipping of 1957. It quotes a description of the Presley charm by a Pittsburgh, Pa., girl. It reads as follows:

"First of all, may I say that if I knew exactly what it is that Elvis has, I'd bottle it and make a million dollars. It isn't one thing, it's everything. There are many singers who have a good voice, a good personality and good looks, but none has that electricity about voice, looks and personality that Elvis has.

"So you take this electricity, combine it with sweetness, sideburns, a Southern accent, and a smile that is the most devastating thing since the atom bomb. You sprinkle all this liberally with musical and dramatic talent.

"You pour this mixture into a form capable of style, magnetism and excitement which is unbelievable. You bring this form to life with love—his love for his fans and theirs for him—and you have Elvis."

So much for Presley as one admirer saw him.

In Memphis, we saw him as a good, well-behaved citizen. He was known for his generosity, not only for the expensive cars he gave away to friends and sometimes strangers, but for his generous contributions to numberous charities.

Death struck unexpectedly yesterday. · Thus ended a glamorous career underscored by the sustained admiration of fans throughout the world.

But in Presley's life his most abiding love was for his mother. She, too, died at age 42.

The Meridian Star

Meridian, Mississippi, August 17, 1977

Era Ends

An era has ended.

Whether or not you were a fan of Elvis Presley, you'll have to admit that the rock and roll king made an impact on music, on the country and throughout the world that won't be soon forgotten.

Rising from a meager background in Northeast Mississippi, Presley went on to become what may prove to be the last of the real "superstars." His name became magic for both recording companies and at motion picture theater box offices.

Yet, with the wealth and adulation accompanying such fame, Presley never seemed to forget his beginnings.

When called on to serve in the armed forces, he went without protest and served in a regular army unit in Europe.

When he build a palatial home, it was in Memphis rather than in Hollywood.

He remembered and cared.

He was generous with his wealth and his talent and never refused to offer aid for victims of such tragedies as Hurricane Camille. He recently did a benefit performance in Jackson to raise funds for tornado victims in Mississippi.

In the late 1950s, when at the beginnings of his meteoric career, Presley performed in Meridian at the Mississippi-

Alabama Fair, once for a relatively meager amount of money and next for free, donating his money to parks.

We cannot recall an instance when he dishonored either his family or his native soil.

He remembered us, and hopefully, we will not soon forget him.

Miami Herald
Miami, Florida, August 18, 1977
Elvis Presley: The King Is Dead

Elvis Presley's death at age 42 has left a significant segment of the nation in shock, a fact which again confirms the impact the man had on the American scene.

He was more than a popular entertainer with the ability to capture the elusive light of success for more than 20 years. He was the personification of a certain spirit that resides within the nation. It is one that many, especially the elite and the churchgoing, would have chosen to ignore. But Elvis Presley was too formidable to ignore. Instead, many chose to disdain him. But an equal number held him in adulation or nearly so. Although he never learned to read music, he was able to capture a sense of the times. Some critics who wrote kindly

about Elvis believe he portrayed the image of a working class rebel.

Of course he enjoyed his share of the good luck that is bestowed on most successful people, the most notable slice coming perhaps when he teamed up with his promoter, "Colonel" Thomas Parker, "Don't explain it, just sell it," was the Colonel's rule. In time, Elvis even was given some credit for his musical ability, or at least for the feelings he was able to evoke with it.

The Presley power resided in rock and roll, a new expression from the underside of America that reflected powerful yearnings and painful isolation. His life exemplified his music.

The Milwaukee Journal
Milwaukee, Wisconsin, August 18, 1977
Elvis Really Started Somethin'

Upon his death, Elvis Presley received one of the highest honors his society can bestow—television specials. There was David Brinkley, more accustomed to solemnly noting the passing of some head of state, presiding over film clips of such last rites as a special commemorative at a New York record store.

Brinkley's obvious discomfort was somehow fitting. When a sneering Elvis swaggered onto the scene in 1956, he made a lot of grownups uncomfortable. They didn't like his music, his haircut or the unseemly conduct that he provoked among their children. The only consolation that parents had was their supreme confidence that it all would pass quickly.

It didn't though. How was anyone to know that those midsection motions, which Ed Sullivan kept off camera to protect the

morals of society, were actually among the first twitches of the sexual revolution? How could anyone know that once young people wrested popular music from their elders, Rosemary Clooney and Eddie Fisher would never get it back again?

In a way, the parents were right. Rock 'n' roll was dangerous. Not long after the young got a music of their own, they started having more thoughts of their own, too. Although Elvis himself sang songs about hound dogs and teddy bears, it didn't take long for the curled lip of rock to turn to other matters.

By the 1960s, rock was the center of something called the youth culture, which had its own dress, its own recreational substances, its own politics and its own morals. It had little respect for the patriotic wars of its elders or even the armed forces, in which Elvis himself had served so loyally for two years at the height of his career.

It doesn't really matter that in recent years Elvis had become an overweight caricature playing for adults in their Las Vegas dens. It doesn't matter that rock musicians who came after had a grasp of such niceties as how to play their own instruments or write their own songs.

Elvis was an idol. He was also a beginning.

Milwaukee Sentinel
Milwaukee, Wisconsin, August 18, 1977

Elvis Symbolized A Changing US

When Elvis Presley swiveled onto the entertainment scene more than 20 years ago, they said he wouldn't last.

"They," in this case, were a substantial number of the older generation of the 1950s who looked upon the Memphis truck driver as something of a curiosity with a weird haircut and singing style to match. Rock 'n' roll just wasn't swing and sway.

Nonetheless, with the support of legions of teenage Americans—many of them among today's middle class middle agers—he changed the tempo of the country and helped write the obituary for the crew cut generation.

Offbeat for its time, Presley music added character to his sullen personality, which was not unlike that of James Dean, who died in 1955 only to give birth to a cult that lives on even today.

In retrospect, it is obvious that Presley's rise to popularity was not a personal victory over the establishment but a manifestitation of a new and unfamiliar—though widespread—attitude that young Americans were to acquaint the country with in the years to come.

In the decade that followed his first success, conventional morals, discipline and dress went the way of what had been conventional music. For good or bad, Presley was a symbol of his time.

Presley died Tuesday at 42 and will be entombed near his Tennessee home Thursday. To say he will love on is not a cliche. Millions of fans still carry memories of Elvis' personal magnetism and his records already are collector's items. The term "living legend" fit few performers as it did Presley.

Even in death, of course Presley will have his detractors—those who didn't appreciate his lifestyle or like his music.

There is a lesson for all of us, however, in the fact that many of them will be wearing sideburns.

The Montgomery Advertiser
Montgomery, Alabama, August 19, 1977

Elvis & Hank

In reflecting on the death of Elvis Presley and the reaction to this unexpected event, we find ourselves drawing parallels to the life & death of the King of Rock'n'Roll and the life & death of another legendery figure in popular music, the late Hank Williams. Anyone living in Montgomery, where Hank is buried, would inevitably make comparisons.

Although a generation apart, they had mjch in common. Both were poor boys, country boys from the South, who hit the top fast—perhaps too fast. Both died young—Presley at 42, Williams at an even earlier age, 29. Both, through their music, managed to tap the great undercurrents of emotion which their fans felt in their souls. And in death both had great throngs of grieving followers and fans who turned out simply to be near the body. Montgomery may never again see such an extravaganza as Hank Williams' funeral.

And yet there was a difference. Without wishing to be ungenerous to Elvis, we must say that he was not an especially creative man, and the emotional chords he stroked in people were essentially earthy and sensual and passionate.

Hank Williams reached much deeper into the soul. He wrote and sang of love and yearning and sorrow and loneliness. Who could ever forget the poignancy of his "I'm So Lonesome I Could Cry," or the pathos and humor of his attempted conversation with the wooden Indian "Kow'liga" on the banks of Lake Martin? He was in every sense, the minstrel of the common man.

They had much in common, Hank & Elvis, and yet they were also light-years apart, even though removed by only one generation. It will be interesting indeed to see whether the legend of Elvis proves to be so durable, dark, and mysterious as the legend of Hank Williams.

Nashville Banner
Nashville, Tennessee, August 17, 1977

Elvis: A Memory For A Generation

Elvis Presley

His death is as incomprehensible as his life.

The picture pops quickly into place—whatever image you prefer. But it is probably one of gyrations and sideburns, a white linen suit or black leather, the mouth curling, the song a shout—not only from style but to rise above the screams from the front seats clear back to the last, sold-out row in the balcony.

Elvis Presley was something never previously experienced, and the imitators of both song and style ranged from makeshift groups performing on a high school stage to the other side of the world, to Europe, to a club act in Tokyo. He did not originate rock 'n roll, rhythm and blues—that bane of parents during the Eisenhower years—but he brought it out into a mass and mostly white audience.

And fame took it from there. Popular music, in some cases better, in some cases worse, has never been the same. And never will be.

Men of state normally have first claim on history. Elvis Presley, certainly, can claim none of the traditional distinctions. He was a celebrity, an entertainer—a creature who often flies close to the lamp for a few moments before falling to the floor.

But his case was different. An influence was there, upon a society and upon a generation. It is not easy to describe, because it worked itself in different ways on different poeple; but it is much more difficult to consider the times of more than 20 years if he had not existed. Perhaps it was a new voice for youth to find its own voice. Perhaps it was just excitement, better enjoyed than rationalized.

The Colonel—Tom Parker—helped him along on this roller-coaster to wealth. His records, some recorded here and with Nashville backup, were automatically dipped in gold. The movies, seemingly made in consecutive weeks and keeping to a stale but successful formula, added to the treasure.

He bought Cadillacs and motorcycles and pickup trucks, for himself and for strangers. He made money, and he gave away a lot of it. He went into the Army amid tears and jeers, and did honor to himself as a simple soldier. A tough image onstage and on-screen gave way to sentiment. There was intelligence under the rough fabric. And he could crack jokes and smile—at Elvis Presley.

A complicated person, really.

And yet there was something else that could touch the observer, by now accustomed to Elvis Presley. Loneliness. It's not unusual for it to keep company with fame, but here both came so sudden. Despite the girls, the good ole boys, the hangers-on, the millions of fans, self-isolation became a necessity. A long-awaited marriage wouldn't work. And something kept driving him, driving, despite bouts with ill-health.

It is, then, back to the original image, the picture to stay in a generation's mind.

The girls who screamed when Elvis first appeared, the boys who first disliked and envied him and then came to admire and imitate him, have aged a bit since those earlier days. And despite their parents' original fears, most of them have turned out pretty well over the years.

So did Elvis Presley. His death Tuesday was a shock, leaving many people feeling slightly older and empty, and quite concious of immortality.

The Tennessean

Nashville, Tennessee, August 18, 1977

Elvis: The King is Dead

The death of Mr. Elvis Presely was a sudden and shocking event and it removed an entertainer who was exceptional and unique.

He had rocketed from driving a truck to being one of the world's best known entertainers. In the 1950s, he simply dominated the field and almost any record of his turned to gold.

It is difficult to gauge the musical influence that he had. He didn't invent rock and roll, but he made it roll with songs like "Heartbreak Hotel," recorded at the RCA studios here.

The Beatles were influenced by his style and so were any number of others, such as British singer Tom Jones, who at least picked up his gyrations for live performances. But until the Beatles came along with a new sound and created a new craze, Mr. Presley was king.

Whatever else may be said of his talent, timing had something to do with his success. He burst on the music scene when the big band sounds of the pre-war years were quietly fading away and when Mr. Frank Sinatra, the idol of the bobbysoxers of the war years, seemed to have lost his music.

Something new and different was what the industry talked about and suddenly, Elvis Presley was it. The gyrating, hard-driving trucker captivated the nation's young—at least the female portion—and pop music had a new king.

There were those who predicted that his vitality and reckless burning of energy would flame out early. But if the Beatles got the teenagers, Mr. Presley kept the audience and the fans of the '50s into the 1960s and the 1970s.

Thanks to the canny management of Col. Tom Parker, Mr. Presley was never "over-exposed" even though he made movies by the dozen. He could still pack them in at age 42, although there were those who thought that age and success had taken something from him.

Perhaps they did. Those who knew him well talked of his restlessness, his poor health and his emotional insecurity. Perhaps only he knew the price he paid for fame and fortune, but he gave his fans their money's worth and a lot of happy memories—as Mr. Kris Kristofferson put it, "For the Good Times."

The Virginian-Pilot

Norfolk, Virginia, August 18, 1977

Elvis

The blue suede shoes have been laid away. Elvis Presley, dead in Memphis at 42, has moaned his last ballad. His leaving will be mourned by millions, many themselves slipping through middle age, who idolized the sultry singer.

The King of Rock and Roll erupted 21 years ago as a Pied Piper of the youth culture of the Fifties, the symbol of implied if not actual adolescent rebellion against parents in particular and adult values in general. Suggestive as his delivery was then, punctuated with primal grunts and hip gyrations, it was bland stuff compared with anarchic rock movements, from acid to punk, that were to follow.

Elvis hit the big time in 1956 with "Heartbreak Hotel." He went from there to sell more than 250 million records, appear in 33 movies, amass a fortune in multiple millions, and acquire the Memphis mansion where he was stricken this week. While teenyboppers of the Fifties adored him and their male counterparts aped Elvis's sideburns, pompadour, and pouty manner, alarmed elders perceived him as a corrupting influence. He was denounced as a sex maniac, a lousy singer, and a moral leper; it was a minor sensation when his notorious twitching pelvis was censored out of a 1956 Ed Sullivan telecast.

The country survived Elvis. Some of his

early idolators now are grandparents who pay their taxes, trim their lawns, and don't speed through school zones. His career had peaks and valleys, and at the end his songs weren't heard much on juke boxes. Yet to the last, though pudgy and ailing, he had the power to pack arenas with the faithful. Adore or deplore him, Elvis was an authentic folk hero.o

Sentinel-Star

Orlando, Florida, August 18, 1977

Elvis: Mr. Entertainment, nice guy

Elvis Presley was like Franklin D. Roosevelt, Frank Sinatra and Hank Aaron—he had lasting power.

Most performers flash on the stage for a short time—almost a fad—and disappear into real estate, family life, the fringes of show business or the gutter.

Not so with the Mississippi-born pelvic gyrator who was Mr. Entertainment for a generation. He became rich and settled into a Memphis, Tenn., mansion, somewhat of a recluse. Had he lived another 30 years, he might have been a latter-day Howard Hughes.

His reclusion was part of his basically shy personality.

He didn't go Hollywood or even go political, as so many entertainers did. He limited his circle to a few friends, mainly truck drivers, as he once was. No rat packs for him.

Presley was devoted to his parents and generous to an unusual degree. His favorite gifts to people he liked were luxury automobiles.

He had a Memphis reputation as a nice guy, a public-spirited citizen, and he was well loved there as a result.

Elvis came along in the '50s, became a symbolic executioner of the big band era, the forerunner of various forms of rock music, and the advance man for anything but subtle sex in entertainment.

He served in the Army without complaining or a hassle, had a marriage and a divorce, packed them in on tour, sold records, made box office biz movies.

And died at 42.

Pensacola Journal

Pensacola, Florida, August 18, 1977

The King

Elvis Presley was the 1950s, and for two decades his musical style revolutionized the industry, sparked the Beatle age, changed dress styles and won the affection of rock 'n roll fans worldwide.

One does not have to like the Presley music to appreciate his impact upon contemporary American culture, from the ducktail, leather-jacketed generation to the ritualistic Woodstock explosion that is more cult than music.

He came at a time when the Memphis sound was regenerating the music industry with rhythm and blues, saving it after the decline of the big bands; and he was the King from the beginning.

In his last years, millions of fans crowded the giant arenas of the world to hear Elvis imitating himself, still the strong, smooth singer and still the sensual stylist who began with a few hip movements on the Ed Sullivan Show in the early 1950s.

Millions mourn his death at 42, and all who study social transition know the country boy from Tupelo, Miss, was the central figure in the scenario. Critics say he was rock 'n roll. He gave us an age—long-hair, loud sound, a revolution in music that led to other revolutions by young America.

We prefer to remember him singing "Love Me Tender," or during his many concerts—including Mobile and Pensacola—where his humble country manner came through despite screaming teenagers and aging mothers who remembered his beginning and cherished his Kingdom.

No one can deny Elvis Presley his rightful place in American social history. He developed a style that has produced many imitators, including inspiration for the Beatles and Bob Dylan; he may well have provided the roots for the current popularity of country music with the rock beat. Certainly every rock singer and band is from the assembly line developed in the Presley era.

He might have been rock 'n roll, but his roots were in the primitive country poetry of Southern music—the gospel, the Memphis and Nashville sounds, western swing.

Like Gable in the movies, Elvis was king.

His legacy is a slice of social history for the 1950s, 1960s and 1970s.

And he gave joy to millions.

The Philadelphia Inquirer
Philadelphia, Pennsylvania, August 18, 1977
Much more than a hound dog

He entered the national limelight almost as suddenly as he departed. As his death is officially recorded as Aug. 16, 1977, at the age of 42, his imprint on the national consciousness can be fixed at Sept. 9, 1956, at the age of 21.

With his guitar in hand, his black greasy hair slicked back, pants molded to his legs and hips moving like a spinning top, Elvis Presley made his first appearance on the Ed Sullivan Show, the first of three he was signed for at the whopping sum of $50,000.

It was the 50s, the age of innocence, so the network protected us from the Memphis singer. We were allowed to see everything from the waist up, including his lip slightly curled with contempt.

From the press clippings and from the frenzy screams of his fans in the audience, we knew much more was happening as he sang his four songs—"Don't be Cruel," "Ready Teddy," "Hound Dog" and "Love Me Tender." But that was left to our imagination.

In any event, the era of Elvis, the King of Rock 'n' Roll, had dawned. To his breathless admirers it would last forever. To his critics weaned on Rudy Vallee and Frank Sinatra, it was a fad. After his television appearance, one local critic wrote, "What will happen to Presley when the craze has ended—and all of them end—is anybody's guess of course. But it seems to many that he will be through as an act. And the big reason for that is his voice—to use the word loosely."

To the extent that everything eventually ends the critic was right, perhaps. But 250 million records, 33 films and millions of dollars later, his fans had a far more accurate pulse on the national mood than the pundits.

Elvis didn't invent Rock 'n' Roll anymore than Beethoven invented classical music. Yet, it is hard to imagine the music flourishing if he hadn't been around. There was more to Elvis, however, than his music or his voice—to use the word loosely or not.

He was despised by the older generation, and, thus, revered by the younger. He was a symbol of rebellion, the generation gap. In an age of moderate politics, peace abroad as well as at home, he was, in retrospect, a hint of what was to come— the sexual revolution, fighting in the streets, protests in the universities.

It is no wonder then that his death, sudden as it was, not only reminds us of how mortal we all are but of another time when life seemed simpler, Elvis's gyrating hips and all.

Arizona Republic
Phoenix, Arizona, August 18, 1977
Elvis Presley

Elvis Presley was much more than a show business phenomenom. He was the cutting edge of a cultural revolution whose blade of change sliced through the traditions of music, fashions, television, and fan worship.

In life, and in death, few celebrities on the American scene have evoked or stirred public passions to such extremes. Only Watergate and the assassination of President John Kennedy produced as much media attention.

In his early, controversial television appearances in the 1950s, the Presley pelvic gyrations created a storm of protest from parents, but instant adulation among millions of young and not-so-young. One TV rating service reported that 85 per cent of the nation's sets were tuned to a Presley performance on the Ed Sullivan Show—a greater audience than a presidential inauguration.

Yet, for all the fame and fortune, Presley remained a genuine personal introvert who shied away from off-hours theatrical soirees, and was never known to be given to theatrical tantrums.

He gladly and proudly went off for two years to serve in the U.S. Army, risking show business obscurity. But, he returned to an adoring and loyal public, and resumed a career which took him to even more spec-tacular heights of popularity and wealth.

Even as news of his death spread across the nation, millions of Americans flocked to stores to buy up every available Presley album. It was the response of a cult worshipping a fallen hero.

Elvis Presley's death at 42 years of age may have been the tragic consequence of a frenzied love affair for his public. Associates concede he needed medication to wake up, medication to sleep, and to thus maintain a professional life which filled the demands of an eager public.

No matter what the Presley detractors may say. The onetime Mississippi country boy who elevated hip movements and rock guitar to high art forms brought change to a nation's lifestyle.

The Pittsburgh Press

Pittsburgh, Pennsylvania, August 18, 1977

Elvis

Elvis Presley was a cultural phenomenon, a precursor of a new generation that was to stray even further from the Victorian precepts of an earlier America.

When he first appeared onstage, swiveling his hips, slinging his pelvis and groaning sensuously into a microphone, he was regarded by mothers and fathers across the nation as an evil Pied Piper who would make the still-whispered word "sex" a shout. They consoled themselves that he was "just a fad."

But there was nothing faddish about what he was heralding—a less inhibited society more willing to express its emotions, whether through music or protest marches.

It was a tribute to Elvis Presley that, whatever his private life, his public image remained impeccable. He was a loving son, unabashedly religious; a loyal, patriotic American who served his time in the Army without a whimper.

In these ways he seemed almost a contradiction to the changing lifestyle he represented. And unlike many of the "stars" who followed him, he shared his wealth—with his friends, his loved ones and his hometown, Memphis, where he was involved in a variety of charities.

Clearly his most significant contribution to our scene was his popularization of a music too long hidden in the rural South and the beer joints of its major cities.

Others had tried with minor success. But it was Elvis Presley who did it with an electricity that defies explanation.

Elvis is gone from the scene, but not from the memories of the millions who were oh-so-young in the '50s and the '60s.

Press Herald

Portland, Maine, August 19, 1977

The King Is Dead

Millions of Americans felt a deep sense of personal loss at the death of Elvis Presley, the man labeled the king of rock 'n' roll.

Most of them had never met him. Many had never seen him. Yet they related to him as to no other figure in show business. Elvis sang and gyrated himself into a per-manent and perhaps somewhat curious chapter in the long and colorful history of that business.

He was not a great singer. He never achieved the quality of a Frank Sinatra, Perry Como, Robert Goulet, Bing Crosby, Nat "King" Cole or many others. He made no pretense about it. As an actor, his ability was even more limited- But his films did well at the box office.

It is not extravagant to suggest that Elvis was to his medium and his fans what Rudolph Valentino was to his fans and the early motion pictures. And perhaps the key is that word "early."

Valentino came before the public when the country was embracing a new and exciting medium. Presley was a product of the times too. When he strode upon the scene, the scene was ready for him.

Television was becoming a fixation with the American people. The big band era had faded into history and nothing had come along to replace its excitement. The public was ready for someone to generate that ex-

citement. That someone would have to be an audio-visual standout. Elvis was it.

Elvis was handsome, youthful, and different. He was excitement. He had his scoffers, of course, but he established a rapport with people of several generations. He reached people in a manner that scores of more talented performers never achieved.

His initial success was a well orchestrated blend of imagery and performance. But his enduring success was the result of his uncanny ability to touch the hearts of so many, to become "just like an old friend," as one sorrowful Portland fan put it.

The king is dead. But as surely as he has a permanent place in the history of show business, so does he occupy a permanent place in the affection of millions.

The Oregonian
Portland, Oregon, August 18, 1977

The death of Elvis

The death of America's first and greatest rock 'n' roll star has stunned and depressed millions of his fans, although for more than a decade Elvis Aaron Presley had been a self-imitator, leading a lonely private life, fighting the effects of fame, fortune and fat.

His death at age 42 is a painful reminder to his middle-aged fans of the 1950s and their elderly parents that rock 'n' roll, that loud amalgam of both real and contrived folklore and spiritual music that once shocked the world, is now more than 25 years old. But even those who censored Elvis and his grinding, bumping hips in the mid-1950s must now feel a deep nostalgia and sadness that their children's golden idol is dead.

In the end, his heart, which seemed so boundless to the many who received his kindnesses and expensive gifts, failed him. He was found fully clothed, face down on the red carpet of his bathroom, probably already dead in his own "Heartbreak Hotel," the white-columned Graceland mansion near Memphis, Tenn., where he had lived as a virtual recluse for 20 years.

As he was being rushed to the hospital in a vain attempt to revive his failed heart, the legend was being expanded. Old bodyguards had accused him of being a drug addict, but Presley's physician, who

had been treating him for an overweight condition, and the Shelby County medical examiner discounted the drug reports. Drugs, they said, did not cause his death.

Elvis recorded 48 "golden" records, not all of them memorable, each of which sold more than a million copies. He made 30 movies during his 23-year career, all with virtually the same plot and all bad pieces of film. He did not invent rock, he simply energized it and tossed it at the world, pulling together the gaps between black and white music.

Few will forget the intensity of the young Presley appearing on the Ed Sullivan Show. His famed hip gyrations, copies of a stripper's bumps and grinds, might go unnoticed today at a Bible college concert. But they shocked part of a nation (the older part) and caused Sullivan to censor Presley from the chest down when he was performing before the show's cameras.

But Rockabilly Elvis, straight out of a poverty pocket shotgun shack in Tupelo, Miss., where he had worked as a truck driver, made rock music a world sensation. He was also a white man with a black man's rich voice—the dream combination of music promoters for a decade. He brought style and energy to pop music and paved the way for the English mopheads, John, Paul, George and Ringo, and for the Jefferson Airplane, the Rolling Stones and Bob Dylan.

Pop music was never the same after Elvis. His impact on his age has stretched across the generations, uniting not only black and white music, but widely scattered world cultures. He lived long enough to see his revolution become an establishment, even respectable, a fate not necessarily worse than death.

Nevada State Journal
Reno, Nevada, August 17, 1977

None Bigger

He was a Twentieth Century legend, along with Chaplin and Garbo, Mary Pickford, Marilyn Monroe and the Beatles. His death has drawn attention once reserved for the funeral processions of monarchs. Even former presidents of the United States have not received the attention at death that this pop-rock idol has drawn.

Elvis was an original, a prototype, the model for a generation of other performers. As the first big rock star, even performers young enough to have been his sons acknowledge their debt to him. He growled and crooned to the beat of a new kind of music. And his dark, heavy-lidded good looks and his gyrating abandoned manner onstage created waves of shock and excitement that never stopped. The value of shock and outrage was capitalized on by the Mick Jaggers and Alice Coopers of latter day rock but none parlayed it to the living-legend status of Elvis Presley. Twenty years after his fame began, he was still one of the biggest draws in the entertainment world. And he was so popular in Nevada that even a reasonably accurate imitator of Elvis drew good audiences in Reno.

To those who were never caught up in the Elvis mystique, the survival of his performing career into the seventies was a mystery. Long past his prime, overweight and sluggish onstage, he still provoked the same mass hysteria and the crowds groping for his handkerchiefs that he did at the beginning of his stunning career.

Much of this endurance was undoubtedly the result of the management of his career by Col. Tom Parker. Parker directed his early concert and movie career. And when it appeared that his career as a film star was waning, Parker built him by means of hype and shrewd publicity to one of the biggest attractions in Las Vegas and Lake Tahoe. Presley seldom granted interviews, undoubtedly at Parker's advice. It was probably recognized that the Garbo-like silence created more publicity than daily interviews. As Howard Hughes proved, silence can create more copy than overexposure.

Presley's contribution to the Nevada entertainment scene should not be underestimated. The descent of the legend onto showroom stages at both ends of the state created matchless excitement and his performances were inevitably sold out. The capacity to attract the biggest and the best is the essence of the Nevada entertainment scene, as the Frank Sinatra and John Denver co-billing has shown at Lake Tahoe.

And while there may have been better performers, there is little doubt in anyone's mind that there was none bigger than Elvis.

The Richmond Times-Dispatch
Richmond, Virginia, August 18, 1977

Elvis

When Elvis Presley burst into public view more than 20 years ago, shaking his mane of ducktail hair, gyrating his hips and shouting the likes of "Hound Dog" and "Jailhouse Rock," he was denounced as an affront to music, morality and the established order of American life. When he died Tuesday, Mr. Presley was the brightest star in the galaxy of heroes of millions of working men and women, the backbone of the social order that had felt so threatened by his emergence.

Though he is eulogized as "the king of rock'n roll." Mr. Presley's public esteem has little to do with the musical style. He was a contemporary manifestation of the Horatio Alger story—an ordinary young man with a commonplace job who, through luck and hard work, attained a life of luxury and adulation.

On a more direct level, he was one of the most potent sex symbols of his generation, a blue-collar Valentino who mixed boyish vulnerability with a surly toughness. That symbol was to prove a model for scores of singers and actors, and it persists to this day.

Mr.Presley's music was tailored long ago to reflect and promote an image, spawned by the fantasies of his admirers and honed by an efficient corps of publicists. Romantic ballads, dramatic production numbers and inspirational songs supplanted rock'n roll in his concert recording repertoire. A

series of crowd-pleasing films cast him as a romantic lead, slightly detached and seemingly bemused by his effect on the starlets and fans who surrounded him.

Mr. Presley himself retreated to the seclusion of a well-guarded Memphis mansion, venturing out periodically for sold-out concert tours. Gossip columnists and scandal sheets nibbled at the edges of the public person; but his carefully crafted image remained intact, because his fans wanted it to. His death has prompted an outpouring of public grief, the kind usually reserved for heads of state, military heroes and religious leaders.

The death certificate and obituaries note that Elvis was 42. But to legions mourning him, he was much younger. Mr. Presley's death marks, with compelling finality, the passing of his fans' youth.

The Morning Star
Rockford, Illinois, August 18, 1977

'The King' Is Dead

To those who were young in the Fifties, he was a reminder of youth, of oat-sowing days.

To their parents he probably will always be a symbol of the risque, regardless of how tame in comparison to those who came later.

To a generation of Americans, he was Mr. Rock 'n Roll, a swivel-hipped singer whose brand of music and gyrations made the girls scream like they had not screamed since the advent of Frank Sinatra.

He had this charisma, a Southern boy gone wild with guitar and song.

And he is dead, incredibly say some, at the age of 42.

Elvis Presley.

"The King."

Whether you were a fan, and there were many, or whether you were a detractor, and there were many, you could not ignore Elvis because he was indefatigable.

He was never casual before an audience.

He cared about his following and he performed with a zest and abandon that is rarely seen on any stage, whether the music is genteel or cast in a more classical mold or whether the song was twangy and declared that "You Ain't Nothing But a

Hound Dog."

Or how about that Elvis "classic," the one about "Blue Suede Shoes" that caused a fashion fad for many while instilling self-consciousness on others who just happened to be wearing a pair?

His records sold in millions. His impact on musical trends was staggering—and remains.

He garnered—and kept—more fans after he entered military service as a dutiful citizen who never complained about the interruption of his career but went about his business—as he always did.

Elvis Presley was asked once if his life had gotten back to "normal." He replied, "If it did, I'd be truck driving."

That's how this son of Mississippi started out—as a truck driver.

And when he achieved stardom, he just kept drivin', with everything in high gear, forget the brakes. He made 25 films, all of them forgettable.

What was unforgettable was the entertainment value of Elvis himself, a man with a way with music and a self-effacing way that made him known as a generous guy in private life.

Elvis Presley. Dead of a heart attack at 42. He remains phenomenal.

St. Louis Post-Dispatch
St. Louis, Missouri, August 18, 1977

Elvis Presley

In 1956, Elvis Presley shocked the United States and became rock's first superstar. He offended parents who found his appearance, performing style and music vulgar and offensive. But teenagers, who had money to spend to support such art, which at the time was using the word loosely, embraced the man and the music called rock 'n' roll. His greased-back hair style, his mannerisms, his tight slacks were copied as one generation's expression of independence from the preceding one. Elvis was a leader of a national protest—not over war and injustice, as rock would later become the chosen medium—but over conformity and blandness. And despite prophesies that nation degeneration was right around the corner, Elvis and his music left the country stronger rather than weaker. The teenagers who came under his influence became adults, most of them working—the solid citizens their parents had hoped they would become.

Along with helping to forge an acceptable place in American society for the protests of new generations, Elvis popularized a type of music that introduced many white Americans to black artists. Rock 'n' roll was a blending of black rhythm and blues and white country and western. Once Elvis gained a white national audience for this kind of music, the way was eased for black performers to achieve the wide recognition they had long been denied.

Rock has become an American musical form of recognized substance, one that is modified by the musical and social demands of successive generations. Elvis, through the years, adapted his music but as he gathered new fans he retained the gratitude and admiration of those who were young in the fifties. The death of Elvis Presley leaves no other rock figure who spans that music's evolution. A poor Southern country boy, he enriched the nation in ways that few if any of us could foresee.

Deseret News
Salt Lake City, Utah, August 17, 1977

Elvis Presley: a sad saga

Few entertainers have made as big an impact on their times as did Elvis Presley, who unexpectedly died Tuesday afternoon.

More than 250 million copies of Elvis Presley records have been sold all over the world. Until the Beatles came along, his recorded voice was said to have been heard by more people than that of any other recording artist.

He changed the shape of American popular music, influenced the personal and entertainment tastes of American teenagers, and opened the way for many of the musical fads that have come along since the mid-1950s.

Surely someone with so much influence should have left something of lasting value. But what? Maybe his donations to various charities, though sometimes seemingly prompted more by whim than by need, will qualify. But what else?

Not his movies. Though generally light and inoffensive, such froth is quickly dated. And certainly not his music. In his field, yesterday's best-seller is today's quaint curiosity, quickly forgotten as the wave of one fad washes over another.

In the saga of Elvis Presley, there is something profoundly sad because of what it says about this country and some of its values. Some mourning is definitely in order.

The Salt Lake Tribune
Salt Lake City, Utah, August 18, 1977

Elvis Ever After

Popular music is remorselessly fickle for those who perform it as a career. The current favorites occupy center stage for fleeting periods only to be replaced by a new arrival. It is the rare such entertainer who remains at or near the top of the commercial heap through succeeding decades. Elvis Presley was one of those.

Perhaps if his untimely death, at age 42, had not forever cancelled his act, Elvis would have become as much an honored perennial as Frank Sinatra, Bing Crosby, Johnny Mathis, Count Basie, Ella Fitzgerald and Lawrence Welk. The style and impact of Elvis Presley had little in common with any of those other long-time headliners, but he shared their apparently permanent claim on audience enthusiasm.

The Elvis allure has been traced to the unique influence he brought to popular music. There's no contesting that. Predecessors developed the rock and roll sound well before the Memphis guitar strummer adopted it to his own earthy delivery. Yet it was Presley who gave the music an identifiable personality, an established appeal that decided what direction popular music would take for the next 20 years.

Elvis Presley himself suffered the cruelty of his occupation—shouldered aside, almost forgotten as newcomers capitalized on the markets he and his promoters discovered. But he was proving his durability, with sell-out concerts and a new hit record, a country single: "Way Down." It might have been Elvis on top again if he hadn't been fatally stricken.

Whatever the speculation, it's a cinch the prominence of Elvis will live on, as long as the traditions, lineage and recognized contributors to popular music are discussed.

The San Diego Union
San Diego, California, August 20, 1977

Man Of The Times

The death of Elvis Presley is inspiring huge sales of his records and reruns of his movies, and emotionally affecting millions of followers. Presley could not have been what he was, save for his massive following. And it will be a final measure of Presley that as his followers die so will the memory and music of Elvis Presley.

To his credit, of course, Presley never pretended that his music would transcend time. But it is a commentary on the '50s—an age obviously with subterranean currents lasting through the '60s and gushing into the '70s—that Presley's music and style lifted him to cultural royalty. This was a new type of royalty, for Presley was not a hero in the profound and usual sense of having human excellence worth striving for. He was not Lou Gehrig or Charles Lindbergh or Winston Churchill.

Nor was he an anti-hero, a cultural species evident when Presley was shooting to fame. In Presley, rather, were evident good feelings and benevolence, if also sensuality. Presley was supremely a man of the times.

Ironically, in Presley's final years one had the sense that the man was less shallow than the era he lived in. His music took on a metaphysical twinge here and there, and his private life seemed full of the kind of gravity that settles in a man upon the realization that all, or so much, is vanity. It is true, as his friend Pat Boone once said, that it was hard to image an old Elvis. But it seems true as well that though he died so young, at 42, Elvis already was quite old. And in this, surely, he was far ahead of the times.

San Francisco Examiner
San Francisco, California, August 17, 1977

Elvis Presley

Elvis Presley, whose death yesterday came as a shock to millions, overnight is changed from man to legend. In the 1950s he established what Harper's Magazine then called "a stunning rapport" with his own teen-age generation and 20 years later he could still transmit the same magic.

In a curious coincidence of timing, Moscow's "Literary Gazette" the other day charged that the "American system mercilessly tossed Presley onto the scrap heap." Hardly. The ol' country boy maintained his unique hold on the public to the last.

The Times
Shreveport, Louisiana, August 21, 1977

Elvis, and youth

He was barely out of boyhood himself when he stepped onto the stage of Shreveport's Municipal Auditorium that December night in 1954, but the young Mississippian with the then-odd-sounding name of Elvis Presley at that moment was on his way to becoming a symbol of America, rock 'n' roll and youth for two decades.

He played here for a year and a half, enjoying his growing popularity at the Louisiana Hayride and perfecting the sideburns-and-swivel-hips image that was to be a national rage by 1956.

The kids loved him, idolized him; their elders saw him as a threat to the very foundation of the civilized world. Eventually, both sides regained composure and acknowledged that he was not quite a god, but not the devil incarnate either.

By then he was an American institution. The first name alone was known worldwide. The low-throated voice was instantly recognized by millions. If he actually grew older, few noticed it. Or at least, few admit-

ted it. He was, after all, a symbol of our youth; if he got older, we got older too, and that was not allowed.

In a way, then, it was surprising to realize at this death that he was 42—barely middle-aged, certainly, but hardly a kid any more. This was no Valentino nor James Dean, flaring briefly only to die tragically while still young. This was a youthfulness that lasted, that seemed to be going on and on.

Was he more than an entertainer? Sociologists insist that he was, but they're less sure about where, exactly, Elvis fits into the youth revolution of the 50s and 60s. He was not one to sing songs designed for social change in the manner of the 60s folk singers, yet the very fact of his performances seemed to bring on changes.

His greatest effect may well have been that ongoing image of youth—an image that made us almost believe we could all just keep on being young together.

The Spokesman-Review
Spokane, Washington, August 18, 1977

The impact of Elvis Presley

To his millions of fans he was "the king" of rock and roll.

To many teen-agers' parents, however, and other critics of his emergent sound and style—the beat, the gyrating hips, the sneering look, the black leather outfits—he was a worrisome influence.

But to most Americans living today, whether fan or critic, Elvis Presley was a

phenomenal figure in the world of entertainment.

The teen-age girls who screamed and swooned at his exaggerated sexuality on stage and their male counterparts who adopted his slick looks and mannerisms in the 1950s have survived to become today's adults, despite the concerns expressed at that time. And some who worried most about his early influence even came to enjoy his music, once the novelty of his style had passed.

His death this week marked the end of an era for many Americans. But he is not likely to be forgotten soon.

In the years since 1954, when the 19-year-old truck driver paid $4 to make his first musical recording for his mother, the public has bought some 250 million copies of Presley records. Forty-five of his recordings sold more than one million copies each.

He appeared in more than 25 motion pictures, some of which are now likely to be reissued. And in hundreds of concert performances across the nation, including Spokane, he entertained millions of rock and roll fans.

His entertainment career spanned nearly a quarter-century, and though there were the inevitable highs and lows, he was about to embark on several sold-out concert engagements at theaters.

The many fans he acquired over those years no doubt will take comfort in recalling the lack of accuracy shown by one of his early career forecasters:

"It isn't enough to say that Elvis is kind to his parents," wrote jazz musician Eddie Condon after Presley's first appearance on the Ed Sullivan television show in 1956. "That still isn't a free ticket to behave like a sex maniac in public before millions of impressionable kids. According to a scholarly friend of mine, Jackie Gleason, we'll survive Elvis. 'He can't last,' said Gleason, 'I tell you flatly, he can't last.'"

Summary: The career of Elvis Presley produced a remarkable impact on the world of entertainment.

The News Tribune
Tacoma, Washington, August 18, 1977
Gone but not forgotten

The death of Elvis Presley, at the "young" age of 42, has shaken his millions of fans and given pause to those who may not have been overly fond of his vocalizing but who recognized his place in the world of popular music.

It seems like only yesterday that Presley was featured on Ed Sullivan's TV show, stirring national debate over whether his gyrating hips were a bad influence on the morals of the youth.

That was 20 years ago. And Presley's gyrating hips seem so bland today, in our sexually open society, that one cannot help but wonder what the fuss was all about.

At his best, Presley's singing—emphasizing a throbbing, almost primal beat—caused even the most unmusical to tap their feet.

When Presley appeared at Tacoma's Lincoln Bowl 20 years ago, he sang, among other things, the memorable "Houn' Dog," which he called his National Anthem.

Few who lived through the Presley era will ever hear that song or "Heartbreak Hotel" without thinking of the handsome young man, in tight-fitting pants, holding an audience in the palm of his hand.

Charisma is an overused word. But Presley had it. He lasted much longer than his detractors thought he would. He was no flash in the pan.

The Presley cults, which sprang up years ago among teenagers, still continue today— even though those teenagers are now married, settled down and, in some cases, getting a bit gray on top. There is no evidence that exposure to Elvis Presley harmed their lives in the least.

Through his concerts, his films and, most of all, his recordings, Elvis Presley has secured a niche as one of the major influences on American life over the past 20 years.

The King of Rock is dead. The memory will linger on.

The Tampa Tribune
Tampa, Florida, August 19, 1977

Eras End for America ...

For some he was the devil risen up to claim the nation's children, for others he was incomprehensible, but for most of a rising generation he was a relief from the staye, quiet Fifties. Now, at 42, the life of Elvis Presley has ended and so has an American era.

He was sandwiched between 1940s heart-throb Frank Sinatra and the middle-60s Beatles but he was distinctly himself, slicked hair, bushy sideburns, a continuing sneer and the gyrating hips in skin-tight pants. He went from driving a truck in 1955 to driving women mad and before long the top of his torso was gracing the new television screens across America. When he appeared on the Ed Sullivan Show in 1956 to sing "Heartbreak Hotel" and "You Ain't Nothin' But a Hound Dog," the first two of his more than 30 gold records, he was shown only from the waist up.

That show on a single television network was viewed by more people than watched President Eisenhower make his acceptance speech on three networks. Later his world-wide fan club would number 400,000 members and millions watched his 31 films.

The rock 'n' roll era he cemented into the nation's culture with his throaty baritone changed the country more than it altered him. Besieged by fans, he did his tours and made his films but remained a semi-recluse in his Memphis mansion. Unlike many of the early rock 'n' roll stars, Presley maintained his public attention, even through the most recent years when he grew fat and began cutting some shows short. But though his physical appearance changed his generosity never did. His gifts of cars to strangers who touched his fancy were more than public relations posturing, and he once donated proceeds from a world-wide televised concert to the family of his deceased drummer.

Tampa came to know him early, when he played on the bottom part of a Fort Homer Hesterly bill prior to his Sullivan appearance. A return a year later produced a packed house and by then Presley was under the solid management of Col. Tom Parker, who in Tampa was better known for his work with animals (at the Humane Society) than with rock superstars.

Perhaps the most lasting irony of Presley's life is the public perception of him at the end. Compared to the sex-exhibition of a Jim Morrison or the bestiality of an Alice Cooper, Elvis Presley at his most torrid was tame.

On the day he died of a heart attack, he was preparing for another national tour, already sold out. Whatever the truth of Presley's personality, his impact on today's generation of Americans was like a kick in the pants with a blue suede shoe—disruptive but pleasantly memorable.

The Arizona Daily Star
Tucson, Arizona, August 18, 1977

The king is dead

Elvis was king.

The voice got richer over two decades, and the vibrant charm of the one-time Mississippi truck-driver, well, it prospered too as he wailed his way through his youth.

The creation of Col. Tom Parker, who packaged the gyrating guitar-player/ vocalist and doled him out in measured amounts to an adoring world of fans, Presley was symbolic of an affluent, all-conquering, but still-rebellious America.

He came on the show-business scene amid controversy over his sideburns and pelvic thrusts. He left it amid critics' jabs over recent performances.

He lived a legend and left one when he died Tuesday at 42.

Daily Journal
Tupelo, Mississippi, August 19, 1977

Elvis Is Gone But Not Silenced

"THE KING IS DEAD."

That explicit headline atop Page One of Wednesday's Daily Journal said it all.

Elvis Presley, who rocketed from a simple childhood in Tupelo to the pinnacle of his chosen profession, will perform no more for his legion of loyal subjects the world over.

Though Elvis was buried yesterday in his adopted home-town of Memphis, the moments of happiness he provided for more than two decades will live forever.

The golden voice of the young man who lived here for the first thirteen years of his life will never be stilled. Through the medium of records, tapes and the golden screen, the captivating musical beat peculiar with Elvis remains.

We have enjoyed the comments of those who knew Elvis when he grew up in East Heights. All have been complimentary and agree that the relatively hard times he and his family experienced here served him well when he was no longer a stranger to fame.

Elvis kept a soft spot in his heart for those less fortunate than he and gave away literally thousands and thousands of dollars during his career to charitable causes throughout the wide area, including Tupelo and Lee County.

We felt sorry for Elvis in a way after he had made his way to stardom. He was idolized to the point that he was literally a captive to his success. Much of his life away from the theater was spent behind gates of iron, protection against his adoring fans.

Thus Elvis reaped the benefits of being The King, but paid dearly in that he was denied a normal lifestyle. His remark, "I'm here, but how do I get back?" says much for the envy Elvis must have felt for those of us who have no trouble going unnoticed in a crowd.

But Elvis loved to sing. He reveled in making people happy, helping them forget their troubles for an instant as he maneuvered around a stage as only Elvis could, working his unique musical magic on young and old alike.

Though Elvis himself is gone he has not really vacated his throne. We doubt that ever again will one come along to capture the hearts and loyalties of so vast an audience and for so long a time as did Elvis.

He was one-of-a-kind. And we're glad that not even the grave can silence such uniqueness.

The Washington Star
Washington, D.C., August 18, 1977

Elvis Presley

A strange, fascinating figure, Elvis Presley. The newsprint and television time expended on the death of the singer at 42 was, to us, astounding. Statesmen and poets, generals and philosophers, do not often command such attention at their passing.

We have been aware of Mr. Presley for over two decades now—who could not have been? We were aware that he was credited as a progenitor of rock and roll and, to his fans, was a cult figure intensely adulated. But his dimensions in popular culture came, we confess, as something of a revelation.

Not just that a performer became enshrined as a national idol of sorts—nothing new in that, indeed we seem to have an appalling appetite for celebrities. Not just that he was perceived as a rebel, a sort of outlaw—the American head has long reserved a worshipful corner for those who flamboyantly defy. And not just that his curious style of life, whether adopted through volition or self-defense, was so disproportionate—bizarre habits irresistibly intrigue those of routine habits and excess frequently is the partner of fame.

No, it strikes us that another aspect of Elvis Presley's career was more responsible for the public niche he occupied. In one appraisal of his career, the writer noted that his ascension coincided with the coming to age of a new kind of youth music, "one that swept aside the gentilities of the adult-oriented pop of previous decades and reflected the swelling youth market of the postwar baby boom." That was John Rockwell commenting in the *New York Times* and he is onto something, we think, even to Mr. Presley's presaging trends in more than music.

Mr. Rockwell ended his piece by saying: "He was as much a metaphor as a maker of music, and one of telling power and poignancy."

There is a tendency toward over-indulgence in social metaphors. In this case, however, Elvis Presley as metaphor is fairly persuasive. If a metaphor is to an extent self-defining, though, it also begs questions or assumes answers to them not particularly evident. In the case of Mr. Presley, for instance, it is not terribly clear why so many elements of fame, notoriety, fad and trend crystallized around him rather than some other performer. Or why Elvis Presley was able to retain the relentless devotion of so many fans, for goodly numbers of whom 1956 represents antiquity.

Well, perhaps it is fatuous to attempt to analyze such phenomena or to speculate on the how and why of their genesis. Like mythic figures in a minor key, they apparently mirror and reflect so many elements of a time and circumstance that the response to them has a quality that extends beyond the merely rational. They simply are.

Those ruminations may be out-sized to the memory of Elvis Presley. But the awesome response to his death suggests that they may not be wholly inapplicable.

Wilmington Morning Star
Wilmington, North Carolina, August 18, 1977

'50s belonged to Elvis, and generation thankful

To those of us who grew up in the fifties, Elvis Presley provided an era. The old folks had World War II and Korea, the new model cars of the early 1950s, and the first inklings of an affluence sprung from a newly-molded economy.

Those to follow would have more money—the benefits of new-found affluence—color television, encounters with the drug culture, hard rock, acid rock, "relevant" education and the protest movement.

We had poverty, white socks, penny loafers with real pennies, souped-up cars, drive-in movies (entered clandestinely by hiding in car trunks) and Elvis Presley and rock and roll.

It could be argued we were better off.

Elvis was a savior, particularly if you were from the South. Dirt poor, marginally educated and driving a truck to a dead-ended future, Presley rode a guitar—played poorly—and a unique style to fame and fortune. Elvis adapted rhythm and blues and legitimatized it for white audiences. Heretofore the exclusive domain of black entertainers, R&B was music heard late at night—when interference lessened—over a Nashville radio station.

But, Presley having broken the mold, singers, black and white alike, found a whole new audience just coming into affluence, and rock and roll sprung forth.

It changed the face of American music, nurtured a generation into adulthood. It endured, permeating rock, country and pop music.

There are few of us from that generation who can hear a Presley lyric and not be instantly reminded of a specific moment of 1956, '57, '58, or '59.

The success of Elvis Presley was ours, whether from one of his 45 million-record sellers, or two years endurance in the Army.

And we block from our mind those recent years, when Elvis was a shadow of Elvis the Pelvis, when his voice was gone and, as Dave Marsh of Rolling Stone wrote, he no longer sang as if he really cared.

We remember the 1950's and early '60s: Heartbreak Hotel, Hound Dog, Teddy Bear.

Elvis Presley is dead at 42. Long live Elvis.

The Intelligencer
Wheeling, West Virginia, August 20, 1977

Elvis Presley

The term "end of an era" cannot be applied to this week's untimely death of Elvis Presley, the undisputed King of Rock and Roll.

The 42 year old singer began an era in American music, which ushered in a resultant change in the country's lifestyle, but did not live long enough to see the end of what he had wrought.

Ironically, many people in the late 1950s, when Elvis became a household word, said Rock and Roll would die a quick and, to them, justified death. However, rock music simply branched out in dozens of directions and grew into the multi-million dollar business it is today.

Elvis Presley changed with the business. As rock became more sophisticated, so did his songs. In recent years, he rarely appeared on the singles charts but his albums continued to sell well to a large group of hard core fans, all of whom mourned his passing in an outpouring of love last seen only when Marilyn Monroe and Rudolph Valentino died while still young.

It was Elvis Presley's sexy hipswiveling, sideburns and bedroom eyes, along with his unique music, that helped him eclipse Bill Haley and the Comets and other early Rock and Roll stars.

His early films, though sometimes simplistic, were far superior to the later movies which usually paired Elvis with up and coming starlets with only slight variations in theme and locale. It was the early films which moved his manager to boast that if he wanted to, Elvis could win an Oscar.

In addition, his live concerts many times were sellouts days after being announced.

His career, therefore, which encompassed records, films, television and concerts, became the type of career to which all rock stars aspired.

His music, though, was the impetus for and most influential aspect of other rock stars' careers.

There was only one Elvis and his talent and phenomenal career created a business and an idol for other singers to emulate and for the public to hold dear.

Sources and Notes

INTERVIEWS

Aberbach, Joachim Jean. Art dealer, holder of Presley music copyrights, New York, March 26, 1980.

Albritten, Nanci. United Press International, Atlanta; formerly with UPI, Memphis, October 10, 17, 18, 1979.

Ames, Robert. Associate editor, *U.S. News & World Report*, Washington, D.C., April 9, 1980.

Anthes, Connie. Manager of communications, The Arbitron Company, New York, June 5, 1979.

Bain, Jackson. Evening news anchor, WTTG-TV, Washington, D.C.; formerly with NBC News, September 7, 1979.

Bakke, John. Professor of rhetoric and communication arts, Memphis State University, August 14, 1979.

Behanna, William R. Director of press relations, A. C. Nielsen Company, New York, March 26, 1980.

Benjamin, Burton, Jr. Executive producer, *CBS Evening News*, New York, January 30, 1980.

Benton, Charles. Chairman, Films, Incorporated, Wilmette, Ill., December 6, 1979.

Bezshehowski, Peter. International Communications Agency, Washington, D.C., May 24, 1979.

Bond, Ron. Producer, CBS News, New York, January 17, 1980.

Boren, Charles. WAMY, Amory, Miss.; formerly with WELO, Tupelo, Miss., August 19, 1979.

Boyd, Mrs. Billy. Former curator, Elvis Presley Birthplace, Tupelo, Miss., March 30, 1979.

Brewster, The Reverend W. Herbert. Pastor, East Trigg Baptist Church, Memphis, August 16, 1979.

Brinkley, David. NBC News, Washington, D.C., April 28, 1980 (letter).

Britten, Milton. Editor, *Memphis Press-Scimitar*, April 2, 1979.

Brown, James. Entertainer, recording artist with Polydor Records, New York, January 10, 1980.

Browne, Raymond. Professor of popular culture, Bowling Green State University, Bowling Green, Ohio, November 14, 1979.

Butler, Don. Executive director, Gospel Music Association, Nashville, Tenn., October 16, 1979.

Carey, Robert. United Press International, Little Rock, Ark., October 27, 1979.

Carter, Vicki Helms. Music director of *Eubie*, New York, August 17, 1979.

Cody, W. J. Michael. United States Attorney for West Tennessee, Memphis, April 3, 1979.

Cole, James. Free-lance writer, Memphis, April 1, 1980.

Compton, Margaret. Memphis Convention and Visitors' Bureau, April 3, 1979.

Connelly, Richard. Vice President, Public Affairs, ABC, New York, June 7, 1979.

Danskin, The Reverend Warren. Pastor, The American Church, London, December 17, 1978.

Deary, Joan. RCA Records, Los Angeles, August 17, 1979.

Dombrofski, Tamara. Voice of America, International Communications Agency, Washington, D.C., January 8, 1979.

Doolittle, Jerry. Public affairs, Federal Aviation Administration, Washington, D.C.; former presidential speechwriter, April 23, 1979.

Duncan, Nathan. Editor, *Lee County News*, Tupelo, Miss., March 31, 1979.

Dunn, Ed. Reporter, *Memphis Press-Scimitar*, former communications director, Memphis Area Chamber of Commerce, September 15, 1979.

Fadal, Eddie. Sports editor, *Waco Citizen*, Waco, Texas, August 17, September 27, 1979.

Fletcher, Raymond. Member of Parliament from Derbyshire, London, December 15-16, 1978.

Ford, Harold. Member of Congress from Tennessee, Washington, D.C., July 23, 1979.

Franklin, Jerry. Producer, WKNO-TV, Memphis State University, April 17, 1979.

Gaugher, Tom. Disc jockey, WMAL, Washington, D.C., March 1, 1980.

Geissler, Harry. President, Factors, Etc., Inc., Bear, Del., August 17, 23, 1979.

Graham, James. Editor, *Daily Journal*, Tupelo, Miss., March 31, 1979.

Granum, Rex. Deputy press secretary, The White House, Washington, D.C., May 15, 1979.

Green, Pam. Music director, WHN, New York, January 15, 1980.

Harris, Art. Reporter, *The Washington Post*; formerly with *San Francisco Examiner*, January 3, 1980.

Harrod, Jack. International Communications Agency, Washington, D.C., May 24, 1979.

Helman, Herbert. Vice President, Public Affairs, RCA Records, New York, March 19, 1980.

Hertzberg, Hendrick. Chief speechwriter to the President, The White House, Washington, D.C., February 19, 1979.

Holditch, Kenneth. Professor of English, University of New Orleans, April 28, 1980.

Holmes, Charles. Director of public affairs, Memphis State University, August 14, 1979.

Ivins, Molly. Bureau chief, Denver, Colo., *The New York Times*, March 24, 1980.

Jennings, Robert. Entertainment editor, *The Commercial Appeal*, Memphis, April 2, 1979.

Johnson, Diana. Deputy director, Country Music Foundation, Nashville, Tenn., May 28, 1979.

Kieckhefer, E. W. Chief editorial writer, *The Commercial Appeal*, Memphis, April 2, 1979.

Knoller, Mark. Reporter, Associated Press Radio, Washington, D.C., November 15, 1979.

Lerner, Louis. Publisher, Lerner Newspapers, Chicago; former U.S. ambassador to Norway, November 19, 1979.

Lewis, Wanda Davis. First Family secretary, The White House, Washington, D.C., April 5, 1979.

Lomax, Alan. Folklorist and musicologist, New York, June 6, 1979.

Lomax, John, Jr. Oral historian, Country Music Foundation, Nashville, Tenn., July 23, 1979.

McComb, Janelle. Chairman, Elvis Presley Memorial Commission, Tupelo, Miss., March 30, June 23, August 16, 1979, April 16, 1980.

McDaniel, James. Managing editor, *The Commercial Appeal*, Memphis, April 3, 1979.

McEachran, Angus. Editor, *Birmingham Post-Herald*; former metro editor, *The Commercial Appeal*, Memphis, April 27, 1979.

McLean, George. Publisher, *Daily Journal*, Tupelo, Miss., March 30, 1979.

Manning, Gordon. Producer, NBC News, New York, June 12, 1979.

Mitchell, Henry. Reporter, *The Washington Post*, January 10, 1980.

Montgomery, Harold. Former state representative, Tupelo, Miss., August 17, 1979.

Morris, William. Mayor of Shelby County, Tenn., Memphis, April 26, 1978.

Mudd, Roger. CBS News, Washington, D.C., December 10, 1979.

Nichols, Larry. Manager of WTUP, Tupelo, Miss., August 17, 1979.

Palmer, Robert. Critic, *The New York Times*; formerly with *Rolling Stone*, New York, August 16, 1979.

Pierce, Clifford, Jr. Memphis city attorney, April 3, 1979.

Pollack, Jason. Publicist for West End show, *Elvis*, London, December 13, 1978.

Porteous, Clark. Reporter, *Memphis Press-Scimitar*, April 2, 1979.

Prewitt, Cheryl. Miss America 1980, Ackerman, Miss., February 4, 1980.

Rhea, John. Manager, WLVS, Memphis, September 13, 1979.

Richman, Joan. Producer, CBS News, New York, September 14, 1979.

Rivera, Geraldo. ABC News, New York, August 17, 1979.

Rosenthal, Harry. National correspondent, Associated Press, Washington, D.C., May 9, 1979.

Rosellini, Lynn. Reporter, *The Washington Star*, March 3, 1980.

Salamon, Ed. Program director, WHN, New York, March 26, 1980.

Schroeder, Patricia. Member of Congress from Colorado, Washington, D.C., March 20, 1979.

Seago, Les. Associated Press, Memphis, October 10-11, 1979.

Sears, Dan. Announcer, WREC, Memphis; formerly with WMPS, Memphis, January 21, 1980.

Seibert, Fred. Promotions director, WHN, New York, March 26, 1980.

Slaughter, Todd. President, International Elvis Presley Fan Club, Heanor, England, December 15, 1978; August 17, 22, 1979.

Smith, Griffin. Former presidential speechwriter, Washington, D.C., January 12, 1979.

Stevens, Don. News director, WHBQ-TV, Memphis, January 31, 1980.

Strick, Philip. Managing director, Harris/Films, Ltd., London, December 31, 1979; March 6, 1980 (letter).

Thompson, Asa. Disc jockey, WELO, Tupelo, Miss., April 2, 1979.

Thompson, Charles. Producer, *20/20*, ABC Television, Washington, D.C., August 17, 1979; April 1, 1980.

Tornabene, Russell. NBC public affairs, New York, June 5, 1979.

Townsend, Lee. Editor, CBS News, New York, January 7, 1980.

Venardos, Lane. Producer, CBS News, Washington, D.C., March 5, 1980.

Walls, Wayne. Band director, Nettleton, Miss., August 19, 1979.

Ward, Beverly. Reporter, WTVA (formerly WTWV-TV), Tupelo, Miss., August 17, 1979.

Welch, Billy. Psychiatrist, Mississippi State Hospital, Jackson, September 6, 1979.

Whitburn, Joel. Director, Record Research, Menomonee Falls, Wisc., September 14, 1979.

White, Susan. United Press International, Memphis, September 27, October 2, 1979.

Wick, Arthur. Formerly with KING-TV, Seattle, Wash., March 24, 1980.

Williams, Robert. Photo editor, *The Commercial Appeal*, Memphis, April 2, 1979.

Wilson, Gordon. Producer, WHBQ-TV, Memphis, January 31, 1980. Wolfe, Kathy. Former news assignments editor, WHBQ-TV, Memphis, February 20, 1980.

Wolfe, Kathy. Former news assignments editor, WHBQ-TV, Memphis, February 20, 1980.

BROADCAST SCRIPTS AND TAPES

Abstracts of news items concerning the death of Elvis Presley that were broadcast by the three U.S. commercial television networks are compiled in the August 1977 edition of *Television News Index and Abstracts*, published by the Vanderbilt Television News Archive of Vanderbilt University, Nashville, Tennessee.

Transcripts of comments broadcast from Memphis by Jackson Bain on the *NBC Nightly News* and *Today* for August 17-19, 1977, were made available to the authors from Mr. Bain's personal file. Transcripts of all CBS Television news broadcasts are compiled by the network and published on microfiche. (See *CBS News Index, 1977*, Glen Rock, New Jersey: Microfilming Corporation of America, 1978.) A partial script from the *ABC Evening News* of August 16, 1977, was obtained from ABC News, New York.

Broadcast logs and transcripts of programs aired by the British Broadcasting Corporation during this period are in the BBC Library, London.

A record of Elvis Presley's early television broadcasts, featuring the entertainer's comments and descriptions of his performances, has been compiled by fans and included in various issues of *Elvis Monthly*, published in England since 1959 by Albert Hand Publications, Heanor, Derbyshire.

In addition to interviewing radio and television personnel, the authors reviewed tapes and scripts or monitored the broadcasts of the following special programs that were aired after Presley's death:

Elvis, NBC Television. Broadcast August 16, 1977, 11:30 p.m., EDT.

Elvis: Love Me Tender, ABC Television. Broadcast August 16, 1977, 11:30 p.m., EDT.

Untitled radio news special, produced by Chuck Connor of WELO, Tupelo, Miss. Broadcast August 17, 1977, 8:00 p.m., CDT.

Elvis, CBS Television. Broadcast August 18, 1977, 11:30 p.m., EDT.

Untitled radio news special, produced by Mark Knoller of Associated Press Radio. Broadcast several times during the weekend of August 22-23, 1977.

$3 One Side, $4 Two Sides, WKNO-TV, Memphis, Tenn. Broadcast September 4, 1977, 9:00 p.m., CDT.

Elvis in Concert, CBS Television. Broadcast October 3, 1977, 9:00 p.m., EDT.

Nashville Remembers Elvis on His Birthday, CBS Television. Broadcast January 8, 1978, 8:00 p.m., EST.

Elvis, ABC Television. Broadcast as the ABC Sunday Night Movie, February 11, 1978, 8:00 p.m., EST.

20/20, ABC Television. Broadcasts of September 13, 1979, and September 20, 1979, 10:00 p.m., EDT.

"Elvis Memories . . .." Interview segments with Presley friends and associates by Marge Thrasher on *Straight Talk*, WHBQ-TV, Memphis, Tenn. Broadcast daily during July and August 1979, 9:00 a.m., CDT.

NEWSPAPERS

Copies of the following newspapers were examined for the period of August 16-21, 1977. Various articles, editorials and headlines are cited.

United States

Alabama
  Birmingham News
  Birmingham Post-Herald
  Mobile Register
  Montgomery Advertiser
Alaska
  Anchorage Times
Arizona
  (Phoenix) *Arizona Republic*
  (Tucson) *Arizona Daily Star*
Arkansas
  (Little Rock) *Arkansas
                Democrat*
              Arkansas Gazette
California
  Los Angeles Herald Examiner
  Los Angeles Times
  Oakland Tribune
  Sacramento Bee
  San Diego Union
  San Francisco Chronicle
  San Francisco Examiner
  San Jose Mercury
Colorado
  Denver Post
  (Denver) *Rocky Mountain News*
Connecticut
  Hartford Courant
Delaware
  (Wilmington) *Evening Journal*
District of Columbia
  Washington Post
  Washington Star
Florida
  (Jacksonville) *Florida Times-
                 Union*
  Miami Herald
  Miami News
  (Orlando) *Sentinel Star*

  Pensacola Journal
  St. Petersburg Times
  Tampa Tribune
Georgia
  Atlanta Constitution
  Atlanta Journal
Hawaii
  Honolulu Advertiser
  Honolulu Star-Bulletin
Idaho
  (Boise) *Idaho Statesman*
Illinois
  Chicago Daily News
  Chicago Sun-Times
  Chicago Tribune
  (Rockford) *Morning Star*
Indiana
  Indianapolis Star
Iowa
  Des Moines Register
Kansas
  Topeka Daily Capital
Kentucky
  Lexington Herald
  (Louisville) *Courier-Journal*
Louisiana
  (Baton Rouge) *State-Times and
                Advocate*
  (New Orleans) *Times-Picayune*
  (Shreveport) *Times*
Maine
  (Portland) *Press Herald*
            *Maine Sunday
             Telegram*
Maryland
  (Baltimore) *News American*
             Sun
Massachusetts
  Boston Globe

Boston Herald American
Michigan
   Detroit Free Press
   Detroit News
Minnesota
   Minneapolis Star
   Minneapolis Tribune
   St. Paul Pioneer Press
Mississippi
   (Biloxi-Gulfport) *Daily Herald*
   (Jackson) *Clarion Ledger*
   Jackson Daily News
   Meridian Star
   (Tupelo) *Daily Journal*
      Lee County News
Missouri
   Kansas City Star
   St. Louis Globe-Democrat
   St. Louis Post-Dispatch
   Springfield Leader and Press
Montana
   Great Falls Tribune
Nebraska
   Omaha World Herald
Nevada
   Las Vegas Sun
   (Reno) *Nevada State Journal*
New Hampshire
   Manchester Union Leader
New Jersey
   (Cherry Hill) *Courier Post*
   (Hackensack) *Record*
   (Newark) *Star-Ledger*
   (Paterson) *Evening News*
New Mexico
   Albuquerque Journal
New York
   Buffalo Evening News
   (Garden City) *Newsday*
   (New York) *Daily News*
   New York Post
   New York Times
   (New York) *Wall Street Journal*
   (Rochester) *Democrat and Chronicle*
   Syracuse Herald-Journal

North Carolina
   Asheville Citizen
   Charlotte Observer
   Greensboro Daily News
   (Raleigh) *News and Observer*
   Wilmington Morning Star
North Dakota
   (Fargo) *Forum*
Ohio
   Akron Beacon Journal
   Cincinnati Enquirer
   Cleveland Press
   (Cleveland) *Plain Dealer*
   Dayton Daily News
   Toledo Blade
Oklahoma
   (Oklahoma City) *Daily Oklahoman*
   Tulsa World
Oregon
   (Portland) *Oregon Journal*
   Oregonian
Pennsylvania
   (Philadelphia) *Bulletin*
   Philadelphia Inquirer
   Pittsburgh Post-Gazette
   Pittsburgh Press
Rhode Island
   Providence Journal
South Carolina
   (Charleston) *News and Courier*
   (Columbia) *State*
   Greenville News
South Dakota
   (Sioux Falls) *Argus-Leader*
Tennessee
   Chattanooga Times
   Knoxville Journal
   (Memphis) *Commercial Appeal*
   Memphis Press-Scimitar
   Nashville Banner
   (Nashville) *Tennessean*
Texas
   Amarillo Daily News
   Corpus Christi Caller
   Dallas Morning News

Dallas Times Herald
El Paso Times
Fort Worth Star-Telegram
Houston Chronicle
Houston Post
San Antonio Express
San Antonio Light
Utah
(Salt Lake City) *Deseret News*
Salt Lake Tribune
Vermont
Burlington Free Press
Virginia
(Norfolk) *Virginian-Pilot*
Richmond News Leader
Richmond Times-Dispatch
Roanoke Times and World-News

Washington
Seattle Post-Intelligencer
Seattle Times
(Spokane) *Spokesman-Review*
Tacoma News Tribune
West Virginia
Charleston Gazette
(Wheeling) *Intelligencer*
Wisconsin
(Madison) *Wisconsin State
Journal*
Milwaukee Journal
Milwaukee Sentinel
Wyoming
(Cheyenne) *Wyoming State
Tribune*

Foreign

Argentina
(Buenos Aires) *La Prensa*
La Razon
(Cordoba) *La Voz del Interior*
Australia
(Brisbane) *Courier-Mail*
(Canberra) *Australian*
(Sydney) *Daily Mirror*
Sydney Morning Herald
(Sydney) *Sun*
Austria
(Vienna) *AZ (Arbeiter Zeitung)*
Neue Kronen Zeitung
Brazil
(Rio de Janeiro) *O Globo*
*Journal do
Brasil*
Canada
Montreal Star
(Montreal) *La Presse*
(Toronto) *Globe and Mail*
Toronto Star
Vancouver Sun
Winnipeg Free Press

Chile
(Santiago) *El Mercurio*
La Tercera de la Hora
Colombia
(Bogata) *El Tiempo*
El Siglo
Denmark
(Copenhagen) *Politiken*
Finland
(Helsinki) *Ussi Suomi*
France
(Paris) *L'Aurore*
Le Figaro
France-Soir
L'Humanite
L'Humanite Dimanche
Liberation
Le Monde
Germany
(Berlin) *Berliner Morgenpost*
(Cologne) *Kolnische Rundschau*
Express
(Frankfurt) *Frankfurter
Allgemeine Zeitung*

(Hamburg) *Die Welt*
(Munich) *Suddeutsche Zeitung*
(Stuttgart) *Bild*

Israel
    Jerusalem Post
Hong Kong
    South China Morning Post
Japan
    (Tokyo) *Japan Times*
Kenya
    (Nairobi) *Daily Nation*
Korea
    (Seoul) *Korea Times*
Mexico
    (Mexico City) *El Dia*
        La Prensa
Netherlands
    (Amsterdam) *Trouw*
New Zealand
    (Auckland) *New Zealand Herald*
    (Christchurch) *Press*
    (Wellington) *Evening Post*
Norway
    (Oslo) *Aftenposten*
        Morgenbladet
Peru
    (Lima) *La Prensa*
Philippines
    (Manila) *Evening Post*
Singapore
    Straits Times

South Africa
    (Johannesburg) *Rand Daily Mail*
Sri Lanka
    (Colombo) *Ceylon Daily News*
Sweden
    (Goteborg) *Goteborgs-Posten*
    (Stockholm) *Aftonbladet*
        Expressen
        Ny Dag
Switzerland
    (Zurich) *Neue Zurcher Zeitung*
Thailand
    Bangkok Post
United Kingdom
    Birmingham Evening Mail
    (Edinburgh) *Scotsman*
    Liverpool Daily Post
    (London) *Daily Express*
        Daily Mail
        Daily Mirror
        Daily Telegraph
        Evening Standard
        Financial Times
        News of the World
        Observer
        Sun
        Sunday Telegraph
        Sunday Times
        Times
    (Manchester) *Guardian*

BOOKS AND PERIODICALS

Ackerman, Paul, "The Revitalization of American Music—Rock," *Billboard*, November 14, 1970, p. 12.

Alden, Ginger, "Girl Elvis Was Going To Marry Tells Her Heartbreaking Story," *National Enquirer*, September 6, 1977, p.20.

Allen, Steve, "TV Is Junk Food for the Mind," *U.S. News & World Report*, March 13, 1978, pp. 76-77.

Ayres, Tom, "Elvis Off-stage," *Country Music*, December 1977, pp. 25ff.

Baker, Howard (U.S. Senator), " 'The King' Is Dead," (editorials from *The Commercial Appeal, Memphis Press-Scimitar,* and *The Tennessean*), *Congressional Record*, September 9, 1977, p. S14480.

Baker, Jackson, "Elvis: End of an Era," *City of Memphis*, September 1977, pp. 25-32.

Baker, Morris B., "Dateline: Memphis, Aug. 16, 1977," *Public Relations Journal*, October 1977, pp. 10-12.

Belz, Carl, *The Story of Rock*. (New York: Oxford University Press, 1972.)

Berglind, Sten, *Elvis: Fran Vasteras till Memphis*. (Stockholm: Askild & Karnekull, 1977.)

Blotner, Joseph, *Faulkner: A Biography*. (New York: Random House, 1974.)

Bonafede, Dom, "Carter's Favorite Speechwriter," *National Journal*, April 14, 1979, p. 611.

Booth, Stanley, "A Hound Dog to the Manor Born," *Esquire*, February 1968, pp. 106-8.

Cleaver, Eldridge, *Soul on Ice*. (New York: McGraw-Hill, 1967.)

Cocke, Marian J., *I Called Him Babe*. (Memphis: Memphis State University Press, 1979.)

Cocks, Jay, "Last Stop on the Mystery Train," *Time*, August 29, 1977, pp. 56-59.

Cohn, Nik, *Rock from the Beginning*. (New York: Stein and Day, 1969.)

Cole, James, "Mr. Crump's Town, After 20 Years," *The Commercial Appeal*, October 13, 1974, p. VI-1.

Consoli, John, "Presley Photo Sparks Press Freedom Case," *Editor & Publisher*, January 13, 1979, pp. 34-35.

Coppock, Paul R., "Elvis: The Memories, the Fans, the City He Left Behind," *The Commercial Appeal*, March 4, 1979, p. G-7.

Dawson, Walter, "Presley and Phillips Had Nothing to Lose by Being Different," *The Commercial Appeal*, August 13, 1978, p. B-3.

Dornan, Robert (U.S. Representative), "An American Tragedy," (article from *National Enquirer*), *Congressional Record*, September 7, 1978, p. E4836.

Dunleavy, Steve, et al, *Elvis: What Happened?* (New York: Ballantine, 1977.)

"Echos of Love: Elvis' Friends Remember," *Rolling Stone*, September 22, 1977, pp. 48ff.

Eisen, Jonathan (ed.), *The Age of Rock: Sounds of the American Cultural Revolution*. (New York: Random House, 1969.), Vol. II (New York: Random House, 1970.)

"Elvis' Total Gross Already $4.3-Billion," *Variety*, August 24, 1977, p. 1.

Escott, Colin, and Hawkins, Martin, *Catalyst: The Sun Records Story*. (London: Aquarius Books, 1975.)

Europa Year Book, 1979. (London: Europa Publications Limited, 1979.)

Everett, Todd, "Elvis Presley, 42, Rock Pioneer, Dead of Heart Attack in Memphis," *Variety*, August 24, 1977, p. 50.

Ewen, David, *All the Years of American Popular Music*. (New York: Prentice-Hall, 1977.)

Flippo, Chet, "Funeral in Memphis," *Rolling Stone*, September 22, 1977, p. 38.

Fong-Torres, Ben, "Broken Heart for Sale," *Rolling Stone*, September 22, 1977, p. 42.

Forkan, James P., "Elvis: The Song Is Ended, but the Legend May Sell," *Advertising Age*, August 22, 1977, p. 2.

Green, Paul, "A Consistent Champion on the Charts," *Billboard*, August 27, 1977, p. 60.

Grehl, Michael, "Presley Memory Lives In Pocketbook Pandering," *The Commercial Appeal*, August 29, 1977, p. 4.

Guild, Hazel, "Presley Posthumous Disk Boom Also Echoes in German Market," *Variety*, December 7, 1977, p. 69.

Guralnick, Peter, "Faded Love: A Personal Memoir," *Country Music*, December 1977, p. 36.

———, *Feel Like Going Home*. (New York: Outerbridge & Dienstfrey, 1971.)

Haas, Charlie, "Heartbreak Hotel: a Brief Encounter with the Living Elvis," *New West*, October 23, 1978, pp. 54ff.

Haspel, Randy, "Tell 'em Phillips Sencha: Dewey Phillips—the First Rock and Roll Deejay," *Memphis*, June 1978, pp. 52ff.

Heilbut, Tony, *The Gospel Sound: Good News and Bad Times*. (New York: Simon and Schuster, 1971.)

Hiaason, Carl, "The Untold Story of the National Enquirer," *Miami Herald*, June 11, 1978, *Tropic* magazine, pp. 8-15.

Hodenfield, Chris, "Shake, Rattle and Roll 'em," *Rolling Stone*, September 22, 1977, p. 47.

Hoffman, Abbie, "Too Soon the Hero," *Crawdaddy*, November 1977, pp. 39-41.

Hollingsworth, Ron, "Farewell to Elvis," *Melody Maker*, August 27, 1977, p.1.

Hollstein, Milton, "The Changing Press of Paris," *Journalism Quarterly*, Autumn 1978, pp. 438-44.

Hopkins, Jerry, *Elvis*. (New York: Simon and Schuster, 1971.)

"Hound Dog Days in Memphis," *Time*, August 28, 1978, p. 22.

Jacobson, Harlan, "Not Many Presley Prints Exist As Posthumous Demand Explodes," *Variety*, August 24, 1977, p. 2.

Jahn, Mike, *Rock*. (New York: Quadrangle, 1973.)

Johnson, Derek (ed.), "Elvis' Last Ride," *New Musical Express*, August 27, 1977, p. 3.

Jones, Peter, "Album Demand Reflects His Popularity," *Billboard*, August 27, 1977, p. 1.

Kaye, Elizabeth, "Forever Elvis," *New Times*, November 13, 1978, pp. 36ff.

Kennedy, Caroline, "Graceland," *Rolling Stone*, September 22, 1977, p. 40.

Klein, Jack, "Tupelo," *Rolling Stone*, September 22, 1977, p. 41.

Kozak, Roman, and Traiman, Stephen, "RCA 'Pressing' To Satisfy Unabated Presley Demand," *Billboard*, September 3, 1977, p. 1.

Kroll, Jack and Orth, Maureen, "All Shook Up: Heartbreak Kid," *Newsweek*, August 29, 1977, pp. 46-49.

Kuncl, Tom, and South, John, "Emergency Medics Tell Inside Story of Elvis' Death," *National Enquirer*, September 6, 1977, p. 26.

Landau, Jon, *It's Too Late to Stop Now*. (San Francisco: Straight Arrow Books, 1972.)

Lazar, Jerry, "Front Page Blues," *Crawdaddy*, November 1977, pp. 37-39.

Leroux, Charles, "A Visit with Charles Kuralt," *Chicago Tribune Magazine*, January 25, 1976, pp. 14ff.

McLuhan, Marshall, *Understanding Media.* (New York: McGraw-Hill, 1964.)

_____, *Verbi-Voco-Visual Explorations.* (New York: Something Else Press, 1967.)

Marcus, Greil, "Elvis: Spirit and Flesh," *Rolling Stone*, September 22, 1977, pp. 56ff.

_____, *Mystery Train.* (New York: E. P. Dutton, 1975.)

Marsh, Dave, "Elvis in the Promised Land," *Rolling Stone*, September 22, 1977, p. 58.

_____, "The Singer, Not the Song," *Rolling Stone*, February 9, 1978.

Martin, Tom, "Stalking the Grim Reaper: How ABC Unearthed the Elvis Story," *Memphis*, March 1980, p. 44.

Miller, Jim (ed.), *The Rolling Stone Illustrated History of Rock & Roll.* (New York: Rolling Stone Press, 1976.)

Miller, William O., *Mr. Crump of Memphis.* (Baton Rouge: Louisiana State University Press, 1964.)

Morgenthau, Tom, et al., "Carter's Wordsmith," *Newsweek*, April 30, 1979, p. 31.

Morthland, John, "An Oral History of Elvis: The King Remembered," *Country Music*, December 1977, pp. 46ff.

_____, "Producing the King," *Country Music*, December 1977, p. 31.

Mulherin, Joe, "Taking Care of Business? " *Memphis*, August 1979, p. 20.

Needs, Kris, "Elvis," *Zigzag*, September 1977, p. 2.

"Newspapers cash-in on Elvis' death," *Editor & Publisher*, August 27, 1977, p. 9.

Nusser, Dick, "Run on Catalog Heats Up RCA Presses," *Billboard* , August 27, 1977, p. 1.

Palmer, Robert, "Big Boss Man: Working with the King," *Rolling Stone*, September 22, 1977, pp. 54ff.

_____, "Sam Phillips: The Sun King," *Memphis*, December 1978, p. 32.

Pascall, Jeremy, *The Illustrated History of Rock Music.* (London: Hamlyn, 1978.)

Paulu, Burton, *Radio and TV Broadcasting on the European Continent.* (Minneapolis: University of Minnesota Press, 1967.)

"Phenom Disk Sale Continues in Wake of Presley Death," *Variety*, August 31, 1977, p. 1.

"Presley Changed Face of Culture," *Variety*, August 24, 1977, p. 50.

Presley, Vernon, "Elvis" (as told to Nancy Anderson), *Good Housekeeping*, January 1978, pp. 80ff.

Presley, Vester, *A Presley Speaks.* (Memphis: Wimmer Brothers, 1979.)

"Presley's Posthumous B. O. Power Tapped Once More at Las Vegas Hilton," *Variety*, September 13, 1978, p. 1.

Rector, Lee, "Disk Sales in Phenom Spurt, Post-Presley," *Variety*, November 9, 1977, p. 1.

"Remember Him This Way," *New Musical Express*, August 27, 1977, pp. 23-25.

Rice, Jo, and Rice, Tim, *The Guinness Book of British Hit Singles.* (Enfield, England: Guinness Superlatives, Ltd., 1977.)

Rolling Stone Interviews. (New York: Paperback Library, 1971.), Vol. II (New York: Warner Paperback, 1973.)

"Sale of Elvis Tribute Section To Top 2 Million," *Editor & Publisher*, October 1, 1977, pp. 12-13.

Schroeder, Patricia (U.S. Representative), "Blue Suede Shoes," (article from *The New Yorker*), *Congressional Record*, September 8, 1977, p. E540.

Schruers, Fred, "What Price Glory? Peddling the Relics of Royalty," *Crawdaddy*, November 1977, pp. 35-36.

Shaver, Sean, and Noland, Hal, *The Life of Elvis Presley*. (Kansas City: Timor Publications, 1977.)

Siegelman, Jim, "Playboy Interview with Geraldo Rivera," *Playboy*, November 1978, pp. 79ff.

Slaughter, Todd, *Elvis Presley*. (London: Mandabrook, Ltd., 1977.)

Smith, Anthony D., "Press Lord of Mass Ignorance," *The Nation*, November 18, 1978, p. 535.

Stambler, Irwin, *Encyclopedia of Pop, Rock and Soul*. (New York: St. Martin's Press, 1974.)

Staten, Vince, *The Real Elvis: Good Old Boy*. (Dayton, Ohio: Media Ventures, 1978.)

"Stations Hustle To Air Their Tributes," *Billboard*, August 27, 1977, p. 15.

Stoppard, Tom, *Night and Day*. (London: Faber and Faber, 1978.)

Tharpe, Jac (ed.), *Elvis: Images and Fancies*. (Jackson: University Press of Mississippi, 1979.)

Tosches, Nick, "The Rise of Rockabilly," *Country Music*, December 1977, pp. 18ff.

" 'Tributes' Abound As Many Cash In On 'The King' " *Variety*, August 24, 1977, p. 50.

Truscott, Lucian K. IV, "Final Tribute: Elvis Presley's Deep-Fried Demise, " *New Times*, September 2, 1977.

Von Meier, Kurt, "The Background and Beginnings of Rock and Roll," *Art International*, October 1969, pp. 28-38.

Walton, Samuel B., "The Rebel Who Became a Legend," *Saturday Evening Post*, December 1977, pp. 56ff.

Ward, Robert, "Down at the End of Lonely Street," *Crawdaddy*, November 1977, pp. 29-34.

Watts, Michael, "The Phenomenon," *Melody Maker*, August 27, 1977, p. 6.

Welles, Chris, "The Americanization of Rupert Murdoch," *Esquire*, May 22, 1979, pp. 51ff.

Welty, Eudora, *Place in Fiction*. (New York: House of Books, 1957.)

Wheeler, Tom, *The Guitar Book*. (New York: Harper & Row, 1978.)

Whisenhunt, Elton, "Shock Waves Linger After Presley's Death," *Billboard*, August 27, 1977, p. 3.

Whitburn, Joel, *Top Country & Western Records, 1949-1971*. (Menomonee Falls, Wisc.: Record Research, 1972.)

————, *Joel Whitburn's Top LP's, 1945-1972*. (Menomonee Falls, Wisc.: Record Research, 1973.)

_____, *Top Pop Records, 1955-1972*. (Menomonee Falls, Wisc.: Record Research, 1973.)

_____, *Joel Whitburn's Pop Annual, 1955-1977*. (Menomonee Falls, Wisc.: Record Research, 1978.)

Williams, Jean, "Boy from Tupelo Did Much to Bridge Black-White Gap," *Billboard*, August 27, 1977, p. 82.

Wilmer, Val, "Still Got the Blues," *Observer Magazine*, London, December 17, 1978, pp. 32ff.

CHAPTER NOTES

All dates are 1977 unless otherwise specified.

Introduction
1. Emergency at Graceland

Interviews with McDaniel, McEachran, Seago. *The Commercial Appeal*, Aug. 17; *Memphis Press-Scimitar*, Aug. 17; Alden article and Kuncl and South article, *National Enquirer*, Sept. 6. Quote from Vester Presley and his daughter, from his book, *A Presley Speaks*, p. 109. Vernon Presley quote from his article, *Good Housekeeping*, p. 84.

2. The Word Goes Out

Interviews with Albritten, Britten, Cole, McEachran, Porteous, Seago, Sears, Stevens, White, Wilson, Wolfe.

3. Airwaves of Grief

Interviews with Benjamin, Bond, Knoller, Mudd, Salamon, Townsend. Ratings from Arbitron, Anthes interview. TV scripts. Radio reaction from "Stations Hustle ...," *Billboard*; "'Tributes' Abound ...," *Variety*, various newspapers of Aug. 18-19, as follows: *Baltimore News-American, Philadelphia Inquirer, Chicago Sun-Times, San Diego Union, Charlotte Observer, Tampa Tribune, Boston Globe, Detroit News, Cincinnati Enquirer, Miami Herald, Seattle Times*. Camphonse quote from *Elvis Monthly*, Nov. 1977.

4. Elvis: Front Page

Interviews with Albritten, Harris, Ivins, McDaniel, Seago, Charles Thompson, White. *20/20* TV scripts. Newspapers, as cited in text, for Aug. 16-17. Background on Dunleavy book, *Washington Post*, Aug. 18. Bob Greene column, *Chicago Sun-Times*, Aug. 17, 22.

5. Late-Night Reflections

TV scripts. Interviews with Bain, Brinkley, Connelly, Manning, Montgomery, Richman, Rivera, Tornebene. Background on Rivera, Siegelman interview in *Playboy*; background on Kuralt, Leroux article in *Chicago Tribune Magazine*. Early television, *Elvis Monthly*; Hopkins, pp. 123, 136-41; Staten, pp. 130-45. Precht quote from Frank Swetlow, *Chicago Daily News*, Aug. 17. Ratings from Arbitron.

6. Gathering in Memphis

Interviews with Albritten, Bain, Carey, Cole, Fadal, Knoller, Rosenthal, Seago, Charles Thompson. Tripper brothers from *New York Post*, Aug. 18; story on free photos from *St. Petersburg Times*, Aug. 18. Background on Hawaii from *Honolulu Advertiser*, Aug. 17. TV scripts. Newspaper circulation figures from newspapers, as cited, usually on day following special section; "Newspapers Cash-in ...," *Editor & Publisher*. Background on *National Enquirer* from Hiasson article in *Miami Herald*.

7. The Tears of August

Interviews with Albritten, Dunn, Fadal, Gaugher, Green, Ivins, Knoller, Mitchell, Rosenthal, Rosellini, Salamon, Seago, Sears, Stevens, Venardos, White. Newspapers, as cited, of Aug. 17-18. Background on flowers, *Atlanta Journal*, *Courier-Journal*, Aug. 18. Morris Baker article in *Public Relations Journal*. Krebs story, *New York Times*, Aug. 26. Bob Greene column, *Chicago Sun-Times*, Aug. 18. Molly Ivins essay, *New York Times*, Aug. 18.

8. The Final Farewell

Interviews with Albritten, Bain, Cole, Harris, McEachran, Rosenthal, Rosellini, Seago, White, Williams. Newspapers of Aug. 18, as cited. TV broadcasts of Aug. 18, as cited.

9. Roots of the Legend

Interviews with Boren, Boyd, Brewster, Brown, Duncan, Fadal, Ford, Graham, Green, Holditch, Alan Lomax, John Lomax Jr., McComb, Morris, Salamon, Seibert, Asa Thompson, Walls, Welch. WELO special, TV broadcasts, as cited. *Daily Journal*, Tupelo, Miss., Aug. 17-20; *Lee County News*, Aug. 19, 26. *Washington Post* editorial, Aug. 20; *Chicago Sun-Times* editorial, Aug. 18; Gary Deeb quote, *Chicago Tribune*, Aug. 21; William Steif quote, *Cleveland Press*, Aug. 17; *Oregon Journal* editorial, Aug. 18; Williams article in *Billboard*. Cohen column, *Washington Post*, Aug. 23; Cleaver, p. 179; Penneman quote, *Rolling Stone Interviews*, I, p. 371; *Billboard* music terms from von Meier article in *Art International*, p. 31. Background on Dewey Phillips, Haspel article in *Memphis*. Background on Sam Phillips, Palmer article in *Memphis*; Dawson article in *The*

Commercial Appeal; Escott and Hawkins, chapters 1, 2, 3, and 10. Analysis of '50s music from Belz, pp. 130-36; Eisen, introduction and H. F. Mooney chapter; von Meier article in *Art International*; Booth article in *Esquire*. Burch quote from Cole article, *The Commercial Appeal* Elvis's quote on leaving Memphis from Hopkins, p. 32. Background on Handy, Ewen, p. 220. 'Son' Thomas quote from Wilmer article in *Observer Magazine*, p. 37. B.B. King reminiscence from Escott and Hawkins, p. 8. Background on gospel music from Heilbut, introduction and pp. 12-15, 127-35. Hovie Lister quote from *Atlanta Constitution*, Aug. 27. Maschal quote from *Akron Beacon-Journal*, Aug. 18; Hayakawa quote from Eisen, pp. 25-26. Faulkner quotes from Blotner, p. 706 and p. 811. Welty quote, *Place in Fiction*, n. p. General background on Presley's music roots, see Marcus, *Mystery Train*, pp. 148-53, 160-64, 176-81, and 189-99. [Alan Lomax was quoted in New York *Daily News*, Aug. 18, *Cleveland Press*, Aug. 17, and *The Australian*, Aug. 19, as saying Elvis freed American music from the European tradition. In an interview, Lomax denied saying this.]

10. Interpreting the Myth

Interviews with Ames, Browne, Kieckhefer, McDaniel, Schroeder. Quotes from editorials and columnists and cartoons are from newspapers cited, Aug. 17-20. (For full text of editorials, see "Selected Newspaper Editorials" in this book.) Skitch Henderson quote, *Memphis Press-Scimitar*, Feb. 3, 1967; Crosby, Simon, and Frampton quotes, *Chicago Tribune*, Aug. 21; Muddy Waters quote, *Chicago Tribune*, Aug. 19; Beatlemania reaction, *Washington Star*, Aug. 17; Carl Wilson quote, *Denver Post*, Aug. 17; Pat Boone comments, *San Francisco Chronicle*, Aug. 17; *Washington Post* editorial, Aug. 20; Steve Allen, article in *U.S. News & World Report* (full page of letters, April 24, 1978, p. 55); Board of Alderman statement, *Daily Journal*, Tupelo, Miss., Aug. 17; Blanton statement and constitutional convention tribute, *Nashville Tennessean*, Aug. 18; Jerry Brown statement, *Los Angeles Times*, Aug. 18; George Wallace statement, *Montgomery Advertiser*, Aug. 17; Biaggi, House Joint Resolution 589, introduced Sept. 12, 1977; James Thompson proclamation, *The Commercial Appeal*, Aug. 13, 1978; Esensten quote from (Portland) *Maine Sunday Telegram*, Aug. 21.

11. The President Himself

Interviews with Cody, Doolittle, Granum, Hertzberg, Lewis, Smith. Background on Hertzberg, Morganthau article in *Newsweek* and Bonafede article in *National Journal*; Carter statement at Ford's Theater, Oct. 2, 1979, from *Compilation of Presidential Documents*, Vol. 15, No. 40, pp. 1815-16.

12. The World Joins In

Interviews with Aberbach, Bezshehowski, Britten, Dombrofski, Harrod, Lerner, McDaniel, McEachran, Seago, Slaughter. Shaupe quote, *Cleveland*

Press, Aug. 17; Elias quote, AP story, Aug. 18; tape sales in Iran, *Washington Post*, Dec. 20, 1979; Kominowski quote, cited in *Elvis* theatre program, Astoria Theatre, London; Associated Press story on foreign coverage, *Denver Post*, Aug. 17, *Times Picayune*, Aug. 18, and *San Francisco Chronicle*, Aug. 18. Welty quote, *Place in Fiction*, n.p. *Neue Zurcher Zeitung*, Zurich, Aug. 18. Background on Radio Luxembourg, Paulu, pp. 21-22, 85-86. Foreign newspapers as cited, Aug. 16-21. General articles on foreign reaction, *Elvis Monthly*, Dec. 1977, Jan. 1978; *The Commercial Appeal*, Dec. 11; Tharpe, pp. 24-26. Quebec record sales from Richard Galibois, sales manager, RCA Quebec, quoted in *Montreal Star*, Aug. 18. Parley quote, *Elvis Monthly*, Dec. 1977. Background on French press, Hollstein article in *Journalism Quarterly*. Quote from W. J. Cash also cited in Marcus, *Mystery Train*, p. 151.

13. The Special Case of Britain

Interviews with Danskin, Fletcher, Slaughter, Strick. Rice and Rice, p. 147. Needs editorial in *Zigzag*; Lennon quote from Joseph Sasfy, *Washington Post*, Aug. 24; description of British fan club from Slaughter, *Elvis*, p. 119. Hollingsworth article and Watts article from *Melody Maker*; Johnson article from *New Musical Express*. Logs and transcripts, British Broadcasting Corp. Newspapers, as cited, Aug. 16-21. *Elvis Monthly*, Sept.-Dec. 1977, Jan. 1978. Background on Murdoch, Welles article in *Esquire*, Anthony Smith article in *Nation*. Stoppard quote from *Night and Day*, p. 61. Year-end comment from *The Times*, Dec. 30.

14. Seeking the Image

Interviews with Benton, McComb, Pollack, Slaughter, Charles Thompson. TV programs, as cited. Alan Meyer quote, *Las Vegas Sun*, Aug. 19; Rusk incident from *Atlanta Constitution*, Aug. 17; King quote from *St. Petersburg Times*, Aug. 18; Saucedo quote from *Chicago Sun-Times*, Aug. 18; Haney quote, *The Commercial Appeal*, Dec. 4. British reviews of West End play, *Elvis*, from newspapers, as cited, Nov. 29-30, Dec. 4. Harold Thompson review, cited in Shaver and Noland, p. 11; Taurog quote, Gene Siskel column, *Chicago Tribune*, Aug. 17. Colonel Parker quote by Linda Deutsch, (Portland) *Maine Sunday Telegram*, Aug. 21. Gary Smith quote, *Minneapolis Tribune*, Oct. 2; Parley quote from *Elvis Monthly*, Dec. 1977. Other background on West End play, *Elvis*, and ABC-TV's *Elvis*, press materials. Ratings from A. C. Neilsen Co. Flander review, *Washington Star*, Feb. 10, 1978.

15. Buying a Memory

Interviews with Deary, Duncan, Geissler, Harris, Helman, McComb, McDaniel, McEachran, Pierce. RCA Records reaction from *Philadelphia Inquirer*, Aug. 17; *Chicago Tribune*, Aug. 17; *Atlanta Journal*, Aug. 18, 28; *Los Angeles Times*, Aug. 28; *Nashville Banner*, Aug. 18. Guild and Rector articles in

Variety; "Phenom Disk Sale...," " *Variety;* Kozak, Jones, and Nusser articles in *Billboard; Billboard,* Oct. 1, Oct. 29; *Rand Daily Mail,* Johannesburg, Aug. 18; *Memphis Press-Scimitar* , Aug. 26. Felton Jarvis story from *Nashville Banner,* Aug. 17. Grehl comments from *The Commercial Appeal,* Aug. 29. Background on licensing of Factors, Etc., Inc., Consoli article in *Editor & Publisher; Memphis Development Foundation* v. *Factors, Etc., Inc.* 2nd Circuit Court of Appeals, March 26, 1980 (from UPI wire); *Factors, Etc., Inc.* v. *Pro Arts, Inc.,* 579 F.2d 215 (2d Circ. 1978), *cert. denied,* 40 U.S. 908 (1979); *New York Times,* Aug. 25. Mulherin article in *Memphis,* p. 21. Newspapers, as cited, for dates following special sections. "Newspapers Cash-in ..." and "Sale of Elvis Tribute ..." from *Editor & Publisher.* Liz Smith comment from *Chicago Tribune,* Aug. 27. *Rolling Stone,* Sept. 22, 1977, issue; *Crawdaddy,* Nov. 1977 issue; *Country Music,* Dec. 1977 issue. Cocks article in *Time;* Kroll and Orth article in *Newsweek.* Other comments on media coverage, Lazar article in *Crawdaddy.* [*The Washington Post,* quoting industry sources, reported July 13, 1980, that Presley record sales had passed the *one billion* mark, compared with sales of 500 million or less for Paul McCartney, Frank Sinatra, or Bing Crosby. RCA Records announced it was pressing 250,000 copies of a new album titled "Elvis Aron Presley," marking the 25th anniversary of the singer's exclusive recording contract with the company. The four hours of music, which retails for $69.95, includes 87 songs— 65 of them in versions previously unavailable, a 1956 live performance, and a 14-minute monologue on life.]

16. Epilogue

Interviews with Carter, Fletcher, Hertzberg, McComb, McDaniel, Pierce, Charles Thompson, Williams. *The Commercial Appeal,* Aug. 16-18, 1978. *New York Times* unpublished editorial of Aug. 16, 1978 (part of microfilmed archival record for period when *Times* was on strike). "Presley's Posthumous B.O. Power ...," *Variety.* "Hound Dog Days in Memphis," *Time.*

Elvis Bibliography

When Elvis died, dozens of books were published about the man and his music. Some earlier works were reissued but few gave the reader any solid information about the entertainer. Libraries had tended to ignore most of the hundreds of Presley magazines, concert programs, and other ephemera that had been published through the years. But the British Library had gathered Presley information from the start. It holds a complete set of *Elvis Monthly*, a magazine published in Heanor, England, for more than twenty years and written primarily by the fans. The Library of Congress has not collected similar American publications in any systematic way. Indeed, the only items from this category are a few assorted photographs and booklets and a 1956 souvenir photo album listed in the Library of Congress card catalogue with "Parker, Tom" named as the author.

Much additional information about Elvis Presley is available from a wide range of periodicals, and many books contain references to the entertainer. In mid-1980, for example, the Library of Congress listed in its computerized files two-hundred-sixty-one items on rock music and musicians and fifty-five on country music. The forty-two page chapter on Elvis in *Mystery Train* by Greil Marcus (New York: E. P. Dutton, 1975) is probably a better source of information than most of the books listed below. This bibliography, however, is a compilation of those books exclusively about Presley that have been collected by the Library of Congress and the British Library.

Adler, Bill, *Bill Adler's Love Letters to Elvis*. (New York: Grosset & Dunlap, 1978.)

Alico, Stella H., *Elvis Presley—The Beatles*. (West Haven, Conn.: Pendulum Press, 1979.)

Bagh, Peter von, *Elvis! Amerikkalaise Laulajan Elama Ja Kuolema*. (Helsinki: Love Kustannus, 1977.)

Barlow, Roy, et al., (comp.), *The Elvis Presley Encyclopaedia*. (Heanor, England: Albert Hand Publications, 1964.)

Barry, Ron, *All American Elvis*. (Phillipsburg, N.J.: Maxigraphics, 1976.)

____, *The Elvis Presley American Discography*. (Phillipsburg, N.J.: Maxigraphics, 1976.)

Berglind, Sten, *Elvis: Fran Vasteras till Memphis*. (Stockholm: Askild & Karnekull, 1977.)

Bowman, Kathleen, *On Stage With Elvis Presley*. (Mankato, Minn.: Creative Education, 1976)

Bowser, James, *Starring Elvis*. (New York: Dell, 1977.)

Canada, Lena, *To Elvis, with Love* (New York: Everest House, 1978.)

Carr, Roy, *Elvis Presley: An Illustrated Record*. (New York: Harmony Books, 1980.)

Cocke, Marian J., *I Called Him Babe*. (Memphis: Memphis State University Press, 1979.)

Cortez, Diego, (ed.), *Private Elvis*. (New York: Two Continents Publishing Group, 1978.)

Dunleavy, Steve, et. al., *Elvis: What Happened?* (New York: Ballantine, 1977.)

Elvis Lives! (London: Galaxy Publications, Ltd., 1978.)

Elvis Presley: A Photoplay Tribute. (New York: Cadrant Enterprises, 1977.)

Elvis Presley—1935-1977: A Tribute to the King. (Wednesbury, England: Bavie Publications, 1977.)

Farren, Mick, (comp.), *Elvis in his own Words*. (London: Omnibus Press, 1977.)

Fraga, Gaspar, *Elvis Presley*. (Madrid: Ediciones Jugar, 1974.)

Gregory, James, (ed.), *The Elvis Presley Story*. (London: Thorpe & Porter, 1960.)

Gregory, Neal, and Gregory, Janice, *When Elvis Died*. (Washington, D.C.: Communications Press, 1980.)

Grove, Martin A., *Elvis: The Legend Lives*. (New York: Manor Books, 1978.)

____, *The King Is Dead: Elvis Presley*. (New York: Manor Books, 1977.)

Grust, Lothar, F. W., and Pommer, Jeremias. *Elvis Presley Superstar*. (Bergish Gladbach, Germany: G. Lubbe, 1978.)

Hand, Albert, (comp.), *Elvis Special*. (Manchester: World Distributors, issued annually since 1962.)

Hanna, David, *Elvis: Lonely Star at the Top*. (New York: Nordon Publications, 1977.)

Hansen, Mogens, *Elvis—Er Ikke Dod.* (Copenhagen: SV Press, 1978.)

Harbison, William Allen, *Elvis Presley: An Illustrated Biography.* (London: Joseph, 1975.)

——, *The Illustrated Elvis.* (New York: Grossett & Dunlap, 1976.)

——, *The Life and Death of Elvis Presley.* (London: Joseph, 1977.)

Harms, Valerie, *Tryin' to Get to You: The Story of Elvis Presley.* (New York: Atheneum, 1979.)

Holzer, Hans, *Elvis Presley Speaks.* (New York: Manor Books, 1978.)

Hopkins, Jerry, *Elvis.* (New York: Simon and Schuster, 1971.)

——, *Elvis: The Final Years.* (New York: St. Martin's Press, 1980.)

James, Anthony, *Presley: Entertainer of the Century.* (New York: Belmont-Tower, 1976.)

Jones, Peter, *Elvis.* (London: Octopus Books, 1976.)

Kling, Bernard, and Plehn, Heinz, *Elvis Presley.* (New York: Music Sales, 1979.)

Lacker, Marty, et al., *Elvis, Portrait of a Friend.* (Memphis: Wimmer Brothers, 1979.)

Levy, Alan, *Operation Elvis.* (New York: Holt, 1960.)

Lichter, Paul, *Elvis in Hollywood.* (New York: Simon and Schuster, 1975.)

——, *The Boy Who Dared To Rock.* (Garden City, N.Y.: Doubleday, 1978.)

Lohmeyer, Henno, *Elvis Presley Report: Eine Dokumentation der Lugen und Legenden, Thesen und Theorien.* (Frankfurt: Ullstein, 1978.)

Loyd, Harold, *The Graceland Gates.* (Memphis: Modern Age Enterprises, 1978.)

Mann, May, *Elvis and the Colonel.* (New York: Drake Publishers, 1975.)

Matthew-Walker, Robert, *Elvis Presley: A Study in Music.* (Tunbridge Wells, England: Midas Books, 1979.)

Nash, Bruce M., *The Elvis Presley Quiz Book.* (New York: Warner Books, 1978.)

The Official FBI File on Elvis A. Presley. (Chicago: MEM Publishing Co., 1978.)

Panta, Ilona, *Elvis Presley, King of Kings.* (Hicksville, N.Y.: Exposition Press, 1979.)

Parish, James R., *Elvis Presley Scrapbook.* (New York: Ballantine, 1979.)

Parker, Ed, *Inside Elvis.* (West Orange, Calif.: Rampart House, 1978.)

Parker, Tom, *Elvis Presley Souvenir Photo Album.* (Madison, Tenn.: Elvis Presley Enterprises, 1956.)

Presley, Dee, et al., *Elvis We Love You Tender.* (New York: Delacorte, 1980.)

Presley, Vester, *A Presley Speaks.* (Memphis: Wimmer Brothers, 1978.)

Roggero, John, *Elvis in Concert.* (New York: Dell, 1979.)

Rosenbaum, Helen, *The Elvis Presley Trivia Quiz Book.* (New York: NAL, 1978.)

Saville, Tim, (comp.), *International Elvis Presley Appreciation Society Handbook.* (Heanor, England: Albert Hand Publications, 1970.)

Shaver, Sean, and Noland, Hal, *The Life of Elvis Presley*. (Kansas City: Timor Publications, 1979.)

Slaughter, Todd, (ed.), *The A-Z of Elvis Presley*. (Heanor, England: Albert Hand Publications, 1976.)

_____, *Elvis Presley*. (London: Mandabrook, Ltd., 1977.)

Staten, Vince, *The Real Elvis: Good Old Boy*. (Dayton, Ohio: Media Ventures, 1978.)

Stearn, Jess, *The Truth About Elvis*. (New York: G.P. Putnam's Sons, 1980.)

Taylor, Paula, *Elvis Presley*. (Mankato, Minn.: Creative Education, 1974.)

Taterova, Milada, and Novak, Jiri, *Elvis Presley*. (Prague: Supraphon, 1969.)

Tello, Antonio, and Otero Pizarro, Gonzalo, *Elvis, Elvis, Elvis: La Rebelion Domestica*. (Barcelona: Bruguera, 1977.)

Tharpe, Jac, (ed.), *Elvis: Images and Fancies*. (Jackson: University Press of Mississippi, 1979.)

Thornton, Mary Ann, *Even Elvis*. (Harrison, Ark.: New Leaf Press, 1979.)

Tribute to the King of Rock'n'roll: Remembering You. (London: IPC Magazines, 1977.)

Verwerft, Gust, *Elvis, de Koning die Niet Sterven Kon*. (Ghent, Belgium: Het Folk, 1977.)

Wallraf, Rainer, *Elvis Presley: A Biography*. (Munich: Nuctern, 1977.)

Werteheimer, Alfred, *Elvis, Fifty-Six: In the Beginning*. (New York: Macmillan, 1979.)

West, Joan Buchanan, *Elvis: His Life & Times in Poetry & Lines*. (Hicksville, N.Y.: Exposition Press, 1979.)

Yancey, Becky, and Linedecker, Cliff, *My Life With Elvis*. (New York: St. Martin's Press, 1977.)

Zmijewsky, Steven, and Zmijewsky, Boris, *Elvis: The Films and Career of Elvis Presley*. (Secaucus, N.J.: Citadel Press, 1976.)

Index